The Thai Way of Counterinsurgency

by

Dr. Jeff M. Moore

19 March 2014

A Muir Analytics Book

About the Author

Dr. Jeff M. Moore earned his PhD from the University of Exeter in the UK. His subject material was counterinsurgency in Thailand. Dr. Moore has worked as a defense contractor and security consultant since 1998, including three years in the Pentagon supporting the U.S. Army's G-3 (Plans and Operations Division). Dr. Moore has lived in several countries in Southeast Asia and currently runs Muir Analytics, LLC, which helps corporations in conflict areas reduce risks and increase the protection of their employees, assets, and investments.

Books by Dr. Jeff M. Moore

Spies for Nimitz; Joint Military Intelligence in the Pacific War, US Naval Institute Press

The Thai Way of Counterinsurgency, a Muir Analytics Book

Lifeblood: Oil & Gas in Asia (tentative title, mid-2014), a Muir Analytics Book

ISBN-13: 978-1497395701
ISBN-10: 1497395704
Library of Congress Control Number: 2014905524

Cover and maps by Business Image Solutions
Greenville NC
243.341.1821
www.businessimagesolution.com

Executive co-editors: Kathryn N. Hoey, Riplee N. Royster, and K. Mei Lee Dozier

To Robert J. Gowen, PhD: mentor, friend, & world-class
Asia scholar

Foreword

With his first book, *Spies for Nimitz*, Jeff Moore gave us a penetrating account of how intelligence collection and management for Joint Operations were born during the Pacific theater campaigns in World War II. In doing so, the author made a great contribution to our understanding of effective operations within the context of a global conventional war, and did so on the basis of innumerable primary sources that had not been analyzed previously.

With this latest book, Dr. Moore has delved into the highly relevant arena of Irregular Warfare (IW) and given us the most up-to-date and comprehensive analysis and critique of the Thai way of counterinsurgency (COIN) available so far. Again, he does so not on the basis of exposition extrapolated from secondary references, but utilizing primary sources, extensive fieldwork, and interviews with the commanders and decision makers involved in fighting the Communist and Islamist threats to Thailand.

Given that America has since 9/11 been involved in several IW campaigns in more than one theater and has yet to defeat al Qaeda and its affiliated threat groups, the tome is most timely.

While it is fair to say that each insurgency is *sui generis* in nature, there are lessons that can be learnt from any such conflict and certain principles that pertain across different battlefields, be they in Asia, Latin America, or the Middle East. The author illustrates this in part by comparing the Thai case to the approaches and subsequent advice given by the French COIN practitioner David Galula and the British legend Sir Robert Thompson. His conclusion is that the Thai followed the advice of Galula and Thompson for three fifths of their approaches, but added their own methodologies to arrive at their own "edgy" Thai Way of COIN. This indigenous recipe, which has been at times "clumsy and messy," and at other times "sleek and elegant," has proven itself on the whole to be effective.

The most interesting aspect of Dr. Moore's work, besides the eternal IW verities it illuminates, is how his analysis clearly demonstrates how a nation can learn and adapt if it has the will to do so, and how it can so become more effective against a deadly unconventional opponent. This is all the more relevant given how the US was forced to adapt during Operation Iraqi Freedom after it finally realized that the nature of the threat it faced was not solely driven by foreign fighters but by disaffected indigenous actors that had lost so much with the fall of the ancient regime and the outlawing of the Baath Party in Iraq.

The author succinctly identifies for us the 10 strategic objectives that informed the Thai approach to COIN over the last 50 years as well as the hard lessons learned when the means used to realize these objectives proved less than fruitful. Ultimately, the Thai government came to understand that legitimacy is not solely measured in terms of the popular vote, but, as General Carlos Ospina, the commander of the Colombian Armed Forces who was so pivotal in bringing the FARC to its knees expresses it, in the intangible quality of the relationship *between* the government and the people. (This is really what was meant by General McChrystal, the US commander in Afghanistan, when he expressed, in more military parlance, the idea that the people are the "center of gravity" in the COIN campaign being waged by America and her NATO allies).

The Thai Way of Counterinsurgency is invaluable to the modern practitioner and scholar of IW in that it underscores the little understood difference between a counterterrorism campaign and a counterinsurgency. The difference between a terrorist organization and an insurgency lies predominantly in their individual capabilities. A terrorist group is just that: an organization that uses violence to terrorize and intimidate. An insurgency by definition has effectively leveraged grievances to catalyze mass mobilization of fighters into its ranks. As a result, a counterterrorism campaign can concentrate on attacking solely the organization and its membership. A COIN campaign must attack the dynamic that facilitates thousands, if not hundreds of thousands, of the nation's citizens deciding to take up arms against the government. The Thai understood that to do the latter one must use economic development as a weapon to address the tangible complaints of the population and at the same time use psychological operations and information warfare to delegitimize the ideology of those calling for Communism and jihad. This dual-track approach provides much food for thought in America's war against al Qaeda.

On the latter point, one must commend the author for not shying away from the ugly truths of the situation, as is so often the case since 9/11. With his understanding of the negative involvement of the Organization of the Islamic Conference in the Thai scenario and sophisticated religious concepts such as *taqiya* - theologically justified dissembling - Dr. Moore reveals his understanding of the true nature of the threat so many nations face today. In fact, his identification of how the Thai took an insurgent concept, in this case *da-wah*, or the use of religious proselytizing as a cover for subversion, and turned it around to use a positive version of the same tool as a weapon against the threat is most significant for any other nation with a large "at risk" Muslim population.

Hopefully, another author will apply as systematic an eye to the American experience in Afghanistan and Iraq as Dr. Jeff Moore has applied to *The Thai Way of Counterinsurgency.*

Dr. Sebastian L. Gorka   8th May 2014
Associate Dean   Fort McNair
War and Conflict Studies Department   Washington, DC
College of International Security Affairs
National Defense University

Acknowledgments

There is a host of people to thank for helping with this PhD dissertation-turned-book. First and foremost, very special thanks go to Dr. Gerd Nonneman, an internationally recognized subject matter expert on Islamic, Arabic, and Middle East affairs, currently dean of the School of Foreign Service at Georgetown University's campus in Qatar. Dr. Nonneman bravely accepted my subject material and me as his PhD candidate at the most excellent University of Exeter in Devon, and provided superlative tutelage along the way. Likewise, special thanks to Chris Donnelly CMG, and Ms. Emma McCarthy of the UK defense establishment for searching for, and finding, the right professor for my PhD. Without these people, this project would have never gotten off the ground.

Sincere appreciation also goes to Dr. Gareth Stansfield, Professor of Middle East Politics at the University of Exeter, and Dr. Feargal Cochrane, Professor of International Conflict Analysis at the School of Politics and International Relations at the University of Kent. Both provided superb inquiry during my most exciting viva ("PhD defense" in American parlance) and made this work more vigorous, especially the conclusion regarding comparing the Thai way of counterinsurgency (COIN) to David Galula's and Sir Robert Thompson's irregular warfare theories.

In Thailand, the ever-connected and highly knowledgeable Professor Panitan Wattanayagorn of Chulalongkorn University was instrumental in providing broad guidance and specific contacts to interview, as were various persons in Thailand who preferred to remain anonymous. Professor Srisompob Jitpiromsri of the Prince of Songkhla University in Pattani provided multiple contacts as well, plus he gave copious and detailed information on all three wars unavailable from any written source. Thank you, Khun Panitan and Khun Srisompob.

Another exceptional source was former National Intelligence Agency Chief Professor Bhumarat Taksadipong, a living national treasure to Thailand and currently a professor at a Thai university. His insights into all three wars covered in this book were absolutely indispensable. Somchai Rakwijit, former intelligence official and COIN advisor to General Prem Tinsulanonda, likewise provided true insider information, especially on the communist COIN, much of it never written down until now.

Brigadier General Harn Pathai (RTA, RET) did as well. His observations on what it was like being an infantry officer fighting communist guerrillas in the jungles was invaluable. As an aside, thanks also to General Pathai for his service to America while serving in the Vietnam War alongside US troops, where he was wounded and decorated for valor with the Silver Star on 16 April 1971.

Chuan Leekpai, who twice served as Prime Minister of Thailand, was gracious enough to take time out of his busy schedule to grant an interview, which proved priceless. He is surely one of Thailand's most intelligent and effective prime ministers. Thank you, kind sir.

Retired Lieutenant General Kitti Rattanachaya, former Fourth Army commander, granted a highly informative interview that lasted several hours. He dedicated his life to serving Thailand and ran the war in the far south for years. He has also written several books in Thai on the subject. Other exceptional Royal Thai Army interviewees included General Akanit Munsewat, Lieutenant General Waipot Srinual, and Major General Perapong Manakit. Gentlemen, you have my gratitude.

From the Ministry of Interior, top-ranking and highly able Pranai Suwannarat, Director General of the Southern Border Provinces Administrative Centre (SB-PAC), offered tremendous information on political and social programs for the current COIN. One of his predecessors, Samacha Potavorn, Deputy Director of the SB-PAC in the 1980s–90s, did as well. Charnchao Chaiyanukij, Deputy Permanent Secretary of Justice, granted me an interview that was critical in understanding justice facets of the war.

Other hospitable and knowledgeable Thai officials that allowed me their time included: Dr. Gothom Arya, Director, Mahidol University; Professor Amara Pongsapich, Rotary Peace and Conflict Studies Program; Police Major General Tritot Ronnaritivichai, Deputy Commissioner, Special Branch; Professor Arun Bhunupong, former Thai Ambassador to the Soviet Union, the United States, and France, plus former Undersecretary of Ministry of Foreign Affairs; Colonel

Suwan Chirdshai, RTA/ISOC officer; Dr. Khunying Pornthip Rojanasunand of the Justice Ministry's Forensic Science Institute, and Democratic Party Head Abhisit Vejjajiva. Many thanks to each of you for imparting upon me your expertise on Thai COIN.

There were scores of other Thai personnel—some high-ranking officials, some low-ranking officials, and others simply rank-and-file civilians in the southern insurgency zone—that provided intricate commentary on Thai COIN issues. To them, I extend my genuine gratefulness.

There were a handful of Americans with penetrating knowledge of Thai COIN who should be recognized as well. They helped me understand not only Thai COIN, but also Thai culture, or they helped me with sources and editing. They include: Denny Lane, former Assistant US Army Attaché to Thailand; Jeffrey Race, author of the venerable *War Comes to Long An: Revolutionary Conflict in a Vietnamese Province*; Matt Wheeler, currently of the International Crisis Group, who located several hard-to-find sources; Bob Elston, Southeast Asia subject matter expert, who helped with editing; and the legendary Colonel John Cole (US Army, RET), former US Army defense attaché to Thailand.

Two others provided intricate Thai COIN information, too, and deserve many thanks: Nick Nostiz, a freelance photographer who has covered the far south on combat patrols, and Colonel Ahmed Ghazali (Malaysian Army, RET), Faculty of Defence Studies and Management, National Defence University of Malaysia.

TABLE OF CONTENTS

INTRODUCTION

This book analyzes how the Thai conceptualize and wage counterinsurgency (COIN). It does not make COIN recommendations for Thailand's current war, a highly controversial subject. The Thai way of COIN deserves analysis because Thailand has defeated two insurgencies and is currently fighting another. The first of these involved a nationwide battle against communist insurgents between 1965 and 1985. The second, from 1980 to 1998, was on Thailand's southernmost border against a hodgepodge of separatists and criminal groups that touted everything from increased political participation to secession to jihad. The current insurgency, also on the southern border, fights for a separate state under a combined impetus of Pattani nationalism, Malay racism, and Islamist jihad. This movement makes extensive use of terrorism by regularly targeting civilians.

In order to proceed, definitions are necessary. Islamist here refers to those who believe in the global spread of ultraconservative and intolerant Islam via preaching, politics, manipulation, and violence. Moderate Muslims do not believe in this radical interpretation and assert it has nothing to do whatsoever with Islam. Additionally, jihad to moderate Muslims means "utmost effort." Getting up early in the morning to pray falls in this category. To Islamists, however, it means warfare and terrorism.

The US Department of Defense (DoD) defines insurgency as "an organized movement aimed at the overthrow of a constituted government through the use of subversion and armed conflict."[1] Irregular warfare is also a term commonly applied to the whole insurgency/terrorism spectrum. At any rate, insurgents live and operate among the people, essentially militarizing swaths of the population to join their underground army as secret logisticians, intelligence agents, bomb makers, assassins, and light infantry fighters. They usually do not wear uniforms and they never field massive standing armies. Instead, the insurgents' most important weapon is usually political—namely, the ability to convince a nation's people that the state is illegitimate, and the insurgents' cause is just. This is political warfare, and it requires extensive propaganda, indoctrination, and psychological operations (psyops). In many cases, it also involves politically inspiring the downtrodden population to rally against the state's genuine failings. As guerrilla warfare theorist and practitioner Mao Zedong prescribed, insurgency is a massive clandestine movement that depends on popular support, whether that support is offered voluntarily or secured through force or trickery. Insurgency experts Thomas A. Marks, Seb Gorka, and Robert Sharp of the United States National Defense University decisively sum up what insurgency is about: armed politics creating a counterstate within an existing state.[2] The communist Vietnamese National Liberation Front, commonly known as the Viet Cong, is a prime example.

Regarding force, all insurgencies use subterfuge warfare—hit-and-run raids, ambushes, assassinations, and bombings, for example. Some use subterfuge to drive the state into exhaustion where it sues for political settlement. Others use it to buy time and amass an army to eventually battle the state on equal military terms. This is where insurgency ends and conventional war begins.

It is important to differentiate insurgency from terrorism. Insurgency seeks to win the people over to its cause through political warfare and violence and usually targets and attacks government forces. While terrorism also uses political warfare, it punishes the population by targeting it with violence. Terrorism does not try to win over the population. The DoD, in the 2010 Joint Publication 3-07.2, *Antiterrorism*, describes terrorism as, "the unlawful use of violence or threat of violence to instill fear and coerce governments or societies. Terrorism is often motivated by religious, political, or other ideological beliefs and committed in the pursuit of goals that are usually political."[3]

Marks, Gorka, and Sharp describe terrorism as armed political communication in which the terror group itself is the counterstate entity. They assert that while terrorists do on occasion attack state security forces, their main target and enemy is the population. The Japanese Red Army and Germany's Red Army Faktion are two prime examples.

The DoD defines COIN as "those military, paramilitary, political, economic, psychological, and civic actions taken by a government to defeat insurgency."[4] This is vastly different from conventional warfare and heavy suppression. Conventional warfare is typically state versus state, army versus army. It has clearly defined battlefields where the end goal is destruction of the enemy's forces and the surrender of the opposing state at bayonet point. Heavy suppression— what some states use to battle insurgents—is the liberal use of conventional force against guerrillas, their civilian supporters, and even civilians that have nothing to do with a rebellion. It is, in essence, the extermination of swaths of people in a rebellious zone in order to kill as many insurgents as possible and intimidate the survivors into total submission. Heavy suppression, like terrorism, punishes a population and does nothing to repair broken political, social, and economic issues that fuel insurgency.

COIN is different. COIN requires not only precise force application operations based on quality intelligence, but also lasting social and economic programs, counterpolitical warfare, political remedies for the disenfranchised, and government acceptance of previously ignored cultural realities. All these efforts have to be coordinated under a single strategy and command authority. If they are not, COIN will not work. All this is easier said than done, however. COIN is a difficult type of warfare for five reasons: (1) it can take years to succeed and results are hard to define; (2) the battle space is poorly defined; (3) insurgents are not easily identifiable; (4) war typically takes place among a civilian population whom the guerrillas depend on for auxiliary support; and (5) it requires coordination of civilian, military, and police assets at the strategic, operational, and tactical levels.

As Sir Robert Thompson stated in his 1966 classic *Defeating Communist Insurgency: The Lessons of Malaya and Vietnam*, COIN assumes the at-risk population is part of the state and is worth saving. It is the prize to win. Thompson and his British cohorts formulated this idea and others like it while successfully defeating communist insurgents in the Federation of Malaya in the 1950s.

David Galula, French COIN theorist and anti-insurgent fighter in Algeria in the 1950s, developed similar theories about protecting and insulating the population from insurgents in his 1964 book *Counterinsurgency Warfare: Theory and Practice*. Both Galula and Thompson are considered "classical COIN" theorists, and some modern COIN thinkers assert their tenets do not apply to today's hyperactive, asymmetric warfare environment, especially in the face of Islamist jihad. There is some truth to this assertion. Close study of Galula and Thompson, however, proves that most COIN theories, even modern ones, are indeed rooted in the thoughts of these two founding fathers. They were pioneers in their field and their lessons are relative to today's threat environment.

COIN is typically characterized as "population-centric" instead of "enemy-centric." Population-centric generally means focusing on protecting the population from insurgents. Enemy-centric means destroying enemy fighting units. While insurgent fighters need to be neutralized, exclusively doing this does nothing to reduce the root causes of an insurgency. That is why politics and economics are also necessary in COIN.

States that adopt COIN usually base their strategies on some semblance of what insurgency expert David Kilcullen calls the "three pillars of COIN": security, politics, and economics. Kilcullen is an Australian Army Lieutenant Colonel with a PhD in political anthropology who specializes in insurgency and COIN. In 2005, the George W. Bush Administration hired Kilcullen to head counterterrorism strategy for the US State Department. This was more of a station for him to work from as he advised key government and military personnel, including General David Petraeus, on how to hone US counterterror and COIN strategy. He, along with a host of other high-level military thinkers such as Kalev Sepp, Eliot Cohen, and Conrad Crane, helped fix American COIN strategy in Iraq and save the United States from a Vietnam-style geostrategic disaster.

So why is the Thai way of COIN relevant? First, no one has ever written a holistic professional military study of Thailand's COIN strategies and tactics. Several foreign and Thai authors have examined Thailand's insurgencies individually, and many have done so quite well, but none have analyzed all of Thailand's major COIN efforts to decipher just how this nation has succeeded. Moreover, numerous foreign writers on Thai national security affairs are pure academics, and many of these are decidedly leftist. They tend to lambast the government for its national security decision making and ignore its successes. This book corrects these wrongs and seeks to do so objectively.

Second, the United States and its allies, including Thailand itself, could use the lessons summarized in this book to improve their COIN doctrines. Since the United States' retooling of its COIN methods resulting from its involvement in Iraq, Afghanistan, Pakistan, the Philippines, and other countries, the US government has ordered scores of COIN studies of lessons learned. One of the most significant was the 2006 US Army and Marine Corps COIN manual *FM-3-24*, which included lessons from Vietnam, Ireland, Malaysia, Algeria, the Philippines, China, ancient Persia, Lebanon, Spain, and Haiti. The manual overlooked examples from Thailand's successful COINs despite their positive value. The 2012 US COIN manual rewrite, which I participated in, has some lessons from Thailand, but not in any depth.

Third, this book explains Thai national security issues and decision making in intricate detail. This information is critically important as America and the world intensify their focus on the Asia-Pacific region as of 2013. Understanding Thailand's defense priorities and processes, both internal and external, means more effective engagement with it, and that translates to more effective regional interaction.

Finally, this study explains how to wage COIN on multiple levels—strategic, operational, and tactical. The fact that it comes from the Thai perspective is irrelevant. Explaining COIN is necessary because, despite having waged COIN in Iraq, Afghanistan, and other theaters in the Global War on Terror, large portions of the US national security community still do not understand COIN. The United States and its allies must continue to study COIN and master it in addition to conventional warfare. Insurgency is not going away. Even while the Obama administration withdrew from Iraq and is withdrawing from Afghanistan, its January 2012 defense guidance, contained in the document *Sustaining U.S. Global Leadership: Priorities for 21st Century Defense*, asserts that America will utilize Special Forces (SF) and continue to fight terrorism and insurgency around the world, but more from a foreign internal defense angle. To accomplish this, the United States and its allies need to keep their COIN capabilities sharp.

This book has its origins in my dissertation project. It has since been honed and shaped for a broader national security readership. Discovering the Thai way of COIN entailed a lengthy, nontraditional process that combined academic research and investigative journalism. It involved four months of research on the ground in Thailand interviewing pertinent people and visiting former and current insurgency areas. It also included two years of follow-up interviews and research using books, monographs, and articles ranging from the present back to the 1960s. The main approach used to analyze Thailand's three internal wars is my own "COIN Pantheon," a subjective analytical model that filters various aspects of each war in order to discern patterns of Thai irregular warfare actions and behavior.

The COIN Pantheon Model of Analysis

The COIN Pantheon is adapted from David Kilcullen's "three pillars of COIN" model. Kilcullen's model consists of a base of intelligence and other information sources that support security, political, and economic columns. These are the general types of operations that must be applied to reduce insurgency and uplift and protect the population. The roof of Kilcullen's model is control: a government seizes control of the insurgency zone and then stabilizes it. The overarching goal of the state, says Kilcullen, is to achieve legitimacy in the eyes of the population over the insurgents.

The three pillars strategy is loosely based on British efforts to defeat communist insurgents in Malaysia in the 1950s, as described in Thompson's book. While very well conceived, the three pillars offer no magic formula for victory—and Kilcullen asserts this up front. And neither Thompson nor Galula disagrees. As Kilcullen argues, every insurgency offers unique challenges, and the application of the three pillars must be tailored to each conflict.

I created the COIN Pantheon because I needed a simpler model to help filter a voluminous amount of complex Thai insurgency material that spanned from 1965 to the present. The model looks like a Greek pantheon (see illustration 1).

ILLUSTRATION 1

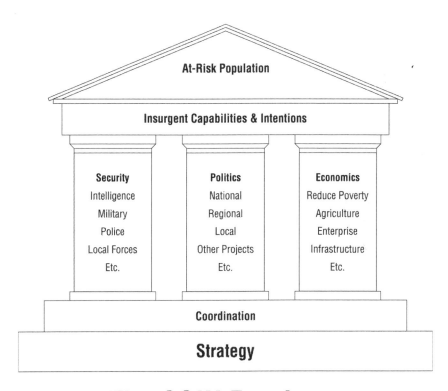

The COIN Pantheon

The base consists of strategy, which asserts the end goals of the COIN effort. Ideally, end goals need to be realistic, clear, and decisive. They should address root causes of an insurgency, such as extreme poverty and government corruption, and the outputs of an insurgency, such as violence and propaganda. Usually, strategy involves (1) ends, (2) ways, and (3) means—what is to be achieved, the methods and programs used to attain these achievements, and the assets used to fulfill them. In this model, however, strategy means simply the end goals. Ways and means come later.

The next edifice is coordination. It reflects the central command-and-control authority that manages the war. It synchronizes all operations and funnels material and manpower where needed. Coordination is critical in COIN because multiple civilian, police, and military entities need to work in conjunction with one another in order to successfully apply ways and means to achieve specific ends. If coordination is muddled, it has the same effect as having too many cooks in the kitchen. Nothing effective gets done.

As Kilcullen prescribed, the three pillars, or columns, consist of the ways and means of security, politics, and economics. All three pillars overlap in places, and they all benefit from each other as well. Politics cannot move forward without security, for example, and security operations are more effective and population-friendly when accompanied by effective information operations that describe the government's security goals and calm the population's fears. Likewise, economic operations nearly always need some type of security, and security operations alone rarely achieve government legitimacy. Poverty reduction is necessary as well.

In broad terms, the security pillar entails quelling guerrilla and terrorist operations. The ultimate goal of security is to protect the population. Destruction of insurgent forces is of secondary importance, but if the chance arises, COIN forces usually make it a priority. The military is but one component in the security pillar. The police, intelligence services, and local forces have critical roles, too.

The political pillar entails instilling effective and just governance that reduces the political reasons for revolt. Government over insurgent legitimacy is the ultimate goal. Tasks in this pillar might include, but are not restricted to, amnesty programs, reintegrating surrendered insurgents into society, instituting population-friendly government reforms, correcting grievances, increasing the at-risk population's political participation, and all forms of psyops.

The economic pillar includes micro- and macroeconomic initiatives designed to build capacity to grow and develop a sustainable economy, including resource and infrastructure management. Poverty reduction is key here. Local buy-in regarding what development projects will work is pivotal. Development is rarely decisive, however. It is more commonly a tool that erodes insurgent prowess by reducing the economic angst of a population, which reduces grievances and increases government legitimacy.

These three pillars push against the next edifice, the enemy. Here, the model is concerned with insurgent capabilities and intentions—what they can do militarily and ideologically. If these things are competently defined, then they can be addressed, curbed, thwarted, and in some cases, halted.

The roof of the COIN Pantheon is the population that the government structure aims to uplift and support. Not only must COIN practitioners thoroughly understand an at-risk population, they must also identify the nexus between the insurgency and population. COIN means severing or eroding that nexus.

Filtering each Thai COIN through this model reveals patterns on how the Thai organize for and wage COIN (see illustration 2). Each of the main chapters of this book is organized along the lines of the COIN Pantheon. Each chapter is prefaced by an overall synopsis of each war, providing the reader with a bird's-eye view of what happened, followed by detailed sections on how the Thai developed strategy, organized coordination, and waged security, political, and economic operations. Sections that describe the insurgents and the at-risk population are included, too.

While these chapters help reveal the Thai way of COIN, Gareth Stansfield of the University of Exeter, and Feargal Cochrane of the University of Kent, suggested the author filter these COIN Pantheon findings through the theories of Galula and Thompson. While this exercise could be a separate PhD, these

ILLUSTRATION 2

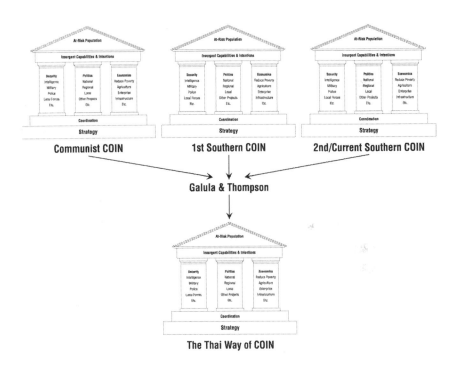

Communist COIN   1st Southern COIN   2nd/Current Southern COIN

Galula & Thompson

The Thai Way of COIN

professors were thoroughly correct that even a cursory look at this subject would strengthen the COIN Pantheon's findings, as illustrated in the concluding chapter.

Glancing at the conclusions of this study, it is evident that the Thai, once they understand the insurgent situation, use a decisive strategy of politics leading the military and staunch coordination to drive forward their COIN operations. Having said this, they use a commonsense balance of security, politics, and economics where and however needed to quell insurgent violence, political warfare, and to uplift the at-risk population from poverty. The Royal Thai Army (RTA) usually leads these efforts, and under its supervision, local forces also play a significant role. The Thai well understand that insurgency is people's war, and they believe in countering insurgency with the state's version of people's war. In keeping with politics leading the military, the Thai understand the necessity of reducing the insurgents' angst and popular support via political programs, including wider political participation, amnesty, and psyops operations, just to name three.

The Thai go to great lengths to define and infiltrate the insurgents, which means they put tremendous stock in intelligence. Moreover, they strive to treat the population as the object of victory.

Having mentioned these, it is pertinent to note the Thai have not always applied these principles flawlessly. Indeed, some of their efforts have been unrefined, clumsy, and even counterproductive. Thai political infighting is a chronic problem that has delayed effective COIN programs and even exacerbated negative situations, especially in the current war.

At the same time, the Thai have won their past COIN engagements. This cannot be ignored. There are reasons for these victories. They have, moreover, experienced some success in their current ten-year-old COIN. Old bad habits, however, are weighting down their better efforts.

A Need for Analysis by National Security Professionals

There is some excellent literature on Thai COIN, but it is not too copious. Two Americans wrote must-read studies of the communist COIN: Thomas A.

Marks's *Making Revolution* and George K. Tanham's *Trial in Thailand*. Marks is a department head at National Defense University and an irregular warfare expert. His book served as an anchor for this book's chapter on the communist COIN. Tanham was a State Department official engaged in the fight against the Thai communists and was ahead of his time as an American COIN thinker. Tanham's work helped clarify the scope of scores of Thai security, political, and economic programs.

From the Thai side, General Saiyud Kerdphol wrote *The Struggle for Thailand, Counter-Insurgency, 1965–1985*. It is a most superb collection of speeches that the general gave over two decades about the direction of the war, enemy activities, and Thai government successes and failures. Other indispensible Thai works include Kanok Wongtrangan's monograph "Change and Persistence in Thai Counter-Insurgency Policy"; Suchit Bunbongkarn's *The Military in Thai Politics, 1981–86*; and the masterful *From Armed Suppression to Political Offensive: Attitudinal Transformation of Thai Military Officers since 1976* by Chai-Anan Samudavanija, Kusuma Snitwongse, and Suchit Bunbongkarn. These Thai authors captured the essence of Thai COIN during the communist era like no others. Gawin Chutima's "The Rise and Fall of the Communist Party of Thailand, 1973–1987" was a critical and brutally honest look by a Thai communist at the strengths and weaknesses of his insurgent movement writ large. Some Thai officers who strategized the defeat of the communists wrote works in Thai, but these, tragically, were either poorly published or ignored.

A handful of bold authors have tackled the southern insurgency of the 1970s, '80s, and '90s. This is a little-researched and scantily understood conflict, and the researchers who took on this subject should be commended. Without them, this book would not have been possible. This author fully acknowledges that more needs to be investigated on this particular war and hopes Thai researchers seize upon this important mission. Critical works on this war include Panomporn Anurugsa's 1984 University of Texas doctoral dissertation, "Political Integration Policy in Thailand: The Case of the Malay Muslim Minority"; Ornanong Noiwong's 2001 Northern Illinois University doctoral dissertation, "Political

Integration Policies and Strategies of the Thai Government Toward the Malay-Muslims of Southernmost Thailand (1973–2000)"; and Surin Pitsuwan's 1982 work, "Islam and Malay Nationalism: A Case Study of the Malay-Muslims of Southern Thailand." Surin went on to serve in high-level positions within the Royal Thai Government (RTG), including as Minister of Foreign Affairs. Ladd M. Thomas, a Northern Illinois University professor, covered the south in the 1970s–80s in several works, including "Political Violence in the Muslim Provinces of Southern Thailand," written for Singapore's Institute of Southeast Asian Studies (ISEAS). While indispensible, none of these works approached the southern insurgency from a COIN angle.

A handful of writers have looked at the current war in the south from a security point of view, including Thailand's General Kitti Rattanachaya, who authored the highly informative *Thailand's Southern Insurgency: Creation of Pattani State*. Australian Marc Askew has done groundbreaking work on the current insurgency and has published penetrating, must-read studies such as "Fighting with Ghosts: Confronting Thailand's Enigmatic Southern Fire." Simmons College professor Zachary Abuza has likewise produced highly utilitarian studies and books such as *Conspiracy of Silence: The Insurgency in Southern Thailand*. Duncan McCargo has written several works on the south, including *Rethinking Thailand's Southern Violence*, to which he both contributed a chapter and served as an editor. This book's many contributing authors provide historical material that peers into the causes of current conflict along with offering good commentary about the war's early period. Still, with the exception of General Kitti, none of these respected studies have taken a COIN point of view.

A host of other authors have provided crucial information on Thailand's insurgencies but produced less than utilitarian analyses. Katherine A. Bowie's *Rituals of National Loyalty: An Anthropology of the State and the Village Scout Movement in Thailand* is a prime example. Bowie expertly describes Thailand's main counter-communist, political-paramilitary program, the Village Scouts. She details the foundation of this decisive program and how it functioned. This book certainly benefited from her diligent research. She admittedly uses a Marxist model, however, to analyze the Scouts and the war, which negates her objectivity. Because she uses Marx to analyze a communist rebellion, her final analysis is predetermined. More, Bowie does not admit the Chinese and North Vietnamese supported the Thai insurgents, a point even the rebels themselves admit.

The International Crisis Group (ICG), a Brussels-based think tank, has also produced exceptional research on Thailand's current war, but its analyses of Thai COIN have been lacking. In October 2007, for example, the ICG published a monograph titled "Southern Thailand: The Problem with Paramilitaries," which critiqued the government use of local forces in COIN programs as brutal, ineffective, and only adding to the carnage of insurgency. It suggested that these forces should be replaced with Thai soldiers.

In presenting this latter argument, the ICG demonstrated a poor understanding of COIN in general. While the ICG is certainly correct that bad local force actors can derail good-intentioned COIN, inserting conventionally trained soldiers from Bangkok, Korat, Chiang Mai, and other such places with their M-16 rifles into Thai Malay Muslim villages does not address core security, political, and economic problems at the village level. Conventional forces do not take into account the social and religious nuances that are required to wage COIN. COIN is local and irregular. Local irregular forces are necessary, at the very least, to guide national forces through insurgent territory. Optimally, local forces fight the insurgents as agents of the government in their own neighborhoods and villages since they know the local "human terrain"—that is, the culture, the socioeconomic connections, the individual characters, local politics, etc. This practice is common in nearly all COINs, and local forces have proved decisive in Thailand's past wars. If improperly managed, however, local forces can exacerbate the negative issues that feed insurgency. This has happened in Thailand on occasion, which the ICG correctly points out. As an aside, Matt Wheeler, an exceptionally talented researcher and writer with a dedication to thorough field investigations, recently took over the ICG's Thai desk. The material he has since produced has been outstanding.

Overall, however, the field of Thai COIN begs for examination by national security professionals. If this subject is left to pundits who do not understand COIN, the truth of Thailand's national security history and its COIN lessons—the positives and the negatives—will remain hidden. This book capitalizes on professional studies that came before it, breaks new ground on Thai COIN theory and practices, and creates opportunities for other researchers to explore. Hopefully, the Thai will "Charlie Mike"—military nomenclature for "continue mission"—here with vigor. It is, after all, their country, and their national security, that is at stake.

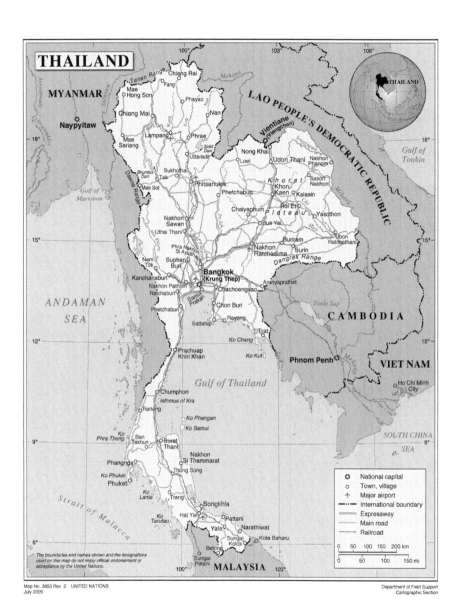

United Nations, Thailand Map No. 3853 Rev.2, July 2009.

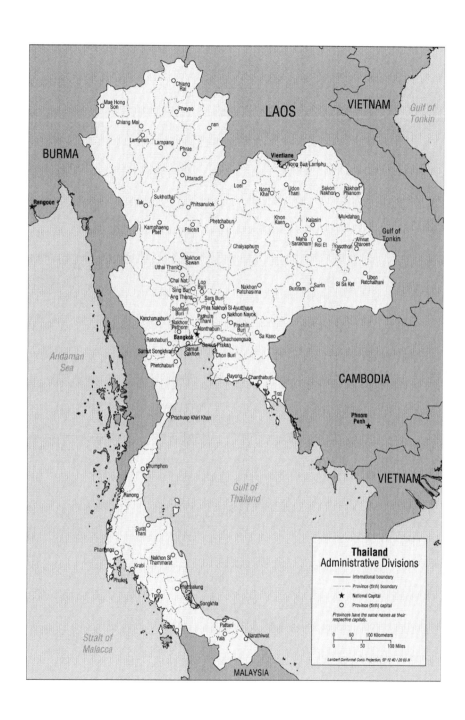

US Government Map

SOUTHERN THAILAND

Trang

Songkhla

Hat Yai

Sada

Pattani

Yala

Narathiwat

Langkawi

Kedah

Sungai Kolok

Tumpat

Kota Baharu

Betong

Sungai Petani

Perak

Kelantan

MALAYSIA

United Nations, Thailand Map No. 3853 Rev.2, July 2009.

THAILAND IN HISTORICAL CONTEXT

Thailand's rich history need not be repeated here, but some historical issues that helped set the stage for insurgency and also counter it should be mentioned. These include a societal rank system called *sakdi na*, Theravada Buddhism, Thailand's countrywide administrative system, and "Thainess." None of these issues were intended to hurt or suppress the Thai population. They were political or cultural mechanisms that in some cases inadvertently helped fan the flames of insurgency. In other cases, however, they helped quell them.

The *sakdi na* class system was imposed on Thailand by Siamese royalty in the 1400s. Literally translated as "field power," it was a feudal rank system based on points and proximity to the throne. High *sakdi na* points (such as five hundred thousand) meant one was a part of, or close to, the royal court and thereby afforded privileges such as education, special legal rights, and land. Low *sakdi na* points (such as one hundred) indicated peasantry, which meant fewer privileges and a meager life. *Sakdi na* also established client-patron relationships throughout society, locking lower-level citizens into the orbits of those above them for business, government, and/or military purposes.

Even though *sakdi na* was officially eliminated after a coup ushered in constitutional change in 1932, the phantom of its class and rank system remained.[1] The poor can rise in Thai society today and become successful in most any endeavor, but there is still a hazy class division wherein the lower ranks, such as workers and farmers, defer politically and socially to higher classes that rule the country. The upper ranks, characterized not only by money and power but also by central Thai traits such as light skin, softer facial features, and/or Chinese blood, are sometimes referred to as *amart*. The lower ranks, typically characterized by not only lesser socioeconomic status but also by darker skin and sometimes by tinges of Khmer and Lao blood, are sometimes referred to as *prai*.

Again, these are not clear and dogmatic distinctions. They are much softer, and they are rapidly fading as Thailand progresses into the future, but they exist, and they are controversial. More, when the *prai* have become politically disgruntled, they have occasionally clashed with the *amart*, a de facto violation of the ghost of *sakdi na*. This societal rank has exacerbated insurgency; the ruling class balks at lower-class audacity, and the lower class is inspired to rebel against the vestiges of this social ranking system.

Theravada Buddhism came to Thailand with Ceylonese monks in the sixth century. Siam (the historical name of Thailand) adopted it in the thirteenth century as its national religion. Theravada Buddhism became a centerpiece of Thai society, and even today it is part of the country's core identity. Buddhism introduced ideas of *karma* and fate to Thailand and provided it with a set of standardized ethics. The Buddhist understanding of fate, coupled with the remnants of *sakdi na*, has made Thailand generally a nation of politically demure people with strong central leaders. On the other hand, Thailand's citizens became more politically active in the 1970s. And since then, especially since 2006, they have become hyper political as Thailand's 2014 political crisis demonstrates.

Buddhist monks, collectively known as *sangha*, have held a special place in Thai society as sacred advocates of the teachings of the Buddha. The *sangha* were supported with money and daily food donations or *alms giving*. In return, the monks bestowed blessings on the people, helping them earn good *karma*. Buddhism gradually became the national moral compass for the people and the government as well.[2] Regarding insurgency, Buddhism's extensive influence on Thai society and government has sometimes clashed with the cultures of rebellious groups, specifically the Malay Muslims who see their religion as a dominant societal core. At the same time, Buddhism has helped the Thai harness incredible compassion and understanding for insurgents that have committed extreme acts of violence. For example, Buddhism provided the ethical foundation for hundreds of rural development programs and encouraged COIN campaigns to offer amnesty to thousands of insurgents in the 1970s, '80s, and '90s.

The history of countrywide administration in Thailand dates back to the 1800s, when Kings Rama IV and V went to great lengths to consolidate Siam's borders. They sent emissaries to Europe to learn how central governments ruled their respective countries via provincial systems and then applied these lessons in Thailand. Over time, this effort (1) kept European colonial ambition from seizing Thailand's unmarked border areas, and (2) formally made citizens out of most outlying ethnic groups, such as the Lao/Thai Issan people in the northeast (the region is also called Issan), and Malay Muslims in the far south.[3] Never having been fully consolidated under Thai rule, these groups resisted central government control, and many of them would eventually become insurgents.

"Thainess" (*kwam-pen Thai*), or Thai culturalism, has also contributed to insurgency in Thailand. Foreigners (*farang*) explain this concept as "what it means to be Thai," though few understand it. Certainly, Thainess is a positive, unique, and enriching cultural phenomenon. Far more than just language, mannerisms, and food, Thainess is based on hundreds of years of cultural history and encompasses Thai thought processes and spirituality—not Buddhism explicitly, but the Thai version of what it means to be a human being and a member of Thai society. In itself, Thainess is uplifting. If, however, Thainess is used as a filter to evaluate security, governmental, and economic policies, it can reduce objectivity. This has occurred among certain officials charged with carrying out COIN. Moreover, when Thainess has clashed with other cultures' unique and rich ways, such as those of Malay Muslims, the results have exacerbated insurgency.

For example, in 1939 Prime Minister (PM) Phibun Songgram (formally, Plaek Phibunsongkhram) passed the National Culture Act, which consisted of decrees that promoted both Thai nationalism and Thainess. The act forced all citizens, regardless of religion or ethnicity, to adopt uniform cultural practices. By law, for instance, neither Hmong tribes in the north (technically not Thai citizens), Issan peoples in the northeast, nor Malay Muslims in the south were allowed to wear traditional garb, and they had to speak Thai instead of their local dialects. Thai historian Thanet Aphornsuvan says that the act "required women to wear hats and Western dress, forbade the chewing of betel and areca nuts, and instructed the use of forks and spoons as the 'national cutlery.'"[4]

Rulers in other countries have taken similar steps. For example, Turkey's President Mustafa Kemal Atatürk in the 1920s–30s forced Turkish citizens to adopt Western ways, dress, and government. But whereas Atatürk was successful, partially due to the homogeneous nature of Turkish society, Thailand was less homogenous, and its outlying ethnic communities recoiled. Malay Muslims in the far south rejected the act because it tampered with their deeply rooted dress, language, and heritage. Many southerners felt their culture was at stake. While the Issan people's Lao heritage was not unlike Thai culture, they also rejected Phibun's policies for stomping out their deeply ingrained customs. All of this created societal angst, which fed oxygen into insurgency when it infiltrated Thailand from abroad.

THE COMMUNIST COIN: 1965–1985

Prelude

The international communist movement targeted Asia (and other regions of the world) at the first meeting of the Communist International (COMINTERN) in Moscow in 1920, according to former Communist Party of Thailand (CPT) member Gawin Chutima and COMINTERN histories. COMINTERN sought to replace right-leaning or democratic governments around the world with communist ones typified by command economies, central ruling committees, and rigid Marxist rules and regulations. COMINTERN cheerily referred to these systems as democracy, but no communist country in history ever had an authentically representative democracy—witness Lenin's Soviet Union, Pol Pot's Cambodia, and Wilhelm Pieck's East Germany.[1]

At any rate, as Mao's influence spread throughout China, communist Chinese in Thailand established several subversive parties: the Communist Party of China, the South Seas Committee, the Communist Party of Siam, and the Communist Party of China in Thailand (CCPT).[2] Most were Chinese-led, though there were also Vietnamese-led factions. Ho Chi Minh operated in Thailand as a communist agent provocateur in 1928.[3]

On 20 March 1930, the CCPT published its "Draft Statement Analyzing the Government and Economy of Siam and the Procedures for the Associations." It was a blueprint on why and how to infiltrate Thailand through clandestine networks of secret cells inside clubs, organizations, and unions so as to more effectively spread communism throughout the population. Gawin says the document was nearly a carbon copy of Mao's *Analysis of the Classes in Chinese Society* and was short on population analysis and substance.[4] It worked well enough, however. The "Draft Statement" provided the strategy for thirty years of methodical communist infiltration of Thailand. Bangkok responded with a series of anticommunist laws and law enforcement campaigns, but none stemmed the rising tide of communist subversion.

The first government offensive against communism was the Anticommunist Act of 1933, which restricted communist activities and membership.[5] In 1936, the government launched a massive crackdown on communists, arresting hundreds of people in Bangkok and northern Thailand. While the crackdown destroyed the Communist Party of Siam, many agents escaped and founded the Thai Communist Party on 1 December 1942. In the early 1950s, this group changed its name to the Communist Party of Thailand (CPT), and its two hundred members accepted the CCPT's four thousand members, mostly Chinese, into their ranks. These newcomers added badly needed experience to the fledgling CPT and kept it in China's orbit.[6]

In 1948, more crackdowns occurred as the Royal Thai Police (RTP) raided Chinese schools, clubs, and associations, arresting hundreds of people. In addition, PM Phibun limited the number of Chinese entering the country to two hundred people per year, down from ten thousand.[7] Still, the communist cause grew, especially in the Issan region, which resulted in incidents such as the March 1949 "Kilo 11 Incident."

The Kilo 11 Incident involved the deaths of four major politicians from Issan, including former Minister of Industry Nai Thong-In and former Deputy Commerce Minister Nai Chamlong Daoruang, highly visible men with respected backgrounds. The RTP arrested them and their cohorts for several serious offenses, including communist activities, lobbying for Issan's autonomy, and for joining a Marine-backed coup led by former PM Pridi Phanomyong. Authorities also accused Pridi of being a communist, partly because of his extreme, Soviet-style command economy proposals that the rest of the government firmly rejected.

While Nai Thong-In and his associates were being transported to prison, his supporters attacked the RTP convoy. A firefight broke out and chaos ensued. Police claimed afterward that the prisoners were killed in the crossfire, while the rebels said they were executed. Regardless, the Kilo 11 Incident reinforced northeasterners' angst over the government's centralization policies that they believed were diluting their culture. They also felt politically rejected and resented their plight as the poorest region of Thailand. While most of this poverty was due to dreadful agricultural conditions, the government had done little to help Issan.[8] The infiltrating communists increasingly used these grievances to rally the population to their cause.

From 1952 to 1953, the government uncovered yet another communist plot to overthrow the government and raided over 150 Chinese-owned businesses. They made 250 arrests and closed scores of Chinese-sponsored clubs and schools accused of communist activities. At the same time, the legislature passed the Anticommunist Act of 1952 (a.k.a. the "Un-Thai Activities Act") that made it a criminal offense to be a communist.[9]

The Thai government, contrary to the accusations of left-leaning historians, was not paranoid, nor was it using the false specter of communism as an excuse to torment the Chinese or the people of Issan. Communist infiltration of Asia unquestionably occurred during the post–World War II era. Mao was the main inspiration. After defeating the nationalist Chinese government in 1949, he said one of his main goals was to spread communist revolution around the world.[10]

Indeed, communist revolutionary wars surrounded Thailand in the 1950s. To Thailand's north and east, Ho Chi Minh's forces were fully engaged in communist revolution in Vietnam, and they spread their war to South Vietnam, Laos, and Cambodia with Chinese and Soviet assistance. (Chinese-Soviet cooperation crumbled in the 1970s, however, and these early allies became staunch enemies by 1975.) To the south, Chin Peng's forces, which the British and Malaysians called the Communist Terrorist Organization (CTO), had been engaged since 1948 in full-scale guerrilla war and terrorism in Malaya.[11] To the west, the communist Revolutionary Burma Army and other groups had been waging insurgency since the end of World War II. Farther afield, the Communist Party of the Philippines had been attempting a revolution since the 1930s. The Communist Party of Indonesia was doing the same. All these groups, while political in nature, also waged wars of assassination, bombings, and subterfuge. Some, such as the North Vietnamese, fought major infantry operations at places such as Dien Bien Phu, exhibiting highly effective ground combat prowess. The North Korean invasion of South Korea in 1950 represented the hallmark of violent communist expansion in Asia via a swift and heavy-hitting conventional military strike.

Amid these wars, China increased pressure on Thailand in 1953 when it announced, via radio, the most powerful psyops tool of the era, the establishment of the Thai Autonomous People's Government (TAPG) in Yunnan Province. Establishing a shadow government outside Thailand by another nation-state was an act of war. To soften this bold maneuver, China said that the TAPG would represent a "Greater Thailand," something that PM Phibun and the Thai population had generally supported since the 1940s—that is, an expansion of Thailand's borders to include its historical, ethnic, and economic claims. In a brilliant psyops maneuver, then, China had stolen a popular Thai nationalist sentiment and made it a communist one.[12]

In 1954, North Vietnam added to the pressure on Thailand. Ho Chi Minh's Viet Minh troops crossed into Laos and established a Free Laos government, a Marxist administration outside Vientiane's jurisdiction. Bangkok perceived this act as an immediate threat because of (1) Issan's cultural and geographic links to Laos, (2) Issan's rebellious streak, (3) the presence of communist activists in Issan, and (4) the fifty thousand Vietnamese loyal to Ho Chi Minh living along Thailand's side of the Mekong River.[13]

In 1961, came yet another act of aggression. According to Thomas Marks— the premier foreign Thai communist insurgency specialist—the CPT held its Third Party Congress, declaring that war was its method of revolution for Thailand. The CPT planned to set up a Northeast Region Jungle Headquarters from which to wage this war, and it designed support networks that included leftist and communist organizations such as the Farmer's Liberation Association.[14] For the communists, their revolutionary designs on Asia and Thailand were unfolding according to plan, specifically the 1930 "Draft Statement Analyzing the Government and Economy of Siam."

China and its surrogates then launched a series of propaganda attacks to lay the groundwork for war. From November 1964 to January 1965, Radio Peking, Pathet Lao Radio, and Radio Hanoi announced that Chinese, Laotian, and North Vietnamese communist forces were supporting revolutionary front organizations in Thailand, namely the Thai Independence Movement and the Thai Patriotic Front. Adding fuel to the fire, Chinese Marshal Chen Yi stated in January 1965 that Thailand was next on the list of wars of liberation.[15] Finally, on 7 August 1965, the CPT officially launched its war against the RTG.[16]

For Thailand's revolution, then, there was no spontaneous peasant revolt cloaked in communist red glory, no sudden citizens' uprising demanding more political freedom, and no workers' movement gallantly driven to strike, as frequently heralded in leftist lore. To be sure, poverty, government corruption, and lack of political opportunity for many Thai citizens made them ripe for revolt, but the ideology, the people, and the organizational mechanism that rallied them came mainly from China and North Vietnam. It was a prepackaged, franchised revolution—an invasion—that would claim thousands of lives over the next few decades. Eventually, however, the war would also establish Thailand as one of the best counterinsurgency fighters in history.

Overview of the Communist COIN

1965–1967

The CPT launched its war to overthrow the government and replace it with a Marxist one on 7 August 1965. The communists termed it "gun-firing day." Here, an armed CPT propaganda team clashed with a police unit, a firefight ensued, and the war began.

Unlike many countries that refuse to acknowledge they are facing an insurgency, the Royal Thai Government quickly understood this irregular threat and how it fit into broader wars of communist liberation throughout Asia. The government responded with a lucid COIN program. Says Professor Arun Bhunupong, former RTG diplomat in the Ministry of Foreign Affairs (MoFA): "At the time, people were alarmed by the spread of communism and spoke of the domino theory, and many thought the next to fall would be Thailand." Thailand was determined not to fall victim to the communists, however. "But when they arrived at the Thai border," Arun says, "the domino struck back. Ultimately, this was the Waterloo of the spread of communism in Southeast Asia." [17] Professor Bhumarat Taksadipong, former head of the National Intelligence Agency (NIA), echoes this sentiment. "We refused to be the next domino," he says. "We said, 'We can fight back. We can do it.'"[18] Ultimately Thailand did, in fact, fight back, and quite successfully so, but the RTG's response was neither quickly planned nor easily executed. In fact, until 1977, it was messy and haphazard.

Field Marshal Sarit Thanarat, who was also the Prime Minister (20 October 1958–8 December 1963), Minister of the Interior, and Acting Director of the RTP, assigned his deputy PM (DPM), General Prapass Charusathiara, the responsibility of taking on the CPT. Prapass was also Commander-in-Chief of the Army. PM Sarit remained involved in strategic planning, but at a higher level.

Prapass understood that COIN entailed more than suppression, and he solicited the assistance of Royal Thai Army (RTA) General Saiyud Kerdphol, a student of COIN, to help organize and manage the fight. They saw the insurgency as both a security threat and a socioeconomic problem, so in response decided to use kinetic operations to destroy the CPT's military units and development operations to raise the population from poverty, hoping that these measures would also prevent the CPT from gaining recruits. Bangkok did not perceive the insurgency as political, so it launched no political operations against the CPT save for a handful of weak psyops, thinking them tertiary to security and economics. This was a mistake that took years to correct.

To coordinate the war, the government established the Communist Suppression Operations Command (CSOC), headquartered in Bangkok with satellite stations throughout insurgent areas. CSOC's mission was to coordinate all kinetic and development operations. General Prapass placed General Saiyud in charge of CSOC. Under the CSOC was the RTA, RTP, development-related ministries such as the Ministries of Health and Education, and agencies such as the Accelerated Rural Development program (ARD). The government also established the Civilian Police Military (CPM) program, which entailed civilians, police, and military forces all working together to quell the insurgency. CPM units were intended to work as mutually supportive teams, bringing both development and security to CPT-threatened and -occupied areas. Local forces were a pivotal aspect of this formula.

From 1965 to 1967, CPM operations reduced CPT strength by about half and resulted in the arrest or killing of more than one hundred CPT leaders. In 1967, for example, the RTP arrested twenty CPT leaders in Bangkok, including Central Committee members Prasert Eeowchai, Prasert Sapsunthorn, Pin Bua-orn, and Thong Chaemsri, who eventually returned to the jungle and remained active in the rebellion. The government eliminated scores of local CPT leaders as well, which hurt its field capabilities.[19]

The RTG's efforts were not flawless, however. It suffered from a lack of coordination among civilians, police, and the military. Worse, the military on occasion used too much force, attacking entire villages with napalm even for just allegedly supporting the CPT. Additionally, RTA operations did not target the multitude of CPT bases and logistical lines stretching across to Laos, North

11

Vietnam, and China. Without striking these bases and interior lines, CPT infiltration from its many sanctuary areas would not stop.

By January 1967, the RTG realized that local Thai people could play a greater role than previously realized in fighting the insurgency, and it developed a new version of the CPM plan called the 09/10 Plan. Through this scheme, the government drafted the people into the government's fight, just as the CPT had drafted the people into its fight. General Saiyud believes that, had the government stuck to this program and kept its momentum, it could have won the war before 1975. But it did not.[20]

Instead, the RTA's regional commanders felt threatened by General Saiyud's power, and they revolted against CSOC's command and control. General Prapass gave in to their demands in 1967, granting them the power to run their own anti-CPT operations as they saw fit. They still used the CSOC name, and they adopted some CPM concepts, but overall, they mostly conducted heavy suppression operations, and the war continued on, uncoordinated and sloppy.

This shift was unfortunate. In February 1967, the CPT increased its terror operations to panic the RTA. The CPT knew the military would overreact and implement unpopular, massive sweeps, which is exactly what happened. "From that moment," says General Saiyud, "the emphasis shifted toward military operations of the Vietnam type," by which he means American-style search-and-destroy operations using large formations of troops to find, fix, and then destroy the enemy.[21]

That was not all, however. In the northeast, the RTA's Second Army dropped the CPM scheme that had covered two hundred villages in seven provinces. In the north, the Third Army used excessive force in multiple cases, leading to deaths of innocent civilians in Nan, Chiang Rai, the Phetchabun-Loei-Phitsanulok tri-border area, and Tak. In the south, RTA commander Major General Cherm Preutsayachiwa did not see the communists as a threat, and he ceased operations altogether. CSOC was able to influence the sacking of Cherm, and Major General San Chitpatima took his place. He began CPM-style operations, but the CPT had solidly established itself in the south and put up staunch resistance.[22] The war was not going well for the government.

1968–1973

By the late 1960s and early 1970s, the CPT had become adept at evading the RTA's large sweeps, and it had infiltrated more villages, since local defense forces had sloughed off with the demise of most of CSOC's CPM operations. The CPT's clandestine agents increased ties to leftist organizations throughout the country and shored up their cell structures to tap domestic sources of support instead of relying solely on logistics from China, Laos, Vietnam, and Cambodia. The CPT established the Supreme Command of the People's Liberation Army of Thailand (a.k.a. the Thai People's Liberation Armed Forces, or TPLAF) on 1 January 1969 and intensified radio propaganda via its Voice of the People of Thailand (VOPT) against the government and the Thai royal family.

Because the government's efforts were getting nowhere, in May 1969, CSOC and a small but influential group of COIN-minded RTA officers convinced the PM to adopt a new war plan, the 110/2512 Plan. It entailed harnessing even more local forces, increasing development, and building trust between villagers and the government, which to date had been lacking, especially because corrupt government officials scammed and extorted villagers in many cases. The CPT had exploited this corruption to recruit villagers, with great success. Unfortunately, the RTA, except for some officers in the Second Army, largely ignored the 110/2512 Plan. By 1970, the CPT had infiltrated thirty-five of Thailand's seventy-two provinces. The insurgency had become endemic.

Armed communist propaganda platoons intensified their activities from an average of 6.4 instances per month in 1966 to 16.4 a month by 1970. Assassinations of villagers who did not cooperate with the CPT increased from 5.6 to 11.6 per month during the same time period. Murder of government officials increased from 3.6 to 10.0 per month.[23]

By 1971, the CPT had doubled its strength to five thousand members and recuperated from its earlier losses, even in the face of several government successes. During that year, military offensives resulted in 1,500 CPT weapons seized, 540 insurgents killed, scores of bases overrun, and the surrender of some three thousand communists.[24] The government was severely bloodied too, however. The RTA withdrew the First Division from the tri-border area in the north as a result of high casualties from clashes with the CPT, effectively giving the communists a sanctuary within Thailand, something they previously had only in Laos, North Vietnam, and China.

Still, the RTA was beginning to understand irregular warfare. General Saiyud says that, from 1971 to October 1973, the RTA learned from its mistake of applying heavy suppression. "Military sweep operations," he says, "contributed only to the statistics of clashes, killed, and wounded."[25] Accordingly, RTA commanders slowly began to reapply the CSOC/CPM concept, first to CPT areas in Na Kae District, Nakhon Phanom province. The army then expanded these operations into the Phetchabun, Loei, and Phitsanulok provinces.[26]

1973–1976

Despite the RTA's efforts, chaos lay ahead. As the RTA slowly began to improve its COIN operations, the government lost control of domestic politics, which further fed the insurgency. Supreme Commander and PM Thanom Kittikachorn (9 December 1963–14 October 1973) and General Prapass controlled all diplomatic, justice, and national security ministerial portfolios. They enforced heavy-handed domestic policies such as suspension of due process and assumed the power to arrest and execute any enemy of the government without trial, despite great popular protest. Thanom, Prapass, and several successive administrations banned all political parties in attempts to curb communism and quell dissent, but these policies disenfranchised large swaths of the population, not just the communists. Widespread government and military corruption added to the popular anger. Against this backdrop, the CPT eventually came to provide the only opposition to a repressive government, thereby winning support from people who were not even communists.

As a result, the CPT increased its infiltration of intellectual, labor, and university groups. These organizations clashed with police on numerous occasions, leaving scores dead and wounded on both sides. A major student-police clash occurred on 14 October 1973 in Bangkok. About two hundred thousand people had gathered to protest Thanom's policies, and police killed as many as seventy while trying to contain the crowd. The *New York Times* reported that "rampaging students" took over the First Army headquarters, stealing weapons from the armory and burning buildings.[27]

The violence caused King Bhumibol Adulyadej, upon personally hearing the concerns of student protest leaders, to intercede and force the resignation of the government, a rare move for a monarch removed from active governing. This bold action triggered what both Thai and foreign historians commonly refer to as "Thailand's experiment with democracy," marked by a three-year era of civilian rule. None of this, however, assuaged the CPT, which grew by 6,500 personnel by the end of 1973.[28] Because of a lack of leadership, the government was unable to handle the domestic political and insurgent crises at the same time. Thailand's COIN campaign temporarily halted in 1973.[29]

The government changed hands between four administrations from October 1973 to October 1976, when Thailand's insurgency and domestic turmoil came to a head with the Thammasat University massacre. On 6 October, thousands of students and intellectuals, some simply anti-autocratic and some pro-CPT, clashed with police and several government-sponsored paramilitary groups developed to counter the communists. These included the Red Gaurs, a small, secretive organization that used force and intimidation against the left, and the Village Scouts, a nationwide political and paramilitary organization. The violence left multitudes of dead and wounded. Some dead students' bodies were hung and beaten by right-wing fanatics. The nation was horrified, and some three thousand students fled to the jungles to join the CPT, swelling its ranks with organizational expertise and antigovernment fervor. Popular support for the government wavered as the number of CPT fighters swelled to fourteen thousand.[30] Communist auxiliary support expanded to more than one hundred thousand.

With this new injection of manpower and political support, the CPT was able to exert direct control over four hundred villages and indirect control over six thousand. Furthermore, the CPT was able to conduct combat operations in seventy-one provinces, or practically the entire country.[31] As a result, it held sway over millions of Thai citizens.

In 1976, CSOC, which had changed its name to Internal Security Operations Command (ISOC), upgraded the CPM program with a special village self-defense and development scheme called *Asa-samak Pattana lae Pongkan ton-eng* (Development and Self-Defense Volunteers Program), or *Aw Paw Paw* for short. Part of the impetus behind the new program was an intelligence report saying the CPT's strength would rival that of the government by 1977 or 1978.[32] This would be the point in Mao's theory of warfare when the guerrilla army has achieved parity with the state's army and can begin to engage the latter on an even military footing in a conventional war. The report was a doomsday estimate for the RTG, and Bangkok's highest priority became defeating the CPT. Accordingly, programs such as *Aw Paw Paw* took on new urgency. In 1976, a year before real COIN reform began, a discombobulated Thai government still managed to apply *Aw Paw Paw* to 3,754 villages. While government mismanagement, jealousies, and turf disputes kept it from expanding further, the program did nevertheless represent an effective way to secure the countryside, and the government would eventually build upon this.

1977–1980

Amid the tumult of the early 1970s, officers in the Second Army area began to run CPM operations in a style akin to the ideology that had spurred the original CSOC concept and the 110/2512 Plan. Among them were Second Army Commander General Prem Tinsulanonda and his second in command, General Harn Leenanond. They also added their own ideas and began to perfect COIN operations that hinged on focused force operations paired with Civil Affairs (CA) missions and well-crafted psyops. Their initiatives made slow progress against the CPT in separating the communists from the population, but they did indeed make progress. Eventually, that progress would have a nationwide impact, as the Second Army's actions would soon form the basis of Thailand's victorious COIN strategy, but no one in Thailand's national security sphere could see this at the time. In the meantime, and despite these improvements, the CPT increased its operations by 20 percent. Moreover, the rest of the RTA was not aligned with the Second Army or CSOC, so the fight at the national level continued at an ineffectual pace.

In the south, for example, the government's effort fell apart. The Fourth Army commander there, CSOC's own Major General San, "withdrew from the field for no good reason," writes General Saiyud, who describes friction between Bangkok, the governor of Phattalung province, and General San.[33] One of the sticking points between them was that the governor thought General San's tactics were too harsh and requested the withdrawal of all RTA forces from the field so that the police and local forces could fight the CPT instead. Regardless of who was right or wrong, the south became Thailand's most active insurgency zone during the 1976–77 time frame.[34]

Communist forces surrounding Thailand had gained strength, too. Laos, South Vietnam, and Cambodia all fell to Chinese- and/or Soviet-supported communists in 1975. From Bangkok's point of view, the regional situation looked dire, but a complicated string of fissures in the communist alliance eventually ruptured their solidarity, which created weaknesses and opportunities.

Vietnam invaded Cambodia in December 1978 over the latter's terrorist border raids. This invasion caused a row between Vietnam and China, the two main supporters of the CPT, which caused an internal split between the Vietnamese and Chinese factions of the CPT. Thailand committed diplomats to take advantage of the divide and lobbied Beijing (then called Peking) to cut off Chinese support for the insurgents. The tactic worked. In 1979, the Chinese shut down the VOPT, and Vietnam and Laos punished the Chinese faction of the CPT by ousting it from their territory.[35] These events began the end of foreign support for the CPT. After 1979, the CPT had little to no external sanctuary, a key ingredient needed for insurgent success.

Simply cutting off the communists' external support was not enough to defeat them, however. There were still fourteen thousand CPT fighters and over one hundred thousand active supporters in the field, plus more than a million passive supporters. And the CPT had broad internal sanctuary areas as well, such as in the Khao Kho basin area in Phetchabun province, where the RTA had not dared venture for many years. To defeat the CPT, then, the government would have to apply all three pillars of COIN better than it had done in previous years.[36] But who would lead this new challenge?

RTA General Kriangsak Chomanand (11 November 1977–3 March 1980) answered the call when he took over the government by coup in 1977. Kriangsak initiated countrywide economic and democratic reforms that undid many of the autocratic policies of previous regimes, including civilian ones, and he offered amnesty to the Thammasat students who had joined the CPT after the 1976 massacre.[37] Democratic reform relieved pressure on the population, and broad support for the CPT dwindled. Because of these significant political changes, Chai-Anan, Kusuma, and Suchit write, "It is generally considered that the real turning point in [counterinsurgency] policy took place during the Kriangsak administration which took over from the ultra-right Thanin Government."[38]

Not all COIN reforms during this time were political, however. In 1978, RTA General Chavalit Yongchaiyudh, Chief of Army Operations, designed a new local force unit to "out-guerrilla" the CPT guerrillas: the *Thahan Phran*, or, literally, "Soldier Hunters." This strike force was divided into companies and regiments that would operate in the areas from which their recruits were drawn, primarily because they knew the human terrain of their villages better than RTA forces. (Human terrain is a modern COIN term referring to the schematics of a local population's economic, social, and anthropological makeup.) The *Thahan Phran* were ideally placed to root out and eliminate CPT insurgents on a mass scale, and they did so with ruthless efficiency.

Other security reforms followed, some of them seemingly opposed to democracy. Specifically, Kriangsak enacted the Anticommunist Act of 1979, which gave security forces wide-ranging power. Police, for example, could conduct warrantless searches and seizures and could detain insurgent suspects for more than one hundred days. The new law gave RTA commanders and governors the power to impose curfews, ban demonstrations and meetings, monitor phone conversations, and access corporations' personnel files.[39] These focused and methodical security measures, carried out by more professional security forces than Thailand had previously known, put pressure on the CPT's abilities to move and communicate. The results of these measures also helped security forces identify key communist personnel so that these people could be arrested, neutralized, or turned into double agents. While these reforms were essential, they did not solve all the government's woes. Additional COIN innovation would come in 1980 with General Prem and his cohorts.

1980–1985

General Prem, former head of the Second Army, Commander-in-Chief of the Army, and Defense Minister, took over by coup in 1980 and continued Kriangsak's democratic reforms.[40] Prem (3 March 1980–4 August 1988) placed other COIN-minded leaders in positions of power throughout the RTA— namely General Harn—and forced the country's entire national security complex to accept his plans to defeat the CPT through the 66/2523 Plan, also known as the "Policy to Win Over Communism." Prem also put into action the 65/2525 Plan, or the "Plan for Political Offensive." Amnesty was a major component of Prem and Harn's ideas, and they made democracy the main tool to defeat communism. The plan mimicked CPT political mass-mobilization strategies without apology. Aptly applied, the CPT fell into disarray.

Prem moreover forced the military to accept ISOC's coordination authority, and he implemented the CPM program nationwide since it had served him well in the northeast. Thailand's intelligence services by now had gained the upper hand on the CPT and correctly interpreted its capabilities and intentions. Government clandestine services had effectively penetrated the communist infrastructure with informants. These measures further eroded the CPT's prowess, and high-profile surrenders began.[41]

In a major public relations blow, CPT student leader Seksan Prasertgul and communist labor leader Therdpoom Chaidee surrendered in October 1980. Therdpoom accused the Chinese of dominating the CPT, a debilitating propaganda blow against the movement, since the Thai people disliked any hint of foreign control of their politics. The indictment caused the CPT to lose more popular support.[42]

In January 1981, Khaiseng Suksai, a former deputy of the Thai Socialist Party, surrendered, followed by Thirayuth Boonmee, leftist student leader and senior organizer of the communist front organization known as the Coordinating Committee for Patriotic and Democratic Forces (CCPDF). In April 1981, authorities captured CPT Politburo member Damri Ruengsutham at a road checkpoint in the south's Surat Thani province. In the same year the RTA picked up the pace of its operations in Khao Kho, a CPT stronghold area, in the largest offensive that the war had seen. CPT forces in Petchabun province fell in defeat.[43] The CPT's army began to decline, falling from 14,000 to 12,500 fighters.[44]

From March through May 1982, the RTA continued to attack the CPT's previously impervious base camps: one at Surat Thani in the south, another at Doi Pha Chi in Nan province in the north, and the CPT's main northern base at Phu Khad in the Phu Niang Mountains. During this time period, RTA Chief of Operations Major General Chavalit proclaimed all major CPT bases destroyed. At roughly the same time, the Secretary General of the CPT, Mit Samanan (a.k.a. Charoen Wangnarm), died.[45] His passing was a blow to the morale of the CPT, which further weakened it.

About 9,000 CPT supporters and some fighters also surrendered in 1982, many of them Hmong tribesmen and their families. CCPDF chief and Politburo member Odom Srisuwan surrendered in September. In December, 216 CPT fighters gave themselves up in Yasothon province, a year after the CPT's Fourth Party Congress had reiterated its dedication to armed struggle.[46]

When 1982 ended, the CPT's fighter strength was reduced by about half to seven thousand, many from kinetic operations, but most from surrenders.[47] This was a dramatic setback for the CPT and signaled the movement's national failure—not yet its capitulation, but that was coming soon. Facing ever-tightening government security and political pressure, CPT personnel continued to defect in 1983. By September, ISOC declared that only four provinces still had active CPT operations. By 1984, the CPT had dwindled ·to twelve hundred fighters countrywide.[48] In October, ISOC declared victory over the CPT, but defections continued throughout the rest of the year.

By 1986, all senior-level CPT leaders had surrendered, their strongholds had fallen, and the war was over.[49] Of the victory, General Prem remarked in 1995, "Together, the Thai nation found the way—our way—to end the hatred and killing between brothers and compatriots. The result, as you know, made us all very proud."[50]

The Insurgents

The CPT was a large, centralized insurgent organization with fighting units, political units, and staff officials. Its highly organized structure, Maoist ideology, unity of purpose, and fervent motivation made it incredibly formidable. The CPT's sanctuary, logistics linkages, and training areas in neighboring communist countries provided it with critical supply lines and support functions. The CPT's international communist support base added punch to its political messaging. All these factors, combined with government mistakes, provided the CPT with the capabilities to take over Thailand and turn it into a communist regime. And it nearly succeeded.

Strategy

In January 1965, the Thai Patriotic Front (TPF), speaking for the communist insurgency, published a vague six-point strategy for the coming war against Thailand. The TPF strategy was to:

1. Overthrow the current government, rid the country of US imperialism, and cooperate with "international peace forces."
2. Develop the national economy.
3. Improve the standard of living.
4. Institute land reform.
5. Eliminate corruption.
6. Develop health, education, and social welfare.[51]

In 1969, the CPT replaced the TPF strategy with a new one containing ten points that were decidedly more communist in their language and goals. The 1969 strategy followed these specific end goals:

1. Unite all working class, petty bourgeoisie, and "national capitalists of all nationalities" to overthrow the government, expel all US forces, and establish a "democratic" government with representatives of all members of the united front.

2. Allow voting at age eighteen; allow freedom of writing, speech, press, and assembly, including strikes; release all "democratic-loving detainees" from prison; and "abrogate all popular laws."

3. Seize all US and "hooligan landlord" properties and distribute them among the people; bring to justice all those who fought against the CPT.

4. Nullify all foreign relations and treaties with the Soviet Union and the US; align with nations that respect each other's territorial integrity and independence; and support "oppressed peoples" globally.

5. Promote equal rights and access to education regardless of ethnic background; respect ethnic differences and create autonomous "nationality regions."

6. Discard feudalism and initiate an agricultural revolution in which all unjust financial, banking, and legal policies are undone; grant land ownership to farmers.

7. Protect national resources; develop industry and "commerce of national capitalists."

8. Ensure that all people, regardless of gender or creed, are employed and paid equally according to their production.

9. Grant equal rights to men and women; encourage women to join "the revolution and production"; encourage young people to become educated while embracing the nation and helping to build a new society; provide benefits to CPT fighters.

10. Remove from Thai culture and education "imperialists and feudalists"; promote "revolutionary culture" (scientific, democratic, and nationalistic); promote Thai culture; expand development work nationwide, especially in rural areas.[52]

These points left wide room for interpretation. Some of them, like equal rights and jobs for people of different ethnicities, could have reflected the US civil rights movement of the 1960s. Others, such as removing "imperialists and feudalists" from Thai culture—perhaps by rewriting history and eliminating large portions of the population—might reflect Pol Pot's genocidal reign in Cambodia, Mao's China, or Stalin's Soviet Union. Other points, such as allowing farmers to own land, were already Thai law.[53] This particular demand, however, was one of many CPT propaganda ploys. It gave the impression that no farmers owned their land. This created a false basis for the people to rally against the government.

The anti-US stance of the CPT was not simply nationalistic. Since the CPT was largely a Beijing-controlled organization and aimed to expand communism throughout the region, it wanted the US military out of Thailand and the rest of Southeast Asia. US deployments across the region were hindering the communist takeover of Vietnam, Laos, Cambodia, and Thailand. The deployments in Thailand were based on the 1962 Rusk-Thanat Agreement, which linked Bangkok and Washington in defense matters such as protecting Thailand from invasion—Chinese support for the CPT made the insurgency tantamount to an invasion.[54] US forces in Thailand, some forty thousand personnel on seven Thai air bases, were also staging air support operations into Vietnam to fight the communists there, all with Bangkok's blessing.[55]

Maoist Warfare

At the behest of its Chinese benefactors, the CPT chose to use Maoist warfare as its method of achieving power.[56] In theory, Maoist strategy is "people's war." Thomas A. Marks, an expert on Maoist warfare, describes the crux of it as "the greater military power of the state [being] negated by mobilizing the people against it."[57]

Marks says Maoist warfare happens in three broad phases.[58] First comes the political phase, which is the most important phase and the foundation of the entire movement. Here, an insurgency establishes secret political cells throughout society and wins over as much of the population as possible before ever firing a shot. These cells infiltrate social clubs, labor and farmers' unions, political parties, teachers' associations, and other such organizations. Front groups emerge from these cells, showing solidarity in a singular cause. From there, the insurgents establish a shadow government to compete with the state's government structure at all levels. The movement also gathers international political backing.

Popular support for the movement then pits the people against the government, which is made illegitimate by politicking about genuine grievances such as poverty and government corruption, and also by concocting fake issues or interweaving small bits of truth with large amounts of lies. This latter action is political warfare. Political organization and psychological operations are key tools at this stage.

The second phase, insurgent movement, ideally from difficult terrain, begins guerrilla warfare, and terrorism if necessary, against the state and its supporters, including civilians. Maoist warfare advises that violence should begin in the countryside to secure it first, and then proceed to the cities, which are attacked last. The strategy calls for starting with light attacks, such as occasional assassinations and acts of sabotage, and gradually increasing to more forceful hit-and-run operations, including light infantry operations and bombings. The emerging guerrilla force also establishes an internal security unit to protect the fledgling shadow government. It develops far-reaching power to eliminate opponents of the insurgency, both internal and external.

Popular support is critical to this phase as well. It provides fighters with auxiliary support such as food, war materiel, sanctuary (places to hide and reconstitute), and intelligence. Without this popular support, guerrilla warfare is nearly impossible. Similarly, without some kind of international political and logistical support, guerrilla warfare is quite difficult. Having access to a neighboring country as sanctuary is ideal.

In the third phase, the guerrilla army gains sufficient strength, manpower, and materiel to engage the state's forces on an even footing in conventional warfare. Victory would be assured not only because of this military parity, but also because of the political strength of the sympathetic masses, the insurgency's success in political warfare (delegitimizing the state), and the state's exhaustion from being besieged by guerrilla warfare.

"People power" was crucial in all three phases of Mao's theory of warfare, and the CPT in Thailand applied it as best as it could. Scores of insurgent movements through history have used this model. Many have never needed to apply the third phase because the state was exhausted by phases one and two. Even radical Islamist jihadist movements use a version of Maoist warfare.

Ex-CPT member Gawin says the CPT did not wholly follow Mao's instruction, as the armed conflict phase started early. "Gun-firing day," says Gawin, was an accident. A police patrol happened across an armed CPT propaganda unit and a firefight erupted, leaving a guerrilla killed and a police lieutenant colonel wounded. Because newspapers sensationalized the story, the CPT went along with the momentum and proclaimed that its war of liberation had begun.[59] From that point on, the CPT sought to spread communism by both political warfare and by fighting.

On the ground, the CPT applied its strategy systematically, one region at a time. Issan was first. Professor Bhumarat Taksadipong says, "The CPT began fighting in Issan, Sakhon Nakhon…in the northeast. It was the poorest region in the country, just one day's drive to the Vietnamese border, and communist philosophy attacks the poor. And there was some sentiment of fighting the government in the past."[60] He also says that the CPT started in Issan because of its difficult terrain, just as Mao prescribed: "It has rough mountain ranges and the jungle, so the CPT started in the jungle, and from the jungle to the villages, and then later, all over."[61]

Professor Bhumarat continues: "From Issan, the communists then went north, because the northerners were the second poorest in Thailand. The terrain was very suitable for communist insurgency."[62] This occurred in 1967. The CPT targeted not only ethnic Thai in this area, but also ethnic hill tribes who had migrated from Burma, Thailand, Laos, and Vietnam. Thailand's hill people consisted of six major tribes. The most prevalent was the Hmong, also called the Meo or Miao. Others included the Mien, Lahu, Lisu, Akha, and Karen. The hill people numbered in the hundreds of thousands.[63]

Infiltration of the south happened throughout the rest of the 1960s. In the 1970s, having penetrated every outer region of the country, the CPT began to infiltrate the central areas in earnest, which entailed recruiting university students and urbanites in cities such as Bangkok. The CPT needed educated talent to further its cause and also wanted to reach a wider swath of the population than just poor farmers. Otherwise, its revolution would remain rural.

Organizational Structure

The CPT's shadow government provided an approximation of what its government should look like if it won the war. Structurally, it was hierarchical and vertical, like the Communist Party at large. According to Marks, the CPT's organization "followed standard Leninist lines."[64] Gawin describes Leninist lines as strictly hierarchical, with all communication between units being funneled through higher units, a system the CPT called "democratic centralism." Democratic centralism meant, according to the communists, an "iron discipline" with the following stipulations: (1) the party's authority was final and supreme, (2) the minority had to follow the majority, (3) lower ranks had to follow the upper ranks, and (4) the Central Committee had power over every unit, every branch, and every person in the CPT. To be sure, this was not democracy by any means, though the CPT touted it as such to the poorly educated Thai population.[65]

Marks says a seven-man Politburo ran the CPT. The second-highest level of governance was a twenty-five-man Central Committee that managed military and political operations. Its members also served as heads of Party Provincial Committees, which oversaw Party District Committees, which in turn oversaw CPT operations at the town and village levels. These organizations roughly followed the Thai government's countrywide structure. At the local levels, however, CPT organization was nebulous, and some commanders divided swaths of territory into what they simply called "zones."[66]

Local CPT commanders managed party committees at the village level. Village committees consisted of seven-man teams headed by a chairman. They supervised eight committees of as many as thirty people that ran services such as military affairs, propaganda operations, youth and women's affairs, and labor activities. The CPT tried to grow these organizations by persuading people to join the communists' ranks and either provide auxiliary support or become part of combat units.[67]

The CPT's fighting wing, the Thai People's Liberation Armed Forces, was not a true standing army during the war's early years. It was more like a series of platoons and squads. In the mid- to late 1960s, the CPT referred to their fighters as *thahan pa*—literally, "soldier jungle." In the northeast, people called them *tap*, which is a local word for a "temporary shelter in the jungle" for loggers or criminals on the run. Similarly, in the north they were called *pang*, which means "hideout." General Saiyud writes that these names, since they were military rather than political, represented the CPT's early move toward using war to spread communism.[68]

On 1 January 1969, the Chinese took steps to centralize the CPT's military structure by establishing for it a military Supreme Command inside China. At this point, the CPT began to refer to all its fighting units as the TPLAF. From there the organization grew into a standing army with both small and large units, but it still fielded part-time fighters and clandestine operators as well.

Insurgent Numbers

It is nearly impossible to calculate the CPT's exact size. Without precise rosters of troop formations, clandestine networks, and secret cells, only rough estimates can be made. In the years following the 1976 Thammasat University massacre, the CPT's ranks swelled to an estimated fourteen thousand, with what Marks calls its "rural base" adding another twenty thousand supporters, making total membership thirty-four thousand. [69] General Saiyud, however, said the government's estimate of CPT auxiliary support in 1968 was twenty-five thousand for twenty-five hundred fighters, which roughly equates to ten auxiliary or support personnel for every fighter in the field. If this was accurate, then the CPT might have had 140,000 auxiliary supporters at its peak, which is possible because it had cells and political support throughout the entire country. This assumption would have placed total CPT membership as high as 154,000. Passive support for the communists appears to have reached into the millions. Regardless, the CPT had enough fighters and supporters to operate in nearly every province in Thailand during the mid- to late 1970s. Clearly, it had enough people to push its agenda forward, and it had enough supporters to achieve victory.

Logistics and Sanctuary

No insurgent movement can survive without a logistics chain and sanctuary with space for resting, refitting, training, and administration free from government pressure. Sites just across a target nation's border are ideal for this type of support. The CPT's main supporters were China, North Vietnam, Laos, and, to some extent, Cambodia under the Khmer Rouge (KR). Toward the middle of the war the CPT also carved out sanctuary zones within Thailand, indicating its remarkable progress and the serious threat that it posed.

The CPT's primary logistics providers were China, North Vietnam, and Laos. The CPT was purposefully positioned in the northeastern and northern border areas to exploit of these lines of communication through difficult mountainous and jungle terrain.[70] This three-country arrangement provided operational security and kept the RTA from raiding training camps.[71] Thai Special Forces tried to raid CPT camps in Hoa Binh, North Vietnam, but were never successful.[72]

Says Professor Bhumarat, "Issan has a border with Laos and Kampuchea, both areas where the communists were very active. It was easy to get supplies and people through their rear lines."[73] RTA General Harn Pathai observes, "The Hmong from Laos were fighting in Thailand, too, to spread communism, but more in a logistics and transport role than a direct combat role. There was continual infiltration into Thailand via Laos."[74]

In the war's early days—the 1960s—the CPT's financial flow, a key logistics concern, was not too great. By the 1970s, writes George K. Tanham, "money seems to be more plentiful for the party, which makes recruiting and buying of supplies much easier."[75] Tanham was Special Assistant for Counterinsurgency at the US Embassy in Bangkok during the 1970s. It is notable that he lobbied successfully for a small American COIN footprint in Thailand as opposed to the large Vietnam-style COIN effort. Tanham was ahead of his time regarding American COIN thinking.

Regardless, Gawin notes that the CPT in the south and west did not receive Chinese support. It had to be largely self-sufficient for the duration of the war, but it did receive some supplies from the North Vietnamese through Cambodia.[76] "The CPT in the [south]," Gawin writes, "seized guns and everything they wanted from the government and, especially in the south, acquired so much money that for some years it supported other regions."[77]

According to Tanham, Chinese weapon shipments to the CPT in the early years of the war were not immense, but they greatly increased in the 1971–73 period.[78] China also provided trainers for these weapons starting in 1971.[79] From 1975 to 1978, the Chinese provided approximately six hundred tons of materials that included clothing and weaponry and one thousand tons of rice each year.[80] The 1970s rice deliveries were probably arranged because food had been the CPT's biggest logistical concern in the late 1960s. The CPT was forced to sneak small amounts of food out of villages via friendly relatives, and hunger was a continual concern during the first five years of the war.[81]

For the most part, the CPT used light infantry weapons. In the early days of the war, the then young RTA Lieutenant (and later General) Harn Pathai says, "They did not have very good weapons to fight with when I was [first] there. They had some M-1 carbines, M-3 'Grease Guns,' things like that."[82] These were World War II–era American firearms, likely obtained from the regional stocks of a host of neighboring countries.[83] The Thai police used some of these weapons as well, so the CPT could have obtained them from dead officers or by raiding arsenals.

A CIA report noted Chinese-supplied AK-47s flowing to the CPT in 1969, and heavier weapons such as rocket-propelled grenades (RPGs), 60 mm mortars, and captured American M-79 grenade launchers followed. Radios, medical supplies, and uniforms came in, too.[84] Tanham writes that the CPT took considerable shipments of "bloc weapons, mostly Chinese."[85] These included antiaircraft weaponry and mortars used in defense of CPT mountain fortresses.

Later, in 1980, when General Harn was an infantry battalion commander, he found the CPT much better armed: "The CPT was stronger than when I first fought them. They had better weapons and more people. They had AK-47s, RPGs, and a lot of mines, too. Lots of mines."[86] By this date, the CPT also had recoilless rifles.

Aside from logistics, China, North Vietnam, and Laos also provided sanctuary for the CPT. Gawin says the CPT's headquarters was in northern Laos, but he does not specify exactly where: "This capital, as Wirat Sakchirapapong, a Socialist Party Central Committee member, has stated, comprised hospitals, at least six children's schools, the CCPDF [Coordinating Committee for Patriotic and Democratic Forces] office, the research office, training camps, storehouses, and other buildings, and it could not possibly have existed without enormous help from China."[87]

Thai insurgency expert Jeffrey Race, author of *War Comes to Long An*, said a major CPT base in Laos existed near the Thai border at Phu Miang. He writes that it was "the site of a major communist base camp and training area. Infiltration of men would thus be easy southward down the ridgeline connecting Phu Miang with the tri-province boundary area."[88] A CIA report claimed that a Chinese cultural school in Laos kept the CPT linked to the Chinese Communist Party. The school focused on reading, writing, and indoctrination.[89] The forty thousand North Vietnamese Army troops in Laos kept CPT lines of communication to its allies secure.[90]

The CPT had foreign training areas in China, North Vietnam, and Laos, but it also conducted training in its Thai sanctuaries. The diversity of training areas and their vast geographic distribution reflect the massive size of the CPT support operation. This was no simpletons' army.

The CPT's main school for political thought, based in Beijing, was reserved for promising recruits who demonstrated leadership potential. Ideological training lasted for two to five months.[91] Gawin quoted a CPT leader as saying, "Most of [the CPT leaders] graduated from the Marxist-Leninist Institute in Beijing, so we have been doing what we learned from that institute, setting up a form of revolution like the one we saw in China."[92] While some ideological training also happened in Laos and North Vietnam, the Beijing connection made sure that the CPT remained under Chinese control.[93]

The CPT trained in military tactics in North Vietnam, in Long Mu near Hoa Binh. Courses lasted three to six months, with six months being a more typical time frame for basic training. After this preparation, many CPT recruits fought alongside the communist Pathet Lao against the Lao royalist government in order to gain combat experience.[94]

The CPT also trained with Pol Pot's Khmer Rouge in Cambodia. KR tactics emphasized extreme violence, grotesque torture, and mass executions, none of which sat well with the majority of the CPT. Gawin asserts:

> The most alarming incidents occurred in the southern region of the northeast, on the Kampuchean border, where the local CPT, trained and supported by the Khmer Rouge, began using Khmer Rouge style revolutionary terror not only against government personnel but also villagers. Large areas were declared war zones and villagers were told either to join the struggle by moving into CPT camps inside Kampuchea or risk being killed.[95]

Gawin insists the main body of the CPT saw these tactics as "unreasonable and excessive" and preferred to "keep killing and acts of terrorism to a minimum."[96]

Political Operations

Politics in insurgency is mission critical at every turn. It is the core of any such movement, and fighting is useless without it. Upon overturning the state, the CPT's shadow government would transition from running parts of Thailand in secret to running all of it in the open. The CPT's infiltration of nearly all of Thailand's provinces proves the organization's political prowess. But how did the CPT accomplish its political objectives? How did it infiltrate Thailand's society so broadly? It did so by clandestine activities, political organization, indoctrination, and propaganda—all key facets of political warfare.

Clandestine Activities

Clandestine infiltration entails spy tradecraft—covertly inserting people into companies, government offices, and organizations—and reporting on these organizations or influencing them secretly from the inside to adopt an insurgent group's ideology and goals. Nowhere was the CPT's clandestine infiltration more apparent than in Thailand's 1970s student movement. According to Gawin, the CPT "succeeded in getting its agents into key positions in student organizations, and was able to use journals such as *Athipat* [of the communist National Student Center of Thailand] and *Asia* magazine to provide guidelines for the movement."[97] Gawin says the CPT's student leaders did not lead from the front. They led from the shadows. He says they "formed part of clandestine groups that discussed and analyzed the political situation and decided on the action to be taken."[98] Gawin adds, "It is likely that, without the CPT's infiltration of the student movement, the student activities would not have adopted the extreme, far-left strategies they did."[99]

The CPT penetrated university student groups, teacher training institutions, high schools, and vocational institutes throughout Thailand. These personnel established links between urban and rural communists, bolstered recruiting, and provided communist literature on the correct political positions to adopt.[100]

This infiltration would not have been possible, however, if Thai students were not already agitated by the government's autocratic policies and a faltering economy. Moreover, the time was ripe for student rebellion. In the 1960s–70s, student agitation sprang up on campuses across the world over a host of social issues, a waning global economy, and US involvement in the Vietnam War. It was telling, however, that few, if any, major student movements protested Chinese and Russian support for the war, nor North Vietnamese atrocities such as the mass execution of at least two thousand civilians at Hue and Phu Bai in 1968. The global student movement strictly opposed Western actions. And it produced violent campus and street clashes in Germany, the UK, and America. It gave birth to terrorist movements such as the Baader Meinhoff gang (Red Army Faktion) in Germany and the Weathermen in the United States. It is not surprising, then, that around the same time, the CPT was able to burrow into, and build a nest inside of, the Thai student movement. These actions were, after all, "Terrorism and Insurgency 101."

Political Organization

The CPT was equally effective in political organization. In democracies, political organization means forming political parties and campaigning on issues. For communist revolutionaries, in accordance with Maoist strategy, it means establishing front groups to make it appear as if different segments of the population are ideologically united. These groups would later merge under a single umbrella group as a solid, united front. The united front then evolves into a single Communist Party, politically encompassing the masses.

An excellent example of how the CPT executed its front group strategy comes from an indoctrination document written in 1978 by one such group, the Union of Democratic Thais (UDT). This document accompanied an album of communist propaganda songs titled *Thailand: Songs for Life Sung by Caravan*.[101] In it, the UDT describes how a student leader, Thirayud Boonmee, organized student protests in 1972 against the Thai-Japanese economic relationship under which Thailand was providing low-cost raw materials to Japan, while Japan was then sending higher-cost finished products made from those materials back to Thailand. The theme of the protests was a nationalist call to "Buy Thai!"—hardly a communist mantra. Nevertheless, the protest served the communist cause.[102]

How so? The UDT said student actions in this case "helped build further bridges between the student movement on the one hand and the workers and petite bourgeoisie on the other."[103] The UDT further explained, "This process would prove invaluable later in the building of a national front."[104] It also said the protests provided the students with excellent experience and education on the struggles of the various classes of Thailand. Perhaps most importantly, the UDT confessed that student leader Thirayud was, in fact, chair of the CCPDF, the organization responsible for uniting and coordinating "the Thai Communist Party, Socialist Party, and many peasant, worker, and intellectual organizations in the liberation struggle."[105]

Because of the 1972 "Buy Thai!" protest, along with CPT clandestine infiltration of the universities, the UDT asserts students ventured into Thailand's rural areas where they taught illiterate farmers about equal rights and economics. They also bonded with farmers by helping harvest their crops and singing songs around campfires with them. The UDT left out the fact that all this activity happened under CPT supervision that advised communist solutions to rural problems. As for the effort's impact, the UDT asserts the "distinctions" between the educated urban students and uneducated rural farmers were "blurred" and a "sense of trust [between them] deepened."[106] This type of political organization and infiltration demonstrates exceptional cunning, patience, and expertise. This is one of the reasons the CPT was so successful at spreading its influence all over the country. It would not have been possible, however, without the Thai government's mistakes and inadequacies, which Bangkok later corrected in order to expose the CPT's real identity and ultimately defeat it.

The CPT also used personal ties for political organizing. Writes Gawin, "A new recruit was often a friend or relative of an existing member…For those who were not relatives, the ties were likely to be those of a patron-client relationship."[107] The latter refers directly to the *sakdi na* system—an interesting reference since the CPT was allegedly fighting against the ghost of *sakdi na* and everything it stood for. Gawin further implies that the *sakdi na* system made recruiting easier: "The peasants, who had *sakdi na* attitudes of submission inbred into them, therefore turned against government personnel to a relationship with CPT activities and the party itself, which became a new source of patronage and security."[108]

The UDT also provides an excellent example of the CPT's international organizational linkages, another linchpin of Maoist warfare. For example, the propaganda document that accompanied the Caravan album was printed in both

Thai and English. It was copyrighted by Paredon Records—not in Thailand, but in Brooklyn, New York. The UDT had offices across the United States, in Washington, DC, Chicago, and Los Angeles. It covered Europe from a headquarters in France, with additional offices in Germany and Sweden. The UDT also had a presence in Hong Kong, New Zealand, and Australia.[109]

Moreover, the UDT sought out and connected with other international leftists such as Don Luce of the communist-leaning Asian Center in New York City—yet another propaganda organization. Luce, in the Caravan document, proclaimed to be against dictatorship in Chile and apartheid in South Africa, and he criticized South Korea's dictatorial government. At the same time, he neglected to condemn one of the harshest dictatorial regimes in history, North Korea.[110] But he would not, because it was communist, which was his brand of politics.

The UDT Caravan document also mentioned other Western community sympathizers who were assisting the Thai "struggle for liberation" with production and messaging. One of these was communist propagandist Barbara Dane, also touted as an accomplished jazz, folk, and protest singer who had apparently performed with scores of musical greats such as Muddy Waters and Bonnie Raitt.[111] She wrote songs for albums such as *FTA! Songs of the GI Resistance* in 1970 and *I Hate the Capitalist System* in 1973.[112] Again, the CPT's political savvy in reaching out to singers such as Dane was brilliant. Knowingly or not, her support furthered not simply a political cause, but a violent, autocratic movement.[113]

Indoctrination

CPT indoctrination—the education of its own membership to keep it thinking correctly and focused on revolution—was prolific. The CPT's main target, Thailand's peasant class, was poorly educated, so intricate instruction on the founding fathers of communism such as Engels, Marx, and Stalin was unnecessary. Instead, CPT leaders simply told their subordinates to follow the party's leadership and Mao's philosophy. Writes Gawin, "The CPT's educational system was narrow and conservative," and this kept the movement from "becoming a true Marxist-Leninist party."[114]

The CPT distributed booklets and held educational lectures instructing its ranks on how the CPT viewed Thailand's ruling elite, its government, international trade, the United States, the Soviet Union, and other issues. The booklets contained CPT-approved worldview realpolitik, and members were not supposed to think otherwise.[115] Gawin indicates that few CPT members were sufficiently educated to receive formal classroom instruction on political theory. "The trainees' perception of social problems and sophisticated revolutionary theories," he writes, "was limited and their intellectual potential could not be developed much by such a short period in school." Gawin says one CPT leader in the south went so far as to forbid his troops to read Mao in case they misperceived his teachings.[116]

Gawin acknowledges the CPT even violated Mao's tenets by keeping its cadres only partially indoctrinated. Mao said followers should be both "red," meaning communist, and "expert," or politically informed to an authoritative degree. But the CPT just wanted its cadres red and obedient, which satisfied democratic centralism.[117]

CPT indoctrination changed somewhat when the student movement joined its ranks. Having a greater background in communist and other political philosophies, leftist students increased the effectiveness of the CPT's indoctrination messages and taught "revolutionary morality," which asserted that rebelling for "justice" and "equal status for all" meant being a true human being, a morally correct person.[118] Of course, the CPT's version of "justice," and "equal status for all" came from Mao, not Plato, Jefferson, or John Locke.

The students' vision of revolutionary morality, however, clashed with the CPT's version of indoctrination for the uneducated. The CPT's emphasis on keeping the peasant ranks red and obedient frustrated the students, who wanted all CPT members to be fully "enlightened."[119] Students also believed in a cultural revolution—that art, music, and literature needed to be taken from the upper *sakdi na* class and rewritten for the people by the working class.[120] This mass indoctrination strategy never happened because the CPT leadership did not allow it. In hindsight, this CPT-student clash further reflects how autocratic a CPT government might have been had it won the war.

Propaganda

CPT propaganda was profuse. Control over people's minds is vital to communism. As long as everyone sees history, economics, politics, and outside threats through Marxist eyes, extreme leftist systems can flourish. Propaganda takes genuine political, economic, and social grievances and twists them to a particular purpose with political spin and outright lies. In some cases, the outright lies are carefully manufactured and intricately designed to fend off cursory investigation and questioning. And as Marks points out, propaganda also relies on real grievances that alienate the people from the government. This gives some credibility to propaganda.[121]

As already noted, Thai citizens had copious political, economic, and corruption grievances in the 1960s and '70s. These grievances increased the effectiveness of CPT propaganda and made it easy to win over large portions of the population. The CPT delivered its propaganda through four methods: the Voice of the People of Thailand (VOPT), armed propaganda teams, word of mouth, and the written word. The first two were the most prolific.

As rural Thai families were generally quite isolated, radio was vital in connecting villages all over the region to the rest of the world with news and various programs. The VOPT used this arrangement to its great advantage.[122] It used radio, for example, on 1 January 1969 to announce the establishment of the TPLAF, and shortly thereafter to declare that the CPT had combined Maoism with Marxism-Leninism as its key ideology. It followed that announcement quickly with its ten-point strategy for revolution.[123] In short, the CPT used the power of radio to announce its army, its governing philosophy, and its strategy. This "educated" the people, which gave more power and legitimacy to CPT organizers when they approached villagers. Radio paved the way for political organization on the ground.

The CPT used armed propaganda cadres both to protect propagandists and to intimidate their audiences. Student CPT members like Srisompob Jitpiromsri carried an AK-47 for protection against Thai police and army patrols and ambushes. To Srisompob and his CPT colleagues, the people were their most precious assets, and they were dedicated to getting the CPT's message out and fixing Thailand's broken government, even at the risk of being ambushed and killed by an RTA patrol.[124]

Other armed CPT propaganda teams behaved in ways more akin to the Viet Cong, which is fitting because the North Vietnamese Army trained many of them. Tanham asserts, "Early in 1966, the CTs [communist terrorists] in the northeast began to conduct armed propaganda meetings, which combined propaganda with terror. On these occasions a guerrilla band would appear in a village, intimidate the population by show of arms and sometimes violence, and then deliver long lectures on the failures of the Royal Thai Government (RTG) and the unhappy lives of the people."[125]

Word-of-mouth propaganda worked similarly. It consisted of rumors of an alleged government offensive against the peasant class, conversations in student groups, and CPT propagandists disguised as peasants intermingling with locals to complain about government policies and praise communist ideas. Word of mouth and the VOPT made tactical guerrilla victories in minor firefights seem grander than they really were, rallying the people behind an allegedly winning army.[126] For written propaganda the CPT used propaganda chits and newspapers such as *Athipat* and *Asia* magazine.[127]

The CPT put out several types of written propaganda: educational materials, threats of violence, anti-US tirades, manipulation of cultural mythology and current events, and attacks on the monarchy. Educational propaganda explained the benefits of Mao's communism, the perils of Bangkok's policies, and the wealthy's exploitation and hatred of the poor. This education was necessary because most rural people were apolitical and wanted to be left alone to farm and live day to day. After demonstrating all these negative issues, the CPT told the peasants that Maoism offered them a path to justice.[128] Through CPT propaganda, writes Saiyud, "Rural people slowly awoke to the realities of their relatively deprived existence."[129]

While there is no evidence Thailand's wealthy hated the poor, as the CPT claimed, it is certainly true that many rural poor Thai citizens had no idea, until the arrival of the CPT, that other people in their own country were leading far more comfortable lives. Thailand was an incredibly fractured nation in the 1960s, and rural residents knew very little about the rest of their country, making them easy picking for CPT propaganda.

Other educational propaganda focused on corruption of local officials, police tyranny, the lopsided justice system that favored the rich, inadequate schooling and health systems, and agricultural problems such as the terrible water shortage in Issan. All these were indeed real problems, and in many cases the RTG was unnecessarily slow to address them. The CPT easily exploited Bangkok's apathy.[130]

In offering to solve rural problems, Tanham writes that the CPT offered villagers "tractors, food, regular salaries for guerrillas, and official status within the government."[131] For the young, the CPT offered opportunities for travel and education.[132] In reality, however, the CPT had relatively meager resources to aid poor communities, and it rarely told the population that its assistance came with Maoist strings attached.

Justification of violence—a key Maoist propaganda requirement, says Marks—was high on the CPT's agenda. The communists needed to trick the masses into viewing the CPT as a benign organization that used violence only as a last resort. And it had to excuse that violence by painting those in power as so heinous and so dastardly that they were, in effect, dehumanized, making their destruction justifiable.

A simple but classic example of justification of violence propaganda comes from the UDT Caravan document. The UDT stated that, as a result of the Thammasat University massacre and the coup that followed, "all hope for a peaceful struggle for social change was dashed for the Thai masses."[133] This seemingly simple statement is actually a brilliant but pivotal piece of strategic messaging. It gave the impression that, until the massacre, the insurgency had been a "peaceful struggle." This was a lie. The CPT had been assassinating, bombing, raiding, and ambushing civilians and security forces since 1965. Additionally, the communist insurgency was about war, not "peaceful struggle" as the UDT proclaimed. Violence was the communists' remedy from the beginning. The contention that the CPT had not been fighting, coupled with the shock value of the massacre, allowed the communists to cast an illusion over the politically docile population, making it seem as if self-defense was the people's only recourse.

The Caravan document also said, "To sing to them in a group is a call to arms, for no one in Thailand now believes there is a peaceful road to a new society."[134] Here, the communists played the wounded victim while urging their audience to respond with violence. By claiming the government had forced the population into war, the communists depicted violence as a popular and necessary response, thereby making it easier for each individual to justify supporting the insurgency. Accordingly, responsibility for the decision to kill was dispersed, which made it easier to do.

The other big lie from the first Caravan statement was about the "struggle" for "social change," as if the revolution was about some utopian concern for the people's welfare. In reality, it was all about turning Thailand into a Maoist regime. Maoism does not allow opposition political parties, it wholly rejects religion, it insists upon command economies, and it either imprisons, exiles, or murders royal personnel. This is brutal dictatorship. In truth, the CPT and all its front organizations were fighting one autocratic government simply to replace it with another.

Anti-US messages were a constant of the CPT, dictated in part by Beijing. As earlier stated, the communists wanted the United States to stop aiding Thailand, Laos, Cambodia, and South Vietnam. They moreover wanted to stop the RTG from sending military forces to fight communists in Laos and South Vietnam.[135]

CPT propaganda also aligned the United States with the RTG in situations where no such linkage actually existed. For example, a post–Thammasat University massacre message titled *Resolutely Oppose the Coups by the Fascist Warlord Clique, the U.S. Imperialists' Lackeys* said:

> Our people will remember the old and new blood debts of
> the enemy and will consolidate forces to advance along the

trail of heroes' blood in order to drive out the U.S. imperialists, completely destroy fascist dictatorship, and build an independent, democratic, and prosperous Thailand.[136]

Here, the CPT partially blamed America for the massacre, as if US soldiers or policy makers had somehow intentionally targeted and killed those students. This was, of course, sheer fantasy, but because Washington supported Bangkok economically and militarily, such verbal trickery could be persuasive.

CPT threat propaganda involved warnings about future violence if people did not do as the CPT wanted. In the northeast, for example, Tanham asserts that the CPT used terror and fearmongering against the population, but not indiscriminately. "Key people," writes Tanham, "such as village leaders and teachers, have been harassed to the point that they could not or dared not perform their duties. Others have been assassinated or threatened with death."[137]

A clear example of CPT threat propaganda comes again from the Caravan document, which contains this joint statement by Caravan and another UDT-associated band, Komchai, after the 1976 Thammasat massacre:

> Listen up, you feudal lords, big capitalists, fascist warlords, and all of your lackeys: you have betrayed the masses who labor so that you can stuff yourselves with curry and rice. The time is now ripe for the victorious revolution of the people. It approaches so rapidly that you no longer have time sit at your ease. The wheel of history is turning fast and it will smash all of you into a million pieces.[138]

The CPT also used manipulative propaganda that cleverly leveraged the cultures of Thailand's outlying populations for recruiting purposes. For example, the CPT told hill tribes that it aimed to establish for them a Meo kingdom including like peoples from China and Laos, while nothing could have been further from the truth.[139] Citing evidence from prisoners of war and field reports,

Marks says the CPT told the Hmong that their mythical savior king of legend had returned, reincarnated in Beijing as "Miao Tse-tung"—capitalizing on the similar sounds of "Meo" and "Mao."

Hmong myth stated that, one day, a Meo king would arrive to unite all Hmong under one kingdom. When he returned, all tribesmen had a duty to fight in a campaign called *Oa Phoa Thay*, or "To Make a King." The CPT told the tribes to come to Beijing to meet their "Miao" leader, and that they should adopt communism. The ploy worked for a time. Some hill tribesmen were indeed trained in Beijing and then returned to the Thai mountains to spread the word that the *Oa Phoa Thay* campaign had begun.[140]

Finally, propaganda attacks on the Thai royal family were necessary for communism to sweep into power. Communist regimes cannot have royalty in their midst. Point ten of the CPT's ten-point plan for revolution called for the dissolution of feudalism from Thai history and culture. The Thai, however, deeply loved their royal family, and the CPT was hesitant to attack it. When it did, Marks describes a slow and indirect propaganda campaign that eventually cascaded into direct attacks.

Marks analyzed thirty-six VOPT attacks on the royal family from 26 February 1977 to 10 January 1978. Eight were "oblique," as Marks calls them, twenty-two associated the king or his family with enemies of communism, and six were direct attacks. Marks's analysis further shows that most indirect attacks took place from 22 February to 23 June 1977, with one oblique attack on 4 November 1977. The creeping nature of this political campaign might have been a test to see if the population would accept it.[141]

An example of an oblique attack happened on 26 February 1977. It stemmed from the CPT's killing of Princess Wiphawadi Rangsit ten days earlier by shooting down her helicopter. (One highly placed interviewee says bad weather forced her helicopter to low altitudes in mountainous terrain and it crashed.) She had been in southern Thailand while tending to a royal housing development project when she diverted her flight plan to evacuate two wounded police who had been fighting the CPT. Her helicopter came under fire, and the entire crew died. The public decried the event, and the CPT fought back with a broadcast entitled "Who Is Really the Cruel and Savage One?" It labeled the princess a "feudalist," a psychological trickster, and a murderer, thereby justifying her killing in the CPT's eyes.[142]

On 23 September 1977, the CPT launched a direct attack on the king, titled "Who Is the Father of Thai Medicine?" In this message, the CPT said that the king had sent troops to kill students at Thammasat University in October 1976. They said this because the Village Scouts were close to the king, and they had been part of the attack force. This was, however, a major overreach. The king had interceded on behalf of students just before the 14 October 1973 massacre, where he forced the government to resign. If anything, the king had demonstrated his desire for stability and justice, and the assertion by the CPT that the king had ordered the Thammasat killings was farcical. More, saying so linked the king with the most heinous government act perpetrated against the Thai population in modern times, marking him as one of the communists' most loathsome enemies.[143] This was, as Marks points out, a huge mistake. Not only was it patently false, the population adored the king, and having a government without his lofty guidance was, for most Thai citizens, unthinkable.

Military Operations

The CPT's combat operations consisted mostly of ambushes, raids, and maneuver warfare. It also conducted sabotage and assassinations. The CPT executed some classical conventional operations, especially in defense of its mountain strongholds that were protected by fixed fighting positions, bunkers, and trench warfare. It used terrorism to a certain extent, but this was not a primary operational tool for the duration of the war. Chai-Anan, Kusma, and Suchit, in their 1990 analysis of the war, said that the Thai military concluded that the CPT used terrorism frequently from 1965 to 1969, but from then on relied mostly on guerrilla warfare.[144]

CPT units used the jungle, difficult terrain, and night to their advantage as part of their doctrine. "They stayed deep in the jungles," says General Harn. "In the day, they stayed in the villages. At night, they fought in the jungles."[145]

Harn adds, "The CPT…they did patrols and ambushes. And [they deployed] land mines. They used land mines to place on trails where they thought the army would walk. They mostly targeted soldiers, not so much the population. They did not fight the people because they wanted their support. But if they knew you were helping the army, they'd kill you."

Harn says despite the CPT's lack of heavy weaponry such as artillery and armored fighting vehicles, the insurgents had hard and skilled fighters who did not shy away from combat. "They had more advantage because they knew the landscape. Their fighting skill was good. Normally, they would have the advantage of maneuver because of terrain appreciation. And for the same reasons, they could set up ambushes easily. When we first began fighting them this way, you never knew where they'd hit you. There was some trepidation when the troops went through CPT-prone areas."[146]

Though the RTG never publicly admitted it, the CPT seized and controlled significant areas of Thailand, such as the Khao Kho basin in Phetchabun province (northern Thailand), Bar Thong in Chonburi province (southeast Thailand),[147] and Khao Chong Chang in Surat Thani (southern gulf coast Thailand). Most of these are now tourist spots in national parks.

The CPT's military operations kept up a brisk tempo. On occasion, government operations forced the CPT to curtail its activities, and the wet season usually put a damper on guerrilla and government military operations alike. In the early years of the war, the CPT avoided major operations, most likely to prevent attracting forceful military responses.[148]

By 1968, in places such as the tri-border area between Laos, Thailand, and Burma, the CPT demonstrated real light infantry prowess, as Jeffrey Race describes. On 20 November 1968, the CPT raided an army-sponsored hill tribe self-defense force at Huai Sai Tai. A week later, in broad daylight, it ambushed a Public Welfare Department unit in their jeep at the Phu Lomo development center, killing one and wounding two. Shortly thereafter, the CPT laid siege to the Phu Lomo development center with twelve Border Patrol Police (BPP) officers inside. The BPP was a paramilitary police unit with light infantry and CA capabilities set up with help from the CIA. When the police sent a quick reaction force (QRF) via helicopter, the CPT battled it for seven days. When the army sent in another QRF to help, the CPT delayed its progress with roadblocks and harassing ambushes. When the army finally made it through to the besieged BPP, the guerrillas dispersed.[149] The CPT was indeed a professional fighting force.

Tanham writes the northeast saw 150 CPT-related acts of violence in March 1970, a record number for that region and time period.[150] Thousands of attacks occurred in 1970 alone, and the barrage continued past 1975. Tanham writes, "As 1970 unfolded, the CTs turned more and more to armed encounters and attacks on communications. A number of bridges were burned, ambushes were laid on the main Sakon Nakhon-Nakhon Phanom highway, and the first armored personnel carrier was mined."[151] Tanham cites a 28 February 1970 CPT attack in Nakhon Phanom as proof of the CPT's combat expertise. Here, a formation of eighty to ninety fighters divided into six units attacked several village security teams, blocked two roads, ambushed an army column, and set fire to nine bridges.[152]

As for assassinations, Marks writes, "Terror was an essential ingredient, but it was selective, generally aimed at recalcitrant villagers or symbols of government authority (village headmen and school teachers, for example)." [153] Several assassinations bear out Marks's findings. On 30 September 1968 in Ban Pa Wai, Nakhon Thai district, Phitsanulok province, the CPT assassinated a village chief. In the following six weeks it made two more attempts on other village officials.[154] In 1970, the CPT assassinated village heads that opposed them in four provinces: Nan, Chiang Rai, Lamoang, and Chiang Mai.[155] On 8 June 1970, the CPT shot three Thai who were working for the US Information Service in Nan province. In September, communist assassins murdered the governor of Chiang Rai province.[156]

The At-Risk Population

As Mao said, the people are the critical linchpin for revolution. They are the "sea" in which the "insurgent fish swim." In Thailand, the people most vulnerable to CPT revolutionary ideas lived in the northeast and north, followed by southerners. The rest of the population was not at risk until poor economic conditions combined with extremely autocratic government policies, which pushed the population to the brink.

At the time of the communist COIN, Thailand was still organized along almost feudal lines according to General Saiyud. Thai people lived in seventy-three provinces (now seventy-six) ruled by appointed governors and district administrators. It was largely an agricultural society that Saiyud described as "docile and politically apathetic," typified by "master-client" and "tolerant Buddhist" ethics.[157] In 1966, farming employed 80 percent of the national labor force, accounted for 32 percent of the Thai gross domestic product, and produced 80 percent of the total value of exported goods.[158]

The northeast region, Issan, was highly susceptible to the CPT. Its terrain is flat, dry, and dotted with forest-covered hills that rise to elevations of three thousand feet. The wet season is not enough to sustain effective agriculture. Droughts plagued Issan in the 1950s–60s, and its soil is not very fertile. Regardless, rice was the region's main product. In the 1960s, Issan held one-third of Thailand's 40 million people. Saiyud says that substandard communications, inferior medical services, and a second-rate educational system left the northeast chronically impoverished.

Issan's population is closely related to that of Laos, but, as Tanham writes, the region was "definitely Thai in their political and economic allegiance." Paul Handley, author of *The King Never Smiles*, points out, however, that Thai was the third most popular language of Issan in the 1960s, after Lao and Khmer. The people there had their own customs and an independent political streak.[159]

General Prem wrote of Issan, "Generally, villages were inaccessible. One day, having covered some distance on foot on the way to a village, we came across coconut trees. Tired and thirsty, we asked the owner who was standing nearby if we could buy some coconuts. He happily brought over the coconuts, [and when we] asked how much we should pay for the coconuts, he said that he didn't know because he had never sold a coconut in his life. To me, this showed the extent of the neglect. People were abandoned to an existence beyond the pale of society."[160]

The north of Thailand is mountainous and jungle-clad, with peaks reaching eight thousand feet. As a result, much of it is accessible only by foot, helicopter, or aircraft capable of taking off and landing on short runways. Four major rivers run through the north, including the Chao Phya, which flows through Bangkok. Rain is prevalent and the soil is ideal for agriculture. Lowland farmers—ethnic Thai—grew rice at the time, and there was some phosphate mining and teak tree logging. The road network was limited in the 1960s–70s, hindering development work and economic expansion. As many as five hundred thousand hill people occupied the north's mountain ranges.[161]

The two main tribes in the north were the Yao and the Hmong. The Thai hill tribes were fiercely proud of their own customs and religions, and they viewed outsiders with suspicion.[162] The rest of the northern population, some 5.5 million people, were Thai and occupied the foothills and lowlands.[163] The lowland farmers were by no means destitute, but government services did not reach them readily because of geography. They had no allegiance to a central government they knew little about.

The hill tribes' relationships with the Thai and the Thai government were bad. Some Thai ridiculed and conned hill people when they brought their goods to market. Many viewed the tribes as inferior peoples. Their citizenship status was in limbo for decades. During the 1960s–70s, Bangkok categorized them as refugees because they were nomadic and did not recognize national or internal borders. (In the mountainous jungles, borders were not well marked.) Since they were not citizens, they could not own land, nor could they have government jobs. The hill tribes lived by hunting, gathering, and slash-and-burn agriculture. The latter destroyed the mountain ecosystem and clogged rivers with dirty runoff. And because they lived in what the RTG considered a royal nature preserve, Jeffrey Race asserts that, technically, they were illegal squatters.[164] They also grew opium, which was illegal.[165]

Southern Thailand is divided into two sections, the mid and far south. The midsouth runs from north of Songkhla to Prachuap Kiri Khan province. Rice and rubber cultivation, tin mining, and fishing were its key industries. When tin and rubber prices were high, the region prospered. In the 1960s, when such commodities declined, the economy faltered. A rice shortage added to the difficulties. During the 1960s and 1970s, the crime rate was exceedingly high in Nakhon Si Thammarat province. It had one of the highest murder rates in all of Thailand.[166] No one was sure why.

The far south was, and by most statistics still is, Thailand's third-poorest region after the northeast and north. It is 80 percent ethnically Malay and Muslim, with Thai Buddhists making up most of the remainder. Songkhla has a large Chinese population, replete with Chinese-style pagodas in Hat Yai city. Malay Muslims have their own customs. Many prefer sharia law to Bangkok's laws. Low-level resistance to Bangkok's rule festered there for decades. As with the northeast, Bangkok neglected the far south's welfare for years, and many government agencies sent bad civil servants there as punishment. The area was crime ridden, and government corruption was also high, especially regarding cross-border smuggling. Few Malay Muslims held local government positions, and resentment toward the government was widespread.[167]

All the negative issues in each of these regions made the people there susceptible to the CPT. And as earlier stated, government neglect and mistreatment only added to the risk. In retrospect, the communists' infiltration of these areas is proof that effective government administration, even at the lowest level, matters on a strategic scale.

In any case, the central Thai also became susceptible to the communists in the early to mid-1970s. During that time, the government had become extremely repressive, and a global recession had set in. Wages fell, while inflation soared to 3 percent per month. A million Thais were unemployed. It was not uncommon in 1976 to have two hundred thousand workers go on strike in Bangkok. The government arrested political opponents without due process, allegedly executing many. With no room for even loyal political opposition, thousands of central Thai that never would have considered rebellion became vulnerable to the CPT. Student protest groups, full of idealism and zeal for confrontation with the police, made the situation worse.[168]

Without a just central government, then, societal weakness resulted. Under these conditions, the Thai people were prime for communist infiltration. But exactly why did many of them join the CPT?

Gawin, writing from the CPT side of the issue, contends that the main reason people joined the CPT was not communism, but the "oppression and exploitation of the ruling class, and indirectly, to some extent, of imperialism."[169] Here he is referring to the *amart-prai* issue, the ghost of *sakdi na*, and the US involvement in Thailand and the Vietnam War. As Gawin previously stated, however, the poorly educated, low-ranking CPT members knew little about political philosophies such as those of Marx and Mao. It is also likely they knew little about regional power politics, the United States, and the Vietnam War until the CPT told them America was trying to take over Thailand and colonize the rest of the world.[170] This was propaganda fantasy, but it worked on the gullible.

Saiyud, on the COIN-minded government side of the issue, also blames societal and political problems associated with the remnants of the *sakdi na* system. These problems, he says, included limited political participation by rural people, a lack of social mobility, and disputes over the citizenship status of ethnic minorities such as the Hmong and Malay Muslims. Poor and rural people were also tired of having no status in the country and of being treated like second-class citizens.[171]

Tyrell Haberkorn, in her detailed and insightful work on the subject, describes how landowners heavily exploited farmers. She writes, "In both the 1950s and the 1970s, farmers organized to challenge what they perceived as unjust practices which forced them to often give more than half the yearly rice harvest to the landlords from whom they rented land."[172] She further asserts that some landowners cheated farmers and were not sympathetic to their indebtedness.[173] Such corruption and lack of compassion left scores of farmers desperate. They either turned to the CPT or were easily recruited by it. Greedy Thai landlords, then, invited revolution upon themselves.

The macroeconomics of the agricultural sector in the 1960s was beginning to misfire as well, causing friction in the farmer-government relationship. A declassified 1968 CIA report on the situation stated that, although Thai farmers' incomes were rising, the rest of the country's incomes were leaping forward more dramatically as a result of industrialization. Agricultural production was not advancing as fast as manufacturing. Because 80 percent of the population depended on some aspect of agriculture for their livelihood, and because agriculture equaled one-third of GDP, the report said income discrepancy would become a major friction point. The CIA concluded that these macroeconomic issues would provide opportunities for Maoists to exploit. And they did.[174]

After petitioning the government via several student-assisted protests in Bangkok, farmers, led by groups such as the Farmers' Federation of Thailand (FFT), managed to get the government to pass the 1974 Land Rent Control Act. This measure cut landowners' share of tenant farmers' rice crops by a third or more. Some landlords ignored the order, however. According to Haberkorn, this problem, coupled with assassinations of activist farmers by right-wing paramilitaries and the Thammasat University massacre, pushed thousands into the arms of the CPT.[175]

Scores of activist farmers were already in the CPT, however. The FFT was aligned with the National Student Center of Thailand (NSCT), the powerful student group that had been thoroughly infiltrated by the communists. The FFT used CPT nomenclature, as front organizations are supposed to do in Maoist warfare. It referred to landlords as "capitalists," a sharply insulting term when used by the extreme left. After all, say extremist leftists, capitalism is the enemy to be stomped out by violence—and these farmer and student groups blamed capitalists for many of the people's woes.[176] Moreover, Haberkorn cites activists in the farmers' camp who "called into question the sheer ethics of land possession and personal profit."[177] Such a statement is pure CPT and Maoist thinking. It represents command-and-control economics of the Stalinist type. It also advocates for an economic system that has never worked in any modern society.

While Haberkorn notes the ugly trend of assassinations of leftist, activist farmers, the reality was that, regardless of their legitimate grievances, the more extreme farmers had joined a violent revolution. CPT agents were equally ruthless, assassinating government personnel and government-friendly villagers. In turn, the government and its civilian allies assassinated CPT agents and communist-friendly villagers. These were "big boy's rules," as Mark Urban wrote when describing Britain's war with the IRA.[178] That, however, is the unfortunate nature of insurgency and counterinsurgency.

Agricultural economics was not the only fiscal reason for revolt. Thailand's overall economy was in dire straits as well. Financial motivations for joining the CPT included the desire for a higher standard of living, higher incomes, and wider educational opportunities. The CIA, in a report on the CPT, wrote that the average income of Thai citizens in 1968 was $140 a year, a pittance that gave people ample motivation to search for a better way of life. Even though Thai incomes were rising by 4.5 percent per year, and the economy was growing by 7.5 percent a year, bleak news was on the horizon. The CIA estimated Thailand's economic growth was expected to drop to as low as 6 percent by the early 1970s because of floods, droughts, and poor global economics.

This economic trouble came to a head in the 1970s. Thailand's poor, especially those in areas most affected by rebellion, understood by then the discrepancy between rich and poor, and they knew that their government was not providing adequate aid programs or social safety nets. The CPT easily played on these grievances and told poor villagers that communism would boost their incomes and improve their economic lot.

In some cases, however, popular grievances were unrealistic. Thai officials indicate there was a difference between what economic improvements people wanted and what the government could actually do.[179] This issue is a sticking point in COIN. When poorly educated villagers finally understand the government is there to help, how much help is realistic? If the government supplements villagers' livelihoods to an excessive degree, then it bankrupts national coffers, as Greece experienced in 2012. If the government does not help the people enough, then they remain susceptible to rebellion. It is a difficult balancing act that requires careful calibration.

Aside from these agricultural and political issues, both Saiyud and Gawin cite widespread abuse of power by arrogant government officials as another reason why people joined the CPT. There were few checks and balances to keep corrupt officials from extorting the public for cash or throwing their weight around for the sake of exercising power. Saiyud writes, "In particular, the abuse of power by some government officials has been the single most important factor in alienating people and breeding recruits for communist terrorism in Thailand." [180] Corruption in the business sector compounded government abuse and further disaffected the population.[181]

Villagers termed corrupt officials as "troublemakers" or, even worse, "social robbers."[182] Gawin points out that corrupt officials threatened the safety of rural and hill peoples, and they had no other group to turn to but the CPT. In the south, Gawin asserts, heavy suppression tactics such as burning civilians in red drums and pushing them from helicopters forced people to seek safety in the arms of the CPT.[183]

General Prem Tinsulanonda also said that corruption was a cancer on society and a reason for people to join the CPT:

> Of course, we had heard of oppressive practices which officialdom in remote areas were prone to. But to come across it at first hand made us intensely conscious of the intimidation, the harassment and exploitation, which had become all too routine. Once we succeeded in getting the villagers to talk to us, we learned of extortions, of husbands and sons being summarily "put away" at the slightest suspicion, or of daughters being abducted to satisfy the casual needs of someone or another. In short, officialdom was its own enemy, turning ordinary villagers into communist sympathizers determined to avenge the wrongs perpetrated.[184]

Some who joined the communists were simply stuck in the middle—farmers or tribesmen who wanted to live their lives free from meddling by both Bangkok and the CPT. The CPT forced some of these people into service, but the coerced made poor Maoist rebels, readily surrendering and confessing to authorities during security sweeps. Because of this internal weakness, Saiyud said, the CPT as a whole lacked ideological toughness.[185]

Hill tribe motivations to join the CPT resulted from a combination of them breaking the law and government corruption. According to Jeffrey Race, the government wanted the tribes to cease their slash-and-burn agriculture, which was illegal. It defoliated mountainsides, caused massive erosion, and clogged streams and rivers, which hurt lowland irrigation and agriculture. It also destroyed teak forests, a moneymaker for Thailand's agricultural sector. The hill tribes, in contrast, saw their form of agriculture as a way of life and the land as their own, not something that outsiders could regulate. Bangkok also wanted the hill tribes to halt opium production, though opium researcher and author Alfred W. McCoy asserts that some criminal elements in the RTG and security forces benefited from it and hindered government anti-opium operations.[186]

At any rate, the complications of government corruption involving the hill tribes were horrendous. Race says that they primarily involved Provincial Police (PP) and Forestry Service officials extorting money from hill tribes not to enforce anti-opium and slash-and-burn laws.[187] A classic corruption case occurred in May 1967 in Huai Chom Poo village, Thoeng district, Chiang Rai province. A local authority told the villagers that he would turn a blind eye to their slashing and burning a mountainside in exchange for a cash payment. Later, a second official that did not know about the first extortion episode made the same demand. Then a group of PP went to the same village, demanding yet another payment for the same favor. Curiously, they found only women there. The men were all gone. Then, as the PP left the village, the tribesmen ambushed them, killing one, wounding three, and capturing three. The next day the police raided Huai Chom Poo with sixty-four officers, resulting in a lengthy firefight. Eventually the tribesmen retreated, and the police burned the village and killed its livestock. Episodes like this ruined the government's legitimacy, alienated the Hmong, and drove them into the CPT.[188]

Student motivations to join the CPT had roots in the 14 October 1973 massacre, which, in part, led to the 6 October 1976 Thammasat massacre. As previously stated, the students opposed the existing regime, government corruption, and the Vietnam War, and they associated with protest movements sweeping campuses all over the world at the time. Some were ardent communists, though most, according to Thai historian Yuangrat Wedel, were not, and especially not Maoists.[189] Their heightened idealism, however, made them ideal CPT targets.

Denny Lane, a former US defense attaché to Thailand, saw student motivations for joining the CPT firsthand. "There were lots of young, coffee-drinking, revolution-hypothesizing, chatty students who took to the jungles, wanting to be part of the revolution but in a political, docile way," Lane says.[190] "But when they got there, the CPT said, 'Good, now dig a foxhole.' The students were quite sophisticated to the CPT, and apparently too much so in a philosophical sense, and they were not terribly practical to have around."[191] As a result, Lane says, many CPT members hated and rejected the students: "The students came with all sorts of ideas and wanted to take the insurgency into the cities. And some students were not ready to leave Bangkok behind. They were the Thai upper middle class and were not motivated to wage jungle and guerrilla warfare."[192]

Strategy

The RTG changed its anticommunist COIN strategy, informally known as "the CPM plan," at least four times during the war, in response to CPT progress and COIN shortcomings. According to Kanok Wongtrangan, an expert on the CPT war, "The CPM Plan was gradually developed through learning from the mistakes and experiences of the government in dealing with the communist insurgency."[193]

One major impediment to effective COIN was executive instability. From 1963 to 1980, Thailand had nine different governments. Each time a new ruling clique came to power, it came with its own political and patronage networks—people with different social, economic, political, and military ideas from the previous administrations. This instability impacted all government policies. Six changes of prime ministers took place in a mere four years between 1973 and 1977, a critical time in the anticommunist COIN era.

Prime Minister	Administrative Years
Thanom Kittikachorn	9 December 1963–14 October 1973
Sanya Dharmasakti (Sanya Thammasak)	14 October 1973–15 February 1975
M. R. W. Seni Pramoj	15 February 1975–6 March 1975
M. R. W. Kukrit Pramoj	14 March 1975–12 January 1976
M. R. W. Seni Pramoj	20 April 1976–6 October 1976
Thanin Kraivichien	8 October 1976–20 October 1977[194]

This instability gave the CPT a window of opportunity to grow and expand its political and military operations to the point it nearly achieved parity with the government. It took a new generation of Thai military leaders who were both politically and militarily astute to correct the government's failures. Their strategy took years to develop, but when they applied it, the results were dynamically successful.

1965: The Civilian Military Police Program

In December 1965, the government developed the CPM program, the brainchild of several officers, including General Saiyud.[195] The CPM concept had its origins in anticommunist operations planned in the early 1960s by the National Security Command (NSC). Some sources indicate that this body was, in fact, the National Security *Council*, not the more military-sounding *Command*. Regardless, this body was a Thai security organ roughly equivalent to a combination of the US Joint Chiefs of Staff and the National Security Council. The US Agency for Development (USAID) and the US CIA helped to lay the groundwork for some of these early 1960s operations.[196]

The CPM strategy envisioned applying kinetic force to destroy CPT military units while using economic development to uplift impoverished people, improve their standards of living, and endear them politically to the government. CPM was supposed to entail civilians, police, and the military working together at the village level to provide local security, political orientation, and military support to areas vulnerable to communist infiltration.

According to Chai-Anan, Kusuma, and Suchit, however, the government relied too much on heavy suppression such as search-and-destroy operations. It did not understand the enemy. The RTA mistakenly perceived the CPT as a band of mostly Laotian and North Vietnamese fighters sponsored by their home countries. The government did not grasp the CPT's organizational capabilities, its guerrilla warfare doctrine, or its intentions to bleed political support from Bangkok. Chai-Anan and his colleagues claim that a mere five people in the Thai government understood communism at the time. Even the Chief of Army Intelligence, Prayuth Charumanee, conceded he did not understand how to fight the CPT.[197] His admission reflected a major deficiency for the entire Thai national security establishment. If a government does not understand its enemy, it cannot strategize a defense, and certainly not an offense.

Professor Bhumarat Taksadipong adds, "We did not know the enemy. We did not know their goals or how they functioned…how they were organized. We did not speak to them about these things."[198] He describes a disturbing trend from the early days of fighting communism: "They got arrested," he says, "and they got killed. And when you killed one man, they had relatives and friends, so you created more enemies. In the first ten years of the war, we lost our way."

1967: The 09/10 Plan

In 1967, the government tweaked its COIN strategy based on the lackluster results of its combat operations against the CPT. In those operations, the RTA and Royal Thai Air Force (RTAF), joining together as a special task force known as the 13th Combined Regiment, conducted combined, large-scale suppression operations in Na Kae, Nakorn Panom province. They did not net many CPT members, however, and the RTA's leadership saw the folly. Large-scale suppression operations were ineffective. Accordingly, CSOC upgraded the CPM strategy via the 09/10 Plan.[199] The 09/10 Plan signified the Buddhist calendar years 2509 and 2510, which translate to 1966 and 1967 on the Western calendar.

Essentially, the government concluded the insurgency had taken root among the people, and since the people were serving as an offensive element for the CPT, they could also be a defensive element for the government. The government called its popular defense strategy "mass mobilization." The strategy was the CPT's, but the government turned it around on the guerrillas.

The 09/10 Plan also mandated village self-defense forces. This concept was essentially the same as in the CPM plan, but it formally parsed CPM tasks and made them general orders. It also rejected heavy suppression. The plan had four main tenets:

1. Clear insurgents from target areas.
2. Provide security at the local level.
3. Harness civilians into action.
4. Initiate development projects for villagers.[200]

In the beginning, this plan applied just to the northeast, not nationally.[201] Though the 09/10 Plan was not a sophisticated strategy, it did, at the very least, reflect an orderly approach. Clearing guerrillas from target areas was pure suppression, the job of military and police units with light infantry training such as the BPP. Providing local security encompassed both static security and kinetic operations that combined the military, police, and armed civilian units in the villages. Stimulating civilian action was both a political and security method. The government wanted anticommunist activists in the villages, it wanted villagers to provide intelligence on CPT activities, and it wanted civilians to join security operations against the CPT.

The main weaknesses in executing the plan were poor RTA and RTP coordination and too much focus on suppression, even though the 09/10 Plan disavowed the latter. [202] In addition, the CIA says the 09/10 Plan fell short due to limited manpower. There simply were not enough troops to get the job done. When the ground forces moved into CPT areas, they did inflict heavy casualties on the communists, but the rebels were able to disperse and reemerge in other areas and continue their fight.

1969: The 110/2512 Plan

The government and RTA reexamined their shortfalls and changed strategy yet again on 30 May 1969 to the 110/2512 Plan, known informally as the 110 Plan. Kanok contends several factions within the military influenced this strategy: (1) those who believed in suppression, (2) those who believed development was the key to gaining political allegiance, and (3) those who called for a combination of both.[203] The latter two had the biggest influence on the 110 Plan.[204]

Glenn Ettinger, a former CIA paramilitary officer previously stationed in Laos and Thailand, says the RTP had a hand in the 110 Plan, too. From the beginning of communist hostilities, PM Sarit Thanarat had been involved in strategic planning against the CPT. He understood waging COIN was a multiagency effort, and he wanted a police voice in the matter. So he tapped Police General Phot Pekanan, CPT Action Officer for Special Branch, to find a motivated officer to strategize the defeat of the CPT. General Phot picked Police Special Colonel Ari Kaributra for the job.[205]

Colonel Ari dedicated significant time to studying the CPT, mostly by interviewing captured communist rebels at the Lat Yao district detention center on the Bangkok-Nothaburi line. Chief among his interviewees was Prasert Sapsunthorn, one of twenty CPT captured in 1967. Prasert was instrumental in detailing not only the internal workings of the CPT, but also communist philosophies and Mao's strategies. This information caused Colonel Ari to propose using democracy as a weapon against the CPT to undercut its fake political promises and boost the RTG's legitimacy in the eyes of the population. Winning the people back from the CPT using political means, Ari concluded, was key to victory. This was counterpolitical warfare.

Ari expressed these sentiments to CSOC, where like-minded personnel had reached similar conclusions. Ettinger also asserts Ari took Prasert with him to share his ideas with RTA General Sawaeng Senanarong, Field Marshal Thanom's personal secretary, thereby helping the CSOC to push the 110 Plan through.[206] The new strategy stated the following tenets:

1. By all means, to persuade people from all social strata to have trust and faith in the authorities' work and the government's administration; to win over the people's mind in order to maintain their loyalty to the government.

2. To provide security to people, so they can peacefully live and work in their village.

3. To formulate a system which will facilitate the people's acquisition of adequate knowledge and experience in economic social, political, and military as well as psychological questions in order to protect their families and villages from communist threats, with the support and assistance of the government; this is the "supreme objective" of communist prevention and suppression.

4. In prevention and suppression, political and psychological, to utilize public relations measures as primary instruments and military or severe physical suppression or [judicial] measures only when necessary.[207]

The 1969 strategy marked a significant change from past schemes. The first tenet was political: winning the population's hearts and minds through good governance. It required civil servants, the military, and the police to abandon corruption, become more professional, and put the people's needs first. In adopting this, Bangkok admitted that it had governance problems. Putting the people's needs first included paying attention to the day-to-day, immediate needs of society's downtrodden. General Saiyud stressed the government had to tackle the effects of bad harvests, lack of access to schools, and inadequate care for infants and the elderly. These were core security issues outside the kinetic realm, and they were just as important as destroying the CPT's military units.[208]

The second new tenet was the use of psyops to win villagers' minds, educating them according to Bangkok's policies, and warning them of the perils of communism. This, the government said, was its "supreme objective," a turn from the past when the main objective was to destroy the enemy's military units. The government's psyops included educational sessions and both soft and hard propaganda—that is, gentle political spin and outright lies. This strategy mirrored the actions of the CPT. The government had decided to play by the communists' rules.

The third new aspect was to make sure the public had a broad understanding of the government's security, political, and economic methods. In this way, the people would understand the government's intentions when its various agencies and security forces came to the villages. This is exactly what the CPT did through the VOPT on New Year's Day 1969, when it announced its strategy and governing philosophy, paving the way for its ground forces to organize the people.

The fourth new aspect proclaimed the government would use political means as its primary COIN weapon. Suppression would be secondary. This would eventually become the key philosophical driver behind Thai COIN.

Unfortunately, only a handful of Thai military officers—those of the Second Army in particular—embraced the 110 Plan. Suppression-minded commanders remained at large and did what they pleased, which generally meant fighting. And why not? The 110/2512 Plan was based on concepts alien to Thailand's top field commanders. It did not mesh with traditional RTA doctrine, and most conventional military men are slow to innovate outside conventional realms.[209]

Strategic Reconfiguring in the 1970s: Foundations of the 66/2523 Plan

Various RTA officers and security officials spent the 1970s studying the insurgency and how to defeat it. No Thai leader had the power to institute effective strategic change, however. It would not be until 1980 that a single commander would take charge and apply an effective COIN strategy. Scores of people and agencies influenced the new plan. They included General Kriangsak Chomanand, General Prem Tinsulanonda, General Harn Leenanond, ex-CPT member Prasert Sapsunthorn, the Democratic Soldiers clique, General Saiyud Kerdphol, General Chavalit Yongchaiyudh, General Arthit Kamlangek, Colonel Harn Pongsithanonda, intelligence official Somchai Rakwijit, US State Department and CIA advisors, and King Bhumibol Adulyadej.

General Kriangsak Chomanand took over as PM on 11 November 1977 by coup d'état after nearly a decade of government ineptitude and despotism.[210] While Kriangsak did not come up with a new formal COIN strategy, he did make a national policy change that proved to be the most effective anti-COIN measure taken since 1965. Simply put, he increased civil liberties. Kriangsak eased police suppression, lifted many press restrictions, engaged moderate labor leaders, raised the minimum wage, gave amnesty to all students who fled to the CPT after the Thammasat massacre, and pushed through a new constitution. Kriangsak took pressure off the population and gave it political breathing room. Thai citizens no longer were forced to choose between autocracy and the CPT.[211] Kriangsak restored national balance and reduced severe domestic political division, both important concerns for the Buddhist-oriented Thai people.

With regard to security, Kriangsak knew who the top COIN personalities were in the RTA, and he elevated them. He appointed Prem Tinsulanonda as Commander-in-Chief of the army and Harn Leenanond as Chief of Army Operations. He moreover kept Saiyud close to him as a COIN advisor and senior officer at ISOC.[212]

At the same time, Kriangsak instituted a crackdown on communists by giving security officials specific powers designed to identify, isolate, and neutralize clandestine operators. To achieve this goal, Kriangsak enacted the Anticommunist Activities Act of 1979, which granted wide eavesdropping, arrest, and detention powers to the police and military.[213] Instead of being clumsy and targeting the entire population, however, Kriangsak's law was surgical, specifically targeting key communists and their networks. Ultimately, Kriangsak was able to simultaneously increase population control and civil liberties through brilliant policy making.

As for Prem, as Second Army commander from 1 October 1974 to 30 September 1977, he ran a COIN program based on the best practices of existing strategies combined with his own ideas and those of his staff. His COIN prowess was hard-won, however. When Prem first arrived in northeast Thailand in 1973, he understood little about the CPT. "On the second day of my [arrival]," General Prem said in a speech to the Philippine Army in 1995, "I lost twenty-three of my men in one single ambush. The whole town barely had enough coffins to put them in. I was plunged into the depths of sadness, lost for an answer."[214]

Prem was also at a loss over the extreme mistrust villagers displayed toward the government. "As soon as we set foot in a village," he says, "the villagers would run away; at best, they would ignore our presence and instantly clam up upon our approach. The misperception and the distrust were evidently mutual."[215]

To solve this problem, Prem's forces made efforts to build trust with villagers. His troopers taught children to read, helped villagers tend crops, provided medical aid to the sick, and did other manual labor to prove their good intentions. "I distinctly remember one village, which was especially difficult," he said. "The first time our men went in, they had to pitch camp outside the village because they were not allowed in. Villagers just hurled insults and abuses at them. Luckily, the man we picked to lead that squad was a man of understanding and perseverance. Though repeatedly turned away, he would always be back the next morning, offering help to villagers working in the fields. It took all of seven months before the villagers started to feel sorry for our men and agreed to join in the Self-Defense Volunteers Program."[216]

Prem was a major proponent of the CPM concept. He believed it increased intelligence flow and heightened the political connection between the government and the people. Despite all the political and development strategies, however, Prem and his lieutenants firmly believed suppression was necessary to physically drive a wedge between the insurgents and the people. He understood people could not carry out politics and economics while being shot at.

Prem believed in widespread psyops, educational seminars on the perils of communism, and identifying key CPT personnel in the villages and singling them out for reeducation. Like most Thai COIN advocates, he also stressed the value of development as both a political and economic stability tool. Consolidating all these ideas into a single strategy, Prem arrived at an approach known as "the villages surrounding the jungle," which was the direct opposite of Mao and the CPT's "villages surrounding the cities."[217]

Kanok, in his excellent monograph on Thailand's victorious COIN strategy, credits General Harn with forging the strategic innovations that turned the tide of the war.[218] Harn believed Thailand's autocratic nature invited rebellion. Kanok cites Harn as railing against dictatorship, saying, "A society in which there is no freedom or democracy will remain in the 'Dark Age' and will be dictated by power," only to "become weak and unstable."[219] Harn said popular upheaval and communist rebellion would be the inevitable outcome of repressive governance.[220]

Kanok writes that Harn viewed insurgency as "a consequence of conflict among the people and/or conflict between the people and government officials."[221] Harn and the Second Army learned these conflicts had their roots in many causes, such as "exploitation by local influential people, poverty, social injustice, corruption, and abuse of power by the authorities."[222]

Solving the insurgency, Harn figured, required changing this situation to build trust with the people and increase government legitimacy. He said, according to Kanok, "the only solution for ending the war is to destroy all conditions for the war."[223] Harn believed a large part of this solution entailed adopting democracy.[224]

Harn's vision of democracy was not exactly an American one that required democratic elections. He said, "If the policy and its practice protect the interests of the people, and the people receive the most benefit, it can be called democratic rule."[225] To Harn, democracy consisted of a just government that was absent of corruption, kept the people's best interests in mind, was independent of foreign control, and fostered fair economic conditions where exploitative landlords and others could not harm the people.[226]

While Harn emphasized the role of political solutions in COIN, he also believed in the utility of force. For certain, he cautioned against putting too much faith in force, saying, "Suppressing the communists with armed forces may reduce their resistance but not win the war."[227] Accordingly, Harn's reliance on force was purposeful and refined. He acknowledged the CPT's military capabilities had to be reduced. "As long as the military influence of those on the mountains still casts its shadow over the villages," he asserted, "political approaches cannot be expected to succeed."[228] Military domination, then, was important. "The people will stick with the victor," Harn said.[229] He committed himself to using swift and decisive force against communist holdouts that would not accept the state's peace offerings.[230] In short, Harn was no political pushover. He believed in the use of force, but only against select and stubborn factions of the insurgency.

Another major influence on Thai COIN strategies was Prasert Sapsunthorn, the ex-CPT member captured in 1967 who helped the government understand the CPT. He proved invaluable in deciphering CPT political warfare strategies, helping the government understand the communists from the inside, and guiding the development of psyop strategies. Prasert's ideas heavily influenced the Democratic Soldiers, a faction within the RTA that believed, as Prem and Harn did, that politics should reign supreme in COIN. The Democratic Soldiers formed after the 1973 student movement took shape.

One lesson the Democratic Soldiers took from Prasert's experience was organization. Specifically, the RTG was weak in organizing groups of people and motivating them to achieve a single, national vision. In contrast, until its final years, the CPT experienced little factionalism and was able to persuade much of the Thai population, which traditionally had been politically apathetic, to embrace revolt. The Democratic Soldiers sought to mimic the CPT's organizational expertise, using the army as the political motivator, which would, in theory, spawn support for the government.[231] As Chai-Anan, Kusuma, and Suchit observe, "The Democratic Soldiers' political thinking greatly influenced the formulation of the prime minister's Order 66/2523 which laid down the guidelines for the suppression of communist insurgency."[232]

Another influential COIN leader was General Saiyud Kerdphol, the first Director of Operations and later Chief of Staff of CSOC.[233] He had been instrumental in shaping COIN strategy based on the CPM concept and directed aid programs throughout the war, despite resistance from RTA area commanders and an absence of real leadership through the 1970s.[234]

Interestingly, General Saiyud expressed his conception of COIN in the terminology of algebra. His variables were G for the government, P for the people ("or target villages"), C for the CPT, and V for victory. A failed strategy, Saiyud believed, followed the formula $G - (C+P) = -V$; that is, the government facing a combined force of the people and the communists equals defeat. A stalemate, he figured, would occur if the people were somewhat cooperative, or when P was not on either side of the equation: $G - C = \pm V$. To win, Saiyud wanted a different formula, one where the people and the government were in the fight together, or $P^G - C = V$. In this case, the people, supported by the government as a force multiplier, minus the communists, equals victory.[235]

Two additional officers who impacted Thailand's COIN strategy were General Chavalit Yongchaiyudh, Prem's aide-de-camp and later Commander-in-Chief of the Army, and General Arthit Kamlangek. John Cole, a US Army defense attaché to Thailand during the Cold War and the first American graduate of the Thai Command and Staff College, explains, "Chavalit was a significant proponent of political means and was credited with helping to write Thailand's ultimately successful COIN strategies."[236] This is an interesting comment about the man who founded the *Thahan Phran*. Chavalit, however, believed that politics would be the ultimate knife in the heart of the CPT. After the war ended, Chai-Anan, Kusuma, and Suchit quoted him as saying, "We can say that the real reason behind the halt in the armed struggle was merely the expansion of individual liberty."[237]

General Arthit, Deputy Commander of the Second Army, was a major proponent of Civil Affairs missions. To him, CA was a combination of politics and development. He believed without politics, development projects were only half as effective. General Arthit was also one of the originators of the amnesty program, a decisive political tool in this communist COIN. Chai-Anan, Kusuma, and Suchit quote General Arthit as saying to his CA troops:

> The duties which you have to perform are beyond military functions. Your duties, connected with all forms of mass movement, are aimed at preserving national security, educating the people to understand the democratic form of government with the king as head of state, convincing them that it is the best form of government for Thailand, and persuading the CPT elements to lay down their arms and surrender themselves to the government authority.[238]

Another influential strategist was Colonel Harn Pongsithanonda, a CSOC director of intelligence for nine years who called for more politics in COIN early in the war. Harn believed the government should do four things in COIN: (1) use political means to assuage people's grievances, (2) instill confidence in the people, (3) stop abusing the citizenry, and (4) convince the population that using violence to achieve political ends is pointless. In the early 1970s, however, these sentiments were considered blasphemous. Harn's enemies branded him a communist and forced him to resign by 1975.[239] This reflects how much sway the suppression-minded leaders had at the time. It further shows how quickly the political-minded COIN proponents took over. By 1977, just two years after the sacking of Colonel Harn, they would be in full control of the government and the war effort. Had more officials listened to Colonel Harn earlier, the war might have been won sooner.

Intelligence officer Somchai Rakwijit went beyond mere collection and analysis and moved to influence strategy by becoming General Prem's premier COIN advisor. "When you fight the communists," he says, "you have to demonstrate that you will provide protection and provide for the target population's safety, that you are their friends, and that you can provide for their material needs. At least then you can neutralize the negative situation."[240] This was, according to Somchai, a critical first step in separating the insurgents from the population, as well as a tenet of classic COIN. "Then," Somchai continues, "you can begin to bring them back into society, make them believe that society is fair to them. So if the government is fair-minded and really cares—if it wants to bring peace and prosperity to the country—then fighting the communist insurgents is a matter of the government and the communists adjusting themselves to narrow the gaps."[241] Somchai made clear that separating the population from the insurgents was not enough. The country also had to address the woes of its at-risk population. This entailed seizing upon genuine grievances highlighted by the enemy and fixing them.

In 1977, Somchai wrote a policy paper titled "Politics Must Have Primary Leadership in Conducting COIN." In it, he states that, "A military dictatorship cannot lead COIN. It only creates more problems and adds to violence. The military must be under the civilian government. At the time, the RTA accepted [this principle], because they needed to win. A dictatorship fighting against a communist insurgency cannot win. So the current government at the time promised to return power to the people as a weapon of sorts to fight the communists."[242]

The US State Department and CIA also influenced Thai COIN strategy through an advisory group called the US Operations Mission. The US Ambassador to Thailand, Graham Martin, wanted the United States to help prevent a communist takeover of Thailand, but he did not want it leading the effort as it did in Vietnam. This, Martin figured, would have restricted Thailand from building its own capacity for guerrilla warfare.[243]

The United States COIN advisors investigated CPT activities and then advised the RTG on how it might counter them. The advisors worked at the national level on strategy as well as at the operational levels with the RTA and RTP. In many instances, the United States hired British COIN veterans from the successful Malaya Emergency of 1948–60, such as Gerry Waller and Richard Clutterbuck. Both provided expertise as consultants paid by the US Advanced Research Projects Agency (ARPA), which some say was a cutout organization for the CIA. During the Malaya war, Waller was a COIN police officer and superintendent of the Police Training Centre in Jalan Semarak, Kuala Lumpur (KAL). Clutterbuck, a British Army officer, was on the operations staff. After his retirement he was a Senior Lecturer and Reader at the Department of Politics, University of Exeter, Devon, UK, from 1972 to 1983.[244]

General Saiyud credits Waller in particular as having had a significant impact on Thailand's COIN program. State Department COIN expert George K. Tanham had a close working relationship with General Kerdphol as well.[245] These men and others, such as Ambassador Martin, brought with them know-how on the nexus between security, information operations, and development—three key drivers of early Thai COIN plans.[246] Interestingly, their COIN expertise seems to have had little impact on overall US activities in Vietnam.

The Thai royal family had immense interest in COIN, too. They understood full well that communist regimes had a history of cruelty toward royal families. They courted Richard Clutterbuck and took lessons from his classic book on the Malaya Emergency, *The Long, Long War*. It contained a step-by-step account of the technical aspects of the British/Malaysian victory over communist insurgents. Some of Clutterbuck's lessons were political and stressed building state-sponsored fronts to counter communist fronts. It is likely that this influenced Thailand's incredibly effective political programs such as the Village Scouts.[247]

1980: The 66/2523 Plan

In a 1978 secret meeting, the RTA concluded that the Thai government was gaining ground against the CPT. This happened for several reasons previously mentioned: Prem and Harn's CPM program in Issan bearing fruit, improved village cooperation and security, better intelligence, reduced corruption, and Kriangsak's democratic policies. The RTA also finally realized unwieldy force application operations resulted in increased CPT recruits.[248] Accordingly, the army decided to make politics and other nonkinetic programs their main COIN tools. They called this policy *karnmuang nam karn tahan*, or "politics leads the military."[249]

Few government programs in Thailand moved fast in the 1970s. For the new COIN strategy to take effect, it was necessary for Prem to seize power in 1980. When he did, the government applied his approach at lightning speed, partly because it was ready-made and already in action in Issan. Prem took over the PM position by coup, ousting his ally, Kriangsak, on 3 March 1980. Prem then issued Thailand's final and ultimately successful COIN strategy on 23 April as PM Order No. 66/2523, the "Policy to Win Over Communism."[250] General Harn was one of its main authors.[251] The document consisted of an overview of Thailand's strategic situation (or context of the war), the government's objectives and policies (or end goals), the types of operations to be carried out (or ways/methods), the different agencies and entities necessary to carry out these operations (means), and the administrative structure of the campaign (coordination). These were all key ingredients of a proper strategy. The main points of each section, as presented by Kanok, are summarized below.[252]

Overview

The 66/2523 Plan recognized the existence of an ongoing Cold War with all its associated problems, such as limited energy supplies (likely a nod to the 1973 oil crisis), and the international military balance between the superpowers. War against communism had come to Thailand as a part of such global troubles.

The government recognized the CPT had exploited Thailand's governmental troubles as its primary means to sway the population to its side and that it had spread from the jungles to the cities. It moreover saw weakness in the CPT, noting the communists could not necessarily rely on the proletariat to support a democratic revolution.

The government also stated it would protect "Nation, Religion, and King," a slogan that represented the heart of Thai domestic, international, and defense policy, which included reforms to ensure good governance, uphold the welfare of the people, and instill idealism among the Thai people. The military swore to protect the monarchy and to defeat communism, the chief threat to national security.

Objectives

The objective of the 66/2523 Plan was "to put an end in the shortest possible time to the communist revolutionary war, which is of the utmost significance and danger to national security."

Policy

The plan stated the government's COIN policy was to wage a continual political campaign against the CPT and its front organizations while also using force against its armed members. The primary goal was to "eliminate the revolutionary situation." The policy also sought to adopt international neutrality, a veiled gesture toward left-wing angst over Thailand's alignment with the United States. Another goal was to move the conflict from an armed one to a political one.

Operations

The operations section had nine points. First, the political offensive took precedence, which entailed convincing the people the land was theirs, and that they had a stake in protecting it. The military's role was to support all political offensives. Second, emphasis was placed on eliminating corruption, bad governance, and poverty. Third, rules of conduct were necessary to promote harmony between the many classes of Thai people. Everyone had to sacrifice social position for the common good, putting country first, regardless of one's individual status. Fourth, political participation by all ranks of society was vital not only for a better society, but also to assuage grievances. Fifth, all democratic movements were welcome and encouraged as long as they were not communist organizations in disguise.

Sixth, all elements in the CPM equation were to carry out both armed and political campaigns. Political campaigns had to be uniform across the entire nation. All units had to promulgate the same message, which was the spread of democracy throughout Thailand to ensure individual liberties. (In the long run, democracy would not spread to the extent to which Western circles are accustomed, but it spread enough to help defeat the CPT.) Armed operations were to be executed according to the regional threat level and in proportion to CPT activities. The goal of armed operations was to "pressure, cut down, and destroy armed bands on a continuous basis." Seventh, all prisoners of war and defectors were to be treated as "fellow countrymen," and the government was responsible for integrating them back into society.

Eighth, the CPT infrastructure absolutely had to be rooted out of the towns, eliminated, and blocked from ever returning. Organizations had to be vetted to ensure they were not part of a united front, and no group, surreptitiously or otherwise, could be allowed to separate the people from the government and create war conditions. Ninth, the importance of psyops—"information, psychological measures, and public relations"—was paramount in every aspect of COIN, and it would be carried out at each phase of every operation against the CPT.

Separate from this document was a tenth and unlisted strategy, which was to politically separate the CPT from its regional sponsors, namely China and Vietnam. Thailand's main tool in this regard was diplomacy, one of its legendary strengths. Thailand had been working this particular angle well before Prem took over. Diplomacy could be categorized, however, under the RTA's policy to "eliminate the revolutionary situation" and point eight, rooting out the CPT's infrastructure, which was tied to China, Laos, and Vietnam.

Administration

Since the anticommunist COIN was the highest priority in Thailand, government agencies were expected to develop plans to support the 66/2523 Plan. The NSC was responsible for advising the cabinet on COIN issues. ISOC was repositioned as an ad hoc agency, and a new position, Director of the Prevention of Communist Activities, was created to coordinate the COIN campaign. This would be not an organization but a single person, presumably aided by a staff. This director also had the power to punish corrupt officials. Finally, the COIN budget was to receive priority, and 66/2523 superseded all past strategies.

While the 66/2523 Plan had its roots in the 110/2512 Plan of 1969, it was distinctly different. The 66/2523 Plan was, in effect, a revolution in military affairs (RMA) in Thailand. The overview demonstrated that the government was treating the communist opposition not just as a local problem of bandits but as a deeply rooted insurgency with national political and economic implications and international ties. The objective and policy were clear and decisive: the government set out to end the war and emerge as the victor. This statement was in effect a veiled admission that the CPT had practically seized the country, and the government was going on the offensive to take it back. No previous strategy stated anything so forceful, decisive, or immediate. The Thai government was finally serious about defeating the CPT.

The operations section called for a unified, national political campaign against the CPT. Correcting CPT propaganda with government psyops was one of Bangkok's main new weapons. It had been used previously, but now it would be intertwined with all COIN efforts.

Kinetic operations were a close second in importance. The plan stated force would be critical in retaking the country from the CPT, but it would be more focused than before. Security forces were to concentrate on CPT armed units only and not on wider segments of the population.

Mobilization of the masses in both politics and defense was key in these endeavors. The government was declaring a people's war against the CPT. Fixing corruption and slipshod governance was also an urgent goal necessary for the countrywide spread of democracy, Bangkok's new governing philosophy.

The plan had an immediate effect, as indicated by the chart below, which details incidents and personnel losses beginning after General Prem initiated the new COIN strategy. The trend is clear: once the government executed the 66/2523 Plan, the CPT slid into defeat.

Incident and Personnel Losses, 1980–1985[253]

Year	CPT Losses				RTG Losses		Clashes	Attacks
	KIA	WIA	Arrested	Detected	KIA	WIA		
1980	316	48	316	1,543	423	1,179	770	22
1981	201	34	286	2,322	459	1,264	704	19
1982	94	62	196	2,071	225	742	405	15
1983	23	13	60	941	74	478	193	2
1984	9	4	29	346	105	462	164	-
1985	-	-	11	18	19	68	41	-

Note: KIA refers to personnel killed in action. WIA refers to those wounded in action.

Coordination
The Communist Suppression Operations Command

On 14 December 1965, as Bangkok developed its COIN strategy, it also created a coordinating agency, CSOC, to manage the war against the CPT. CSOC superseded an older coordination center, the Central Security Command, which continued to manage Mobile Development Units and very limited psyops programs that had started just before the war began.[254]

The government made CSOC legal by using the 1952 Anticommunist Act and activated it via PM Order 219/2508. Prapass was technically in charge of CSOC, but General Saiyud ran it day to day as Chief of Staff of Operations.[255] The RTG saw coordination as crucial. Marks interviewed Saiyud on the subject, and the general said, "Coordination is the key to winning, but all must look at the problem through the same eyes. You need a common blueprint upon which to base the plan."[256]

CSOC's mission was to plan and execute suppression operations and development programs to counter the CPT, using the CPM concept. As such, it had control of civilian, police, and military forces assigned to it. Sometimes, however, the parent commands of these CPM forces bypassed CSOC and passed their own orders to their respective CPM elements in the field. This independent activity worked against coordination and muddled COIN operations.[257] Moreover, scores of government agencies other than CSOC ran their own development projects, further crowding the COIN arena.

CSOC was headquartered in Bangkok's Rose Palace. Its Operations and Coordination Center had staff sections, referred to as committees, including intelligence and operations planning. To execute COIN operations, CSOC had multitudes of CPM centers in the field supported by intelligence units.[258]

CSOC placed CPM centers in CPT-affected provinces, with the responsibility of planning missions to separate the population from the communists using CPM ways and means.[259] CSOC did not micromanage CPM units in their daily routines, however. Under CSOC, CPM cells designed their own operations.[260] It was a decentralized command system.

Both provincial governors and Army Regional Commanders ran CPM units at the provincial level. This task was technically reserved for the governors, but the RTA was powerful and wanted a leadership role. An RTA general commanded the first CPM unit ever deployed, called CPM-1, stationed in Mukdahan on the northeast border with Laos.[261]

RTA regional commanders had seniority over the governors. Says Major General Perapong Manakit of the National Security Council, "For example, the Third Army area has seventeen governors, and its military commander could call all seventeen together and get things done. All army areas operated like this. [CSOC] was clever enough to set up area offices. The governors participated in this system via the MoI [Ministry of Interior], a civilian-run agency. But they were all under the Army Area Commanders."[262] Governors, however, had military and police advisors to aid them with security issues and civilians to assist them with development programs.[263]

CSOC had under it five Joint Security Centers (JSCs) at the regional level that fused and analyzed intelligence from all Thai intelligence agencies to feed operations planning.[264] While the JSCs relied on multiple agencies for intelligence collection, CSOC also had a special intelligence team headed by Somchai Rakwijit. He sent undercover operatives into rural areas to collect information on the at-risk population and its susceptibility to the CPT.[265]

CSOC's troops and police came from existing military and police units.[266] If, for example, CSOC needed a battalion-sized formation to operate in Issan, it drew them from the Second Army because Issan was the Second Army's area of responsibility. Similarly, if it needed police in the far south, it drew them from Police Region 9, the RTP's southern regional headquarters. CPM civilians came from three sources: government employees who were expert in niche areas, such as staff from the Ministry of Agriculture or Education; local government bodies such as the Department of Local Administration (DoLA); and the at-risk population itself.

The CSOC-CPM Process

CSOC and its CPM units approached villages in a methodical manner. The village was the heart of Thailand's social structure and the CPT's main battleground. "The question of the security and development of the village, therefore, is at the heart of any government campaign to defeat the insurgency," said General Saiyud.[267] CSOC researched the anthropology of villages and identified five key leaders with whom it needed to coordinate activities. If it could win the trust of these people, then, in theory, it could win the trust of villages. The key leaders were:[268]

1. The village or hamlet headman (*phuyai baan*): The most popular and respected man in the village/hamlet; a wealthy man who typically came from a family line of village leaders. He was elected by popular vote. The *phuyai baan*'s main task was to mediate village disputes and provide security. He had at least one assistant village head, and sometimes two. It should be noted that *phuyai baan* are different from *kamnans*, which are commonly referred to as "village heads." *Kamnans* are actually *tambon* (subdistrict) chiefs in charge of clusters of villages/hamlets and appointed by governors. Above the *tambons* were *amphoe* (districts), and above them were *changwat* (provinces).

2. The religious layman (*makkh-thayok*): The link between the village and the nearby Buddhist monastery (*wat*). *Makkh-thayok* organized religious ceremonies for the village.

3. The teacher (*khru*): The smartest person in the village. He taught village children, ran the local school, and helped to solve general, day-to-day problems. The *khru* was a highly respected position.

4. The family doctor (*mor prajam baan*): The village physician, who used both modern and traditional techniques, of which the latter category might include magic and herbal remedies.

5. The midwife (*mor tam-yae*): The supervisor of childbirth, who used both traditional and modern methods for deliveries.

Identifying Target Areas

CSOC sent CPM units to areas where it thought the CPT was active or might be active in the future. Typically, it tested CPM programs in nonhostile areas and then spread them out from there. Identifying these areas required intelligence on the at-risk population, CPT activities, and CPT targeting trends. Only then could CSOC tell if a tide of CPT infiltration was approaching or had already occurred. Accordingly, CSOC divided at-risk areas into five categories and had slightly different COIN plans for each type. The categories included:

1. External critical areas (the CPT's initial base of operations).
2. Internal critical areas (the CPT's projected next base of operations).
3. Border populations or areas of CPT infiltration.
4. The hill tribe population.
5. Other minority groups the CPT might target.[269]

For external critical areas, CSOC used the classic CPM model, which consisted of a village security team (VST) of local villagers set up and trained by police.[270] This was different from pre-1965 village defense forces in which people from outside the village constituted some security units. These outside reinforcements usually came from of a national reserve force called the *Komg Asa Raksa Dindaen* (Volunteer Defense Corps, or VDC). The Thai nicknamed it *Or Sor.* While its security capabilities were good, the VDC diluted village ownership. CSOC wanted to increase local ownership, believing "local boys" were more likely to fight harder for their own villages, and that the village inhabitants were more likely to support them in the process.

The village headman was chief of the village defense force, but the police were its tactical commanders while on operations. In case a VST needed support, it could rely on a host of forces above it, including troops from the VDC, the

RTP, and the RTA acting as quick reaction forces (QRFs) stationed at nearby strategic areas such as major intersections, rail stations, and towns.[271]

Many rural villages, especially the hill tribes, did not want much interaction with outsiders. For this reason, they frequently rejected having RTA forces camped inside or next to their villages. The presence of security forces next to villages was sure to invite an attack by the CPT. Therefore, the CPM program stationed support units just far enough from at-risk villages to camouflage the linkage between the two, but not too far to negate effective QRF response times.

For internal critical areas, the government focused on CPT prevention using basic security, intelligence, development, and psyops. The goal was to secure at-risk villages before the CPT could do so. This entailed shoring up the capacity—the leadership and administrative abilities—of local provincial and district authorities that had been neglected by the central government.[272]

For border populations, the RTA, RTP, and especially the BPP established relationships with villages along the border with Burma, Laos, and Cambodia to monitor and curb CPT infiltration. The government employed locals because of their intimate knowledge of border town life, local habits, terrain, and border-crossing routes. [273] Operations consisted of patrolling, surveillance, and ambushes. The authorities provided the majority of the kinetic element, while the locals provided intelligence and guide services.

The CSOC plan for the hill tribe populations was more complex. It had three parts: development, security, and rehabilitation of CPT-infected villages. It was broadly akin to the external critical areas approach, but with added political and socioeconomic features specifically designed to appeal to the hill tribes and to conform their behavior to Bangkok's will on halting undesirable behaviors such as slash-and-burn agriculture.[274] In these tribes' uneven terrain, Bangkok began using the "oil spot strategy" to secure lowland villages and then a "loyal ring strategy" in the hills in attempts to surround higher elevations where it could.[275]

As well organized as all these plans were on paper, jealousy and infighting muted CSOC a mere two years after it began. Powerful Army Regional Commanders saw CSOC siphoning off their troops and resources for COIN, so they mobilized against it. They were moreover worried that General Saiyud would gain too much power at their expense, and so they lobbied General Prapass to return operational command back to them. In 1967, he relented.[276] Somchai Rakwijit explains it in this way:

> The army commanders often think that they know the situation in their area better than Bangkok. And the counterinsurgency force deployed in their area was the force under their own command, and they didn't want outsiders to give detailed instructions to them about force deployment. So Saiyud, as director of the [CSOC] operational center, was at the time a lieutenant general, and the commanders of the army areas were also lieutenant generals. They thought they had parity, so far as the level of command was concerned. They wanted Saiyud to give advice only, and they wanted to have detailed operational planning control of their own areas. Military commanders were then, and are now, in fact, very jealous of control of the force.[277]

In lieu of CSOC, the Army Regional Commanders ran their own anti-CPT campaigns, and heavy suppression became the norm.[278] CSOC ran a handful of operations here and there, but the overall effort remained uncoordinated and ineffective.[279]

The Second Anticommunist Act of 1969 attempted to better coordinate the government and military. The act created five regions, CSOC-1 through 5. The regions aligned somewhat with the army regions. The First, Second, and Third Army commanders executed CSOC operations in their respective theaters. Another command, the Fifth Military Circle, headquartered in Songkhla province, commanded CSOC-4 and CSOC-5 in the south. CSOC-4 and CSOC-5 commanders were supposed to report to the Fifth Military Circle, but instead reported directly to RTA headquarters in Bangkok, evidence of still more internal backbiting.[280]

Internal Security Operations Command

In the 1970s, CSOC began to receive widespread and harsh public criticism. This occurred for several reasons. First, critics assumed that CSOC was still in charge of the war and running heavy suppression operations, which it was not. Second, CSOC's head, General Prapass, had ties to the ousted autocratic PM Thanom and was a lightning rod for condemnation. Third, several legislators and political pundits suspected CSOC of supporting right-wing paramilitary groups that were accused of attacking leftist students and assassinating suspected communists.[281]

It is indeed possible this might have happened. In the 1970s, as the civilian government failed to fight off the CPT, secret groups of military, police, and civilians joined ranks to do the job the government would not. One of these groups was called the Red Guars. Loosely controlled, it exercised haphazard force on many occasions, including participating in the heinous massacre at Thammasat University. Any value it might have had in eliminating key CPT personnel and assassins was probably countered by these extremist actions.

At any rate, to deflect the negative attention, PM Sanya Dharmasakti on 10 May 1974, on the advice of General Saiyud, changed CSOC's name to the Internal Security Operations Command, or ISOC. Saiyud recalls saying simply, "If nobody likes CSOC as a name, why don't we change it?"[282] The name change was a psyop, creating the illusion of a brand-new agency, whereas in reality the ISOC remained focused on the CPT.[283]

In 1976, however, ISOC indeed changed part of its internal structure by adding the *Aw Paw Paw* program. According to General Saiyud, its mission was to increase administration, development, and security at the village level. The end goal was to make villagers more self-sufficient, effective, and therefore resistant to CPT penetration.[284]

This program's main contribution was to centralize the government's village support regimen. Up to 1976, most village programs had been a patchwork of security forces working with scattered civilian ministries such as Agriculture, Industry, Health, and Education. *Aw Paw Paw* formalized their collaboration.[285]

This program also involved creation of village-level *Aw Paw Paw* committees. As usual, the village headman ran the committee with two deputies. Under him were six subcommittees on government, finance, defense, development, education and culture, and health. Villagers elected the heads of the subcommittees.[286]

The program had a positive impact. "Between 1975 and 1985," says Saiyud, "a total of 6,960 villages across the country were set up along the lines of the APP program." Slightly more than half of these were set up between 1975 and 1981, indicating that the RTA did in fact allow ISOC to operate its COIN programs and that it gradually began to cooperate with many of them. In the end, *Aw Paw Paw* covered fifty-two of Thailand's then seventy-three provinces.[287]

In 1983, the government revamped ISOC via PM Order 83/2526 and gave it more power. The new plan redefined ISOC's mission:

1. Command and control the government agencies, civilian-police-military forces, paramilitary forces, and all citizen volunteers in joint operations to win over communism.

2. Direct, supervise, monitor, and implement the campaign to win over communism in accordance with orders 66/2523 and 65/2525.

3. Coordinate with other governmental agencies in order to win over communism.[288]

Another one of ISOC's significant COIN coordination innovations was its Civil Affairs Center. The Civil Affairs Center was responsible for coordinating all political and political-military programs run by ISOC. It paralleled the creation of the army's Directorate of Civil Affairs in January 1982. The Assistant Chief of Staff of Army Civil Affairs was commander of ISOC's CA center.[289] By the 1980s, the Thai saw CA as a primary weapon against subversion, a marked turnaround from the days of napalming CPT-controlled villages. Says Saiyud, "In military and government circles, and particularly in the ISOC, there was a growing emphasis on the principle of putting political pressures before military operations in tackling internal security problems. This trend was facilitated by the close relationship between the upper echelons of the military and the government."[290]

The Three Pillars of COIN Against the Communist Party of Thailand

Here, how the Thai carried out the three pillars of COIN—security, politics, and economics—is explored. As stated in the introduction, these are ways and means, or programs and assets, used to carry out strategy. They were most effective when centrally coordinated and carried out in conjunction with each other to apply constant pressure on all fronts to the insurgents, like three infantry regiments marching forward together on a Napoleonic battlefield in mutual support. Without coordination, COIN programs and assets were just agendas and units, muddling along alone.

Security Measures

For the communist COIN, security consisted of military, police, local forces, and intelligence activities necessary to carry out a wide range of missions against the CPT. They included, but were not limited to, identifying key communist personnel, revealing CPT tactics, techniques, and procedures—exerting population control, investigations, village protection, and destroying the CPT's war-making abilities. The latter involved both large and small-scale infantry operations, plus direct action (DA) missions. Special Forces (SF) and local forces carried out the latter. Local forces were absolutely critical to turning the tables on the insurgents and using their own tactics against them, something the Thai excelled at once these indigenous units were well trained and supervised.

The Royal Thai Military

The Royal Thai Military, all of the government's intelligence services, the RTP, and local forces constituted Thailand's security element for fighting the CPT. In short, every Thai security unit was involved. Military units active in COIN were the RTA, the Royal Thai Navy (RTN) and its Royal Thai Marines (RTM), and the Royal Thai Air Force (RTAF). The RTA played the dominant role. The RTAF, with its tactical air support operations, was second in the military pecking order. The RTN and RTM were third. They had small roles. The RTN

84

conducted river and littoral patrols, and the RTM inserted infantry forces where needed, mostly in the south.

These forces had four broad missions: (1) destruction of CPT military forces, (2) separation of the CPT from the people, (3) protection of the people, and (4) population control. Protection from the CPT was the ultimate security goal as Thailand's COIN matured. In the beginning, however, it was simply the destruction of the CPT's armed units and, on occasion, their civilian supporters.

The Royal Thai Army

The RTA used the basic triangular military structure of armies, divisions, regiments, battalions, companies, platoons, and squads. Each Army Area Command, led by a lieutenant general, had under it an infantry division and two Military Circles, or sections of Army Regional Commands led by major generals. For example, under the First Army Command were the 1st Infantry Division, the First Military Circle, and the Second Military Circle. Along with the First, Second, and Third Armies and the Fifth Military Circle (the latter being a unique command for the south), there were a Cavalry Division and SF. In 1967, the RTA had 141,756 personnel, half volunteers and half conscripts.[291]

The RTA had four missions: static security, patrolling, support for CPM units, and offensive operations against the CPT.[292] The combined purpose of these missions was to break up CPT forces, keep them on the run, and destroy them when possible. Static security meant physical security, such as guarding roads, towns, bridges, railways, and other such infrastructure. Patrolling included walking or riding through CPT areas to pressure guerrilla formations and movement. Support for CPM units mainly consisted of QRF missions.

Offensive operations were quite basic. The RTA would obtain intelligence on CPT activities, surround the area in question, and penetrate it using infantry tactics such as "hammer and anvil." One force, the hammer, would sweep through an area and drive the enemy into a static force, the anvil, where destruction of the enemy unit would happen. The RTA would then deploy to another area, leaving small patrols behind to prevent reinfiltration by the CPT.[293]

General Harn Pathai went on multiple operations in 1967 in Nakhon Phanom province, when he was commander of a platoon of Army Rangers in the Second Army area of operations. "We usually operated under the CPM program where all army Special Forces and police worked together. Our arms consisted of M-16s, M-79s [40 mm grenade launchers], and BARs [Browning Automatic Rifles, a squad support weapon]. We had three BARs per platoon. Our mission was search and destroy."[294]

As for command and control, Harn's unit received orders from Second Army headquarters and sometimes from the Second Army's field command stations. "We had a forward CPM headquarters, or *Por Tor Tor*, which was the Thai nickname for CPM," he says. Otherwise, General Harn's unit was fairly autonomous. "We created the mission plans unless it was a bigger operation from Second Army HQ or a field HQ, and we received intelligence from HQ, so we had freedom to do our own missions," he says. "HQ basically said, 'This is your area, this is the overall mission, now go out and do your job!' I was there for one year [in the late 1960s]. I fought three engagements. These were contact engagements, and they lasted about ten minutes, and typically the communists broke contact. They ran away and escaped. Most engagements were platoon-sized."

A US advisor's analysis of RTA operations in the first four years of the war said that bands of twenty to thirty CPT members easily avoided RTA patrols. There were not enough troops to patrol the countryside. The RTA was using two infantry battalions to control 150 square miles. Small-scale operations were inadequate, as they did not maintain pressure on the CPT. US advisors said the Thai needed thirteen battalions (nine for saturation patrolling and security, and four for strike and QRF) to control an area of this size in the absence of more local forces and police. RTA operations were of average quality in the early years, but later they improved, especially in the Second Army's area of responsibility.[295]

One reason for the improvement was increased motivation. In 1976, when students at Thammasat University allegedly hung the prince in effigy—something leftists denied doing—the RTA became highly motivated to engage and destroy the CPT's military forces. The incident, coupled with the CPT's propaganda assailing the royal family, stirred the military like nothing else. They were protectors of the king, a duty they saw as sacred.[296]

The RTA's ability to adopt COIN lessons increased, too. The Second Army's forward staff and commanding officer in 1968 was thoughtful and intelligent, so said a US intelligence report, and they had taken steps to win over the population by treating them fairly, aiding them with development projects, and restricting artillery and air strikes to confirmed sightings of CPT formations only. US advisors reported that the Second Army's morale at the time was high, and it had a zeal for winning.[297]

In the north, the RTA had mostly halted its indiscriminate artillery and air strikes by 1968. The army had indoctrinated not all, but most of its troops to be respectful and considerate of locals, thereby improving its legitimacy. This change resulted in fewer CPT recruits and more intelligence on CPT activities from locals. These were the first reported improvements in RTA performance since 1965.[298] More vigorous patrols led to more contact with the CPT, too.[299] For example, in a five-month period in 1968, there were eighty-one CPT-government clashes, of which the CPT initiated only five. These firefights resulted in 56 CPT killed, 2 RTA killed, 342 CPT prisoners of war, and 286 surrendered.[300] These late 1960s improvements, however, were not enough to stem the rising tide of the war in the CPT's favor. Much higher quality in these endeavors had to be achieved to beat the CPT, something the RTA eventually achieved, but it took many more years.

RTA SF played a significant role in the war in all army missions, but mostly in offensive, direct-action DA roles—ambushes, raids, and QRF duty. Says General Harn of his unit at the time, "We trained at Lop Buri, the SF headquarters, and we deployed from there to Nakhon Phanom. The US Army's 46th SF Company, which was a training company, was there and trained us on some tasks."[301]

Harn says SF frequently recruited local men such as hunters to serve as guides and translators as they negotiated the countryside. Harn and his men did not speak Issan. While the different Army Area Commanders mostly recruited men from the areas in which they operated, SF was different. Its members came from all over Thailand.

In the northeast in 1968, there were twenty-two SF teams of twelve men each deployed throughout the Second Army's area of responsibility. About half of them deployed on QRF missions, patrols, and ambushes, where they excelled in establishing overwhelming superiority in firefights. They bivouacked in public buildings and camps near CPM units.[302]

Special Forces was highly effective in its DA role. Says a former CPT armed propaganda specialist, "What was the thing that put the most pressure on us? The Army Special Forces. They used the small unit tactics and were very good. Like on patrol or walking through the jungle. We always worried about being ambushed. And when they started shooting, it was very heavy. You could not do anything. They shot a lot when they ambushed us. I lost several good friends in ambushes."[303]

Many Thai COIN operations were joint operations. Operation Bunnam is one example. It ran from 10 April to 27 May 1966 in the Sakon Nakhon-Udorn border area. It included RTP, a Mobile Reserve Platoon of the BPP, the VDC, elements of the 1st Battalion of the 3rd Regimental Combat Team (RCT), and one company of the 13th RCT from Udorn. The RTAF provided air support with five helicopters, and the US Air Force aided with six. US analysts wrote that, through six large clashes, Thai forces captured forty-four CPT suspects and killed four, while twenty-three more surrendered.[304]

On the other hand, a larger joint operation from 30 June to 15 September 1966 in Trang and Phattalung provinces demonstrated the folly of engaging the CPT and then leaving the area and its villagers alone in the aftermath. The operation involved twelve hundred RTA troops, including the 15th RCT, plus the BPP and the Provincial Police. Despite intricate planning, the operation resulted in a few clashes and two hundred arrests of suspected communists, but little else. When Thai forces left, the CPT reinfiltrated the area and took revenge on villagers who cooperated with the government.[305]

Conventional Battles

Despite the CPT's primary reliance on guerrilla warfare, there were scores of conventional battles that resembled World War II–style siege warfare. Khao Kho, a CPT stronghold in Phetchabun province, is one example. On 11 June 1976, realizing the importance of the "Khao Kho anchor," King Bhumibol went to Phitsanulok province and visited the Third Army base called *Sa Krit Sae Na* to discuss reducing it. General Harn says, "The king told the army, 'If we win at Khao Kho, then the other strongholds will fall.' He knew it was the strongest CPT base, and this he advised."[306] The king's strategy entailed cutting roads into Khao Kho's jungle and mountainous terrain and using them to infiltrate military units into CPT areas. He also said as the military destroyed CPT fighting forces, the government should inundate villages along the roads with development projects to lift them out of poverty, thereby co-opting the afflicted people to the government's side over time. They moreover planned to set up set up new villages along the roads, some manned by ex-military men and *Thahan Phran*, who would help fight CPT holdouts.[307] Based on the king's guidance, the Third Army drew up a long-term campaign plan on 11 March 1977 for Khao Kho called the Royal Keg Basin Development Project.[308]

One of the most significant actions under the Royal Keg Basin series of operations was *Pha Muang Phadejsuk*. Here, the Third Army waged three offensives—termed 1, 2, and 3/1—that spanned from 20 January to 30 May 1981. The RTA used CPM forces, including local forces and police units, six companies of *Thahan Phran*, several infantry battalions, plus artillery, tactical air support, and helicopter transport units. Jet aircraft and helicopter gunships provided the air support. These forces fought the CPT in places such as the high ridges along Khao Sai Mountain.[309]

Combat here was intense. In one case on 16 February 1981, the *Thahan Phran* had to halt their approach to the face of Khao Ya Mountain because of CPT mortar and recoilless rifle fire, both of which have a range of about three kilometers or less. A Kuomintang (KMT) force co-opted by the Thai government reportedly flanked the mountain base from the rear while the

Thahan Phran served as the fixing force.[310] In other cases, Thai forces had to fight their way out of CPT envelopments in eight-hour battles.[311]

As an aside, the KMT's participation in the battle was interesting. This force consisted of the remnants of Chiang Kai-shek's army. Its members ended up settling in Burma and Thailand after its defeat by Mao. Ultimately, the KMT ran a large portion of the opium trade in the Golden Triangle, a vast tract of mountainous jungle where Laos, Thailand, and Burma meet. The RTG sometimes used the KMT's army to fight the CPT, and corrupt police, military, and government officials trafficked drugs in conjunction with them. The KMT's strategic contribution to the war against the CPT, however, was minimal.

In any case, in the end the Third Army decisively crushed the CPT and its extensive infrastructure in Khao Kho, which demoralized its supporters. CPT killed in action totaled about a company's worth, and as many as three thousand surrendered. Government casualties for the entire Khao Kho campaign were at least one thousand. At least five hundred *Thahan Phran* were killed. Thai government documents say the victory at Khao Kho paved the way for the decisive defeat of the CPT in Thailand once and for all. General Harn agrees, saying, "And when Khao Kho was finished, the other CPT strongholds began to fall, one by one."[312] All this happened, of course, in conjunction with security, political, and economic operations throughout the rest of the country.

The Royal Thai Police

The RTP's main COIN forces consisted primarily of the Provincial Police, the BPP, and Special Branch investigators who ran clandestine networks, stings, and informants. In the 1960s, these forces combined were about forty thousand strong. At the time, the RTP fell under the auspices of the MoI. The RTP had three missions during the communist COIN: law enforcement, maintaining law and order, and criminal investigation. All this amounted to population control, key to separating the insurgents from the population. The government had used the RTP as its main suppression tool against the CPT until open warfare broke out in 1965. At that time the military took control and the police fell under its command. The RTP, however, remained an integral part of COIN operations and received COIN training throughout the war.[313]

Of all the police, the PP had the most extensive COIN role. It had thirty-seven thousand officers and was divided into nine regions. Its chain of command ran from local police chiefs, to regional chiefs, to provincial governors. The PP worked closely with the governors plus the Department of Local Administration. DoLA ran administrative affairs at district levels and below and was highly influential.

The number of police on any given patrol depended on the threat. If it was low, there may have been only three. If it was high, there may have been twenty, a platoon-sized element.[314] Police stations communicated with each other and with headquarters by radio plus bicycle and foot messengers.[315]

Because of their wide geographic deployment and their close proximity to villages, the PP were usually the first to respond to CPT attacks, so they took on a SWAT-type role. If a threat situation intensified to a high degree, and if police manpower was short, they could, via the CPM program, call on local militias and the military for reinforcements.

Close proximity to the villages also made the PP ideal intelligence collectors.[316] For the same reason, the RTP were a linchpin for population control, which put pressure on the insurgent population nexus through checkpoints, random searches, issuing identification (ID) cards, food control, and curfews. Such pressure makes it harder for insurgents to move and communicate, thereby constraining their ability to access critical auxiliary support (i.e., food, medical supplies, intelligence, ammunition, weapons, sanctuary, etc.). Population control, however, also imposes hardships on the at-risk population. Some of the most successful COINs in history, such as the Malaya Emergency, have had to temporarily curtail civil rights to carry out population control.[317]

Thailand's population control measures included requiring all citizens of eighteen years of age to have ID cards. During ID spot checks, the PP could note the names of suspicious personnel and their activities, which might spur an investigation by PP detectives or Special Branch. The PP also set up road checkpoints and searched vehicles for evidence of locals smuggling for the CPT. The police networked with food sellers to acquire information on large acquisitions that might have been destined for CPT units.[318]

While the RTP's role was critical to victory, the police suffered from a bad reputation. Corruption, in part a consequence of low pay, was rampant throughout the police, which alienated the people and devastated the legitimacy of the government. This was a critical fault because people are the ultimate prize in COIN. Every act of police malfeasance was akin to pouring gasoline on the CPT's bonfire while the stated mission was to put that fire out. American COIN advisors in 1965 recommended measures to improve the RTP's reputation, including mass public relations campaigns, radio programs, and mobile exhibits. These worked in some cases, and RTP units who worked with CPM at the village level were generally effective.[319]

The RTP policed itself, too. In 1965, the Director General of the Police relieved several corrupt officers in Region 4 after the military commander of a Mobile Development Unit (MDU) complained about their unseemly activities. Such actions were critical to prove to Thai citizens the RTG meant well and was a legitimate power. These type internal affairs investigations were rare in the 1960s, however. Not until well into the late 1970s, when the country nearly lost to the CPT, did the RTP improve its performance and reputation. This was a tragedy for a force in which scores of valiant and professional officers fought and died trying to improve their country's legitimacy and protect the population from Marxist dictatorial rule.[320]

The BPP was more elite than the PP, and it saw more combat. The BPP was, and remains, a highly trained and motivated paramilitary force with high morale. Originally designed to protect Thailand's borders, it was used for a variety of COIN missions outside border areas because of the unit's exceptional light infantry and CA capabilities. BPP forces frequently led local force security units, and they even taught elementary school classes in areas where the CPT had threatened or killed civilian teachers. Accordingly, they were a flexible force capable of both fighting and CA, skill sets ideal for COIN.

Special Branch was critical to fighting the communist insurgents. As part of the Central Investigation Bureau, its mission was to collect intelligence on subversives and counter them. The government extended Special Branch's reach to the village level in 1963 with the creation of its 7th Division. US advisors helped to spur this expansion. In 1968, there were thirty-three Special Branch offices throughout Thailand, all working on COIN operations. Aside from collecting its own intelligence, Special Branch also received information from various police units via Joint Security Centers, and it interviewed prisoners at two Interrogation Centers founded in 1966, at Bangkok and Udorn.[321]

Special Branch experienced important successes early in the war. In September 1967, in the northeast, it arrested multiple CPT leaders, resulting in the collapse of a CPT financial network. The operation harvested highly effective intelligence on the CPT and its activities.[322] Operations like this were sensitive, complex, and time-consuming, but they slowly illuminated the workings of CPT cells from the inside. Some such operations took years to develop. They usually entailed either clandestinely infiltrating agents into the CPT or auxiliary force, or identifying CPT or auxiliary personnel and then recruiting them as informants. Only when scores of agents had been put in place and only after their information had been confirmed and processed would Special Branch make arrests.

Local Forces

Thailand had a dizzying array of local forces during the anticommunist COIN, all with similar-sounding names and missions. The RTG was a firm believer in recruiting, training, and arming the population to protect itself and also to solidify it as a political ally. The security part of the equation was obvious. The political theory was subtler and based on the theory that, once a villager picked up a rifle to fight alongside the government, he had also chosen a side, taken a political stance. This was the heart of the CPM program and a direct result of the 09/10 plan and its spin-off strategies.

Furthermore, local forces were a cornerstone of the CPT's strategy, consistent with Mao's call for "mobilization of the masses." Part of Bangkok's strategy was to turn this around on the CPT and use government-friendly local forces against the communists. Interestingly, the government called it nearly the same that thing the CPT did: "major mass organization." Ultimately, Thailand's local forces totaled over 1.2 million people.[323] After the war ended, they roughly doubled in size as part of a follow-through effort to ensure that the CPT did not reemerge. Thailand's primary local forces included the following:

- *Komg Asa Raksa Dindaen* (a.k.a. *Or Sor*, the Volunteer Defense Corps, or VDC)
- Joint Security Teams (JSTs)
- Village Defense Units (a.k.a. Village Protection Units, or VPUs)
- Village Security Forces (a.k.a. Village Security Teams, or VSTs)
- Self-Defense Volunteers (SDVs)
- *Thahan Phran*

The *Or Sor* began as a reserve paramilitary force run by the MoI on 10 February 1954.[324] The CIA sponsored it.[325] In 1968, there were three thousand VDC. This was a force the MoI could deploy for a wide range of security missions. Under the 09/10 Plan, the government used the *Or Sor* for JSTs, which were led by two or three police or military personnel. JSTs had a squad-sized element of nine to twelve VDC. The JST mission was to prevent CPT infiltration of villages. In theory, this was supposed to cut CPT units off from the population and restrict them to the jungles, where the military would hunt down and destroy them. VPUs were supposed to do the same thing.[326] The army trained each JST and VPU for one month in weapons, light infantry tactics, and security. They also learned a few hours of CA and psyops.[327]

The RTA supported local forces such as the JSTs with QRF when necessary. A company or a platoon of army troops camped near a village and remained in contact with its fighters by radio. If local forces came into contact with the CPT and low-intensity firefights ensued, then they fought it out themselves. If the combat became too intense, they could call the army for assistance.[328]

The effectiveness of local forces varied. Some units were well trained and led, but their programs were not widespread enough throughout Thailand to make a strategic difference. Other units were poorly trained, suffered low pay, and used passive tactics such as static perimeter defense. Without patrolling to keep the CPT off balance, villages remained at risk. The CPT frequently mauled these weaker local forces. Another flaw of village protection units was agency rivalry. The MoI did not like RTA-sponsored programs and vice versa, and the two did not work well together. In combat situations, this got people killed. This, in turn, exacerbated friction between the military, police, DoLA, and the governors.[329] As a result, Thai COIN strategists and their US advisors labored to produce the ideal village protection force for years, resulting in multiple programs such as the VPUs and VSTs.[330]

It took until 1976 to achieve the correct approach with the SDVs, which were part of ISOC's *Aw Paw Paw* program. Says General Prem, "This Self-Defense Volunteers Program was later to become the thrust of our counterinsurgency campaign in that it served as the organizational framework for dialogue and interaction with the villagers at the grassroots level. The program took on life from an initiative of a local district officer whose commitment to his work was total. He went around recruiting local teachers, village leaders, or just acquaintances, engaging them in discussion on how best to organize and train self-defense volunteers to resist the CPT. We simply amplified his initiative and extended it to cover all other villages."[331]

The SDVs were not significantly different from prior, effective local force schemes, except they were a nationally consolidated force and much better coordinated.[332] The Thai had learned that ad-hoc units with light training, little pay, and loose command and control fared poorly against the CPT, while well-trained, adequately paid, and nationally consolidated units could keep the CPT out of the villages.[333] By 1988 the SDVs numbered 1,226,000 strong.[334]

The SDVs were more than physical security units, however. They provided valuable intelligence on the CPT as well. "Volunteers began to trickle in, and we also started to learn who our friends were," says General Prem. "Even if there were CPT infiltrators among the [defense] volunteers, we would at least be able to keep an eye on them, to monitor their movements." He describes fellow villagers knowing all the activities of the CPT who infiltrated the villages. "Some would vanish into the jungle at night and return to the village in the morning," he says. "In truth, the villagers themselves already knew who these so-called 'jungle people' were. It was a question of gaining their trust and confidence before they were prepared to tell us what they knew."[335]

General Prem also says the SDV helped identify bad government actors. "It was within the framework of this program too that we made sure the villagers could also distinguish between friends and foes, between the good and the bad elements within the bureaucracy," he says. "A mechanism was put into place enabling us to effect the instant removal of the bad elements from the scene once they were identified as such, with diplomatic action taken where needed. Justice had to be seen as done for it to have any credibility."[336]

"Was [local forces] a successful program? Did it work?" asks General Harn. "It worked. The villages were pretty well protected, and just as important, it freed the army from static security duties and allowed it to go into the jungles on patrol and hunt the communists."[337]

General Harn also says the military training endeared the villagers to the government: "After training, they felt as if they belonged, like they were part of a team, something important." More, the military served the king, and by default, local forces also served the king, which further endeared them to the government. "And, also importantly," says General Harn, "the villagers were willing to give information to soldiers on the CPT after training." Overall, Marks writes of the village defense forces, "They had no trouble gaining recruits and grew rapidly. They were [sic] the units which broke the back of the insurgency."[338]

Breaking the back of the insurgency also involved the *Thahan Phran*, the most decisive local force Thailand ever produced. Some refer to the *Thahan Phran* as "Rangers," but they are not RTA Special Forces Rangers. Marks writes the *Thahan Phran* had its origins in three issues: (1) the CPM concept of mass mobilization against the CPT, (2) the fact that large formations of active-duty military had been called to defend the Thai-Cambodian border where Vietnamese forces were poised for invasion, and (3) the idea of fielding a guerrilla force that could "out-guerrilla" the guerrillas.[339]

General Chavalit established the *Thahan Phran* in 1978. Desmond Ball, a prolific academic writer on Thailand's local forces, quoted General Arthit as saying of the *Thahan Phran*, "We must employ guerrilla tactics to fight the CPT. Since they are using local people, we must also use the local people."[340] Recruits, writes Ball, were eighteen to thirty-nine years old and, where possible, recruited from the areas where they would be deployed. Some joined the *Thahan Phran* for adventure and the glory of national service. Ball quotes one recruit as saying, "I liked the jungle, and I liked hunting and shooting, and I wanted to become a fighter. And I wanted to help protect Thailand."[341]

Basic training lasted forty-five days, much longer than that for village defense forces. Training included light infantry tactics and instruction in modern weaponry.[342] The *Thahan Phran*'s motto is "Nation, Religion, King, and Citizens," an adaptation of the national military motto that hails "Nation, Religion, and King."[343]

Says John Cole, former US Army defense attaché to Thailand, "The *Thahan Phran* were formed into companies only, no battalions or regiments, but there could be as many as six to eight companies in one grouping, all run by an active-duty army colonel."[344] Regiments of *Thahan Phran* would form later in the war, however. Initially, SF noncommissioned and commissioned officers commanded *Thahan Phran* units. Later, RTA officers did. In 1981, the *Thahan Phran* reached a strength of thirteen thousand, divided into 160 companies. This force, Ball notes, was bigger than the CPT's 12,500 fighters.[345]

The operational concept behind the *Thahan Phran* was they would deploy in communist-infested areas, collect intelligence on CPT personnel and activities (targeting), and then act on that intelligence by killing and/or capturing CPT personnel. They sometimes engaged in pure hunter-killer operations, as did RTA SF units. In this regard, the government paralleled the CPT's assassination program that targeted governors, village heads, and local personnel cooperating with the government.

Denny Lane, another former US defense attaché to Thailand, explains, "The Thai deployed *Thahan Phran* deep into communist insurgent areas more than regulars. It was an irregular war, so it needed irregular forces. Additionally, if an RTA trooper got killed in a village, he was just a nameless trooper to many. But if it was a *Thahan Phran*, then it was likely a local boy, and it created all sorts of problems, like blood feuds."[346]

Thahan Phran intelligence-gathering prowess came from intimate knowledge of the human and physical terrain of their districts. When *Thahan Phran* deployed in unfamiliar areas, their abilities were weaker. *Thahan Phran* aggressiveness was legendary, and they struck fear into the hearts of the CPT and its auxiliary forces. To collect intelligence, however, they had to have a good rapport with local villagers, something critics of *Thahan Phran* continually overlook.

Some criticism of *Thahan Phran* was indeed justified, however. A number of recruits were thugs, street toughs, and criminals. Predictably, when these bad actors deployed, they acted like thugs, street toughs, and criminals, especially if their commanders were weak. As a result, some *Thahan Phran* units earned horrid reputations for criminal activities such as bribery, extortion, murder, and rape. These units hurt Thailand's COIN efforts and decreased government legitimacy. As evidenced by their success, however, the *Thahan Phran* more often acted professionally and overcame these infamies.

Some pundits criticize the *Thahan Phran* program as an excuse for the RTA not to deploy, not to fight. Using the *Thahan Phran* for combat, these critics say, allows the army to preserve itself and prevent embarrassment from combat losses. There is some truth here. The Thai Army is not just a military force. It is also a highly involved political actor in domestic politics. So preserving the RTA and avoiding heavy casualties is indeed a useful aspect of the *Thahan Phran*. But this was by no means the exclusive motivation behind this force. The Thai believe in drafting the people into the fight against a people's war. They believe in fighting guerrillas using guerrilla strategies and tactics. They have always done so and likely always will.

Border Security

Border security was a major aspect of Thailand's communist COIN. On the borders with Burma and Laos, the Thai used BPP and military units to patrol, reconnoiter, and interdict CPT activities. They had bases and posts in strategic terrain from which they would fan out on their missions. They were similarly positioned on the Cambodian border until the Vietnamese massed there in 1979, forcing Bangkok to respond by deploying conventional forces on that border.

Bilateral security between Malaysia and Thailand increased as threats gathered on that front, including the CPT, the Malaysian Communist Terrorist Organization (CTO), and Thai Malay Muslim insurgent groups. General Kitti Rattanachaya, a former Fourth Army commander and leader of the southern border security effort, asserts Thailand put greater emphasis on border security after the CTO infiltrated Chinese worker groups in Yala province's rubber plantations and the Thai Malay Muslim separatist movement.[347]

To achieve border security, Thailand and Malaysia signed an accord creating the General Border Committee (GBC) on 13 March 1965. It established a bilateral working group that spelled out the duties of the members, intelligence coordination, the content of psyops (which had to be unified), and types of kinetic operations that would help seal the border and reduce CTO forces. GBC membership included senior defense, interior, military, and police officials.[348] GBC operations happened on an inconsistent basis, however. Some were in spurts of a year or longer, and others were much shorter. Accordingly, the sporadic nature of its operations reduced the GBC's effectiveness.

The GBC carried out three types of border operations. The first type was combined operations, in which Thai and Malaysian forces worked together as a single task force to find and destroy CTO forces. The GBC stipulated the commander of the TF would be from the country in which the TF was operating. The second type was coordination operations, which entailed Thai and

Malaysian forces deploying on their own sides of the border at the same time with the same objective. If they overlapped the other's border, they had to report it. The third type was unilateral operations, in which Thai and Malaysian units operated on their own within their respective borders, with no tactical coordination with the other country. Border operations ranged from small patrols to larger deployments complete with armored cars, artillery, and air support. A joint intelligence center in Songkhla supported them.[349]

Colonel Ahmed Ghazali was a Malaysian Army infantry platoon leader on the Malaysian-Thai border in the late 1970s. "Border control was a big thing," he says. "It was the same as Vietnam, but we had it on a smaller scale."[350] He participated in two major, combined Thai-Malaysian border operations: Operation *Daoyai Musnah* and Operation *Selamat Sawatdee*. These, he says, "were real offensive operations where we had artillery hit suspected 'Charlie Tangos' [communist terrorists], and then we'd send in the infantry to conduct sweeps. We based our artillery strikes on intelligence, analysis of all intelligence on communist units, and aerial spotters. The Thai used Broncos as spotters. It was a great aircraft for that kind of mission."

On unilateral operations, Colonel Ghazali says, "Malaysian forces were allowed to go into Thailand as far as five miles, and vice versa. We could go into each other's territory in pursuit [of enemy forces]. There was no alerting ahead of time, normally." Colonel Ghazali also says he had a Thai liaison team attached to his force: "They fought alongside us, and we had liaison units on their side who fought alongside the Thai." Relations were not always smooth, however, as squabbles and mistrust got the best of them on occasion. "We had our ups and downs," says Colonel Ghazali. "In one station, the Thai asked us to leave, but then relations returned to normal," he says without elaborating. This was a sensitive subject then, and it remains so now.

Border operations were not simply static security missions or beating the bush to flush out the enemy. The Thai and Malaysians used a methodical approach that included harnessing intelligence every step of the way. "Intelligence was very important for this type of mission," says Colonel Ghazali. "Border operations used

HUMINT [human intelligence], too." Intelligence drove operations, as the US Army often says. Based on threat reporting, intelligence—once digested by operations planners—dictated where, what type of, and how many forces would deploy in a given area and what type of operation they would conduct.

Colonel Ghazali explains, "On the placement of artillery, we studied every detail of the pattern of activities of the CTs. We studied everything they did. And then we used the intelligence to figure where they might be. For example, there were CT booby traps all over certain areas, and in those areas the CTs did not use the trails. So we knew to strike remote areas in booby trap–prone stretches of jungle where the CT might be lurking. We also studied personalities and figured, for example, if a CT leader was asthmatic, he could not go high into the mountains. He had to stay low, so we hit low areas where we thought he might be." Then they would send in the infantry and see what the artillery had hit.

Regarding static border security, the Thai and Malaysians left no stone unturned when both sides were committed to the mission. "We manned the whole border, every couple of hundred meters," says Ghazali. They mined it, too. "The mines on the border we called the *Naga* belt, or 'Dragon belt.' We used antipersonnel mines. They were homemade devices." The Malaysians got the idea of using mines from the CTO themselves. Ghazali says, "The communists made homemade mines out of fertilizer as the explosive compound, tin cans as the casing, and nails and other metals as shrapnel. They used torch light [flashlight] batteries as a power source, and they did not last long as a result. They wrapped these devices in tar paper to make them waterproof, but this device lasted only a few months." The Malaysian military made the same mines, but with commercial-grade explosives.

Intelligence

RTG intelligence missions during the communist COIN were to (1) identify the CPT's infrastructure and personnel, and (2) provide intelligence on CPT field units.[351] All this was designed to help police and military forces understand, find, fix, and then destroy, arrest, and/or turn the communists. In short, and per usual for all military and police forces, intelligence fed operations. A third intelligence mission became important later—to gain a thorough understanding of the CPT's ideology in order to discern how to defeat it politically. Ideally, this third mission should have come first.

Four main intelligence entities were used against the CPT: Division 7 of Special Branch, the RTP, the RTA's intelligence units, and the Department of Central Intelligence (DCI, later called the National Intelligence Agency, or NIA). Various civil agencies and officials also participated in intelligence missions at the district and village levels. These included village headmen, DoLA personnel, and the governors, but they did not have a formal role.[352]

As previously discussed, to coordinate intelligence collection, collation, processing, analysis, and dissemination, the government established Joint Security Centers under the CSOC structure. Special Branch managed the JSCs, and military, police, and civilians staffed them. The far south had a unique intelligence coordination center, the Combined Intelligence Headquarters, staffed by both Malaysian and RTG personnel.

JSC intelligence flow began with collection by CPM teams, police, and Special Branch in the villages. The information was then pooled at regional JSCs for analysis. From there it was disseminated to the military, provincial CPMs, and CSOC/ISOC. All these entities used the intelligence for operations planning. The first head of intelligence at CSOC was an RTP lieutenant general, but that changed as the organization became more RTA-centric.[353]

The RTA and its organic G-2 section (and associated secretive units) were also active in the anticommunist COIN. In the early 1960s, however, the army's G-2 had just seven staff officers and six intelligence "D Teams" of twelve men each in the field. Among other duties, D Teams processed prisoners and captured CPT documents, and they debriefed defectors. RTA intelligence staff also encompassed photo interpretation, interrogation, and polygraph sections. The Armed Forces Security Center and the Joint Intelligence Agency under the Ministry of Defense had lesser roles in COIN intelligence and were not part of the everyday intelligence machinery.[354]

The DCI, perhaps the most secretive of all Thai intelligence entities, began as the Government Affairs Collation Department in 1954 and changed its name a few years later. It was Thailand's main intelligence and counterintelligence agency. The National Intelligence Act of 1985 altered the DCI's structure and renamed it as the NIA. Throughout its history, the organization's four main missions have been foreign intelligence, domestic intelligence and security, signals intelligence, and protective security.

Local sources of information for all intelligence entities included village heads, teachers, development workers, and rural people. Village security forces were a particularly valued local source. Their members were lifetime members of their villages, as were their families and friends, and they constituted a de facto informant network that was organically activated once a village defense force was in place. These people had access to village gossip and internal affairs that police and other agencies could not obtain directly because, as a CIA report describes, the government operatives were "outsiders."[355]

While most government intelligence units stumbled to find their way early in the war, Somchai Rakwijit's group was effective from the very beginning. He advocated from the start for a greater emphasis on intelligence, not just to ascertain the CPT's capabilities and intentions, but also to find out the intentions and living situation of the at-risk population—atmospherics and human terrain analysis, in today's COIN parlance. Says Somchai of the government's existing intelligence entities, "They were very much concerned about the communist planning, military planning, and their previous actions as to how they took control of certain areas, but they didn't give much thought to trying to understand the communist propaganda appeals, how they infiltrated the villages, and the indoctrination of the villagers."[356]

Somchai lobbied General Prapass to set up his unique group in 1965 and the group lasted until 1983. "I think it was quite effective," he says. His unit received US ARPA funding for its first two and a half years, after which the RTG took over financing. Somchai went on the first several missions himself, taking the extreme risk of wandering into villages alone. Once accepted, he lived there for six months and collected information on a host of issues. "We were more interested," says Somchai, "in understanding their ideological appeal and [the CPT] approach to the people, the way they were organized, how they indoctrinated, and how they motivated the people to fight for their cause."

Somchai's cover was as a book author reporting on village life in rural Thailand. His preparatory studies told him villagers wanted outsiders to know about their lives, so he adopted an approach that fit their desires.[357] When Somchai expanded the team, he came up with rules of engagement and deployment kits. Each operative had a medical pouch to protect against fever, diarrhea, and jungle illnesses. "If we got sick," Somchai says, "we took our pills so we could stay in the jungle. Sometimes the villagers got sick, too, and we gave them our pills. They never needed too much medicine because they had strong immune systems, and they recovered quickly. We healed them with medicine, helped them look after kids when they worked in fields, helped them gather rice, and did village work, so our approach was one of caring." Early on, Somchai discovered the CPT was not yet strong enough to win with violence alone. It wanted to win hearts and minds, so he figured his research teams were safe as long as the CPT took this approach.[358]

Based on his intelligence, Somchai recommended using the "human approach" in COIN to build a bridge between the villages and the government. Development was a key component, he argued: "You have to try to alleviate the troubles of the locals...helping them goes a long way." It is obvious Somchai ran more than just a collection and analysis unit. He also provided recommendations on how to wage COIN, unlike many intelligence agencies that leave such decisions to policy makers.

Somchai and his subordinates used their embedded positions to leverage intelligence opportunities when they arose. This included exploiting captured CTP personnel: "And in the way of talking to the previous communists arrested by the authorities or the returnees, we got the names of other communists who had returned from the jungle to their homes. So often, we would go to their villages, and we'd make a friendly kind of relationship with them. Sometimes, we took them out to restaurants, out to see movies, or we'd hang out in hotels for a week, and we'd talk about the real life of the people and their problems."

Somchai says, "If authorities treat insurgents or antigovernment advocates like criminals, they'll get little information from them. If the authorities treat them well and make them believe they are dedicated to change and helping their people, then you get a completely different kind of information." Of course, this approach did not work with the most dedicated ideologists and violent revolutionaries, but it worked on the less fanatical, and it reaped excellent results.

Toward the mid- to late 1970s, the government had achieved intelligence domination over the CPT. Military intelligence had improved, and the army had a clearer idea of where the CPT was based, what its kinetic capabilities and intentions were month to month, and just as important, its ideological capabilities and intentions. This knowledge strengthened government decision-making, situational awareness, and operational effectiveness. Professor Bhumarat says, "We got tired of arresting these people. We'd identify them, and then I'd talk to them instead of arresting them. I would go to them and say, 'I know you are waiting for your contact to meet you, but he's not going to make it. We captured him earlier. But I'm not going to arrest you. Let's talk.'"[359]

After chatting, Professor Bhumarat says, they tried to turn their captives into double agents: "We arrested them and then often convinced them that they were wrong, and then they worked for us. They cooperated with us." Thai intelligence had infiltrated the CPT and its student factions so well they were able to create paranoia inside the movement and manipulate people to turn themselves in. This, in turn, encouraged even more people to do the same.

"We told them their friends talked to us, and that they should, too," says Professor Bhumarat. "If they did not like our options, we told them they could run into the jungle and live a life in the wilderness, on the run, cut off from their friends and the city." For many, the emotional pressure was too much, and by the 1980s, many CPT members were accepting the government's offer. "They gave us more information on their colleagues, and then we went after the other cadres." As a result of such operations, Thai intelligence decisively hastened the destruction of the CPT.

Political Measures

Politics played a major role in Thailand's communist COIN. In fact, it eventually played the central role, though not at the beginning. It took the government from 1965 until the mid- to late 1970s to develop a winning political formula. Thailand used six primary political tools to fight the CPT: psyops, CA, the Village Scout program, amnesty, diplomacy, and Kriangsak's democratic reforms at the national level.[360]

Psychological Operations

The RTG resisted using psyops and educational programs at the beginning of the war, primarily because it did not understand the CPT and how to best counter it. In the early 1960s, the RTA had but a single psyops company. By 1969, it had plans for two such battalions.[361] Upon gaining a deeper understanding of the CPT and its methods, and with urging from the United States, the Thai government eventually used psyops at every turn, and it became a mainstay of Thai COIN from then on.[362]

Some in the RTG, most obviously CSOC, realized by 1969 the critical nature of psyops in COIN. This is evident from the preeminence of psyops in the 110/2512 Plan. In it, General Harn Pongsithanonda said, "In the prevention and suppression [of communism], political measures and psychological operations and public relations are to be used principally."[363] This man and his cohorts understood that they were facing not just kinetic warfare but also political warfare.

The purpose of psyops was twofold: to weaken and demoralize the CPT, and to sway the population away from the CPT to the government's side. The overall gist was counterpolitical warfare. CSOC had the most active psyops program. Other organizations carrying out psyops included the government's National Information Psychological Operations Organization, the Public Relations

Department, the ARD program, the Community Development Department, the RTP, and psyops units organic to the RTA.[364]

CSOC's first communist psyops operations used radio—the means by which most Thai got their news—and leaflets. Almost 90 percent of urban homes in Thailand and nearly 70 percent of rural homes had radios during the war years. Until the proliferation of television, radios were the most powerful form of media.[365] The CPT relied on the airwaves extensively to get its messages out, and the government followed suit.

As the war progressed, CSOC formed two psyops teams: Modular Audio-Visual Units (MAVUs) and Mobile Information Service Teams (MISTs). RTA psyops teams formed and led the MAVUs in CPM target areas and were an integral part of drafting civilians into the fight against the CPT. The MoI ran MISTs through provincial governors and subordinate civilian administrators.

MAVUs and MISTs went from village to village, preaching the perils of communism and the merits of the government, how Bangkok's governance was improving, and how it wanted to better the lives of the people. They coordinated their visits with village headmen. These were usually the primary radio owners in rural villages. MAVUs and MISTs gave lectures, passed out literature, and showed movies for entertainment, which provided a novel experience to many in the countryside who had never seen such technology. Some lectures featured CPT members who had surrendered, while others showed Cambodian refugees who had escaped Pol Pot's murderous purges. These sessions offered villagers an alternative and scary version of communism compared to the saintly and just version provided by the CPT.

Surveys in the early 1970s demonstrated that many MAVU and MIST operations did not work well. Some MIST teams, for example, visited villages sporadically, only three or four times annually, when more frequent contact was required. Villagers sometimes asserted that these teams were too bent on requiring villagers to follow central government regulations. The same surveys, however, suggested that focused psyops, when coupled with development programs addressing village needs, had a positive impact.[366] In other cases, government psyops successfully persuaded villagers to join the fight against the CPT by presenting films or lectures on communist atrocities and assassinations. These presentations countered CPT ideological rhetoric touting peace and equality.[367]

Aside from CSOC, the Second Army's Village Voice psyops teams had success with their lectures, movies, and pamphlets in combination with distribution of medication. In the south, the military used the same concept but called the teams *Santi Nimit* (Peace Teams). Fielded in 1980, they consisted of twelve to fifteen people, three or four of whom were armed RTA psyops personnel. They supervised paid volunteers, including women, who went from village to village distributing psyops and pro-government public relations through entertainment, songs, and skits.[368]

Another successful psyop program was *Santi Suk* (Peace and Happiness). An MoI program, it used village informants to identify hidden CPT agents. Once identified, the government would detain and reeducate them. Reeducation included taking the captured personnel on tours of towns to prove CPT indoctrination citing widespread abject poverty and persecution of the citizenry was wrong. Once reeducated, the government reinserted these persons into their villages to get them to convince other CPT agents to surrender and attend reeducation.[369]

Thailand's National Security Council ran prolific psyops. The NSC was meant to be a COIN coordination center, but instead, because of government rivalries, it evolved into a development and psyops unit. As part of its regular duties, it deployed Mobil Development Units throughout Thailand. MDUs conducted psyops as they went on development missions. The NSC's radio stations promulgated pro-government and anticommunist messages throughout the country. Its northeast-based Radio 909, funded by the United States early in the war, was the most successful. The RTA, CSOC, and the Department of Public Relations all contributed psyops material to it. Radio 909 was the most popular radio station in the northeast, in part because it broadcast in the Issan dialect, and it frequently delivered messages in the traditional Issan storytelling "singsong" style known as *mohlam*. Radio 909 discussed village development programs, interviewed CPT defectors, and encouraged villagers to report on CPT activities.

CPT members who surrendered indicated that Radio 909 was a major reason why they quit the war.[370]

Civil Affairs

Civil Affairs is both political and economic. On the political side, during the anticommunist COIN, the RTG concentrated on improving village leadership, administration, and connecting that leadership to the government. This was necessary because, as General Saiyud says, Thailand was replete with villages "totally lacking in self-government."[371] In effect, Bangkok had to do nation building in areas that it had neglected for decades. This, in turn, would ideally demonstrate legitimacy and earn the political allegiance of as many people as possible.[372] CA programs depended on establishing good relations with local people, which is pure politics. This is, moreover, exactly what the CPT had done in order to infiltrate Thailand. The main proponents of CA were CSOC, the RTA, and DoLA.

According to the CIA, "The Civil Affairs section of CSOC was charged with coordinating the activities of the ministries, departments, and bureaus concerned with administration, development, public relations, education, local security, and other civil matters."[373] Initially, CSOC had difficulty coordinating all the various government agencies. The sheer number of departments involved and their bureaucracies frustrated these efforts. For example, CSOC had to convince DoLA and the Ministries of Education, Agriculture (and Cooperatives), Interior, Health, Transport, and Industry to cooperate in COIN missions. In the early days of the war, there was little cooperation, contrary to the very heart of the CPM program. Eventually General Prapass, the DPM, had to order DoLA and the various ministries to contribute manpower and know-how to CSOC and cooperate with it.[374]

RTA Civil Affairs changed significantly when Prem took over as PM. He and his cohorts, particularly General Harn Leenanond, introduced to the RTA the use of politics—in particular, advocating the spread of democracy, or at least the Thai version of democracy—as a primary COIN weapon. Accordingly, Somchai

Rakwijit used this sentiment, politics/democracy combined with development, to create the RTA's first-ever Directorate of CA in January 1982. The Thai called it the "J-5," which in US military nomenclature refers to Plans and Policy and includes liaison with foreign forces.[375] The Thai, however, customized this designation to fit their own needs. The Assistant Chief of Staff of the Army's CA unit was also commander of ISOC's CA center.[376] From then on, ISOC and the RTA were essentially one and the same regarding CA.

After Prem's coup, RTA Civil Affairs held educational seminars all over the country for all walks of society on the benefits of democracy, what the government was doing to help the people, and what the people could do to help the country. The government also held talks on the particulars of its COIN efforts, to keep the people aware of the threat and what was being done about it. Additionally, RTA CA assumed responsibility for removing corrupt officials from the field. For these reasons, Saiyud believes that CA was more strategically important to the COIN effort than pure economic development programs: "I am thus convinced that, despite the prodigious sums of money being allocated for economic development, political stability is only likely to come about when people are assured that social injustices are being corrected."[377]

RTA Civil Affairs under Prem also assumed the task of organizing and coordinating most local forces. This fixed the long-standing problem of having an ineffectual chain of command. The addition of this assignment gave RTA Civil Affairs the biggest COIN portfolio in the government.

Similar to other CA entities, DoLA taught better governance, democracy, and carried out development projects. Because DoLA was not armed, it relied on protection from the BPP, VDC, and local forces. On the political front, DoLA's main task was to train local civilians in problem solving and democracy. Since DoLA administered the province, district, subdistrict, and village levels even in times of peace, waging COIN merely required an expansion of staff, programs, and training. By the end of 1967, it had trained four thousand local committee and assemblymen and nine thousand *tambon* leaders in the tenets of better governance.[378]

The Village Scouts

BPP Major General Somkhuan Harikul founded the Village Scout program in 1970. The Thai name for the scouts was *Luk Sua Chaoban*, or Village Tiger Cubs. The program had three purposes: (1) to provide intelligence on CPT infiltration of villages, (2) to build citizenship consensus throughout Thailand to mend internal division, and (3) to build a political movement that could counter the CPT.[379]

Katherine A. Bowie says General Somkhuan developed the idea of the Village Scouts after his troops suffered badly from a seventeen-day CPT offensive against the BPP in December 1968 in Loei province. The general realized that Thailand had descended into civil war, and he sought a political solution. Since he was also a major proponent of the Boy Scout movement in Thailand and had served in its leadership corps, he thought a similar program might help to curb the insurgency. Moreover, the BPP already promoted the Boy Scout program wherever it deployed, so creating an "anticommunist scouting movement" for the whole population was well within its expertise.[380]

General Somkhuan also wanted Thai society to get the personal and societal benefits of the Boy Scouts. Scouts engaged in activities such as camping, knot tying, fire building, pioneering, orienteering, canoeing, first aid, and fireside rituals. These helped perpetuate confidence, team-building skills, leadership, and unit cohesion. Boy Scouts also learned morals and citizenship tenets that were designed to make them better citizens. Boys from all walks of life and socioeconomic backgrounds joined the Scouts on equal footing, just like soldiers entering boot camp. They were all provided with education and opportunities to exceed.[381] General Somkhuan figured that if the government could have at least a portion of Thai citizens join such a program, it would help reduce their fractured society.

The Village Scouts, then, began in select villages as cells of three adults. These initial members shared the organization's pro-state values with others, seeking to recruit more members. In doing so, the cells mirrored CPT infiltration techniques. The Village Scouts' bylaws required that a man and a woman head each group as president and vice president.[382] Scouts took classes on citizenship, Thai history, and personal responsibility, and they held campfire-style banquets to codify the organization's unity. The Village Scouts' royal association gave it high prestige. His Majesty the King ordained each and every scarf worn by the Scouts, causing many to consider the scarves sacred.[383] The end result was a nearly five-million-member, pro-government, pro-Thai royal family movement that was vehemently anticommunist.[384]

One of the key facets of the Village Scout program was its five-day indoctrination process leading up to induction. Candidates from urban, rural, rich, and poor families were thrust together in groups, stripped of their societal status, treated as equals, and deprived of sleep while they carried out team and camping activities. They also learned patriotic songs and put on skits. The induction ceremonies were held on elaborate stages with torches and giant tiger-head archways and were attended by government officials.[385]

Although the BPP started the Village Scouts, the royal family took over the program and worked to expand it dramatically as the CPT war exploded. "ISOC liked the Village Scouts," says Somchai, "but it was not an ISOC program. The BPP did a good job with the Village Scouts, but ultimately they were under the king. So it was a royal issue, not a military command issue."[386]

Politically, the Village Scouts blocked the CPT from recruiting a fifth of Thailand's adult population. These people in turn influenced others against the CPT as well. As a political blocking force, the Village Scouts were a brilliant idea. Says Professor Bhumarat, "At that time, the Village Scouts worked very well because people could see the threat to our national security, and they played the role of bringing people from the communist side to the government. And they did psyops, too. And they were a force to support the monarchy."[387]

Amnesty

Amnesty began under CSOC in the 1960s as the National Open Arms and Rehabilitation Program. It took in surrendered and captured CPT, reeducated them, and placed them in job programs to reintegrate them into society.[388]

Governor Phat of Ubon province had a major hand in developing amnesty in the 1960s, as did one of his district chiefs, a deputy governor which historical documents refer to only as "Mr. Saisit."[389] This person's presence underscores how deeply governors were involved in the war.

As the government took a more political approach to the anticommunist COIN in the late 1970s, it began to call its rehabilitation program *Karunthep*, and it referred to ex-CPT members as "Cooperators in National Development." The government gave them housing assistance and land in some cases.[390] Says Denny Lane, "The government also gave land to surrendering CPT, much to the chagrin of many army personnel who were promised land and didn't receive it. So for the communists, it was a good program."[391] The government also co-opted many surrendering communists into running nongovernmental organization (NGO) projects.[392]

The concept of offering amnesty to enemies was in part rooted in the Thai belief system. Jeffrey Race says, "It boils down to religion, which is a basic building block of any society. It dictates what is wrong, what is right, what is to be rewarded, and what is to be punished."[393] Theravada Buddhism provided the themes that made amnesty possible. Lane adds, "This is unique. It had to do with the Buddhist idea of detachment, compassion, and recognizing the moral capacity of the other person."[394] The Thai did not believe they had to kill all their enemies or even imprison them for long periods of time.

As an example of the mind-set that allowed such latitude, Lane says, "General Surayud Chulanont—an RTA officer and close aide to General Prem—his father was a high-ranking CPT officer [Lieutenant Colonel Phayon Chulanont, head of the Thai Patriotic Front]. And the government didn't mind. It had no bearing on Surayud's abilities or trustworthiness. We Americans could never do this. The son of a felon or antigovernment activist is unlikely to get into the FBI, for example, but in Thailand the son is not accountable for the father's sins."[395] Incidentally, Surayud became PM via coup in 2006, and he was generally well liked and certainly accepted by the military as an incorruptible leader for the transition from coup back to civilian leadership.

The relatively low number of CPT terror operations was another reason why Bangkok adopted an amnesty policy. Says General Perapong, "The CPT did not harm many villagers." [396] Despite occasional assassinations of aid workers, governors, and other officials, most CPT violence was aimed at Thai government security personnel or local forces and their leaders, or "force on force" violence.

"The RTA even had a select group of officers who had undergone training in communist ideology, and they had a hotline to the communists, their enemies," says Lane. "If the communists had problems, the RTA was there to listen and sympathize, and perhaps get them to come in. All their conversations were off-line. The interesting thing to the US mind was that this was dealing with the enemy, which is unthinkable to us."[397]

A trickle of CPT members sought amnesty in the 1960s and mid-1970s, but the flow increased dramatically in the late 1970s and early 1980s. The first broad granting of this came from the Kriangsak government, which in 1978 offered blanket amnesty for all students and intellectuals who had fled to the jungles after the Thammasat University massacre—some three thousand people. It was an astounding political move in a country that had been so harshly divided between right and left for twelve years. More importantly, it had immediate effects. Some two thousand people surrendered in the first ten months after the Kriangsak amnesty announcement.

General Prem's 66/2523 Plan in 1980 increased the impact of the amnesty strategy by better publicizing it. The more the government promoted scenes of CPT rebels returning from the field and being greeted as citizens, the more insurgents surrendered. The number of amnesty seekers tripled from 1978 to 1979. Adds Gothom Araya of Mahodol University, "Some people just returned from the jungles and did not report to authorities. They just quit."[398]

High-profile CPT amnesty seekers added to the bonanza. The press had a field day when prominent student CPT leader Thirayuth Bunmee returned home after five years in the jungle. That publicity triggered more surrenders.[399] In May 1982, 1,500 CPT members and their auxiliary surrendered in Loei. In August, 7,400 hill tribesmen and their entire families surrendered. In December 1982, 216

CPT members surrendered in Yasothon Loeng. In January 1983, 422 more CPT members surrendered in two northeast provinces, Nakhon Phanom and Udon Thani. In November, the surrenders continued with 664 CPT members coming in, again with their auxiliary support. This flood continued into 1984 and beyond until the CPT had withered as a threat.[400]

"And when they came in," adds Lane, "they were not shot, and they were not thrown into the slammer. It was the human approach they took."[401] Former CPT members resumed their former positions in society and even flourished. Some became highly visible professors and government ministers. Thirayuth Bunmee became a professor at Thammasat University and remained a vocal critic of the government on social issues.[402] Surapong Suebwonglee, a CPT student activist who was at the Thammasat massacre, later served as finance minister to PM Thaksin Shinawatra.[403] It is because of this remarkable flexibility that the Thai amnesty program stands as one of the most remarkable initiatives in the history of counterinsurgency.

Diplomacy

Thai diplomatic prowess is legendary, and the RTG used it with great success in their communist COIN. Bangkok aimed its main diplomatic offensive at halting Chinese support for the CPT, exploiting a political rift between Beijing and Hanoi that began in the mid- to late 1960s and became a full-blown fracture after 1970. Hanoi wanted to escape Beijing's orbit as a communist satellite, so it sought support from Moscow, which readily agreed to be its champion. Beijing, no friend of Moscow by this time, feared an independent and militarily powerful Hanoi, and the stage was set for intense communist rivalry.

Taking advantage of this rivalry was easier said than done, however. The RTG and Beijing did not have diplomatic relations at the time, so Thailand used Chinese spies to contact Beijing and try to open a dialogue. "At that time, nobody knew that we had some linkages under the table," says Professor Bhumarat.[404] "We had agents, communist agents, inside their movement [the CPT]. See, the Chinese collected intelligence in Thailand by recruiting local

Chinese businessmen. The businessmen sent the information to their case officers in Hong Kong, who then sent the information to Beijing." Thai intelligence had identified scores of these agents, and it decided to use them to get their diplomatic request to China.

When the Thai made their pitch, the Chinese accepted. Professor Bhumarat describes the meeting this way: "PM Kukrit went to Beijing [in June 1975] and Mao treated him like he was a son. Our PM was very smart. He told the Chinese, 'We love Mao.' In the beginning, Mao's aide said he'd give our PM fifteen minutes. But Mao and Kukrit talked for forty-five minutes. Mao enjoyed talking with him very much. Then Mao's doctor came in and told him to take a rest. At that time, Mao was very sick."[405] The visit proved fruitful for both sides. Kukrit and Premier Chou En-lai ultimately signed a joint communiqué announcing diplomatic relations between Bangkok and Beijing. This agreement set the stage for the future empowerment of Thailand when it would need China's help the most.[406] And it was the first of many secret Thai visits to China and vice versa to persuade Beijing of Thailand's goals.

Thailand increased its diplomatic efforts with China as Southeast Asia continued to deteriorate. Pol Pot's terrorist expeditions into Vietnam throughout 1977 triggered Hanoi's invasion of Cambodia with more than ten divisions on 25 December 1978. That move, in turn, triggered Beijing's punitive invasion of the northern portion of Vietnam on 17 February 1979. Undeterred, Hanoi pressed its ten-division attack into Cambodia to very near the Thai border.[407] Eventually, communist Vietnam had some three hundred thousand troops in Cambodia. Hanoi could have used a portion of these to infiltrate Thailand's porous twenty-five-hundred-kilometer border any time it wanted.[408] At the time, Hanoi had the fourth-largest army in the world, it was flush with combat veterans from fighting the Americans and the French for more than fifteen years, and it had recent graduates from Soviet military colleges in its ranks.

In addition, Thailand had communications intelligence saying Vietnamese forces were asking Hanoi for permission to invade Thailand. [409] As the Vietnamese massed their forces near the Thai border, PM Kriangsak summoned

General Serm Na Nakorn, the Supreme Commander of the Royal Thai Armed Forces. Professor Bhumarat says Kriangsak asked him, "'What shall we do? If they send troops to Thailand, can we fight them, and how long can we fight?' Serm told the PM, 'Seven days, sir.' And he said, 'Seven days for what?' And Serm replied, 'We can hold them for seven days, and that's it.' So the PM said, 'Pack. We are going to Beijing. If we can talk to them, they may help us.'"[410]

Kriangsak went to Beijing shortly thereafter and, like Kukrit before him, made his pitch. However, as Mao had died in 1976, the Thai had to deal with a new Chinese leader, Hua Guofeng. Kriangsak's main request was that Beijing stop supporting the CPT. His secondary request was that China maintain its troop presence on the Vietnamese border to pressure Hanoi. "So we asked them to please keep strategic forces in the northern part of Vietnam to keep Vietnamese forces occupied, because if they moved near to us, we'd be in trouble," says Professor Bhumarat.[411]

In the meantime, Bangkok sent delegations, which included Kriangsak himself, to Russia. Says Professor Bhumarat, "We asked Russia, 'Don't give the wrong signal for Vietnam to invade us.' This was small compared to the big diplomacy of the day. We were small fry, but we did what we could diplomatically to save our country." Bangkok also sent diplomats to the UN, its Southeast Asian neighbors, and Washington, DC, because they, too, were concerned about the impact of a possible Vietnamese invasion.[412]

After playing its many diplomatic cards, in time Thailand got what it wanted. First, China put pressure on Vietnam, not just for Thailand's benefit, but for its own sake as well. "The Chinese began to fire artillery into Vietnam to keep some of their forces in the north," reports Professor Bhumarat. "And it was a lot of artillery. Some days, it amounted to one thousand rounds. The message was, 'If you do anything to Thailand, we will attack you.'"

Second, China began to halt support for the CPT. The China-based VOPT went off the air in 1979, and Chinese logistics for CPT bases in Laos dried up. Communist Laos had neither the capability nor the capacity to support the CPT, and it was trying to balance its relationship between Beijing and Hanoi, so it disengaged with Thailand's rebels. Threatened by China, the Vietnamese backed off from supporting the CPT, too.

China wanted something in return, however: aid for Cambodian insurgent groups fighting the Vietnamese, which the Thai were happy to provide. As long as the Vietnamese were embroiled in an insurgency in Cambodia, and as long as China kept up its intimidation, the Vietnamese in Cambodia were less likely to attack Thailand.

Thailand, along with the United States, Singapore, China, and scores of other nations, supported multiple Cambodian insurgent groups. Among them were the Khmer People's National Liberation Front, the United Free Khmer, and the bloody KR.[413] Bangkok knew supporting the latter was taboo, but Vietnam had supported CPT rebels inside Thailand since before 1965, resulting in the deaths of thousands of Thai. Thailand returned the favor. "We knew the Khmer Rouge was not popular," says Professor Bhumarat, "but the Khmer Rouge was a good boxer. How can we ignore them? So we had to exploit them to fight against the Vietnamese, and years later we would have to pay the diplomatic price, and our image would suffer for supporting them, but at the time it was the thing to do."[414]

Democratic Reforms

Democratic reform had a major impact on the CPT and the population it was trying to co-opt, so much so that it caused General Chavalit to remark that individual liberty helped to save Thailand from the CPT.[415] No single democratic program forced the issue, however. Rather, it was a series of democratic laws, decrees, and programs that replaced autocratic laws on the books. Given a respite from government autocracy, the people were less inclined to support the CPT, which falsely heralded democracy as one of its goals. It was no easy task, however. Autocracy had ruled Thailand for nearly ten years.

When General Thanom took over by coup on 17 November 1971, he scrapped the 1968 constitution and declared martial law. His government also banned all political parties, curtailed freedom of the press, and discarded due-process legal rights for suspected opponents of the regime. These heavy-handed actions led to unrest that strengthened the CPT's hand.

Thanom assumed the positions of PM, Supreme Commander, and Foreign Minister. His brother-in-law, Prapass Charusathiara, took over the DPM, Interior, Police Chief, Deputy Supreme Commander, RTA Commander, and CSOC portfolios. Thanom's son, Narong, held optimum army posts as a favored colonel. Opponents, who included students and everyday Thai citizens fearful of their rights, called these leaders "The Three Tyrants." The civilian political elite joined students and workers in opposing Thanom's apparent aim to perpetuate a political dynasty through his son, Narong, whose rise the military officer corps particularly resented.

According to author Paul Handley, corruption during the Thanom government ran rampant, and the economy, beset by the global recession of the early 1970s, declined. Between 1971 and 1973, some 180,000 Thais engaged in hundreds of strikes, and a meager rice harvest led to shortages and long lines for consumer goods in Bangkok. In the face of internal government opposition, Thanom abolished the election process for the National Assembly (a.k.a. Parliament) and appointed all 299 members in 1972. This abuse of power gave rise to the 14 October student protest movement, the deaths of seventy student protesters, and an overall national dissatisfaction with the government. The king, primarily urged by the students, stepped in and pressured Thanom to give up power.

Successive governments were either paralyzed by lack of consensus or similarly autocratic. The Thanin Kraivichien government, which took over in a 1976 coup, threw out the 1974 constitution, dissolved Parliament, banned all political parties, increased press censorship, harangued unions—even those not penetrated by the CPT—and placed the country under martial law. Some eight thousand people suspected of communist activities were arrested in the first three months of 1976. Thanin also assumed the power to execute without trial anyone deemed a national security risk.[416]

In one case, Thanin's government shut down the *Siang Puang Chon* newspaper for three days for covering the return of exiled General Prapass, an inflammatory event unpopular with most of the public. It also shut down the biweekly *Patinya* journal for criticizing the government for closing *Siang Puang Chon*, calling it "communist agitation tactics." When the right-wing Armoured Radio criticized the closing of *Patinya*, Thanin shut down its popular show, *Meet the Listeners*. In doing this, the PM accused even anticommunist supporters of "dancing to the tunes played by the communists."[417]

Thanin's government also refused to address pressing economic problems, causing further suffering. Inflation was 13 percent under his rule, and he did nothing to control it. Thanin ignored labor groups' requests for a higher minimum wage, and strike breaking caused a passive "go slow" industrial rebellion that hurt national output. Forty percent of 1976 college graduates were jobless. One million farmers harmed by poor growing conditions struggled to make ends meet, but Thanin lifted not a finger to help. His neglect deepened the wedge between his autocratic government and the Thai people.[418]

Thanin fell in a coup on 11 November 1977, and the successor Kriangsak government reversed past administrations' dictatorial practices. The removal of draconian laws helped to restore public faith in government, thereby denying the CPT a pool of large recruits and sympathizers. Kriangsak enacted a law in 1978 releasing the "Bangkok Eighteen," a group of students and labor organizers charged with instigating the Thammasat University massacre. He reduced the number of provinces under martial law, and he narrowed anticommunist laws so they would net only communists and not all those who longed for political change.[419] Kriangsak paved the way for the return to constitutional government by 1978 and the restoration of Parliament by 1979.[420] He raised the minimum wage in Bangkok in both 1978 and 1979. He brought back some press freedoms and released, with full pardons, twelve thousand prisoners who had been detained since 1976 as "dangers to society."[421]

Taken as a whole, Kriangsak's initiatives relieved significant political and economic pressures. By fostering economic growth and nullifying autocratic political policies, he increased the government's legitimacy and earned broad popular support. This, in turn, sapped support from the CPT and set the stage for launching an offensive against the CPT from stable political footing.

Economic Measures

Thailand had too many COIN development programs to count. The main impetus behind them was King Bhumibol. One of his top policies was to develop the poor areas of Thailand through royal development projects. The king urged all government agencies to do the same, and they did so with zeal. In addition, specific development agencies were set up to assuage citizens' grievances as a way of combating the CPT. Many cooperated with the CPM program as a direct result of the 09/10 Plan. [422] Others operated on their own. The main development programs for the communist COIN were royal projects, government agency projects, and RTA Civil Affairs.

"Why did we use development projects to help fight the CPT?" asks General Harn Pathai. "Because the communists told people that the government made them poor, and that the government walked on the people. The CPT brainwashed them, so we went in and took that away from the communists. We showed the villagers that this was not true. We proved it to them with our work."[423] Adds General Perapong, "Our goal [through development] was to help them and give everything to them and win their loyalty. It was used as a way to fight communists."[424]

Royal Development Projects

There were two kinds of royal projects during the communist COIN: official programs and suggested programs. Official programs were standing projects that the royal family managed on a year-round basis. Suggested programs were those that King Bhumibol encouraged government agencies to undertake. When the king toured the countryside, for example, he might suggest to a government minister traveling with him that his or her agency should set up a potable water project in a particular village. The agency in question then set up the project with royal guidance and technical support, but mostly with its own funding. It had the very real honor of running a royal project, however, which brought high esteem to the project manager and the government ministry in question.

Such undertakings were critical to the royal family. King Bhumibol and Queen Sirikit followed the war closely and knew failure would bring their demise, as it had for the royals in Laos and Cambodia. Moreover, both had a real, demonstrated affection for their subjects, who reciprocated in a way that helps to explain why Thailand has one of the few functioning monarchies in Asia. The king spent considerable time touring all the country's provinces, informally meeting his subjects, and assessing their plight firsthand. Even before the war in 1955, King Bhumibol spent fifty-five days touring Issan, meeting with locals, and listening to their needs. The trip spurred much of his charity work.[425]

One of the most notable official royal development projects that helped farmers was the Royal Irrigation Department. Rainfall was not always sufficient for farmers' crops, and irrigation became a significant need. As the communist COIN pressed forward and many farmers joined the CPT, the king had more than two hundred dams built in the northeast, six of them large ones. Some of them suffered from engineering defects, which impacted efforts to deliver water to parched Issan where the CPT thrived. On the other hand, royal irrigation projects were more successful in the Mae Nam Mae Klong Basin, where the king brought water to 175,000 hectares. Dams in this region allowed many farmers over a region of 250,000 hectares to "double crop," or produce two crops on the same piece of land in a single year. On the south region's east coast, the king's projects brought water to about 25 percent of arable land, or seventy-five thousand hectares, and another fifty-two thousand for the Pattani basin. There were five hundred thousand hectares available in the far south for irrigation at the time.[426]

In the north, the Royal Hill Tribe Development Project began in 1969. It was designed to better the lives of the hill tribes and reduce the friction with the government. "[King Bhumibol] went in and helped them, and his efforts were more like philanthropy," says Amara Pongsapich, head of the Rotary Club's Chulalongkorn branch. "His first trips into the mountains mostly involved giving medicine and basic staples to the Meo."[427] It was a chance for the king to establish relations with them and gain their trust. "Then the second phase would include antinarcotics programs, and encouraging them to stop growing opium and instead grow fruits and things like that," says Amara.[428] The project specifically encouraged growing coffee, chrysanthemums, apples, peaches, strawberries, apricots, and lychees in place of opium, and it brought in specialists to teach the tribes how to grow these crops.[429]

Government Development Projects

The most prominent COIN development agency during the communist COIN was the Accelerated Rural Development program, an MoI program run by Prasong Sukhum, a top COIN development strategist and deputy minister of Commerce and Transportation in the late 1970s. Sukhum's transportation background likely accounts for ARD's heavy emphasis on road building. ARD's Committee for Coordination in Bangkok made agency policy, and its activities took place primarily in CPT-prone areas. The RTA and local forces provided security for ARD staff.[430] ARD eventually grew to a staff of 250 and operated in twenty-four provinces.

The road-building aspect was important to the government's COIN strategy because it gave the government easier means to reach people in remote areas where insurgents operated. Extending the national road network also yielded economic benefits, such as integrating farmers with the rest of the country so that they could more easily market their goods, as well as opening up rural areas to industry and commerce. In its early years, ARD built two thousand kilometers of all-weather roads, plus small feeder roads, dams, wells, and storage ponds. It additionally organized thirty youth groups, made the equivalent of $2 million USD in loans through special credit entities, and held one hundred film showings a month in at-risk areas.[431]

Along with road projects, ARD included Mobile Medical Teams, a farmer aid program, and a drinkable water program. The Ministry of Public Health helped to staff the Mobile Medical Teams. An active public relations program promoted ARD's work and helped to promote government legitimacy.[432]

The Community Development Department (referred to as the "CD") began development projects in 1962 before the war, but became a COIN entity in 1965. Unlike ARD, the CD did not carry out development for villagers. Rather, it helped the villagers carry out their own development. Tanham writes its main goals were to "facilitate communications between the government and the rural population, to improve the peasants' economic status, and to help develop local leadership."[433] In modern development parlance, such as that carried out by USAID, the theory was to "teach the villagers to catch their own fish instead of catching fish for them."

The CD trained its staff to find out from villagers what development projects they needed. They organized village committees to vote on projects, thereby encouraging local leadership and political awareness. Once projects were approved, the CD and village staff organized and carried them out. CD projects were small and included miniature dams, canals, and markets. Tanham writes the CD was a novel idea because the Thai were "strongly individualistic" and not accustomed to community programs except in a few areas, such as assisting monks, harvesting crops, or helping a neighbor build a house. Still, the CD program expanded during the war and had a record of success.[434]

Government expenditures for development programs increased as the war continued, indicating Thai confidence in COIN development programs. In 1967, the government spent $21.6 million on development programs. Here, the US government contributed an additional $19.7 million. In 1968, Bangkok spent $26.7 million, and the United States added $17.1 million. In 1969, government expenditures rose dramatically to $51 million, and US funding dropped to $16.6 million as the RTG increasingly took responsibility for its own programs.[435]

COIN development programs operated by other government agencies included, but were not limited to, the Ministry of Public Health's potable water and protein development projects aimed at improving villagers' nutrition. The Ministry of Education ran Mobile Trade Training units to strengthen trainees' business and marketing prowess. The Ministry of National Development ran labor-intensive construction projects.[436] The list goes on and on, and some Thai say there were too many programs by too many agencies; that their impact, while certain, was diluted because of a lack of focus.

Royal Thai Army Development Projects

The RTA had development programs of its own, which ultimately fell under its CA division. The RTA was the most powerful COIN entity in the government, and it well understood the poverty-CPT nexus. "Development spurred the J-5," says General Perapong, "something we never had before. It means political, development, and social programs. So long as you accept the cause of the war is poor people and lack of development, or bad economics, then this is meaningful."[437]

General Prem says RTA development projects were pivotal to COIN. "By far the more formidable task," he says, "was how to tackle the widespread poverty, which we saw as the root cause of insurgency and indeed all social ills. The Second Army region, despite being the unified command of military and civilian resources in the Northeast, had its obvious limitations. We had to do the best we could. We started by identifying three main areas in which we could be of help to the villagers: means of subsistence, schooling and health care. In all these areas, the aim was to 'help them help themselves.'"[438] The RTA dedicated considerable resources to analyzing the poverty problem. It conducted research in the field, identified critical risk areas, designed solutions, and provided the resources to fulfill them. This work began in Issan in 1974. From then on, RTA development of poor areas, not just insurgent-prone areas, became a long-standing tradition.

General Prem recounts the development projects were not easy to implement. "We simply did not have enough budgets to give handouts, nor did we have enough manpower to carry out the work on that scale," he says. "If money was given out, it was for seeds, farming tools, or poultry or fish stocks for the ponds."[439] The RTA's many small projects immediately impacted villagers' lives, casting a blanket of help over one-third of the population. It was a powerful strategy.

The army benefited greatly from local volunteers. Says General Prem, "Volunteers in each locality served as manpower; once trained, they were put to work applying and extending their newly acquired skills, be it in teaching or in rudimentary medical knowledge. The response from the volunteers, all of whom worked without pay or personal gain, went beyond anything I had expected or indeed had any right to expect."[440] There was a groundswell of support for these projects that were aimed not only at shoring up the well-being of the population but also at keeping it from the CPT's grip. This indicates a "whole of country" approach to COIN, especially the fact the volunteers pitched in. This does not mean the whole country aided COIN in this manner, but it does signify the "whole of country" concept was there, and certain parts of the nation participated with vigor.

"I did some development, too," says General Harn Pathai. "We provided land and built houses…a *rai* of land [to each settler]. Lots of people [in CPT areas] got a half *rai* of land. And we gave money, too, and let them buy wood, and had them build their own houses. These were royal projects. We won because of these royal projects in these areas."[441] General Harn recalled a joint royal-RTA project where the army had cash on hand, called "flash cash" in US Special Operations vernacular, to dole out for unique projects. This example illustrates how much flexibility and development know-how the RTA had.

In many instances the military and private development societies worked together. For example, General Saiyud worked with the *Mitrapap* (Friendship) program, which put on skydiving exhibitions to raise money for school construction. He also collaborated with the Rotary Club of Thailand, an international service society that helps the poor and disadvantaged.[442] Founded on 17 September 1930, the first Rotary Club in Thailand began under the sanction of Prince Purachatra Jayakar (1882–36) after he was introduced to the idea by Canadian Rotarian James W. Davidson. King Bhumibol became its patron in 1955. By 1980, Thailand had forty-eight Rotary Club branches.[443] Saiyud helped Rotary projects in the north provide hill tribes with better medical care, education, and assistance with getting their goods to market.[444]

The results of the government's development projects were mixed. Some data suggest that development did nothing to assuage villagers' CPT sympathies. According to Marks, the reverse could actually have been true. "A Cornell University report," he writes, "confirmed a phenomenon which had already been observed by some American officials: namely, that there appeared to be a strong association between rate of structural growth and incidence of insurgent activities."[445] Marks's own analysis of the ARD program indicates little progress. Regarding improvement of living standards, he says that ARD had "no overall impact" and that only a few individuals were able to benefit from "market mechanisms." In other cases, Marks observed, many villagers came to rely too much on government initiatives instead of helping themselves—an ironic result because the very goal of the CD program was to teach village self-reliance. He adds that ARD had little success in passing on technical know-how to villagers, and that any improvement in communication between the villagers and the government was marginal.[446]

Tactical problems with development resulted from some projects being too sophisticated or beyond the capabilities of uneducated villagers. In one case cited by Saiyud, a development team brought a water pump for use at a village well, but villagers still preferred using a bucket on a string, so the pump went unused and rusted. In other cases, rural people felt insulted or embarrassed to have urban government personnel try to modernize them. Says Saiyud, "They felt change was being forced upon them. Usually, they begin to want it only when they have seen it with their own eyes somewhere else first."[447]

Other critics say that some villagers did not like development projects because they believed the government was essentially trying to buy their loyalty and forcing them to take sides in an armed conflict, opening them up to possible retaliation from the CPT. "Some were not happy," says Amara, "because they knew that there was influence swaying here with some of these projects."[448] While acknowledging that the development effort was politically driven, Amara concludes that it did have positive consequences. "They did help," she admits, "but I saw it as a very political issue. It did help improve the lives of the Issan people, and it did bring them to the government side. At the very least it kept many of them from joining the Communist Party. Follow-through was not very clear, but these areas are very accessible today, so it's not like they've been abandoned."[449]

Others say development certainly helped defeat the CPT. General Saiyud noticed in 1969 that, while excessive force had clearly turned villages against the government, development projects, at the very least, kept rural people from sliding further into poverty, fulfilling a key government goal. In other cases, he says, development definitely won many villages over to the government's side, although it also triggered conflicts.[450] Says Saiyud, "These multifaceted [development] efforts have resulted in a full range of government-to-people relations; and, as elsewhere, some have been good, while others have been, frankly, bad. Misunderstandings between officials and hill tribe leaders have, on occasion, led to gunfire," sparked by real or imagined "government-perpetrated inequity."[451]

Some former communists say development helped COIN efforts. Ex-CPT Srisompob Jitpiromsri says, "We did not worry too much about them [development workers] or the development projects. But they did help Bangkok in the end to bring the people to their side."[452]

Denny Lane toured southern provinces during the war years and witnessed good progress. "Regarding development," says Lane, "go to Nan province. The road network the government built there was incredible. And it allowed the villagers to readily get their goods and food to market. And lots of road construction personnel were killed building those roads—as in a staggering number."[453] The total death toll related to road building numbered in the hundreds.

Lane does not believe development projects had an immediate decisive impact on the war, but he believes they helped. "One day," he says, "I visited a southern CPT area of Malay Muslims. It was night. The village head met me, and we spoke about the insurgents. The village head pointed to the next village over in the hills and said, 'See there? They have electricity,' pointing to the lights. He knew he'd get electricity next. Then he said, 'Last night, I told the communist insurgents that only an established government could give me and my village electricity and the paved road the government had recently put in, and you cannot.' And it counted," said Lane. "It meant something."[454]

THE FIRST SOUTHERN COIN: 1980–1998

Prelude

The history of how Thailand acquired its southern border provinces is well told by modern historians. Suffice it to say the region was a Hindu-Buddhist nation called Langasuka in the 1300s that adopted Islam by the 1500s and took on the name Patani, spelled with a single *t*. In the present day, this region consists of Songkhla, Pattani, Yala, and Narathiwat provinces. At one time, an insurgent group also included Satun province in this lineup. Regardless, this region is not geographically vast like Issan. One can drive across it in a single day. It is lush and green, with low mountains, rivers, savannas, swamps, jungle, and forests. Ethnic Malays have populated the area for centuries. For many decades, Patani was a reluctant vassal state of Siam, which it warred with on occasion, sometimes in conjunction with the Burmese where they sacked major Siamese cities.

Patani also had multiple civil wars between competing *raja* rulers who courted Siam to gain power over their rivals. This internal strife kept Patani unstable and in Siam's orbit for centuries. Patani legend says it was a lush agricultural state, rich, and the cradle of Islam in Southeast Asia. Though the area had busy trading ports and Islamic learning institutions, there is little factual evidence to support these notions. Other than scant reporting by travelers such as sixteenth-century Portuguese historian Tome Pires, there is little recorded history of Patani.[1] For sure, however, Patani's power brokers and about a third of its population have resisted Thailand's rule on and off since Bangkok annexed it in 1902.

"The separatists' idea had been there all along," says former PM Chuan Leekpai. "Some separatists came from the families and political power cliques that lost power when Thailand annexed the area. They lost their controlling interests."[2] Adds former NIA Chief Professor Bhumarat Taksadipong, "The idea of separatism began big in the 1940s. But the movement did not have a lot of backing. It was not the intellectuals. It was the Muslim politicians. And at that time, it was not the idea of pure separatism. It was to establish the Muslim minority identity, not quite full-blown separatism."[3]

The idea of full-blown separatism gained popularity in the 1960s, and government ineptitude and maltreatment of these people who were neither Thai nor Buddhists helped pave the way. In many ways, the government treated southern border people similarly to how corrupt officials had treated the Hmong as the CPT was infiltrating the north. It was a recipe for disaster. When the south revolted, it harnessed a "long-time accumulation of wrath, hatred, and alienation which they had suppressed," writes Panomporn Anurugsa, a noted specialist on the southern insurgency during the 1970s–80s time period.[4]

In the mid-1970s, the insurgency gained political momentum as a result of the Pattani Demonstration of 1975. As many as one hundred thousand Thai Malay Muslims—both insurgents and regular citizens—gathered to protest the killing of five villagers by the RTM in Narathiwat. The Marines said the villagers were insurgents. Local political leaders and imams denied this. Whatever the actual case was, massive crowds gathered in front of Pattani's Central Mosque and Provincial Hall from 11 December 1975 through 4 January 1976.[5]

The insurgent group Pattani United Liberation Organization (PULO) was the key organizer. PULO staged highly emotional readings from the Koran and calls to the Prophet Muhammad. "Every Muslim present was engulfed with emotions, sympathy for the victims, and full of hatred," writes Surin Pitsuwan, former Thai Minister of Foreign Affairs, and a Muslim.[6]

The timing of the protest was a psychological operation, too. PULO waited until 11 December to hold the protests because, asserts Surin, it was close to one of the most important Muslim holidays, *Id al Adha* (*Raja Hajji* in Malay), which signified the end of the *haj*, the pilgrimage to Mecca. (Some sources say the end of *Id al Adha* was in October, some say it was 14 December, and others corroborate Surin's research.) The largest protest came on the actual day of *Id al Adha*. Surin notes the holiday marked the intended sacrifice of Abraham's son, Ishmael, as commanded by God. "In such an emotion-filled period," writes Surin, "religious and ethnic consciousness was easily transformed into political solidarity."[7]

On 13 December, chaos struck. Someone in a government building hurled a grenade or two onto the speaker's stage, killing as many as eighteen and injuring forty. In the middle of the carnage, someone shouted the call to prayer and recited the Islamic profession of faith, the *Shahada*: "There is no God but God, and Muhammad is the Messenger of God!"[8]

Incensed, the crowd blamed the government for the attack and issued a five-point demand, including a full investigation of the killing of the five villagers and the withdrawal of all military forces from the south. The Thai government met the protesters halfway. It removed the Marine unit in question, launched an investigation into the killings, and did not penalize any civil servant who left work to join the protests.[9]

The proverbial fuse was lit, however. Insurgent leaders believed the demonstration proved popular support "was always potentially present."[10] More, Panomporn says, Thai Malay Muslims began to distance themselves from Thai Buddhists, labeling them as lackeys of the government.[11] This division further reinforced the "us versus them" sentiment that the insurgents needed to push their war forward.

Echoing this, Wan Kadir Che Man, former leader of the insurgent group *Bersatu*, writes, "Some separatist leaders interpreted this demonstration as an expression of Muslim anger toward Thai Buddhists. They believed that this anger could be manipulated and directed 'correctly' to support the struggle."[12] The uprising, then, was aimed not only at the RTG, but also at another race and religion. This is key in understanding the insurgency. Insurgent leaders not only embraced these prejudices, they encouraged them and shaped them to suit their plans. Accordingly, the southern insurgency was not a purely a political revolt, as some historians have asserted. The Pattani Demonstration of 1975 and its aftermath drove a wedge between two ethnic and religious groups and began fracturing southern society.[13] It would take until the 2000s for those fractures to become extreme, but the seeds were sown here.

The demonstration was a wake-up call for the government. Bangkok came to the sudden realization that the insurgents had real political power. On the heels of the chaos, the far south's voting constituency rejected all Buddhist parliamentary representatives and elected all Thai Malay Muslim candidates to the National Assembly.[14] The insurgency had legs.

By 1979, four years after the demonstration, the insurgency had grown to eighty-four rebel groups with fifteen hundred fighters. The most active groups were the *Barisan Nasional Pembebasan Patani* (National Liberation Front of Pattani or BNPP), the *Barisan Revolusi Nasional* (National Revolutionary Front or BRN), and PULO.[15] The BNPP was the largest group in the late 1970s, but PULO was the most violent. From October 1976 to December 1981, these and other groups carried out 127 major acts of violence that killed two hundred people and wounded three hundred.[16]

To deal with the rising violence, Bangkok stepped up security, political, and economic programs already in place since the 1960s. Unfortunately for the RTG, none of these programs had ever been effective. Coordination suffered as a direct result of hard rivalry between the Yala-based Coordination Center (CC)—the top insurgency-managing agency in the south—and the powerful southern Department of Local Administration. The CC lost that battle. The civilian side of the equation was further weakened by lack of synchronization with security forces. Accordingly, the RTG's efforts at this time cannot be considered true COIN because of their haphazard and flaky nature.

Security programs during this time period consisted mostly of temporary surges and mass arrest operations. None were successful in achieving peace, and some were reportedly cruel, which enraged Malay Muslim southerners and helped to grow the insurgency. On the other hand, they did succeed in destroying the military capabilities of the BNPP, a major milestone. Additionally, two BNPP weaknesses made it ripe for a knockout blow. These included the 1977 death, from natural causes, of its leader, Tengku Yala Nasae, and the loss of support for its Malaysian champion, *Parti Islam* (PI). The PI lost elections in its home country and, as a result, was unable to help its protégés in southern Thailand.[17]

There were scores of political COIN initiatives in the 1960s–70s. One was "integration," the government's master strategy for the south. Detractors, however, called it "assimilation" and "resocialization." Integration entailed bringing Thai Malay Muslims into the state's society via programs that penetrated their isolation. The goal was to make them productive and employable citizens who accepted a pluralistic society.[18]

Bangkok's primary integration instrument was education. The biggest educational program was *pondok* reform.[19] *Pondoks* were private religious schools for high school–level students. They had been in the south for decades, but grew in number after WWII. They taught the Koran, Islamic culture, and little else. Enrollment was free. There were no tests, no standardized system of learning, and no vocational or secular subjects taught such as auto mechanics, math, or history.[20] *Pondok* teachers, or *ustaz*, were not required to have to have official credentials or training. Overall, *pondoks* were hidden from government regulation.[21] They were also a central aspect of Thai Malay Muslim culture.

Because some *pondok* teachers were fostering rebellion among their students, Bangkok sought to recast these schools to include secular subjects and produce learned citizens open to the culture and politics of the rest of the country.[22] People who studied only Islam became unproductive citizens. They could not be doctors, lawyers, businessmen, or technical tradesmen. They could only fulfill religious roles or perform manual labor. Accordingly, in 1961, Bangkok designed the Private Schools Teaching Islam program (PSTI) that imposed on *pondoks* minimum learning standards and a government curriculum, including some secular subjects. The schools could still teach Islam, however.[23]

A 1968 government survey of the government's reforms indicated that a slight majority of parents, 53 percent, saw these changes as positive and a chance for their children to progress. *Ustaz*, however—typically ultraconservative Islamists—rejected the program by 95 percent. They asserted the *pondok* changes were designed to "make [young Malays] deny their ethnic and religious background" and destroy Islamic purity.[24] This competing sentiment created a divide between religious leaders, who were stakeholders with power to lose, and everyday southerners trying to achieve progress. The insurgency developed along these lines as it marched from the 1970s into the 1980s and 1990s.

Other political programs in the educational realm included teaching southern students Thai history, extending the minimum required time in high school, and offering access to universities via quotas and scholarships.[25] A widespread language control program was particularly controversial. Here, Bangkok banned Malay-language newspapers in the far south and put televisions in village headmen's homes to sway the population to watch Thai language news, entertainment, and government policy programs.[26]

Like *pondok* reform, from the government's point of view, these programs aimed to reduce the far south's cultural isolation and help its citizens to become productive and employable. Prominent Thai south researcher Ornanong Noiwong asserts the language program was partially successful. The government recruited many Thai Malay Muslim university students into government service, partly because they could speak Thai. Publicly educated Thai Malay Muslims began to speak Thai at school and home, and speaking Thai became fashionable among many of the region's youth.[27] Ornanong writes that media programs helped to convince many previously isolated southerners to view themselves as part of Thailand's broader society.[28]

Ultraconservative Muslims, however, rejected these programs outright, especially the language programs. They asserted the government was trying to turn Malays into Thais. The government noticed this rebellious trend in 1979, stating, "The Thai Muslims hold that their custom and tradition is part of their religious life, and they tend to refuse anything out of their own realm, thinking that it would be religiously wrong."[29] Many Thai Malay Muslims believed that Malay and Arabic were the only acceptable languages under God.[30]

It was not just cultural identity that was at stake, however. It was power over the population, too. For example, one of Bangkok's integration programs co-opted traditional Thai Malay Muslim inheritance and family law into the Thai legal system.[31] Imams balked at this change because it cut them out of the judicial chain of command. They lost power.

In an attempt to bridge ideological gaps, the government brought more than one thousand southern imams to Bangkok from 1977 to 1979 to meet with high-level, Islamic government officials (who were ethnically Thai Muslims, not Malays) and with RTA psyops officers. [32] RTA psyops officers provided information on insurgents and warned of the dangers of using Islam to stir separatism. [33] The MoI began to send Islamic scholars and Central Islamic Council members to southern Thailand to train local imams—most of whom had no formal Islamic schooling—in the fundamental aspects of Islam. [34] Again, conservative Thai Malay Muslims rejected these programs. To them, non-Malay Muslims were less pure than Malay Muslims, again highlighting the ethnic motivations underlying the conflict.

Some political COIN policies in the 1970s had failed because of bad governance. Says Somchai Rakwijit, "The government did not adjust its administrators to the culture of the Muslim people of the southernmost provinces. The officials have long been looking down on those people. And then when something happens, when a conflict happens, the officials tend to look past the problem through the lens that the Muslims are not loyal to Thailand. They don't have enough cultural understanding and language to communicate with them." [35] As a result, many Thai Malay Muslims believe the government viewed them as second-class citizens, a perception that festered for decades.

COIN development programs in the 1960s–70s were in many cases identical to those of the anticommunist COIN. There were road, agriculture, infrastructure, and village improvement projects. The far south badly needed these. Writes Ornanong, "The 1975–76 socioeconomic survey shows that poverty in rural areas of the Muslim provinces approximated, and in some cases exceeded, the poverty of northeast Thailand." [36] Many southern border communities, however, resented the government for turning their traditional subsistence economy, which they perceived as part of their culture, into a cash economy. At the same time, southerners also lambasted the government for not doing more to help people out of poverty. Bangkok seemed to be facing a catch-22 situation regardless of what it did. [37]

Something had to be done to assuage Thai Malay Muslim rebellion, however. It was growing at the same time the CPT was reaching its zenith. As a result, when General Kriangsak seized power in 1977, he not only improved COIN against the CPT, but also against the southern border insurgents. This included a new six-point strategy put into effect on 24 January 1978.[38] "This new policy," says Chuan Leekpai, "was considered to be the manual or guidance for any policy implementation for the four [southern] provinces for the first time."[39] The new strategy was:

1. To teach Thai Malay Muslims, particularly youngsters, to be proficient in the Thai language.

2. To foster trust between Thai Malay Muslims and the government.

3. To improve the standard of living in the far south.

4. To eliminate terrorist and separatist threats endangering the southern people, the territorial integrity of Thailand, and the king.

5. To persuade Muslim countries that Thai Malay Muslims are not being repressed and to halt support for their insurgent and terrorist activities.

6. Improve government administration of the southern border provinces. [40]

"Doing all this included several things," says Samacha Potavorn, a former Deputy Director of the Southern Border Provinces Administrative Command (SB-PAC), the political-economic coordination center for the southern COIN after 1980. "First was to believe everyone is Thai, regardless of faith. Next was to have the people behold a good attitude, coexist with others, and accept diversification, such as other people's culture, language; we must accept all these things about each other in Thailand. The next task was to upgrade the standard of living, including incomes. By this we wanted to reduce the social gap between rich and poor."[41]

Kriangsak also emphasized to southerners that Bangkok was not out to destroy Malay Muslim culture. A 1979 statement declared, "It is the government's sincere intention to avoid taking any measure which would create conflict with or adversely affect the feelings of the people on matters of education, custom, and religion."[42] This was vastly different from past government sentiments.

Getting all civil servants in the far south to adopt this attitude was not easy, so Kriangsak established guidelines for them. They had to be well-trained and high-caliber, not rejects from other provinces. They had to speak Malay, be Muslims (or at least well versed in the south's predominant Muslim culture), and be beyond reproach regarding corruption.[43] Of course, achieving these criteria was easier said than done, but there had to be a starting point, and Kriangsak provided it.

Kriangsak also placed Thai Malay Muslims in key government posts. He made members of the National Council for Islamic Affairs consultants for the MoI, and he appointed members of Provincial Councils for Islamic Affairs as consultants for provincial authorities.[44] Kriangsak demonstrated to southern border peoples through words and deeds his sincerity about including them in Thai society. He followed the essential COIN principle that deeds must match words, especially with downtrodden populations.

Ultimately, then, as with the communist COIN, Kriangsak set the stage for Prem, Harn, and their lieutenants to make badly needed upgrades to the COIN in the far south. In the end, these strategies showed good results, but Kriangsak happened to take over at a time when the southern insurgents were increasing their violence. This surging rebellion meant the government's new approach would not be so easily applied.

Overview of the First Southern COIN

1980–1983

In 1980, when Prem took over as PM, he applied communist COIN-style strategies and programs to the Thai Malay Muslim insurgency. General Harn, who had taken over as Fourth Army commander (1 October 1981–30 October 1983), tailored these strategies to fit the far south to great effect via the *Tai Rom Yen* Plan (Cool Shade in the South), which was rooted in the 66/2523 Plan. Prem also established two coordination centers to carry out the southern COIN: the Civilian-Police-Military Unit 43 (CPM-43), and the SB-PAC. CPM-43 was in charge of security operations. SB-PAC was in charge of political and economic development and some law enforcement activities, particularly investigations and community policing. These organizations would be the mainstays of Bangkok's southern COIN for decades to come.

Their impact was immediate, and insurgents responded with a rash of violence not only in the south, but in Bangkok as well. PULO bombed five targets in the capital in 1980, including a bus terminal and two rail stations, which wounded forty. PULO claimed responsibility for the attacks through a series of leaflets threatening more attacks if its demands were not met. The leaflets said, "Stop genocide, massacre on Malayu Moslem in Pattani immediately," and "If our demand do not come to term as you all know very well that the terrorism is a weapon of the international politics." PULO said it would bomb embassies, take hostages, and spread mayhem if the government continued its actions. It closed by asserting, "We strictly mean business. Allah akbar, Allah akbar, Allah akbar. Islam and Pattani must be free."[45]

Despite PULO's terrorist attacks, CPM-43's focused kinetic operations severely reduced the military capabilities of all insurgent groups early in the war. This broke up many of them into smaller cells, a positive development. Smaller cells, however, were more difficult to detect. But this is a typical pattern in COIN and part of the process of reducing insurgent forces.

Generous amnesty programs also contributed to reducing insurgent forces. Some 450 southern insurgents surrendered between 1982 and 1983. Orders from the PM for government personnel to treat Thai Malay Muslims with respect had a significant political impact. The RTA and the king's development projects signaled to Thai Malay Muslims that the government cared for them, thereby winning adequate portions of the population.

1984–1988

By 1984, the BRN's *Ulama* (Muslim scholars) faction, led by Haji Abdul Garim bin Hassan, was urging the southern insurgency to cease its war against the state. Hassan told rebels to seek a political resolution.[46] Hundreds complied, and the movement fizzled. Evidence indicates Bangkok also diplomatically courted Saudi Arabia to shut down PULO's main base in Mecca, which severely injured its operations.

The insurgency did not die, however. While politically minded insurgents compromised with the government, fierce Pattani nationalists did not. Neither did ultraconservative Muslims and a small but growing crop of Islamist extremists.[47]

Still, it was not so easy for these extremists to gather supporters. The government's integration programs via the SB-PAC bore fruit politically and economically. This lessened resistance to the state and shrank the insurgents' popular support base. The SB-PAC's full spectrum of large and small development projects greatly contributed to this trend, as did its interaction with Thai Malay Muslim leadership and rank-and-file villagers on a daily basis. As a result, locals held the SB-PAC in high regard, evidence of their increased trust in Bangkok. The SB-PAC directly increased the legitimacy of the central government in the eyes of Thai Malay Muslims. It was a landmark achievement in the far south.

As CPM-43 continued its kinetic operations, the government began a new amnesty program in October 1987, *Muslim Santi* (Muslim Peace). It was more or less the same as the early 1980s amnesty program but repackaged via public relations (PR) to ensure insurgents understood that they could surrender without penalty, so long as they had not committed acts of terror. As a result, 641 insurgents laid down their arms and swore allegiance to Thailand by January

1988.[48] This means beginning in 1980, over a thousand insurgents applied for amnesty, which effectively defanged about half the movement.

1989–1995

Chatichai Choonhavan took over as PM (4 August 1988–23 February 1991) after Prem left office and distanced himself from RTA COIN advisors. He relied instead on his own civilian advisors for COIN advice. While this did not kill COIN progress in the far south, it did not advance it, either. Chatichai's move caused the RTA, Thailand's traditional COIN leader, to lose significant power to Chatichai's civilian clique. For Bangkok, this was unfortunate, as follow-through in COIN is critical to lasting pacification and economic and political development. So much progress had been made in the south, however, that most people could not see this as problematic. In fact, General Chavalit—by 1990 Commander of the RTA—estimated southern COIN programs would end the insurgency by 1992.[49] This did not happen, however. The insurgency again reorganized into small cells as it had done during Harn's offensives.

A savvy Chuan Leekpai became PM in 1992 (20 September 1992–19 May 1995, and again PM from 9 November 1997–9 February 2001). He brought with him a vast array of knowledge of economic development programs, security issues, and local politics, particularly far south politics. His wide-ranging experience as DPM, Minister of Justice, Commerce, Agriculture and Cooperatives, Education, and Public Health was ideally suited for COIN leadership.[50] Under Chuan was the able General Kitti Rattanachaya, Commander of the Fourth Army (1 April 1991–30 September 1994). He was a scholar, a military man, and a diplomat.

During his command, Kitti furthered the demise of the southern insurgency to the point it nearly ran out of manpower. He believed, as Harn did, that although kinetic operations were highly necessary, they must be conducted in tandem with politics and development. He ran aggressive but focused security operations. After insurgents ambushed soldiers in Yala on 17 August 1993, killing two, General Kitti told the press, "We will not stop until the last man is killed," and he deployed RTA search-and-destroy teams with helicopter gunship support to neutralize the culprits.[51]

Kitti also personally interacted with the local population and its Muslim leaders as much as possible. He initiated direct negotiations with insurgent commanders hiding in the Middle East, spearheaded by his efficient and longtime subordinate Colonel Akanit Munsewat, now an RTA general. General Kitti developed an avant-garde amnesty program for the southern rebels that included work programs to give jobs to the poor, but it was not fully implemented at the time because of political constraints.

While Kitti's operations were largely successful, rebels still struck on occasion. From August 1993 to April 1994, insurgents carried out forty-nine acts of arson, four train bombings (plus an additional train-bombing attempt), and two major light infantry operations—a miniscule total compared to the height of CPT operations, but indeed destructive for the far south.[52] There was a rash of shootings and kidnappings as well. Kitti attributed the violence to desperation, saying that the insurgency had lost significant momentum and was lashing out in last-ditch attempts to impress overseas financial donors.[53]

1996–1998

In 1996, Deputy Permanent Secretary for Interior Paitoon Bunyawat took over security duties in the southern border provinces from the Fourth Army.[54] The RTA was still involved in operations, but the civilian-led MoI had commandeered its traditional and lofty authority. This was far more impactful than Chatichai's late 1980s move that pushed the RTA aside as key COIN advisor. The RTA lost some of its intelligence capabilities, which compromised its ability to monitor and thwart insurgent violence.[55] At the same time, though they usually worked closely together, a rivalry developed between the Fourth Army and the SB-PAC. One result of all these above-mentioned issues was coordination of the war began to suffer. None of this was positive, because, unbeknownst to the government, the insurgents had formed a new organization—*Bersatu*—that pooled the remnants of the old groups into one in an effort to revitalize their wilting rebellion.

Insurgent sabotage operations increased in 1996 to the point they scared investors away from a proposed regional trade bloc—the Indonesia-Malaysia-Thailand Growth Triangle—which was supposed to be centered in and bring new wealth to Thailand's far south. Accordingly, on 18 January 1997, PM Chavalit (25 November 1996–8 November 1997) announced an increase in troops and spending for the southern COIN.[56]

It was too little too late, however. *Bersatu* had matured and was ready to launch a major offensive. The RTA's intelligence network was blind to it, and the MoI had not been in charge long enough for its intelligence sources to report on the pending campaign. In essence, the enemy had slipped in during a change of command, a window when coordination, command and control, and intelligence are traditionally weak. *Bersatu* began striking a multitude of targets in the spring of 1997, in what were likely probing attacks to test the reaction of government security forces. By July, it began its Falling Leaves campaign of terror against civilians and security forces with full force.[57]

Falling Leaves entailed grenade attacks, and bombing public utilities, infrastructure, transport assets, and government and civilian buildings. Insurgents also burned schools and houses and assassinated scores of people. Authorities assumed factions of old insurgent groups such as BRN and PULO were responsible. They did not realize this was the work of a united front.[58]

By November 1997, Chavalit had resigned in the wake of the Asian economic crisis, and Chuan Leekpai once again took over as PM. Alarmed at *Bersatu*'s mass violence, Chuan, the MoI, and the RTA cooperated to restore order to the south and crush the insurgency once and for all. Military and government intelligence agencies published a threat report for the PM that analyzed the state of the insurgency as of January 1998. It was damning.

The report said violence had increased when PM Chuan took over, but did not blame his administration. It appears the timing of the offensive was coincidental with Chavalit's resignation. The report criticized local police for not having arrested more insurgents, which impacted public confidence in the government's ability to provide security. Loss of confidence in the government meant, at the very least, an empowered insurgency. At the worst, it meant more local support for insurgents.

Beyond these criticisms, the intelligence report listed six reasons why rebel violence had recently surged. First, it said local politics had fostered instability: "The fact is that community leaders and local leaders each turn to a political party for protection and as a means to build up their clout, because they do not trust the state authorities. At the same time, political parties are looking to the state authorities to help secure their political base and victory in the elections. This results in conflicts of interest. Every time there is a change in the government, a sense of insecurity and fear arises among state authorities and local leaders that they will not get support and they neglect their duties."[59] This was an indictment of the Thai political system and its leadership in the far south, a major weak point that obviously contributed to the insurgency's strength.

Second, the report stated insurgents had increased antistate propaganda. A large portion of the far south, especially rural people, believed the malicious things *Bersatu* said about the government. Third, intelligence said separatist leaders hiding in their Malaysian sanctuaries were still in full command of their personnel, intelligence, and logistics networks in Thailand, even though their personnel pool had decreased.

Fourth, some Thai Malay Muslim politicians neglected local affairs in pursuit of national-level politics. Ignoring local issues made the people feel isolated, which provided a vacuum for insurgents to fill. Fifth, the people of the far south still did not fully trust state security officials. Some police and military engaged in local corruption such as petty bribery, and others were involved in organized crime and possibly disappearances of innocent suspects.

Finally, drug trafficking and use had become rampant and destabilized the far south with increased levels of theft and murder. Conspiracy-minded Thai Malay Muslims believed non-Muslims were trafficking illegal drugs into the south to destroy Islam.[60] Insurgent leaders, on the other hand, relied heavily on drug users and dealers as fighters, especially for the Falling Leaves campaign.

The government's response to the Falling Leaves campaign was the *Pitak Tai* Plan (Renew or Protect the South). It strategized the destruction of insurgent fighting forces and the reintegration of its broader membership back into Thai society with a new and improved amnesty program. Key to *Pitak Tai*, however, was cooperation from Malaysia in shutting down cross-border insurgent sanctuaries, something Bangkok had sought for decades.

Bangkok finally got that cooperation in January 1998. As *Pitak Tai* was in full swing, Malaysian Special Branch raided several insurgent headquarters on Malaysian soil ranging from KAL to Kelantan, the latter being just across the Thai border. By the end of 1998, the vast majority of Thai Malay Muslim insurgent groups had been defeated, with only a handful of isolated members left, their always-tenuous sway with the population gone, their infrastructure destroyed.

For the RTG, it was a second clear-cut COIN success, but it had not come easy. As with the CPT, it had been a roller-coaster ride of changing strategies, commanders, and ways and means. Some of this was due to major government mistakes, such as petty rivalry and not understanding that the threat remained viable even as it seemed to diminish. There was no question about the end result, however. The southern insurgency born in the 1975 Pattani demonstration was over.

The Insurgents

Whereas the CPT was a nationwide, centralized, and politically unified insurgency, the southern insurgency of the 1980s–90s was not. It was localized to the south, fractured, and politically schizophrenic. There were more than fifty insurgent groups at the time, they all proclaimed to be fighting for some kind of independent "Patani state," and they all ran criminal rackets. Despite being splintered and gangster-like, however, they were political and violent enough to threaten Thailand's stability. In fact, Parliament published a report in 1978 stating Thai Malay Muslim separatists had overtaken the CPT as the most dangerous threat in the far south.[61] The main groups were PULO, New PULO, BRN and its splinter groups, and *Gerakan Mujahideen Islam Patani* (Pattani Islamic

Mujahideen Movement or GMIP).[62] There were scores of other, smaller organizations, too, including Black December and *Sabilillah*. And of course, *Bersatu* was active in the latter stages of the war.

Strategy

The Thai Malay Muslim groups were generally both criminal gangs and separatists. To fulfill their separatist goals, they sought to co-opt as much of the southern population as possible by intimidation and through appeals to nationalism, race, Islam, and Islamism while tearing down the government with acts of violence and propaganda.[63] They used both guerrilla warfare and terrorism—the latter in abundance—which made them more harmful to civilians than the CPT. Because of their factionalism, terrorism, and criminal activities, Professor Bhumarat Taksadipong says, "The movements did not have a lot of backing."[64] This lack of popular support was a key reason for their eventual failure.

No single insurgent group could claim to represent the interests and aspirations of the whole southern population. Says former RTG diplomat Arun Bhunupong, "We know that they were not ordinary criminals. They had political motives as well. But did they represent the whole people? We don't believe so."[65] He adds, "PULO and like groups, they emphasized more on nationalism. The BRN was radical revolutionary—leftist. The GMIP had religious motivations. Other groups had different motivations, so who could speak on behalf of the people living in the south?"[66] The answer, says Arun, was no one.

Organizational Structure

The smaller insurgent groups in the far south had gang-like structures. The larger ones, PULO and BRN, were more sophisticated. On a broad scale, these groups had three organizational levels. First, they had headquarters elements in Malaysia that organized and ran their movements. These headquarters included personnel, intelligence, strategic planning, training, propaganda, and logistics sections. Second, they had operational commands in Thailand's southern border provinces that ran violent and political operations. Third, they had foreign-affairs elements in countries overseas to secure financial and political support.

Effective organization of the southern insurgency ended there. In fact, these insurgents could better be described in terms of how they were *disorganized*. They were plagued by factionalism and could never stay united under one commander for too long. Says Police Major General Tritot Ronnaritivichai, Deputy Commissioner of Thailand's Special Branch, "Before, in the 1980s and 1990s, BRN, PULO, *Bersatu*, and New PULO...they all fought to be the leader of the region, but [except for a brief time in 1997–98] they could not unite."[67]

Che Man, the former *Bersatu* leader, asserts this was due to ideological and class differences. Groups such as the BNPP were conservative Islamists, the BRN was socialist Islamic, and PULO was everything to everyone—nationalistic to politicos, conservative Islamist to those recruited in Mecca, and a criminal syndicate to gangsters looking for a place to hide. None of these mixed well. BNPP and PULO managed to join forces in 1979 for a single year with guidance from the Muslim World League, but their disparities broke them up in 1980.[68] In this way, the southern insurgents acted not like the CPT or the IRA, but more like the PLO. The groups and their commanders became more important than their overall cause.[69]

Southern Insurgent Numbers

Because of factionalism, the number of insurgents and their auxiliary support in the 1980s–90s is difficult to discern. PULO, the largest group of the time, claimed twenty thousand members. Andrew Tian Huat Tan, a Singaporean expert on Southeast Asian terror groups, says it had one thousand fighters in the 1970s.[70] The BRN and its supporters might have been half the size of PULO at its height, and the GMIP and others never had more than company-sized units.

Total insurgent fighters at their peak might have reached three thousand. Auxiliary supporters could have numbered fifty thousand, and people who could be mobilized for public protests might have numbered one hundred thousand, as indicated by the Pattani Demonstration of 1975.

These rough figures indicate two things. First, the movement had enough fighters and auxiliary support to operate for several decades. Second, the movement did not have enough strength to triumph in the long run. The insurgency just did not inspire enough southern border people to rise up and overthrow Bangkok's rule. Southern Thai insurgency expert M. Ladd Thomas estimated that in the 1980s, a mere 10 percent of the local population supported the insurgents, 10 percent favored the Thai government, and 80 percent were neutral.[71]

Logistics and Sanctuary

While insurgents secured weapons and material locally, Malaysia was their main source of logistics and sanctuary. Food, weapons, ammunition, explosives, documents, intelligence, and a largely supportive population—all the things that make a guerrilla army work—waited across the border. Thai Malay Muslims living in Malaysia made this support possible.[72] Northern Malaysian citizens and some local government personnel seemed supportive of the insurgency, too. Otherwise, they would not have provided sanctuary.

To ensure ease of cross-border travel, many insurgents had dual citizenship. Border crossings for them raised no red flags with customs and immigration officials. According to Panomporn, "The separatists always have dual citizenship—Thai and Malaysian. This dual citizenship is a result of the 1960s when the Chairman of the *Patani Islam Parti* granted Malaysian nationality to people who resided in Malaysian territory for three years."[73] This comment provides more evidence local Malaysian government officials and politicians supported Thai rebels. It never appeared to be KAL's official policy, however.

Insurgent connections in Malaysia afforded rebel leaders unique status. For example, *Ustaz* Lukman Iskandar, a senior official in the BRN, allegedly was a member of the "Malaysian Voluntary Corps." Malaysia has scores of volunteer security units, in recent times referred to as the Police Volunteer Reserve, Volunteers of Malaysian People, and the like. These forces augment the police, military, and civil services doing security, defense, customs, and disaster relief work. If the assertion is true, then Iskandar and Thai Malay Muslim rebels like him would have been in ideal positions to create sanctuary and cross-border routes for their movements. Iskandar operated from Malaysia for decades, occasionally being arrested for rebel activities, but no charge was ever enough to imprison him long term, and it does not appear he was ever deported.[74]

Sanctuary in, and support from, the Middle East and South Asia were just as critical for the insurgents as Malaysia was. Che Man asserts the largest sources of insurgent funding were Arabic and Muslim charities. Charitable giving, or *zakat*, is one of the Five Pillars of Islam and a requirement of all Muslims. Insurgents exploited *zakat* to fund violence.[75] Funds also came from crime and local donations.

Regarding crime, Chuan says, "The separatists in the higher echelons like PULO and BRN, most of them were concerned with criminal pursuits, such as kidnap and ransom, drug running, extortion, things like that."[76] In 1998 in Narathiwat, for example, *Thahan Phran* clashed with a group of BRN and shot dead one of its members who had on his person extortion letters written in Thai and Jawi with the BRN letterhead.[77] (Jawi is Malay written in Arabic and is in common use in the far south.) As for local donations, active insurgent supporters with jobs were required to donate between forty cents and forty USD monthly. Local insurgent supporters also provided food to fighters that massed in the field for attack operations.[78]

Insurgents trained in southern Thailand, Indonesia, Malaysia, and the Middle East. Training in Thailand was sporadic, informal, and conducted in remote areas. Middle Eastern training took place in Saudi Arabia, Libya, Syria, Afghanistan, and Pakistan.[79] From the nature of insurgent operations, it is clear they trained in light infantry tactics such as raids and ambushes, plus assassinations, bomb making, and intelligence processing. Their endurance and flexibility also suggests training in clandestine intelligence operations such as covert communications, surveillance, and vulnerability assessments.

Political Operations

General Kitti writes that insurgents in the 1990s had nine specific techniques for penetrating local government offices and countering government COIN programs, of which only two were violent—techniques five and seven. The techniques were:

1. Winning enough popular support to get their representatives elected to positions at the local, parliamentary, and ministerial positions.

2. Inserting intelligence agents into state bodies.

3. Maintaining dual nationality to evade capture.

4. Placing their people into as many Muslim leadership positions as possible to preach separatism.

5. Eliminating Muslim leaders who did not subscribe to separatist ideology.

6. Using mosques for secret planning sessions.

7. Extorting money from Thai Buddhists and Chinese.

8. Transferring businesses from Thai Buddhists and Chinese to Muslims.

9. Using Malay instead of Thai in the villages.[80]

Aside from these political infiltration operations, the insurgents made great use of Islam to spread their rebellion. The way Islam is structured and how it functions provides an ideal network from which to rebel. And this was certainly the case in Thailand's far south. Surin writes that the southern insurgency became "a form of religious purification and moral imperative on the part of the religious leadership."[81] Insurgents tried to make it an Islamic duty of all Thai Malay Muslims to support rebellious groups. (This does not mean all groups were touting Islamism, yet. That would come later.) In 1979, the government recognized this trend, asserting, "To achieve this aim [a separate state], the separatists use, as their instrument, the differences in religion, customs, and traditions between the Thai Muslims and the rest of the population to drum up support from the local people."[82]

This was a practical strategy. Islam is not simply a religion to most Muslims. It does not provide just a moral compass or spiritual inspiration. Islam, through the Koran, the *Sunnah*, the *Hadith*, and rulings from Islamic scholars, provides guidelines and laws for politics, war, business, banking, taxes, family life, sex, marriage, burials—virtually every facet of life imaginable. Islam supplies a complete governing system ready-made to supplant rival governing systems. Accordingly, it was not necessary for insurgents in southern Thailand to import an ideology of rebellion and build a political network from scratch, as the CPT did with Maoism and a people's war. Islam, organic to the southern border provinces, provided the rebels with the framework they needed.

As the southern insurgency marched from the 1970s into the 1980s, it did so with a tailwind of global Islamist revival. This revival happened when Iran's firebrand, Ayatollah Khomeini, sought to spread his version of Shia extremism throughout the world, including to Southeast Asian countries such as Indonesia, the Philippines, Burma, and Malaysia. Bangkok viewed this with alarm. Panomporn says, "The most immediate concern of the Thai government [in the late 1970s] is the fundamentalist Islamic movement in Malaysia, which is now pressing for daily prayers at the mosques. They distribute pamphlet copies of speech[es], translated into Malay, by Khomeini."[83] Thailand was worried these ideas would filter across the border into Narathiwat, Yala, and Pattani.

Compounding Bangkok's worry was Saudi Arabia's response to Khomeini, which was to export a competing and equally extremist Sunni brand of Islam, generally known as *Wahhabism*. (While *Wahhabism* is a universally used term, followers of this sect do not use it and instead refer to themselves as *Muwahidun*, or Unitarians. Wahhab was a person, and *Muwahidun* believe using a man's name to label their movement is insulting because it implies placing a person between themselves and God.) Regardless, *Muwahidun* or *Wahhabism* proliferated more than Khomeini's Shia extremism, and it penetrated southern Thailand.[84] This Saudi form of Islam provided a political bonding element the insurgents could rely on to increase their "us versus them" mantra and deny non-Muslims a place in solving the far south's problems. Riding on the back of the global *Muwahidun* movement was a growing sentiment of Islamist jihadism.

In 1982, Surin predicted Islamist fundamentalism would eventually find its way to southern Thailand. "The Supreme World Council for Masjid," he wrote, "had already decided to set up its missionary activities in countries where there are Muslim minorities, such as the Philippines and Thailand."[85] This organization was a Saudi missionary group dedicated to spreading fundamentalist Islamism worldwide.

Thai Malay Muslim insurgents adopted five tenets in their fight. According to Surin, they were "race, language, religion, customs, and the consciousness of a separate identity."[86] All these items were directly related to Islam. The ultimate goal in pushing forward these five issues was to preserve Islamic customs and protect them from "racial pollution" coming from Thai and Chinese culture, Buddhism, and government regulations. Latching on to these issues could also inspire insurgent fighters to commit religiously sanctioned acts of violence.[87]

Insurgents adopted the *dawah* movement as a political vehicle to spread rebellion, propagandize, indoctrinate, and recruit. *Dawah* means "inviting to Islam." It was essentially a roving preacher type of movement where imams went from village to village urging people to adopt the *Muwahidun* brand of Islam. In the far south, insurgents simply merged the call to fundamentalist Islam with the call to revolt.

Interestingly, not all who joined the rebellion in the 1980s–90s adopted Islamist jihad beliefs, and not all the insurgent groups held this view as their core ideological mantle. In short, jihadism was popular, but not yet an ideological mainstay of the insurgency. This sentiment was new to the region and the movement, but it manifested itself in sufficient degree to spur violence and foster an uncompromising ideology among core followers. In short, while Islam provided an excellent mechanism for rebellion, not all southern rebels were jihadists, but it was catching on.

Regardless, according to Panomporn, founders of the *dawah* movement included former Member of Parliament Amin To'Mina, an unnamed chair of the Islamic Council of Pattani, and BRN leader Hajji Abdul Karim bin Hassan. These men's participation indicates the insurgency had penetrated the local Thai government. More, they cleverly set up the *dawah* in such a way as to protect it from government interference. Panomporn writes, "The *dawah* movement is conducted by religious leaders with the hope that the government will not be able to control it because there are no specific institutions in organizing the mission except for individual cooperation and discussion among themselves." [88] It was a stealthy political tool the government could not regulate, similar to *pondoks*. Aside from its Islamist sentiment, *dawah* propaganda and indoctrination contended that the RTG intentionally poisoned the south with gambling, drugs, and prostitution in order to weaken it and that it carried out injustices against the people.[89] Of course, none of this was true, but to the rural poor and uneducated, it worked.

Pondoks were a valuable political tool for the movement, as they were largely hidden from the government and hard to regulate. General Kitti asserts that insurgents focused most of their energies on indoctrinating the far south's youth into separatist ideals so that the movement would take root and fester with successive generations. [90] *Ustaz* could teach rebellion to rural, uneducated children who knew little about life beyond their villages, effectively brainwashing them into believing rebellion was not only a duty, but a normal way of life.

Some groups used Islamist lectures in classroom settings for indoctrination.[91] One of the BNPP's lessons for new recruits—not in *pondoks*, but in formal indoctrination classes—used a stanza from the Koran chapter, Surat Al-'Anfal ("The Spoils of War," VIII: 60) to justify terrorism:

> Against them make ready your strength to the utmost of your power, including steeds of war, to strike terror into (the hearts of) the enemies, of God and your enemies, and others besides, whom ye may not know, but whom God doth know. Whatever ye shall spend in the Cause of God shall be repaid unto you, and ye shall not be treated unjustly.[92]

Moderate Muslims do not interpret this stanza as justifying terrorism. Islamist jihadis do. By fusing rebellion and Islamism together, insurgent leaders insulated members from considering more peaceful alternatives. As an aside, al Qaeda (AQ) would use this very stanza to incite Muslims to violence in a terrorism manual discovered in 2000 by British Special Branch in Manchester.[93] Thai Malay Muslim insurgents would also use it when they launched a new war in the southern border provinces in 2004.[94]

Violent Operations

Southern insurgent operations included bombings, assassinations, and scattered light infantry operations. The fighters mostly used pistols, rifles, and commercial and homemade explosives. They acquired these weapons by smuggling or by taking them from the bodies of security officials whom they had killed. Says General Kitti, "The enemy's weapons were machine guns and assault rifles, but not too many. M-16s were hard for them to get. But they had some M-16s and AK-47s."[95]

They also conducted arson campaigns. Most of these were against state schools in protest of secular programs insurgents said would destroy Malay Muslim culture. In August 1993, for example, insurgents set fire to thirty-four schools simultaneously.[96]

The insurgents' criminal activities were like those of feudal warlords. Panomporn writes that these operations included "extortion, setting up roadblocks [for bribery], kidnapping Thai teachers and officials for ransom…in order to collect funds for strengthening their organizations."[97] Being in a war zone intensified their criminal activities and made it easier for them to engage in violence.

Aliyah Tohbala, the leader of the BRN in 1994, behaved like a warlord while climbing the ranks of his organization as he tore across the countryside, raiding and taking what he wanted from the population. In 1984, he came across a mother and a daughter tapping rubber. According to the *Bangkok Post*, Aliyah kidnapped the twenty-two-year old daughter, Anisah Dueramae, telling the mother, "I am taking your daughter, with or without your consent."[98]

"We were so scared at that time," Anisah told the press. "I cried a lot. My life has been different ever since." She said she wanted Aliyah to come home and be a father to their three children, but every time she urged him to quit the insurgency and surrender, he beat her.[99]

Sometimes insurgents would use separatism as a cover to mask their criminal activities. Says Professor Bhumarat, "They used the separatist image as value added for their enterprises. For example, if some random criminal kidnapped someone, their ransom letter might not hold much weight. Maybe no one cares. But if it's some separatist group, such as PULO—as in 'we, the Patani United Liberation Organization, have your daughter and will kill her unless you deliver to us a million dollars'—then it's very scary. People will be more motivated to bend to their will."[100]

Insurgent Groups

Scores of historians, political scientists, security professionals, and insurgents have written about the southern insurgent groups of the 1970s, '80s, and '90s. Their detailed histories need not be repeated here. Certain details on their activities are necessary, however, to explain the scope of the rebellion.[101]

Barisan Nasional Pembebasan Patani (National Liberation Front of Pattani)
The BNPP was the oldest and largest of the post-WW II southern insurgent groups. It was founded by Tengku Mahyiddin in 1959.[102] Originally, it was an ex-*raja*-driven political movement. The BNPP's 1981 constitution stated, "The basic political ideology of the BNPP is based on *al-Qur'an, al-Hadith* and other sources of Islamic law." [103] Its international connections in Kuwait, Saudi Arabia, Pakistan, and Malaysia also reflected the organization's Islamic commitment.[104] BNPP had a headquarters in Mecca.[105] "In fact," writes Angelo Carlo Valsesia, Thai insurgency author, "the BNPP network maintained relations with external subjects such as the Al-Azhar University in Cairo where they established a center

for advocacy and fund raising, as well as with the Organization of the Islamic Conference (OIC) and the Palestinian Liberation Organization (PLO)."[106] The OIC, one of the world's largest nonstate bodies, seeks to expand Islam around the world and protect and lobby for Muslim interests globally. As a result, it frequently becomes involved with insurgencies where Muslims are involved.

The BNPP funneled southern Thai youth into the University of King Abdul Aziz in Jeddah, Saudi Arabia. It had a headquarters in Kelantan, Malaysia, and maintained good relations with conservative Islamist parties in Malaysia such as the PI.[107] In 1986, the BNPP changed its name to the *Barisan Islam Pembebasan Patani* (Islamic Liberation Front of Pattani or BIPP) to reflect its religious leanings.[108]

BNPP received significant funds from the Middle East. Abdul Aziz Ibn Baz, President of Saudi Arabia's Department of Scholarly Research and Religious Ruling, once issued a *fatwa* saying the BNPP qualified for donations. The Muslim World League donated to the BNPP, and the Islamic Development Bank through the Islamic Solidarity Fund is alleged to have contributed, too. The Kuwaiti government's Welfare Department and the Islamic Call Society, also in Kuwait, were the BNPP's biggest donors, according to Che Man.[109]

Pattani United Liberation Organization

PULO was founded by Tengku Bria Kotanila (a.k.a. Kabir Abdul Rahman) in 1968 at Aligarh Muslim University near Uttar Pradesh in northeast India. Kotanila was a political science student from Pattani. PULO found inspiration for its name from the PLO.[110]

PULO's rallying cry was "national secularism." The movement did not shun Islam or Islamism, however. On the contrary, Kotanila's revolt called for the establishment of an Islamic state. He proclaimed, "The liberation of Patani from the yoke of the Thai imperialist is a matter of life and death for the Patani people in every level at all times. With all our might, the people of Patani will try and will continue to fight for the freedom of Patani and the emergence of an Islamic republic."[111] Islamic republics have some secular tendencies, but none of them are secular in a Western sense—witness Pakistan and Iran, both Islamic republics.

PULO's constitution states its ideology is anchored in Islam, nation, homeland, and humanitarianism.[112] For Islamist jihadists and similar sects, however, humanitarianism applies only to fellow Muslims. These groups believe that, in order to be truly human, one must be the jihadist version a Muslim.

This sentiment was also reflected in PULO's field operations. One PULO fighter's diary claimed he helped carry out twenty-five attacks from 1976 to 1979, resulting in seventy-nine dead and sixty wounded. The attacks included bombings, raids, kidnapping teachers, and, according to the diary, the murder of Muslims who were not sufficiently Islamist. This latter type of killing meant PULO had some radical Islamist tendencies such as *takfir*. *Takfir* is when a Muslim excommunicates another Muslim from Islam, which sets up the outcast to be killed as a *munafik* (a hypocrite or one pretending to be Muslim) or a *kafir* (infidel or nonbeliever). *Takfir* is supposed to be illegal in Islam, but AQ and like-minded terror groups have applied it for decades without a decisive backlash from the *ummah*, the global community of Muslims.[113]

Additionally, Chaiwat Satha Anand, Thammasat University professor and expert on the far south insurgency during the 1970s–80s, asserts PULO propagandized the population into believing it was their Muslim duty to fight *kafir*. PULO also told the southern population it was wrong to live under the rule of non-Muslims.[114] None of this was secular. In all likelihood, PULO wanted broad membership to increase its numbers, so it heralded "national secularism" while also practicing Islamist jihadism, obviously part of its core belief system. It is also possible the "national secularism" angle was a psyop dictated by the Islamist jihadist concept of *taqiya*. *Taqiya* is the duty of Islamists to lie and deceive in the prosecution of jihad. It originated in the Shia sect as a last-resort, self-defense mechanism, but Sunni Islamists adopted and altered it for their own offensive purposes. At any rate, *taqiya* allows jihadists to make political promises and then break them at will, to sign and then violate treaties, and to advocate for peace and justice and then commit murder. It is a built-in requirement for subterfuge, and it provides jihadists with great flexibility along religious, political, and military lines of effort.

PULO had a strong overseas network, including training and headquarters sites in Damascus, Syria, and in northern Malaysia. At one time its headquarters was in Tumpat, a city on the east coast of Malaysia just south of Tak Bai, Narathiwat.[115] PULO was so entrenched in Malaysia it issued identity cards to Thai Malay Muslims living there, which afforded them work privileges. This is yet another indication that many Malaysian officials and businesspersons at least passively supported the insurgency.[116]

PULO's prime recruiting ground in the early 1980s was Mecca, which was also its main headquarters at the time.[117] At least thirty thousand Thai Malay Muslims lived in Saudi Arabia in the 1960s–70s, in part due to Riyadh's lax immigration policies. Jeddah and Mecca were their two main gathering places. About fifteen thousand of them remained in Saudi Arabia through the 1980s–90s.[118]

In January 1980, PULO lobbied the Islamic Summit conference in Mecca and Taif for international assistance. In April 1981, it published an article seeking support for its cause, titled "Pattani Plea for Muslim Help," in the *Journal of the Muslim World League*. Chaiwat notes these missions were successful and resulted in substantial aid.[119] Insurgents scored another success in September 1984 in Perth, Australia, when the OIC's Seminar on Muslim Minorities stated that it should give full "moral and financial support" to safeguard Malay Muslim culture in Thailand and improve their economic situation.[120]

PULO excelled in violence, too. A streak of operations in the summer of 1980 demonstrates its effectiveness. In June that year, PULO set up a roadblock on the Pa-Lud Road in Narathiwat, checked cars for Buddhists passengers, and then executed the five they found. Leaflets at the scene announced the killings were revenge for PULO deaths at the hands of security forces. PULO repeated the roadblock-murder operation the following month, killing four Buddhists.[121] On 1 July, PULO launched a wide array of operations that wounded forty. It deployed five bombs in Bangkok: one in a movie theater in Thonburi that did not explode, one on a city bus, two at rail stations, and one at a bus terminal. On 13 July it burned a school.[122] In one case in 1986, authorities suspected PULO of throwing a small bomb onto the US Consulate grounds in Songkhla.[123] This was odd, because PULO and other southern border insurgent groups rarely, if ever, struck foreign government assets.

New PULO

Dates vary on when New PULO formed, but it was likely 1993. Regardless, PULO had leadership squabbles and it split—hence, New PULO.[124] Thai officials believed it received funds from Saudi Arabia, Kuwait, and Pakistan.[125] One of its earliest operations in August 1993 involved the burning of thirty or more schools in Yala, Pattani, and Narathiwat.[126] Working alongside the BRN in April 1997, it killed four rubber tappers in Betong, Narathiwat.[127] In February 1998, captured PULO insurgent Abdulharem Dorloh told the press that New PULO was continuing its violent operations while PULO had opted not to: "Haji Da-oh [of New PULO] still wants to use sabotage acts in his fight against the government while Haji Sama-aer [of PULO] disagrees with the strategy."[128]

Barisan Revolusi Nasional (National Revolutionary Front)

The BRN formed in either 1960 or 1968 (reporting varies) as a socialist group loosely aligned with the Communist Party of Malaysia and the CPT. For this reason, many imams shunned it. Its nexus with Islam came from Moammar Gadhafi's Libyan brand of Arabic nationalism-socialism. Gadhafi, a prolific sponsor of global terror and insurgent groups in the 1970s–80s, was a patron of several groups in southern Thailand.

The BRN also associated with what Che Man calls "liberal" Muslim countries such as Syria, Libya, and Algeria.[129] Despite its left-leaning roots, its first leader was ex-*pondok* teacher Karim Hajj Hassan. As a result, the BRN was exceptionally effective at recruiting *pondok* students.[130]

The BRN carried out multitudes of bombings and kidnappings. One of its more memorable operations was the 7 March 1980 attack on Yala town with six time bombs, which wounded seven.[131] It also carried out small harassment operations, such as in May 1994 when it placed a land mine that struck a BPP patrol in Yala, seriously injuring an officer. In August 1994, it raided a Yala army post, wounding one soldier.[132]

In 1994, the BRN also formed a "Muslim Commando Unit," which oddly was a religious psyops unit, not a fighting force. Government COIN operations had taken their toll, and the BRN had trouble continuing its violent operations, so it shifted mainly to political activism, just as the BNPP did in the 1980s when the government destroyed its military capabilities.[133] The BRN did not wholly cease its terrorist operations, however, and launched a slew of attacks in 1994.[134] In November 1997, it conducted joint bombing operations with New PULO on military, police, and local government targets to avenge the killing of BRN leader Arlee Torbala by police in Narathiwat.[135] This action seemed to be separate from the Falling Leaves campaign. Even as late as 1998, when all southern separatist groups were fading, BRN assassins were accused of murdering a suspected government informant in Narathiwat.[136]

BRN Splinter Cells

Three factions split off from the BRN: the BRN-Coordinate (BRN-C), formed in 1979; the BRN-Congress, formed in 1984; and the BRN-*Uran*, or *Ulama*, which also started in 1984. Sources vary as to whether the Coordinate or the Congress was the strongest of these.[137] Thai insurgency expert Zachary Abuza asserts the BRN-C sought public support in mosques for its program of separatism and Islam. He describes the group as "distinctly Islamist." In 1992, the BRN-C also formed a youth group, *Pemuda* (Youth).[138] In 1996, its main operations involved extorting protection fees from rubber tree plantation owners in Rangae district, Narathiwat.[139]

Gerakan Mujahideen Islam Patani (Pattani Islamic Holy Warriors Movement)

The GMIP formed in 1989 from disgruntled members of the BIPP and a small group called *Gerakan Mujahideen Patani*. Some analysts say it was more of a criminal organization than a separatist one, while others describe it as a political organization based in Malaysia with more than one thousand members and active in sabotage and extortion. Most analysts agree the GMIP had veterans of the Soviet-Afghan war in its leadership. It is alleged to have trafficked weapons for the Moro Islamic Liberation Front in the Philippines and the Free Aceh Movement in Indonesia.[140]

Black December 1902

This group was small and received little notice except for its assassination attempt by bomb (with help from PULO) on the king and queen on 22 September 1977 in Yala. Black December's name came from the month and year when Thailand and the UK (which then controlled Malaysia) agreed on their common border partition, officially annexing Patani into Thailand. Authorities initially believed that Black December 1902 began operations in January 1975 after announcing its presence via hundreds of propaganda leaflets. Shortly thereafter, Black December allegedly shot three Buddhist hunters in Yala, and it stabbed to death and then beheaded a postmaster in Yala.[141] The group also claimed to have bombed numerous targets in 1977–78.

Sabilillah (The Path of God)

Sabilillah formed during the Pattani Demonstration in 1975, where it handed out propaganda leaflets. It was responsible for the bombing of the Sungai Kolok-Bangkok express rail line on 4 June 1977. It also bombed the Hat Yai rail station in October 1978.[142] In a more daring operation, *Sabilillah* bombed Don Muang Airport in Bangkok on 4 June 1977.[143] In an interview with the *Far Eastern Economic Review* in 1980, the governor of Narathiwat said he "reluctantly respected" *Sabilillah*. It was the only insurgent group that concentrated on urban operations.[144]

Bersatu

Bersatu was an umbrella organization that brought together PULO, New PULO, GMIP, and the BRN.[145] It had its origins on 31 August 1989, when Che Man sponsored a meeting in Malaysia called "the gathering of the fighters for Pattani" and formed the "*Payong* Organization." Its formal name was *Majelis Permesyuaratan Rakyat Melayu Patani* (Patani Malay People's Consultative Council). It sought to unite all Malay Muslim insurgent groups but was unable to do so at that time. In 1991 it changed its name to The United Front for the Independence of Pattani, or *Bersatu* (United) for short. Che Man was the right person to unite the south's insurgent groups because he personally knew many of their leaders from their school days together in Egypt and Saudi Arabia.[146] His international Islamic connections, particularly with the Muslim World League, also gave him clout.[147]

In 1997, *Bersatu* declared jihad against Thailand.[148] This marked the beginning of the Falling Leaves campaign. It mostly targeted RTG personnel and assets such as local government workers, police, and teachers. The attacks included bombings, ambushes, grenade attacks, assassinations, and raids.[149] Because of effective government COIN operations, *Bersatu* was short on manpower, so it recruited drug dealers and users to carry out most of its attacks. They crossed into Malaysia, met with insurgent leaders for their operational orders, and then crossed back into Thailand to carry them out. *Bersatu* paid them five thousand *baht* each to go on the attack. The campaign spanned throughout Yala, Pattani, and Narathiwat.[150] Casualties included at least 146 security forces killed and eighty wounded.[151]

The At-Risk Population

Thailand's southern border population, as researched by Michel Gilquin in the 1990s and early 2000s, says these people were an "inward-looking, rural society" based on subsistence farming and fishing.[152] Aside from being geographically remote from the capital, in the 1970s–90s, the region had religious, economic, political, and cultural issues that, when added to corresponding Thai issues, made it more prone to insurgency. Insurgents in the area effectively used these issues to fuel their movements, highlighting every difference to enhance the "us versus them" sentiment always present in the region's psyche.

With regard to ethnicity and religion, the far south's population was then, as it is today, 75–80 percent Malay Muslim.[153] The remainder of the southern border area is Thai and Buddhist, with a smattering of Chinese. In contrast, about 3.5 percent of Thailand, or 2.1 million people, are Muslim. The total population of Thailand is 64 million and overwhelmingly Theravada Buddhist. There are twenty-seven thousand Buddhist temples in Thailand, but only three thousand mosques, 70 percent of which are in the far south.[154] Most southern Muslims are Sunnis and follow the Shafi'i sect.[155] They commonly speak both Malay and Thai, but rural and older people more often speak Malay. The latter also use Jawi as written script more than Thai.

Thai researchers Utai Dulyakasem and Lertchai Sirichai assert the mosque and the *pondok* have been, and remain, two of the most important institutions in the far south. They refer to the *pondok* as the region's oldest learning institution, which preserves Malay culture more than any other entity. Historians trace the first *pondok* to 1624 in Talomanok village in Narathiwat. Likewise, the imam and *ustaz* have been two of the most influential people in Malay society. They provide wisdom, knowledge, and guidance in all manners of life—spiritual, material, and political.[156] Perhaps a third of the far south's population adheres to conservative or ultraconservative Islam.

Muslims are represented in other parts of Thailand, including Bangkok, Ayutthaya, Chiang Rai, and Chiang Mai, but in those areas they live in harmony with the broader society and do not isolate themselves.[157] In contrast, many, but not all, Thai Malay Muslims reject Thai culture, asserting that it and Malay culture do not mix. Thai Malay Muslim specialist Omar Bajunid notes that they have historically been resistant to assimilating into the Thai state.[158] Malays have generally been willing to exist within the Thai legal framework while striving to be uniquely Malay Muslim, but some have placed adherence to Islam above state laws, causing friction with Bangkok.

Despite their adherence to Islam, Gilquin says many southern border people have traditionally had little knowledge of the Koran. Their knowledge of Arabic, the holy language of Islam, is scant, which has hindered their deeper understanding of the religion. Most locals have learned Islam by word of mouth, memorizing Koran verses by reciting them over and over again in Arabic without fully understanding the actual meaning of what they are saying.[159] Of this practice Gilquin writes, "This way of studying Islam was based on assimilating unchallengeable norms, rather than true acquisition of theological knowledge. Rationality and logic, though central to classic Muslim thought, were annihilated in rigid reading of texts which did not provide a means of facing a changing world."[160]

Since WWII, and especially in the 1990s, Gilquin says ultraconservative Islam has crept into pockets of the far south, clashing with traditional, more lax customs. For example, the *hijab* headscarf is the usual female Muslim garb in the region. *Hijab* suggests faith in mainstream Islam.[161] With the advent of Saudi-style Islam, however, the *niqab* has become more common. The *niqab* is a head-to-toe and face-covering garb that represents strict Islamist interpretations.[162] Of this trend, and the hint that jihadism might be close behind, Gilquin warned, "The development of these microsocieties, which seek a model in a mythical past having little in common with Southeast Asian society, needs to be watched."[163] His words were prophetic for the 2000s.

Radical Islamist insurgents were certainly active in the 1980s–90s. They saw Bangkok as an infidel regime that unjustly ruled over them, forbidding sharia law, ignoring the Koran, and dismissing the *Hadith*. Muslims susceptible to this indoctrination lashed out. "We arrested a Chinese Muslim convert in '92 or '93," says Professor Bhumarat. "We asked, 'Why are you so militant? You were not bred into it.' He replied, 'I must do something big to impress my Muslim friends, to prove I am a good Muslim.'"[164]

Regarding economics, in the 1970s–80s (as in the present), agriculture was the far south's dominant sector, specifically rubber (23.4 percent), rice (9.2 percent), fruit (3.1 percent), and coconuts (1.9 percent). There was/is also a palm oil sector and a robust but local fishing industry.[165] These sectors provide 45 percent of the region's jobs. The trading sector employs 15 percent of the population, tourism 13 percent, and miscellaneous industries account for the remainder. In the 1980s, a small industrial sector took root that included food processing, wood mills, and the like.[166]

Southern border people have traditionally not been big business owners. They are more often the labor pool for Thai and Chinese businesses, resulting in some resentment among Malays. *Pondok* education, however, does not equip its students to own or operate substantial businesses, nor does studying Islam overseas at the college level. The better-educated and business-savvy Thai and Chinese have naturally filled the vacuum.

During bad economic times, southerners have sometimes crossed the border by the thousands to work in Malaysia's service and labor sectors. Their families are scattered on both sides of the border.[167] The region is Thailand's third poorest, behind the north and northeast. While some in the south decry the state for turning the region into a cash economy, ongoing poverty has added fuel to the fire of insurgency.

Politically, the far south's population has been divided in its loyalty to Thailand. While loyalists have outnumbered rebels, rebellion is indeed a part of the region's social fabric and history. In the far south, loyalty to the state does not necessarily mean dedication to nation, religion, and king. For some it means loyalty out of convenience by a population with nowhere else to go. Up until the Pattani Demonstration of 1975, many southern citizens did not understand or care to participate in the national political system. Accordingly, insurgency as a way to expand their political voice offered an attractive alternative for these disaffected people.

Culturally, Thai Malay Muslims herald their identity and see themselves as unique. Malays all over Southeast Asia believe similarly. And Malay culture is indeed unique, fascinating, and rewarding. In Thailand, however, they are a dense minority surrounded by an equally rich and much different culture, which enhances the Malays' elite sentiment. They "cherish their cultural and linguistic distinctiveness," writes Bajunid.[168] Gilquin adds, "It is revealing that the term for converting to Islam in the local language, *masok melayu*, literally means 'to become Malay.'"[169] To a Malay Muslim, then, it is not simply an ethnic or religious issue. It is a merging of the two that has created an essence of deep cultural and historical importance.

Thai south cultural expert Andrew Cornish argues there is an understudied division between rural and town populations in this region. Rural people, at the time of his research (the mid-1980s–90s), far outnumbered town dwellers. He says, for example, in 1986, Yala and Betong, the two biggest towns in Yala province, accounted for only 26 percent of the province's population. Yet those in towns looked down upon country folk. Rural people were embarrassed to wear their "country" clothing to town, and they would even make fun of each other over their inability to navigate cities when tending to town business. More, people in towns were more apt to speak Thai to show their "sophistication." It was a definite divide that caused social friction. Conservative Islam, asserts Cornish, provided a social shelter from that friction, which is one of the reasons it was able to spread in the border provinces.[170]

Malay Muslims moreover believe in what Gilquin calls a "culture of prestige" where "notability seems a permanent quest."[171] It includes specialized hobbies such as top spinning, kite flying, and raising songbirds—all of which entail competitions. Koran reading competitions are common, too. Their culture holds Islamic study and the medical field in high esteem.[172] Despite seeing themselves as culturally unique, Gilquin notes "there is a desire to exist as social, economic, cultural, and political participants in the Thai framework."[173] Rebellion, then, is not necessarily a cultural demand. But insurgents have certainly tried to make it so.

Crime and violence are a part of the far south's culture, too. Historically, Malay Muslims have been hardy survivors in a tough, less-than-friendly agricultural environment. Duncan McCargo writes that theft, a readiness to fight, and an argumentative nature all characterize the region's arduous side.[174] The same traits have been cited in Northern Ireland as one of many reasons the Irish Republican Army adopted insurgency and terrorism.

McCargo adds these rough-and-tumble attributes, coupled with a high level of crime and insurgency, characterize not only the population, but its politics as well.[175] Kidnap and ransom schemes, smuggling, and extortion by criminal gangs are not uncommon. Organized crime heads called *chao pho* (godfathers) were particularly prevalent in the 1980s.[176] Gilquin notes that while Islam forbids gambling, Thai Malay Muslim culture has a "clandestine betting" penchant for animal fights with roosters, buffaloes, and fish.[177]

Gilquin also says many Thai Malay Muslims compound their unique view of themselves with a "nostalgic" and "embellished" history, not because it is irrelevant, but because it is largely undocumented and oral. Some Thai Malay Muslims, however, are fiercely protective of their version of their own history, which is replete with glorious economic, political, and military feats. It also entails some extreme cruelty at the hands of Siam. Rebel-minded southerners believe they are a defeated, colonized, and occupied people. To them, their history proves it. This clashes with Thai versions of the far south's history, which have dismissed the antagonistic parts and held Thailand in a more paternal light. These two contradicting historical views encumbered Thai–far south relations not only in the 1980s–90s, but in the present as well.[178]

Another factor exacerbating Malay-Thai cultural clashes was the use by many Thai of the word *khek* to refer to Thai Malay Muslims. Most political scientists in Thailand assert *khek* is a racial slur. Technically, it means "guest," but southern border peoples took it as a great insult, which fed their feelings of isolation and neglect. Insurgents have used this to their advantage, again to enhance an "us versus them" sentiment—a "They call us *khek*!" kind of attitude.[179]

Who joined the insurgency depended on how all these issues—religion, economics, politics, and culture—impacted individual Thai Malay Muslims. Some fiercely proud Malays may have disliked Bangkok's "Thai-centric" rule but were not willing to kill over it. On the other hand, impoverished individuals who harbored Islamist ideals and had suffered mistreatment by the government found it easier to join an insurgent group.

Religion was indeed key to being a southern rebel in the 1980s–90s, even if a rebel group did not necessarily espouse radical Islamist ideology. Most rebel leaders were religious. Che Man says they were primarily Middle Eastern–educated with a clear religious bent. Of the thirteen leaders of the BNPP, for example, one was a secular teacher, one was a lawyer, and all others were Muslim teachers. Che Man asserts the religious elite were the insurgency's "stronghold of cultural resistance."[180] Islam was an undeniable bonding agent for rebellion.

As in many insurgent and terror movements, some people remained constantly in a state of rebellion simply because it was their job. Much like Yasser Arafat of the PLO, some southern Thai rebels had been professional insurgents most of their lives. Insurgency paid their salaries. War was their profession, rebellion their career. Peace would mean the end of their far-reaching power, salaries, and status. "Even when the insurgency was not too active," says an anonymous Thai security official, "they are rumored to have called the authorities to ask where they could set off a bomb that wouldn't hurt anyone but would still make a dramatic statement. They needed the press coverage so foreign money sources would continue to fund them."[181]

Strategy

As with the war against the CPT, Thai COIN strategy for the far south went through several changes. This was due to many factors. Among them were leadership changes and the ever-fluctuating nature of the war in the south. The leaders of the southern COIN had an advantage their communist-fighting predecessors did not have, however, and that was legacy COIN knowledge. The CPT COIN strategists had to struggle, experiment, fail, succeed, and wait for conventionally minded commanders to leave government service to apply their winning strategies. The southern COIN strategists, on the other hand, had these CPT COIN lessons at their fingertips. Not that all CPT lessons applied to the far south. They did not. As with all insurgencies, the far south required a tailored approach. The general strategic concepts, however, were indeed there. Ultimately, there were three broad strategies for the war—the *Tai Rom Yen* Plan of the 1980s, an "economics leads" strategy of the mid-1990s, and the *Pitak Tai* Plan of the late 1990s.

The *Tai Rom Yen* Plan

The *Tai Rom Yen* Plan was General Harn Leenanond's COIN plan for the far south. Harn produced it on 2 October 1981 as Fourth Army Order No. 751/2524.[182] The plan was remarkably similar to the 66/2523 Plan but tailored to fit the nuances of the far south. "The strategy was to use development coupled with security. It was our Cold War strategy," says General Perapong.[183] The overall goal was to eliminate the terror and insurgent groups operating there, including the CPT, the Communist Party of Malaysia, and Thai Malay Muslim rebels.[184]

Underlying *Tai Rom Yen* were two key motivations not to give up the far south. First, Thailand did not want to give up territory. It had spent most of its pre-WWII days fending off territorial loss, or the threat of it, to Europeans and Asian neighbors. Territorial integrity was not only in Thailand's blood, it was a constitutional mandate.[185] Second, Thailand did not want hostile groups to set up an unfriendly state on its southern border. If PULO, for example, achieved independence, what would that state look like, who would it war with, and who would it ally with? Because of PULO's track record, Bangkok assumed such a state would jeopardize the nation's safety and economy, so it was a national security imperative not to allow secession.

The *Tai Rom Yen* strategy was simple and designed for a small, regional war. It contained four points:

1. To secure the lives and properties of all the people regardless of ethnicity and religion. Both Thai Buddhists and Thai Muslims will be protected by government forces from the threat of communist insurgents, terrorist movements, Malaya communist terrorists, and various influential persons.

2. To establish security on the Thai-Malaysian border area in order to revitalize the economy of the border provinces and to upgrade good relations between Thailand and Malaysia.

3. To eliminate by peaceful means dictatorial, influential, and shady power, which dominate the region, in order to ensure that all the people enjoy their right, freedom, and equality, be it political, economic, or social, under a constitutional monarchy.

4. To establish good relationships and to manage conflicts between the authorities and the people. [186]

This was the first coordinated, long-term strategy the government had ever applied in the south, and the trend continued into the 1990s. In fact, Chuan Leekpai says all southern COIN strategies post-1980 were designed so successive governments would not have to significantly redesign their approaches to the insurgency, although some changes did occur.[187] The strategy also made clear that success depended on treating ethnic Malays as full Thai citizens.

There was a key difference between *Tai Rom Yen* and the communist COIN approach, however—namely, the inclusion of the integration policies that the government had followed in the 1960s–70s. Integration was not specifically stated in points one through four, but it was broadly inferred, and it remained in practice. Even after General Harn left the Fourth Army in 1985, the commanders who followed him adhered to integration policies.[188] The goal of integration remained the same: to get Thai Malay Muslims to accept (1) central government rule and (2) that other races and religions were a part of southern society. One key in shaping these attitudes was to co-opt southern moderates and neutrals in order to isolate the rebels. Secular education, so as to insulate the people from being gullible to insurgent propaganda, was "one of the most important strategies of the army and the Thai government," writes Panomporn.[189]

Amnesty was absent from the specifics of *Tai Rom Yen*, but the 66/2523 Plan applied nationwide, so General Harn did not have to expressly mention it. Besides, amnesty was not a new concept in the southern war. Insurgents had surrendered in the 1970s, and they continued to do so in the 1980s–90s.

Only rarely did the government grant amnesty to terrorists, however. Professor Arun explains, "So our policy at that time was to treat the various organizations as criminals instead of political groups. Their tactics at the time were criminal— extortion, kidnapping, and arson from time to time." [190] Auxiliary support personnel and low-level fighters could, however, surrender without punishment.

General Akanit adds, "Look, PULO and the others might have been insurgent groups aiming for independence, or whatever they thought that was, but they also excelled in extortion, organized crime, and killing civilians with bombings. So, during that time, we fought PULO and the other insurgents by using the criminal law. With the communists, we used the anticommunist law. With [that], we had the authority to grant amnesty. But it was criminal law for the southern insurgents. They murdered civilians."[191]

The Thai included diplomacy as a strategic add-on to *Tai Rom Yen* by the 1990s. This was a new approach because, in the early 1980s, Bangkok tried to handle the insurgency internally, and it did so with a good measure of success. Professor Arun explains, "At that time, you know, we used intelligence, patience, and an internal policy to handle the matter. Without looking far to other countries, even to Malaysia, when their connection was by blood and ethnicity."[192]

When the nexus between the insurgents and foreign support became clear, however, General Kitti, Fourth Army commander in the early 1990s, changed course. He spearheaded a diplomatic initiative with Malaysia and insurgent leaders hiding in the Middle East, which continued after he left. He used *Tai Rom Yen* points two and three to apply diplomacy in order to isolate the rebels from their foreign support base.

Of the several key strategic thinkers on the south, aside from Harn, Kitti was one of the most important. General Kitti spent his entire service in the Fourth Army, some thirty years. He served as its G-2 (intelligence) director for about four years, and he was also in the G-3 (operations and planning).[193] Kitti read classic books on insurgency such as Sir Robert Thompson's *Defeating Communist Insurgency*. He studied the Vietnam War intently, from the French involvement to the US-led campaigns.[194] When he graduated from the RTA's primary military school, his first post was Songkhla. Kitti says, "When I studied at the Army War College, I studied the four southern provinces: Yala, Narathiwat, Pattani, and Songkhla. And when I studied in the Defense College, I studied again the Fourth Army area. It took my whole career." General Kitti began as a lieutenant and ended his career as a lieutenant general.[195]

General Kitti was a subordinate of both Generals Prem and Harn, so he learned about COIN on the job from them as well. "I worked rather closely with Prem, when he was the Supreme Army Commander, and when he was PM, too," he says. "When I was a division commander, we met a lot in Songkhla. Regarding General Harn, I worked with him when he was Fourth Army Area Commander. I was deputy commander of the Fifth Infantry Division." General Kitti drew on this vast experience to author four books on the troubles in the southern border provinces.

Kitti's military upbringing was vastly different from the COIN fighters who took on the CPT. They had to learn about COIN and communism gradually. In contrast, Kitti was seemingly born for COIN, and it appears the RTA groomed him to specialize in the south. And he went along, willingly. He did not have to learn the hard way about politics leading the military, the use of focused force, and securing local advisors and buy-in for COIN. He was bred into it. In a broader perspective, then, it appears the RMA that led to the defeat of the CPT prepared Kitti and others like him to carry on the fight in the far south long after the Prem clique had left the field.

Economic Strategy

In the mid-1990s, the government realized the south had somewhat stabilized, and the time had come to capitalize on that lull. Thai strategic thinking understood the nexus between poverty and insurgency as early as 1965. And while the economic programs of the 1980s had kept the southern border population from falling deeper into poverty, they were still the third-poorest people in Thailand, which helped the insurgency fester. To fix this problem, the government in 1994 changed its strategy from a "politics leads" core to an "economics leads" core. The actual strategy was spelled out as follows: "Economics leads, public relations follows, peace and order supports."[196] The end goal was to develop industries that could employ much of the population on a sustained basis, thereby keeping them working, out of poverty, and, hopefully, disinclined to rebel. As the second part of this equation states, PR would alert the public of this goal and herald economic successes as they occurred, indicating the Thai continued to tout successful psyops methods learned during the CPT COIN. Unfortunately, this initiative it did not end the insurgency. Four years later, Bangkok would alter the strategic mix to deal with new, violent realities.

The *Pitak Tai* Plan

In 1998, in response to the Falling Leaves offensive by *Bersatu*, the RTG drew up a new strategy called *Pitak Tai*. One of its main drivers was PM Chuan Leekpai. *Pitak Tai* differed administratively and legally from past COIN strategies because it did not rely on anticommunist laws.

Specifically, the RTA and MoI both agreed communism had long since been defeated and criminal laws already in existence would suffice to keep domestic peace. The government then ceased its reliance on the 1952 Anticommunist Act, which had previously served as the legal bedrock for previous COIN strategies and moved forward using criminal law.[197] *Pitak Tai* operations began in January 1998, but official sanctioning of the strategy did not occur until July 1998 via PM Order 127/2541.

Pitak Tai was very much like the 66/2523 strategy. It had a force component and two political components: amnesty and diplomacy. Like the communist COIN, amnesty allowed insurgents back into society, but with conditions. The government used hard-hitting kinetic operations to scare insurgents into a choice between fighting—and dying—or accepting the government's generous rehabilitation program. Regarding diplomacy, the main thrust of *Pitak Tai* aimed at getting Malaysia to go beyond border security cooperation and actually identify and arrest Thai Malay Muslim insurgents based in their semiclandestine sanctuary in northern Malaysia. This was a major change in policy, and something General Kitti had attempted but, for unknown reasons, had been unable to achieve.

Special Branch Commissioner Somkiat Phuangsup was the main architect of the amnesty program under *Pitak Tai*.[198] Commissioner Somkiat spent just a year as Special Branch Chief, beginning in mid-1997. He was not a southern insurgency expert like Kitti and Akanit, nor did he have an intricate understanding of southern political and security issues like Chuan. What Somkiat had was incredibly valuable crime-fighting experience. He had been a policeman for thirty-four years and had spent significant time in Bangkok running informants, conducting investigations, and case-building against suspects. These are critical COIN and counterterror skills necessary to any irregular warfare effort. One of his colleagues said of him, "Mention his name and every hired gunman felt a chill down his spine."[199] When he took the Special Branch position, he brought his dedication and long experience in investigative skills to bear, using them to identify, locate, and neutralize insurgent leaders and their networks.[200] Just as critical, however, as one of the highest-level law enforcement officers in the whole of Thailand, he had the authority to make amnesty stick.

Coordination

Under Kriangsak and Prem, COIN coordination became doctrine, not only for the communist COIN, but also for the war in the far south. "According to the army," writes Panomporn, "integration of this area in the 80s must be unified and systematized for security purposes." [201] Up to that point, political, economic, and security affairs had been uncoordinated and done piecemeal. The chain of command was muddled and ineffectual. Thai leaders of the 1980s realized this, and they also knew from their own experiences with the communist COIN that discombobulated agencies and a divided government hindered operations and allowed the enemy to strengthen. In the south, the government used ISOC and CPM-43 to coordinate and execute security programs and the SB-PAC to coordinate and execute most, but not all, political and economic programs.

Internal Security Operations Command and CPM-43

ISOC and the CPM concept proved successful in the communist COIN, so there was no need to reinvent a security coordination scheme for the far south. Prem made CPM-43 official via PM Order 8/2524 on 20 January 1981.[202] The security chain of command for the south was the same as for the communist COIN, except for the injection of the Fourth Army into the mix. The PM was in command of all COIN efforts. The National Security Council served as a security advisory board and policy maker.[203] ISOC, specifically ISOC-4, served as the regional coordinator, and CPM-43 was the on-the-ground implementer. (ISOC 1, 2, 3, and 4 coordinated national security affairs in Army Regional Commands 1, 2, 3, and 4, respectively.) The Fourth Army had major influence at all levels. Says General Kitti, "The Fourth Army commanded the army and police under CPM-43. The PM let the Fourth Army solve the problems. The government made the policy, but the Fourth Army ran the projects, the planning, devised how to fight, figured out the tactics. It executed operations, got in touch with the people and, eventually, the rebels."[204]

Early in the war, General Kitti was the Fifth Division commander of the Fourth Army. There were ten thousand soldiers in a division. He says, "We had the responsibility to deal with this problem in the south, but only some of my unit, not the entire Fifth Division." This was in accordance with Prem's policy of using force, but not too much. Other units assigned to CPM-43 included eight hundred Marines and nine hundred *Thahan Phran* of the 41st and 43rd Regiments.[205] Standard units of the RTP and BPP of Police Region 9, the police command for the entire south, also participated.

"The functions of the combined force, or CPM-43, were many," says Chuan. "First, it gathered intelligence about the insurgency. Second, it engaged in prevention of insurgent attacks, which was like physical security. Third, it carried out suppression operations against insurgents, actively seeking out and engaging them through military operations."[206]

The RTA largely took responsibility for security in rural and mountainous areas where guerrillas might coagulate, and the RTP took responsibility for security in populated areas. The RTA mostly operated at the *tambon* level with rifle companies, sending QRFs to aid CPM forces and react to intelligence concerning insurgents on the move. This is where the RTA identified, fixed, and fought guerrillas with ambushes, raids, and pursuits.[207]

There were exceptions, however, and the Thai stayed flexible regarding deployments. Sometimes, this would result in a seesaw effect with insurgents. When the RTA conducted operations in the mountains, it sometimes forced insurgents into the plains and towns. Insurgents occasionally used these times to stage attacks in areas where the RTA was not. This was a natural guerrilla reaction to government operations that were not entirely seamless, but ideally should have been. More troops were necessary to facilitate more uniform coverage of the war zone.

A side project of CPM-43 was the Land Resettlement Project. It took Thai Buddhist volunteers from the south and other parts of Thailand and provided them farmland on the Thai-Malay border. The farmers not only tilled their plots, they collected intelligence and provided security, too. The government trained and organized these farmers. There is no evidence the program was successful, however. Insurgents penetrated the border at will, and puritanical Thai Malay Muslims protested the program as an effort to dilute their ethnic monopoly.[208]

The Southern Border Provinces Administrative Command

In September 1980, at the Senanarong RTA base in Songkhla, top government officials discussed the pros and cons of establishing a new administrative center for the far south that would focus on political, cultural, economic, and development issues. The existing CC did not work, so they decided to create a new agency that would have the needed clout and competence to get the job done.[209] That agency was the SB-PAC. The Thai nicknamed it *Saw Aw Paw Taw*.[210]

The PM sanctioned the SB-PAC with the same order that established CPM-43, Order 8/2524.[211] It began operations in Yala, in the old CC building, on 23 March 1981 (unofficial SB-PAC documents say it began operations in February 1981).[212] SB-PAC's main job was to apply CA, economic, and political programs at the local level, help the military maintain law and order, and restore peace to the area.[213] An official SB-PAC history states: "Since its establishment in 1981, A.D., SB-PAC had carried out various tasks mainly concerning psychological activities to win the hearts of the citizens of the fivesouthern border provinces and enhance mutual understanding between government officials and the general public of the era."[214]

According to Chuan, "The function of SB-PAC was to command and supervise government agencies in the area as they carried out tasks to improve the plight of the southerners. It worked with the military to transfer corrupt officials out of the south and focused on improving the effectiveness of local officials and the local government apparatus. It moreover drew up plans for development and followed up and evaluated those projects. It had a local advisory board to aid it in its planning and decision making. And it also did other jobs assigned by the Fourth Army commander."[215] The SB-PAC had 175 civil servants in 1981, 132 of which came from the MoI.[216] It added more personnel as needed.

The SB-PAC's chain of command was clear and concise. It was an MoI organization, which meant MoI management of operations and budget. PM Prem directly supervised it, however.[217] This latter arrangement signified the government's desire to circumvent the inadequate DoLA that had clashed with the CC.[218] In short, if the SB-PAC ran up against administrative, political, economic, or security roadblocks, its higher-ups could solve the problem by a single phone call to the PM. This system worked well.

Since the Fourth Army commander was in charge of all COIN operations in the far south, he also ranked above the chief of the SB-PAC. RTA commanders rarely micromanaged the SB-PAC, however.[219] For the most part, the RTA let it run its own affairs, especially since it had a direct line to the PM.

The National Economic and Social Development Board (NESDB) was also in the SB-PAC's chain of command. The NESDB was an agency on par with the lofty NSC, and it planned the SB-PAC's economic and social projects at the strategic level. The Office of the Secretary of the Royal Initiatives Projects (RIP) also had a hand in making development policy for the far south, but royal projects were not under the purview of the SB-PAC. They fell under the Thai royal family.[220]

Tasking

The SB-PAC sought to produce improvement in five areas: social, political, foreign relations with Muslim countries, economic development, and security.[221] Within these areas, SB-PAC had seven main responsibilities:

1. Supervise all government agencies working on political, cultural, and economic projects in the southern border provinces.
2. Manage all SB-PAC projects.
3. Identify corrupt or inept government officials working in the far south and turn their names and transgressions over to the Fourth Army commander for their removal from office.

4. Help develop the capabilities of the government personnel to make them better civil servants, especially with regard to recognizing the culture of the southern border provinces.

5. Insure all SB-PAC projects were coordinated with the appropriate agencies and CPM-43, and to collect and analyze information of such projects to monitor their progress and effectiveness.

6. Assign, from the local community, advisors to SB-PAC to ensure projects were carried out according to local needs and customs.

7. Execute the orders of the Fourth Army commander.[222]

To this set of responsibilities, the government added seven somewhat overlapping objectives for SB-PAC:

1. Promote the Thai language, to improve understanding between the government and people, and to improve the locals' quality of life.

2. Increase "cross-cultural contact" between Malay Muslims and persons of other religions and races throughout Thailand.

3. Consult with local Muslim leaders in all aspects of SB-PAC work.

4. Coordinate all government administrative bodies in the border provinces.

5. Demonstrate to Muslim countries the situation in the far south and secure their help in cutting off outside aid to insurgents.

6. Upgrade social and economic projects to increase the standard of living of people in the southern border provinces.

7. Protect locals from terrorism.[223]

While the central government made broad policy, the SB-PAC had the power and the responsibility to plan and carry out projects in the field. It also dealt directly with Islamic leaders and appointed local advisors.[224] This was one of the organization's strong points. Chuan explains, "The government, no matter the level, got information from local business leaders for plans and projects that were necessary to enhance the south, so these were always reasonable projects."[225] In other words, SB-PAC was not simply executing plans from Bangkok. It listened to locals and was responsive to their needs, a crucial aspect of COIN.

The government intended the SB-PAC to become the continual torchbearer of a specific southern border COIN policy despite changes that might occur in the central government. Says Chuan, "Together with the policies created and following amendments, the SB-PAC was used to guide policy implementation in the area despite government changes in Bangkok. So new governments at the national level relied on the SB-PAC to help maintain stability in the south. We can say that through this national security policy, it helped various agencies execute their policies with continuity, and it helped resolve the problems effectively."[226]

Organization

The SB-PAC began with eight divisions, but in 1981–82 the government changed its structure to seven divisions:

- Planning and Projects
- Information
- Registration
- Personnel
- Education and Religious
- Psychological Operations and Public Relations
- Research and Evaluation[227]

The cabinet, at the behest of the Fourth Army commander, assigned four special committees to SB-PAC that focused on political integration. These were referred to as Advisory, Psychological Operations, Master Plan (for establishing border security), and Educational Improvement.[228]

The Fourth Army commander saw these as political, cultural, and social means that were pivotal to pacifying the far south. Additionally, he would have sway over who headed and served on these committees. The Fourth Army's chief representative to the SB-PAC headed the Psychological Operations Committee, for example. CPM-43's commander headed the Master Plan Committee. Not all committee heads came from the military, however. The Vice Rector of Prince of Songkhla University headed Education Improvement. [229] Regardless, all committees were designed to work closely with the local population, a major switch from the CC's tendency to seek minimal input from Malay Muslims. As a result, the SB-PAC earned the respect of many southerners and became a positive force in the region.[230]

Overall, the ISOC/CPM-43/SB-PAC chain of command worked well until the end of General Kitti's tenure as Fourth Army commander in 1994. Around that time (sources do not say exactly when) the RTA ceded significant power to the SB-PAC and the MoI. Around 1996, the government placed Deputy Permanent Secretary for Interior Paitoon Bunyawat in charge of security in the far south.[231] This included intelligence and command and control of COIN operations, which pushed the RTA and its robust human intelligence network aside. The government then suddenly lost a large part of its situational awareness in the insurgency zone, a dire development.[232]

It is unclear what caused the change in coordination authority. Perhaps successful suppression operations led the SB-PAC and MoI to believe there was no need for a heavy military presence. Maybe power politics played a role, such as when the Army Region Commanders took power from CSOC in 1967. Alternatively, the SB-PAC might have lobbied Bangkok for the army's dismissal over turf issues. Whatever the cause, coordination between the RTA and SB-PAC declined, and the insurgents eventually exploited this weakness with their 1997 Falling Leaves campaign, preparation for which most likely began in 1996, if not earlier.

In May 1997, Army Commander-in-Chief General Chettha Thanajaro recognized the organizational breakdown and subtly warned of the resulting dangers. He told the press these command-and-control changes had resulted in "coordination problems among local officials," but did not elaborate further. He also said, however, he had ordered the Fourth Army to cooperate with the civil service, regardless of who was in charge of what.[233] The implication was the RTA had become less inclined to collaborate since the SB-PAC had taken command.

By the spring of 1997, however, it was too late for the two sides to reorganize and cooperate. *Bersatu's* violent campaign had begun, and people were getting killed. Other government leaders realized the folly of the civil-military breakdown in the midst of the Falling Leaves mayhem. Interior Minister Sanan Kachornprasart said that in December 1997, the SB-PAC did not have the funds to operate security programs. He further stated the various intelligence agencies in the far south were not integrated and therefore ineffectual. He contemplated shutting down the SB-PAC because of the morass.[234] Ultimately, it appears the governors and the SB-PAC did not have the expertise to run full-spectrum COIN operations without RTA assistance.

When the Falling Leaves campaign peaked, it prompted major coordination changes. Many government ministers saw the SB-PAC as having failed to detect and prevent the operation. Deputy Interior Minister Chamni Sakdiset on 23 December 1997 suggested moving all far southern national security issues to the cabinet level, which would have cut out the SB-PAC, CPM-43, and the Fourth Army from local decision making altogether. Minister Chamni said the problems going on in the border region at the time were beyond the SB-PAC's problem-solving abilities, especially since smuggling and drug use had increased during the 1990s. He indicated the SB-PAC needed to be restructured as a coordinator between the RTP and RTA, and talks with KAL were necessary to prevent insurgent violence and crime along the southern border. Obviously, this meant the fragile relationship between the army and police had also fallen into disarray, and the security situation on the ground was suffering.[235] While Chamni's suggested changes did not occur, they reflected the central government's frustration with the south's coordination breakdown. Without proper coordination, the southern COIN was failing.

Instead of making drastic changes in the wake of the Falling Leaves campaign, Bangkok shifted portfolios within the existing coordination structure. The SB-PAC went back to political and economic affairs, and it also took on a new psyops task: educating locals on the perils of insurgent groups, their propaganda, and how to avoid becoming embroiled with them. PM Chuan put the Fourth Army and its CPM-43 back in charge of all intelligence and force application operations. ISOC retained its coordinating and resource-providing role. [236] General Kitti, though now retired, still lent his wisdom to the government. He supported these moves, but reminded Bangkok to follow through on post-operational security measures to ensure insurgents and criminals did not melt away only to reconstitute and return. Surin Pitsuwan was against the return of the military and lobbied for restraint.[237]

Interior Minister Sanan Kachornprasart agreed with bringing back the Fourth Army, an unusual stance since the move usurped authority from his portfolio. He was a former military man, however, and appears to have put the mission first rather than seeking to cling to power at his country's expense. "I would like the military to take over the task," he told the press in December 1997, "with the southern military chief being in overall command. Provincial governors would receive orders from the military."[238] It was a complete turnaround from his previous policy, but the most practical decision amid the severe carnage of the Falling Leaves onslaught.

Immediately following the reshuffling, SB-PAC Governor Palakorn Suwannarat met with the RTP chiefs from Region 9 and liaisons from the Fourth Army to recoordinate the relationship among the SB-PAC, ISOC, and Fourth Army to ensure the southern COIN was fully functional again. A major part of this included giving the SB-PAC a leading role in the amnesty program specified in *Pitak Tai*.[239] This seems to be the juncture where the police became more involved with the SB-PAC's operations, but it might have happened sooner. Regardless, after the PM's official sanction of *Pitak Tai* in July 1998, Fourth Army Commander Lieutenant General Preecha Suwannasri said his forces would remain in the far south to execute kinetic and psychological operations as long as was necessary to destroy insurgent forces that wanted to fight and help those who wanted to surrender.[240]

The Three Pillars of the First Southern COIN

How the Thai applied the ways and means of the three pillars of COIN to fulfill strategy is explored here. Scores of these programs were similar to those carried out against the CPT, especially the security programs. Some of the economic programs were the same, too. Many political programs, however, varied dramatically from the CPT era because the political problems were different and involved unique religious and cultural issues. As with the CPT war, these programs worked best when they were coordinated and supported each other.

Security Measures

While the security effort for the southern border COIN in the 1980s–90s mirrored that of the communist COIN, it was not nearly as large or complex. The size of the rebel forces and their operational tempo did not match that of the CPT. Accordingly, using all of Thailand's security forces was not necessary, but using all its various capabilities was. Security operations resulted in more than one thousand insurgents being arrested and/or killed, and they helped pressure many more to request amnesty.[241]

The Royal Thai Military

Units from all Thai military services were active in the far south in the 1980s–90s, but the RTA was in the lead. RTA forces used in the far south came from the Fourth Army, which was responsible for all security operations in that region. The main units committed were the 5th Infantry Division and the 4th Development Division. Other services used included Special Forces units from Lop Buri, the RTM who were traditionally stationed in Narathiwat, and RTAF units that provided tactical air support, transport, and logistics. They all operated under the CPM-43 banner, however, so the term "CPM" did not only mean village security teams backed by the police and military, as it had against the CPT.[242]

While the RTA fought mostly a light infantry war against the insurgents, it did use technology to its advantage. "In the present war in the south, we have helicopters, but only for logistics, not tactical attack," says General Kitti. "But we had them back when I was in command. We had gunships [Bell UH-1 helicopters], so when platoons made contact, we had fire support. We did not use artillery."[243] For observation and reconnaissance aircraft, the Thai mostly used Cessna 305 Bird Dogs.[244]

Military operations included the same types applied against the CPT: patrols, ambushes, sweeps, and supporting local forces with QRF. Aggressive operations based on actionable intelligence in the 1980s severely damaged insurgent groups and forced them to break up into smaller bands. General Kitti continued this trend in the early 1990s, to the point the main guerrilla units, namely PULO and BRN, suffered from a shortage of manpower. As a result, insurgent capabilities waned.[245] Thai security operations were highly successful.

COIN Operations in the Field

As is typical in conflicts with insurgencies light on manpower, most field operations did not result in enemy deaths. In a typical successful COIN mission on 29 September 1994, RTA forces on patrol engaged in a firefight with the BRN and killed three.[246] Another success occurred in Narathiwat in April 1997, when forces sweeping an area for specific insurgents located and killed BRN Zone 2 leader Ariya Tohbala and his top three aids. Major General Wanchai Kanprapha, CPM-43 commander, said intelligence from locals was a major reason for the operation's success.[247] In the far south, then, there were no pitched battles and no Khao Kho–type operations against CPT-style mountain strongholds, just light infantry missions that whittled away at insurgent forces over time. These missions decreased their manpower and their abilities to move and communicate.[248]

General Kitti says, "We tracked all the time the armed groups. We sent platoon-sized formations to fight them all the time. So we fought them hard and forced them into Malaysia—*pushed* them into Malaysia. We used small-unit tactics. There were no battalion-sized operations. We sent the troops—rifle companies—to stay in the *tambon* in area of operations."[249]

Larger operations were sometimes necessary to blunt and then counterattack insurgent campaigns. *Pitak Tai*, for example, required planning in 1997 for deployments in 1998, as did the buildup of forces, which included seven hundred newly appointed police. On the ground, the RTA sought to engage and destroy insurgent forces, but it did so with the minimum forces required, adhering to the principles of *Tai Rom Yen*. The RTA launched a psyops campaign alongside the *Pitak Tai* surge to inform the population of its goals and neutralize insurgent propaganda that claimed the army wanted to destroy all Muslims.[250] For the RTA, force application and psyops usually went hand in hand in COIN.

Village security operations under CPM-43 were nearly identical to those used against the CPT.[251] The VSTs had *tambon* chiefs, or *kamnan*, as their leaders and RTP or BPP as tactical advisors. CPM-43 put special emphasis on working with locals at every chance because it wanted to demonstrate its good intentions, establish trust, and gain legitimacy. "Regarding security forces," says Chuan, "defense volunteers, the military, the police; they all worked at the village level. CPM-43 always worked in rural communities; it always had contact with village heads and district heads. It was always involved at the community level."[252]

Professor Bhumarat says of the CPM-43 program, "Under Prem, the CPM worked very well. It had *Thahan Phran*, village militias…we recruited people from the villages. They provided access to the villages and good information. At that time they played a major role in maintaining peace and order and in suppressing the separatist movement."[253]

There were flaws, however. Some RTP advisors spent less time in the villages leading tactical formations and more time coordinating with *kamnan*, which weakened the system. This was not by design. Many police in the far south were Thai Buddhists and did not speak Malay, so they had trouble integrating with village security details. Without deeper government penetration of the villages, Bangkok's quest to secure villages, enact CA, and win legitimacy was hampered.

Police Region 9 was responsible for population control and maintaining law and order in the southern border COIN. Aside from patrolling cities and rural areas and leading some village security teams, the RTP and BPP also investigated crimes, arrested suspects, and built cases against suspected insurgents. Basic police participation in the south was key to demonstrating to the population the government system was based on law and order and not the work of a dictatorial regime, though corruption and condescending attitudes toward southerners by some police stymied this. Regardless, the RTG usually had the police, not the army, arrest suspected insurgents and process them into the justice system. The RTA could detain and question suspects, however.

Some police operations were critical to the downfall of southern insurgent cells. In September 1993, for example, police arrested senior PULO leader Da-o Krongpinang, who was responsible for a string of attacks that year.[254] The RTP had followed his trail for months, building a case against him while also trying to pinpoint his whereabouts. Taking Krongpinang off the streets was a critical blow to the insurgency.

In another case, on 29 December 1997, police investigations led to the arrest of five suspects apparently responsible for a bombing at Betong Weera Ratprasarn School in Yala. The attack killed two and injured thirteen. The five, who eventually confessed to working for Malaysia-based PULO leader Hayee Da-oh Thanam, were answerable for a series of bomb blasts and at least one grenade attack.[255] These types of operations, when applied on a regular basis, whittled away at many insurgent cells bit by bit, eventually isolating and demoralizing other insurgents to a point where ideally they lost faith in their movements.

The RTP was not only concerned with investigation and suppression, however. It also contributed to psyops in support of other operations such as amnesty under Pitak Tai. On 1 July 1998, for example, Police Chief Pracha Promnok stood with Interior Minister Sanan and SB-PAC Governor Palakorn at a surrender ceremony involving five insurgents of the Kasdan Army faction of

New PULO. Led by one of their leaders, Lohmae Sa-i Buke, they turned themselves in at a publicized reception at the RTP training school in Bang Khen. Such psyops helped spread the word that *Pitak Tai*'s amnesty was a real program, and those who surrendered would not be maligned.[256]

Unfortunately, as in the fight against the CPT, the police were generally the weak link in COIN in the far south. Much of the southern population held the police in disdain over its widespread corruption. This hurt government legitimacy and spurred support for insurgents. In some cases, police misbehavior created insurgents. Maltreatment of the population told locals the government was out to use them, and it isolated them from the rest of society. Moreover, as already noted, most police officials could not speak Malay, thus reducing their capacity to interact with the local population, especially in rural areas where Thai was spoken less often.

RTA General Perapong says the police were not ideally suited for COIN work. "In the 1980s and '90s," he says, "the military operations in the south were small. The police, they followed the standard 'bad guy versus good guy' scenario. If they saw a bad guy in the south, they arrested and jailed him. But you can't fight an insurgency only like this."[257] Perapong says the police should have investigated more extensively and started case files on insurgents and all of their connections, but this did not happen on a wide scale.

While the RTP certainly had critical flaws, the scores of dedicated police who died while protecting the population from terrorism should be recognized. Additionally, Police Chief General Pracha had the confidence of PM Chuan and briefed him on the southern insurgency, as he did with other top officials. If General Pracha had not been effective, the no-nonsense Chuan would not have received his briefings.[258] Ultimately, while a more effective RTP could have shortened the war and saved lives, without police involvement, the war likely would not have been won at all.

As in the CPT COIN, Special Branch operations were pivotal in the far south but infrequently commented on publicly because of their extreme sensitivity. Special Branch had excellent sources and worked with SB-PAC to accumulate intelligence that would illuminate insurgent activities, frequently from the inside. Says Chuan, "SB-PAC and Special Branch? Special Branch had staff at the SB-PAC. It had personal links to sources in the region. The organization could extract information from the provinces better, not because of strong-armed intervention, but because of its closer relations with the people there."[259] Nationwide, by 1998, Special Branch had two thousand members. A large portion of them worked in the far south.[260]

Special Branch was a key actor in *Pitak Tai* when the Thai and Malaysian governments worked jointly. It cooperated with Malaysian Special Branch to locate safe houses of insurgents in Malaysian territory. As a clear indication of Special Branch's role in defeating the insurgents, when Commissioner Somkiat retired in September 1998 the *Bangkok Post* wrote, "He left behind a legacy that many of his colleagues can be proud of."[261] Specifically, Commissioner Somkiat was behind the arrest of four key PULO insurgents in February 1998. This triggered scores of other insurgents to take advantage of *Pitak Tai*'s amnesty program and surrender.[262] Special Branch can be credited with providing decisive efforts that helped end the insurgency.

Local Forces

Local forces played a major role throughout the first southern border COIN. They were based on nearly the exact same village security concepts as applied in the anticommunist COIN. The forces were nearly the same as well, including the MoI's *Or Sor*/VDC.

For village security, the government relied on the *Chor Ror Bor*. It had both Thai Buddhists and Malay Muslims in its ranks. This was the MoI's 1985 version of a long line of CPM village security forces developed to fight the CPT. The Department of Provincial Administration, one level higher than DoLA, managed the program.[263] The *Chor Ror Bor*'s mission was to provide security in the villages and keep insurgent forces out. The police ceded considerable local law enforcement authority to village heads, in part because the CPM concept called for it, and also because most police could not speak Malay.[264]

Security missions of the *Chor Ror Bor* included setting up checkpoints at village entries and exits to control passage. These forces participated in local patrols when government forces needed them, and they fended off insurgent attacks, which were rare. Occasionally, they provided security at schools, government facilities, and development projects. CPM-43 trained them. Their main weapons were twelve-gauge shotguns.[265] Regarding leadership, says Prince of Songkhla University Professor Srisompob Jitpiromsri, "The village head was leader of the *Chor Ror Bor*. They were an armed militia of about twenty for each village. This was the old way."[266]

Since the *Thahan Phran* had worked well against the CPT, the government used them against southern insurgents, too. "We had *Thahan Phran*," says General Kitti. "They were very good because it was local people fighting local people, so they knew about the intelligence—they got good intelligence from the people in those areas. These were local *Thahan Phran*, not from the north. I think everything should be local. When they send the troops from the north, it's not a correct policy."[267] The 43rd *Thahan Phran* Regiment, headquartered in Narathiwat, and the 41st Regiment, headquartered in Yala, operated in the south. The RTA established the latter in 1984.[268]

Desmond Ball, a prolific writer on paramilitary organizations in Thailand, says the *Thahan Phran*'s mission in the south was to conduct unconventional warfare and special operations in support of ISOC, the Fourth Army, and CPM-43. *Thahan Phran* put much stock in collecting intelligence, including clandestine human intelligence.[269] Overall, they were highly effective.

Poor discipline and criminal activity blighted the *Thahan Phran*'s reputation in many instances, however. Ball says they were responsible for murder, rape, and wanton violence. In 1981, General Harn Leenanond disbanded *Thahan Phran* units in Surat Thani and Phattalung provinces for criminal activities. While these units were not directly involved in the southern border COIN, their activity nevertheless sullied the *Thahan Phran*'s reputation in the region and hurt the legitimacy of the government. Such problems showed the *Thahan Phran* could sometimes be counterproductive.[270]

The International Crisis Group reported Songkhla-based *Thahan Phran* in November 1987 killed four unarmed Thai Malay Muslims suspected of supporting insurgents, causing the RTA to transfer the 43rd *Thahan Phran* regimental commander out of the region.[271] Ball says in the far south "criminal intent related to banditry, illegal logging, drug trafficking, etc., has come to dominate the relations between the Rangers and the so-called separatists."[272]

In 1987, the government began to reform the *Thahan Phran* by recruiting better-quality personnel from its military reserves, but there were still scores of nonmilitary recruits. Bangkok also required additional training aimed at instilling more discipline and skill in the force. In 1995 the RTA said it had increased *Thahan Phran* training to six months, although the ICG doubted this claim based on interviews with military forces in the far south.[273]

Despite the sometimes unsatisfactory behavior of the *Thahan Phran* and heavy criticism from their detractors—including prolific insurgent propaganda—the force nevertheless proved exceptionally valuable in the southern COIN. In many cases the *Thahan Phran*'s expertise resulted in the neutralization of enemy personnel. Even on operations where there was no kill, the *Thahan Phran* still demonstrated their worth by keeping continual pressure on insurgents, a critical tenet of COIN.

In May 1989, for example, a combined force of twenty *Thahan Phran*, RTA, and RTP clashed with a PULO unit in Narathiwat, killing one. In July 1996, *Thahan Phran* battled insurgents in Narathiwat. Two were wounded. In April 1997, *Thahan Phran* killed a top BRN leader in Narathiwat.[274] In August 1997, *Thahan Phran* raided the house of suspected insurgent Samaoong Sulong, who eluded capture. In his house, however, they found forty-nine sticks of dynamite, homemade explosives, an instructional book on how to make explosives, a book on how to wage guerrilla warfare, and maps marking sabotage targets that included government buildings and bridges.[275] By their actions, the *Thahan Phran* prevented Sulong from making and deploying perhaps forty-nine or more bombs that could have killed and maimed hundreds.

Under *Pitak Tai*, the RTA deployed six hundred *Thahan Phran* to hunt down and destroy insurgent forces once and for all. They applied continual pressure on insurgent units through a series of pursuit and ambush operations. In one of these operations on 31 March 1998, a squad *Thahan Phran* located and clashed with a group of fifteen BRN fighters in a brief firefight. There were no reported casualties and the insurgents escaped, but the hunt continued and it paid off. On 2 April, eleven *Thahan Phran* killed several BRN in Si Sakhon district, which severely injured the BRN's capabilities in Narathiwat.[276]

Operations such as these kept constant stress on the BRN, forcing the insurgents into survival mode—constant escape and evasion—which kept them from planning and executing attacks. No other force in Thailand could combine the *Thahan Phran*'s local knowledge and DA capabilities to produce such results. Accordingly, in the final analysis, despite the heaps of criticism and their sometimes counterproductive behavior, the *Thahan Phran* were decisively effective in the southern border COIN.

Intelligence

Intelligence for the 1980s–90s southern COIN came from the same agencies that processed intelligence for the communist COIN: Division 7 of Special Branch, the RTP, the RTA, and the NIA. The NIA's role in this conflict was kept confidential, however. The SB-PAC also collected and processed intelligence since it had continual contact with the people.[277]

The RTA's intelligence units identified threats and processed combat intelligence. The RTA ran the most powerful intelligence network in the region, at least up to the mid-1990s, when the MoI took over most of these responsibilities. Says General Akanit, "Army intelligence at that time was stronger than police intelligence."[278] Chuan adds, "Regarding intelligence, the capabilities of various forces differed. We had to accept the fact that military intelligence capabilities were higher than those of the police."[279]

RTA forces solicited information from villagers on a regular basis. *Thahan Phran* did the same thing but in smaller units, which was ideal for clandestine intelligence work. This is especially true for targeting, which is vital for capture-or-kill operations.[280] Interestingly, the army had sources that led it to identify the whereabouts of insurgents overseas, indicating strong links to Special Branch, the NIA, and the MoFA. The RTA also probably used its defense attachés for this purpose as well.[281]

Locals provided the best intelligence on insurgents because they knew the pulse of village activities and because southern insurgents depended on contact— sometimes voluntary, sometimes forced—with locals for support. Accordingly, while local residents could provide great strength to guerrillas, they became a devastating weakness when savvy intelligence units got them to cooperate with the government. In this case, Chuan Leekpai says, the people became pivotal sources of information. "Village heads were the best sources," says Chuan. "They provided intelligence to both CPM-43 and SB-PAC."[282]

The Thai recognized the importance of intelligence in COIN so much that during *Pitak Tai*, CPM-43 established a tips and information mailbox for citizens who wanted to report anonymously to security forces. It publicly announced the address, which was located outside the far south, likely for security reasons in case insurgents had agents embedded in the local post offices. As of 1998, it was P.O. Box 20, Muang district, Nakhon Si Thammarat province.[283]

Southern Border Provinces Administrative Command Intelligence

SB-PAC needed an intelligence capability because much of its work required information on insurgents and their nexus with the people. "Intelligence," says Chuan Leekpai, "it was not just from the army, but the MoI had good spies, too. We had a good understanding with the local people. We approached them via grass roots, by the SB-PAC, and we could transfer crooks out of the region, which the people liked us for. At the SB-PAC, we used provincial and district-level offices to get things done. We could monitor all things, not just the insurgency."[284]

Specifically, the SB-PAC needed political and cultural intelligence to stay informed of the population's attitude toward the government, development projects, and the insurgency. Intelligence on these issues helped the SB-PAC to assess its progress, as well as to identify corrupt or inefficient civil servants who needed to be transferred out of the southern region. For this program to be effective, the flow of information had to be clandestine and secure. Lastly, since the SB-PAC was so close to the people and therefore close to the insurgency, it collected intelligence on threats and passed it on to CPM-43.

Political Measures

The RTG had more political programs in the first southern border COIN than security programs. The SB-PAC ran most of them. This demonstrated Bangkok well understood that the key facets of the southern insurgency were political. Many of the government's political programs during this time period were the same as those from the 1970s, but better managed. They included, but were not limited to, the following eight programs: (1) political inclusion at the national level, (2) political inclusion at the grassroots level, (3) local advisors for the SB-PAC's COIN programs, (4) political integration through the education system, (5) diplomacy across multiple fronts, (6) amnesty, (7) quality control (i.e., removing corrupt civil servants), and (8) psyops.

Before the SB-PAC developed these programs, however, it surveyed Thai Malay Muslim leaders in 1981 to learn their attitudes toward the government and civil servants. The goal was to gain an understanding of southerners' concerns to more effectively direct resources to problem areas. The survey also gathered information on residents' living environment and asked respondents to comment on four characteristics of government workers: honesty, justness, public devotion, and competence.[285]

Survey results graded civil servants low in all areas. The survey also demonstrated that Thai Malay Muslim leaders were loyal to their imams first, their communities second, and the Thai state third. This information convinced the government to continue integration strategies and to influence the youth of the region to put loyalty to the state above religious leaders.[286]

Political Inclusion at the National Level

Beginning in the 1980s, the government aimed to enhance Thai Malay Muslims' political participation to remove some of the alienation that contributed to the insurgency. "By providing increasing avenues for the participation of the citizenry in the political life of the country," writes Ornanong, "the rulers hoped to enlarge their popular base of support."[287] This inclusion happened mainly through national political parties.

Lack of access to representation was not the issue, however. Southern border people had been participating in the government for years and were not excluded from the democratic process. They had full voting rights and all the other privileges of any other citizens in Thailand. Thai Muslims had served in Parliament since 1932, and Thai Malay Muslims had served since at least 1976.[288] Moreover, Thai Malay Muslims could look up to national leaders from their ethnic group as sources of political hope and aspiration and as proof of their people's political inclusion.

One such leader was Wan Muhammad Nor Matha.[289] Born in Yala, he rose to prominence in the government after completing a BA and MA from Chulalongkorn University in 1974. From 1980 to 1996, he served seven terms as a representative from Yala, receiving nine royal decorations and holding high-profile posts, including Vice Speaker of the House of Representatives, Deputy of the MoI, Minister of Transport and Communication, and Speaker of the House of Representatives and Parliament.[290]

Surin Pitsuwan was another example of Muslim inclusion. Born in Nakhon Si Thammarat, Surin was not Malay, but he assimilated into a Malay Muslim family, so he held considerable influence with the far south's population. After earning his PhD at Harvard in 1982 and working as a reporter for the *Bangkok Post*, Surin held a number of high government posts, as representative of Nakon Si Thammarat, Minister of Foreign Affairs, and chair of the Association of Southeast Asian Nations.[291]

Despite these cases, many Thai Malay Muslims opted out of the political process because of apathy and ignorance of the system. Accordingly, the government sought ways to increase participation. At the national level, this meant encouraging the creation of political parties for the southern border population. In Thailand, no political party is created without the permission of the government. In the case of the far south, major political figures not only encouraged them, they also helped create them.

One such party was the al-Wahdah Party of Thailand. Former Narathiwat Member of Parliament *Ustaz* Sha-roning (a.k.a. *Seni* Madakakul)—who was also a member of the Islamic Council of Pattani—founded it on 3 May 1986. It had the support of Wan Muhammad Nor Matha. The goal of al-Wahdah was to put more Thai Malay Muslims in Parliament and to lobby the cabinet for southern Muslim interests.[292]

Political science scholar Suria Saniwa believes al-Wahdah and its placement of more Muslims in high positions eased southern political grievances, giving people a peaceful way to advocate for change. Suria says, "These ministerial positions have empowered the Muslim political leaders and have become a source of pride to the Muslim community. In fact, the tactical alliance [between al-Wahdah and the New Aspiration Party] has been instrumental in appeasing the needs of the Malay Muslims within the Thai political system."[293]

The New Aspiration Party was yet another southern border political COIN initiative. Nor Matha was a key member. [294] General Chavalit established it after retiring from the military. New Aspiration helped propel him to the PM's position in 1996. General Chavalit courted and won a large portion of the Thai Malay Muslim vote during his campaign, helping to increase their political power further. As Patrick Jory writes in the *Harvard Asia Pacific Review*, "Under the Chavalit government a number of Malay Muslims held influential senior positions, including Wan Muhammad Nor Matha, who remains Parliamentary President and deputy leader of the New Aspiration Party, and New Aspiration Party power broker Den Dohmeena, whose family has a history of Muslim political activism."[295] The fact that General Chavalit spawned the *Thahan Phran* did not seem to bother politically active Thai Malay Muslims.

Because of initiatives such as these, Thai Malay Muslims won six Parliament seats in the September 1992 elections. They helped form Chuan Leekpai's coalition government. He chose two New Aspiration Party members to serve key posts: Surin Pitsuwan as Deputy Foreign Minister and Nor Matha as Deputy Speaker of the Parliament.[296]

The government also used national cultural recognition to counter the insurgency. On the heels of the 1992 election, the government amended the constitution to recognize the right of all minorities to speak and promote their languages. The constitution also authorized "support for the administration of Islamic affairs and the teaching of minority languages."[297] This was a landmark event, a major turnaround from the days of Phibun's 1939 National Culture Act that restricted cultural diversity for Thailand's minorities.

One meaningful tenet of the new constitution officially declared Thailand to be a secular state. Until 1992, it had officially been a Buddhist country. Part of the reasoning behind the secular declaration was to embrace Thailand's other religions, such as the Thai Malay branch of Islam, and to make southern border Malays feel less marginalized. Ornanong cites Thai Malay Muslim students as saying they previously did not feel that they were part of Thailand because "being a Thai is being a Buddhist."[298] They associated being a Thai citizen as being ethnically Thai and religiously Buddhist. The 1992 constitutional amendments sought to change this.

Political Inclusion at the Grassroots Level

The government increased Thai Malay Muslim political inclusion at district, subdistrict, and village levels, first via the SB-PAC and later through the 1988 National Security Policy. This measure was rooted in Kriangsak's 1979 policy of organizing annual seminars for the Provincial Councils for Islamic Affairs to discuss local problems of, and solutions for, Muslims all over Thailand via leadership training.[299] These programs encouraged more of them to join the local governing system.[300] It had both positive and negative effects.

Regarding positive effects, Omar Bajunid cites a 1998 study that states, "The democratization of the Thai political system has significantly contributed to the deradicalization of Malay Muslim opposition."[301] Special Branch Commissioner Somkiat told the *Bangkok Post* in October 1998, "There are now legal channels for those seeking political freedom. It is useless to pursue the old violent way. I think they now realise that violence is not the answer. Have they gained anything during the past fifty years?"[302]

Similarly, the Tambon Administration Organizations (TAOs) and Provincial Administrative Organizations (PAOs) were two entities that fostered Thai Malay Muslim involvement in administering their own provinces. The TAOs, established by the RTG through the TAO Act of 1994, were particularly influential.[303] The PAO Act came later, in 1997.[304] These governing mechanisms were created for the entire country, but they were intentionally applied in the south as COIN measures aimed at decentralizing Bangkok's power.

PAOs consisted of a lead official and staff that supervised public works at the *changwat* (provincial) level. The TAOs, at the *tambon* (subdistrict) level, were composed of two elected representatives from each village in each *tambon*. The MoI appointed the secretary of each TAO. These organizations had thirty-one assigned tasks, which included managing public services in the infrastructure, local business, health, forest, and aquatic sectors.[305] Commissioner Somkiat said of the PAOs and TAOs, "If [insurgents] stop and think about it, these are the same rights they have been fighting for."[306]

Regarding negative effects, some believe decentralization and the increased introduction of democracy enabled religious radicals to infiltrate the government, masquerading as participants of the state system only to subvert it from the inside, a hallmark of the Islamist jihad concept of *taqiya*. "The position of this group," writes Gilquin, "both regional and religious, is a challenge to the country's authority, the more so as there is increased democratization in society."[307]

More, increased electoral competition damaged age-old systems that had previously been in effect, such as village headmen running security. Chuan explains, "So the heads of the villages were strong enough to provide security and to handle any problems, handle any misunderstanding. This man was key in the village structure. In the eighties and mid-nineties, the heads of the villages were strong. Afterward to 2007, they were weak."[308] Chuan says they went from being trusted appointees by governors in the late 1990s—men the government knew would keep order—to being elected, where the best politician took over. Security suffered as a result, and insurgents found it easy to penetrate and manipulate the system.

Special Branch Police General Tritot says this new political elite made many mistakes. "They let the locals build *ponohs* [*pondoks*] again, and they reduced the security presence, all because local pundits kept harping on how the Muslims were not free and that they needed to be free. And ultimately, it's easier for politicians to push these issues, because they get more power as a result."[309] In essence, decentralization enabled and exacerbated the insurgency. Also, these programs became platforms for a new generation of insurgents who would arise years later, though no one could foresee this in the 1990s.

Local Advisory Committees

The SB-PAC tapped Thai Malay Muslims for advisory positions to ensure it was focusing on the most pressing problems and applying the correct solutions. "So the southern border command set up an advisory committee," says Dr. Gothom Arya. "It's the correct approach to have local people as advisors, and they are more people-friendly since ordinary people can walk in [to the SB-PAC] and speak to everyone. People can't just walk into a military camp and speak to the people they need to meet with. There are checkpoints, layers of security, and those types of things."[310]

The results were positive. "Local Muslims and leaders got more access to public decision making and governing," says Chuan. "We had town meetings and got local leaders involved. We worked through imams. We invited them to be members of local committees and advise us on political and development matters."[311]

Bringing imams into the equation sought to ease their worries by showing they could live within the state system and still be Malay Muslims. In this regard, Bangkok tapped moderate imams to broadcast to the villages its new pro-Thai Malay Muslim policies. This is the same method the government used to reach northern and northeastern villages during the communist COIN—by way of harnessing local village leaders to facilitate effective communication.

As an aside, however, even though the government reached out to Malay villages in the first southern COIN, it did not seem to be as intricate and methodical an effort as it was during the CPT COIN. For sure, the southern insurgents were not as threatening as the CPT, but they were indeed threatening, and they had bombed Bangkok. It appears that the deep cultural differences between the Malay village structure and the RTG's national security chain of command might have prevented a more meticulous approach.

Education Systems

The education system was the state's main integration program for the far south. It had been active since the 1960s, though in the 1980s–90s it was improved and more attuned to local sensitivities. Unfortunately, many Thai Malay Muslims did not believe school of any kind would improve their lot in life. Statistics from 1981 said after compulsory schooling, 95 percent of Thai Malay Muslim teens dropped out of the education system. The 5 percent remaining went on to higher learning. By comparison, 43 percent of Thai Buddhists in the far south continued higher learning. Many Thai Malay Muslims complained most of their teachers were Thai Buddhists, which did not sit well with racially and religiously insular-minded peoples.[312]

Bangkok was right to focus on the educational system of the far south, however. The *pondoks* were the main antigovernment program of the insurgents, which the *ustaz* controlled. On the whole, the far south's entire school system became the central ideological battleground for the war, and when the insurgents began killing and kidnapping teachers, it became a physical battleground as well. The Ministry of Education was a pivotal actor in the government's education integration programs.[313]

In 1979, on the cusp of Bangkok's COIN campaign in the far south, there were 1,500 schools ranging from kindergarten to the university level. There were 10,850 teachers and 283,000 students. Up to 23,000 of those students attended *pondoks*.[314] There were five kinds of schools in the far south as of 1980:

1. Public schools not teaching any Islam.

2. Public schools teaching Islam two hours each week.

3. PSTIs offering secular curricula along with Islam.

4. PSTIs with no secular teaching.

5. Unregistered and illegal *pondoks* that were nonetheless tolerated by the state.[315]

By 1985, the government had declared there would be no new *pondoks*, but in 1997, TAO and PAO officials overturned this policy.[316]

There were three primary government education integration programs (and multiple minor ones not mentioned here). They were part of the government's Master Plan on Education for the Malay Muslims (1977–82), which the SB-PAC adopted. The most important ones involved revising the curriculum at Private Schools Teaching Islam programs, using the Thai language for Islamic studies, and expanding the amount of teaching on Islam in public schools.[317]

In 1980, the government and its Thai Malay Muslim advisors launched an effort to revise the PSTI curriculum. They called their resulting product "The Curriculum for the Study of Islam in 1980," and it went into effect on 5 June 1981. It had three levels of study. The first level was *ibtidaiyya*, or grades one through four, which paralleled the government's primary school system. The second was *mutawatsita*, or grades five through seven, which paralleled the government's secondary school system. The third was grades eight through ten, the highest compulsory educational level.[318] Along with secular subjects, PSTI students also studied the Koran, Islamic traditions, and sharia law. The new curriculum was designed to make Thai Malay Muslims more competitive and also assuage imams' angst that the state would turn all educational programs purely secular.[319] In the end, however, since the government controlled the curriculum, it took power away from the *to-kru* (headmasters) and *ustaz*.[320] They were disenfranchised, and the more radical of them rejected the new program.

University affirmative action was another political integration program. In the 1980s, a mere 20 percent of Thai high school graduates enrolled in college, in part because of the system's fierce competitiveness. *Pondok*-educated Thai Malay Muslims, because of their Islamic-focused education, found it difficult to gain entrance to secular universities. The government recognized these students needed greater access to higher learning. As a result, a quota system for Thai Malay Muslim admissions to universities was created in 1971. DoLA ran it. The Prem administration and successive governments continued this university quota system.[321] Between 1971 and 1981, 458 Thai Malay Muslim students went through the university quota program. More than 80 percent of the students in the programs graduated, and many became civil servants. The government considered the program a success and continued it into the 1990s.[322]

Outside the school system, the SB-PAC decreed Thai language education for all peoples of the far south, including at the village level. The government had done this in the 1970s, and it continued into the 1980s–90s. As of 1991, the SB-PAC was running Thai language courses for 288 people in seventy-two villages. Participants included youth leaders, schoolteachers, local leaders, and imams.[323]

Government Employment

Since the far south was 80 percent Thai Malay Muslim, and its civil servants were mostly Thai Buddhists, the government on 30 December 1980 decided to inject more locals into the local administrative system through quotas. The cabinet ordered all government agencies working in the far south to hire four Thai Malay Muslims each from the DoLA-sponsored university quota system. This measure offered greater job opportunities to graduates while enabling the government to staff local administrative positions with ideologically friendly Thai Malay Muslims. Some pundits say this program discriminated against Thai Malay Muslim graduates from foreign universities, but since most foreign graduates studied only Islam, they were not qualified for government administrative jobs.[324]

Diplomacy

The government applied direct diplomacy with rebel leaders as an additional political means to counter the insurgency. General Kitti developed and executed this strategy. In his mind, and based on his prior experience negotiating the end of the Communist Party of Malaysia, diplomacy was an excellent tool with which to end conflict. Moreover, it was culturally in line with the Buddhist sense of restoring balance and calm to a tumultuous situation.

General Perapong echoes this sentiment: "Because the insurgent groups of the eighties and nineties had some political aspirations—PULO wanted political voice in the villages and representation in local government offices—you could negotiate with PULO. It's okay. So we go to the table."[325]

"We talked to them," adds Professor Bhumarat. "Back then, the old PULO, for example, they realized they would never win. Eventually, they stopped."[326] But it took years of frustrating sessions, and when the end came, there was no climatic "peace talk conclusion." Talks served as a slow, droning erosion of insurgent will, with no decisive end.

General Kitti sent then Colonel Akanit Munsewat to several countries—first to Egypt—to meet with PULO and BRN leaders. Akanit was Fourth Army Deputy of Operations at the time.[327] Kitti saw the problem as a security issue, which put the RTA in the lead. "Army intelligence knew [the rebels] were in Egypt. Army intelligence was better than the police. Everything was up to the army," says Kitti.[328]

Diplomats were not integral to the negotiating process, adds Akanit. "They have their own mind-set," he says. "It's different from us because this is a security issue."[329] He and other security and defense types believed fighting men should talk to fighting men.

The government supported the RTA's diplomatic effort via the National Security Council, which was close to the PM. Says General Akanit, "My work was not under CPM-43 or ISOC. I dealt directly with the NSC. I suggested to the NSC to form up a working group. I reported to Kitti, Kitti reported to NSC, and NSC reported to the PM, who at that time was Prem."

Securing a place to hold the talks was sensitive. The exact nature of the talks themselves was classified top secret and remains so. "PULO suggested we talk in Malaysia, Pakistan, or Egypt," says Akanit. So he worked his Thai government contacts to see where they might set up a meeting. "There is one officer from the Ministry of Foreign Affairs…he's a Muslim, and close to me. This officer was not in the working group, but we thought he'd be a good person to cooperate with to help put these meetings together. Our contact in the MoFA contacted all three countries," says Akanit, "and both Malaysia and Pakistan declined. But Egypt allowed us to go. So we agreed to go to Cairo and meet at the Meridian Hotel. The meeting lasted about one week. It was just PULO and us. PULO was the biggest threat at the time."

At the meeting in Cairo, PULO representatives requested one thing: autonomy for "Patani." Akanit asked them to explain their conception of what autonomy would mean in practice, and PULO could not answer. "They did not know what a 'Patani state' would look like, how it would operate, how it would collect taxes, nothing," says Akanit. His counterproposal was simple: stop the violence and join the political process. "I said they should let the people make decisions. I gave them three months to give us an answer."

After the Cairo meeting, however, the leader of PULO gave a statement to a Pakistani newspaper about the peace talks, breaking their agreement to keep them secret. The RTG felt betrayed and figured PULO had no intention of achieving peace through dialogue. "They simply wanted to raise up their status," says Akanit, "and raise up the problem to an international level." In the eyes of PULO, it gave them prestige to be negotiating with the government.

Akanit continued informal talks with PULO for years, however, in kind of a diplomatic cat-and-mouse game. He even had coffee with its leaders in Syria, but they went nowhere. Contact with the rebels languished for two to three years until Akanit heard that a top leader of PULO living in Syria was sick. "So I contacted him and wanted to see him as a friend. I sent a message to him if he'd agree to a visit. Then a newspaper in Saudi Arabia announced, 'The Thai are going to negotiate with PULO again.' So I canceled the trip. Regardless, afterward, I would still call them—the insurgent leaders in Syria, Sweden, and Malaysia—and we kept in touch with them."

Ultimately, Akanit determined the negotiations were a dead end. "In the end," he says, "I realized we could not talk with PULO. I saw that the best way to solve the problem was to get support from the Malaysian government. Malaysia must assist us. Why? Because most of the separatist leaders, they stayed in Malaysia and used it as sanctuary."

While Kitti's and Akanit's efforts did not reach a decisive diplomatic end, they did appear to erode the will of the insurgent leadership over the years, similar to how the North Vietnamese frustrated American war efforts with a "talk-fight" strategy. Thai cat-and-mouse diplomacy seemed to have helped set the stage for the end of the insurgency in 1998, when force, amnesty, and diplomacy (which secured Malaysia's denial of sanctuary) applied tremendous pressure that PULO and other insurgent leaders could not withstand. Similarly, these talks let the insurgent leaders know over time that their negotiation efforts were getting nowhere and their war was fruitless. It must have been demoralizing.

General Akanit sums it up this way. "I know all the leaders of PULO, GMIP, BRN, and all of them know me," he says. "My concept was like tearing the pages from a book. I talked with them, a few pages torn out. I wrote them letters, a few more pages. I kept on until the book went from a hundred pages to only thirty, so they were very weak in the end."[330]

Diplomacy with Saudi Arabia

When PULO increased its violence in the late 1970s and early 1980s, it appears the RTG used diplomacy to help curb the problem. It was probably the several PULO bombings in Bangkok in the early 1980s that pushed the government into action. Committing sporadic terrorism in the far south was one thing, but bombing the capital was intolerable. Accordingly, in 1984, Bangkok appears to have persuaded Saudi Arabia to shut down PULO's offices in Mecca. Officials from both countries have kept quiet on the subject, but evidence suggests diplomacy was involved.

Admittedly, Saudi officials were hesitant to allow too much foreign influence from any entity on Saudi soil. They did not like PULO members based in Saudi Arabia issuing identification cards to, and collecting taxes from, Thai Malay Muslims living there. They certainly did not like PULO interacting with the Baath Party of Syria, either, an enemy to the north. The Bangkok bombings, however, made it appear as if PULO was using Saudi Arabia as a base to terrorize Thailand. And it was. This was too much for the House of Saud, and the Thai knew this. Unlike other regimes in the Middle East, Saudi Arabia did not outwardly tout support for revolutionary and/or terror groups. Because of its prominent position as an international oil provider, it had a place in the global political pecking order, and being a vocal sponsor of insurgency and terrorism threatened this position. Saudi Arabia's support for these groups was usually much more subtle through cutouts, or through royal family members acting on their own, sometimes against the wishes of Riyadh.

But this was no guarantee the Saudis would move against PULO. In all likelihood, they had to be persuaded. This is probably where Thai MoFA diplomats, or the RTA acting in a diplomatic role, went into action. Exactly who did what is a mystery, but something triggered Riyadh to take steps. It could have slapped PULO on the wrist and simply diminished its capacity in Saudi Arabia, still allowing it to operate on a lesser scale. But in 1984, Riyadh went the full distance. It completely shut down PULO's base, it temporarily detained scores of its leaders, and it deported seven hundred Thai Malay Muslims in rapid form.[331]

More than just a pinprick, Saudi Arabia's actions decisively damaged PULO, which was, in effect, a religious ally. The shutdown obliterated PULO's biggest command-and-control, recruiting, and propaganda headquarters—its very core. The incident even forced the resignation of PULO head Tengku Bria Kotanila. PULO was critically dependent on Mecca and had no other location from where it could manage and grow its insurgency with such impunity. While PULO increased its presence in Malaysia in the wake of the shutdown, even with passive local Malaysian government support, it could not risk angering Kuala Lumpur by growing too large.

Che Man wrote of the incident, "The crisis has undoubtedly crippled the PULO, and it may take several years before it can revive its activities in Saudi Arabia. The difficult task of restoring the organization to its original strength is now in the hands of younger generation leaders."[332] The Saudi government's actions, then, were so injurious that PULO never recovered to its early 1980s level of power.

Diplomacy with Malaysia

During General Kitti's tenure as Fourth Army commander, he sent then Colonel Akanit on a special mission to win Malaysia's support for quelling the insurgency. Akanit was a natural choice, having engaged in so much diplomacy with insurgents through the years. His experience with difficult negotiations was excellent. Moreover, this was Bangkok's first major attempt to bring the two countries together on the issue, and the government needed its best people on task.

"So I went to see a high authority within Malaysian Special Branch who was my friend," says Akanit. "After that, he was Inspector of Chief of Police. And I talked with him and said that I needed his support. I said, 'It's time the Malaysian government assisted the Thai government to solve the insurgency problem.'"[333] Akanit even got personal on the issue. He says, "I told my friend, 'I myself helped Malaysia with the Malaysia Communist Party problem. Now, you must help me.'"

General Akanit here is referring to the diplomatic shutdown of the CTO. It happened in 1989, when General Kitti was tapped by Bangkok to solve the Malaysian communist terrorism problem once and for all. It was partly a Thai issue because, after Chin Peng and the CTO were reduced as an effective fighting force in the 1950s through exceptionally effective British COIN programs, the CTO established camps in southern Thailand. From there it occasionally staged hit-and-run operations into Malaysia. In the 1980s, it began carrying out similar operations in southern Thailand, which drew Bangkok's ire. General Kitti then assumed his diplomatic role, and, with the assistance of then Colonel Akanit, worked with Peng and Malaysia to stop the fighting. It was one of the most successful diplomatic negotiations in the history of Southeast Asia, and it stopped a forty-year insurgency that had killed thousands. As a result, both Kitti and Akanit had earned a reputation as warrior diplomats, and they used those skills to harness Malaysia's help with Thailand's southern insurgency.

After Akanit met with Malaysian Special Branch, a series of roller-coaster diplomatic actions began. "The head of the Malaysian police went to Bangkok to see the Secretary of the NSC, the Supreme Commander, the Chief of Thai Police, and also General Kitti," says Akanit. "He said that Mahathir [the Malaysian PM] had agreed to help Thailand solve the problem. So we agreed to form up a working group to work together, the Thai and Malaysian Governments. We drafted a ToR, or Terms of Responsibility. But during the drafting we also cooperated on other matters, such as when the Malaysian police arrested some members of PULO. They seized them and sent them back to Thailand."

In the meantime, by January 1994, Thai diplomacy had led to KAL issuing a warning to Thai Malay Muslim insurgents hiding in northern Malaysia, telling them to cease terrorist operations or face police action.[334] While it was not the sweeping series of arrests Bangkok was hoping for, it was a good start for the Thai-Malaysian COIN relationship. The warning had no effect on insurgent operations, however. It is possible Malaysia's central government had less sway over the outlying states, and the insurgents knew their local contacts would keep them secure.

Then in 1995, an odd interruption halted the working group's progress. General Akanit recalls, "During our work together, General Parnthep took over as Fourth Army commander from Kitti. General Parnthep ordered me to stop the case. He ordered me to go to Malaysia to explain we were stopping. I asked General Parnthep about the reason [sic], and he just said, 'Akanit, you tell them it's the policy of the PM.'"[335] The PM at that time was Banharn Silpa-Archa (13 July 1995–24 November 1996), following Chuan Leekpai's first term.

"I knew that Banharn did not know about this," continues Akanit, "but I had to do this. I sent the message, and said I had something urgent to speak with them about. And when I told them that we wanted to stop the case, they were shocked. Then Parnthep reported to the NSC that he wanted to form a new working group, headed by Major General Leawat Wattanat Pongsai, which would deal with the Malaysian Army. So he went through the wrong channel."

Akanit explains, "Internal security in Malaysia is not under the army. It's under Special Branch. I have many friends in Special Branch. The Malaysian Army didn't know much about this, the terrorists in their country's border lands, because it's not military work. It's not their job. And Parnthep asked for the budget for the working group from the government, but he didn't get it, so he couldn't form the group. The end. No more cooperation between Thailand and Malaysia to solve the separatist problem."

A year later, however, on 19 October 1996, an incident in Malaysia forced the issue and provided an opening for diplomacy once more, but it did not produce immediate results. Malaysian police arrested PULO insurgents Samail Thanam, then commander of the group's military wing, and Jama Sateng, a bomb maker, for possession of several bombs and ammunition. Samail had lived in KAL for several years, running a restaurant in Selangor. They were traveling from Kelantan to Kedah when forced to stop at a police checkpoint forty kilometers from the Thai border.[336] The link between the insurgents and their Malaysian sanctuary was now embarrassingly out in the open. As an interesting aside, it is probable that someone inside Malaysian security who did not like the insurgents using Malaysia as sanctuary leaked this information to the press. Insurgent supporters and those embarrassed by the arrests would have kept quiet.

Shockingly, however, even though the Malaysian penalty for possession of explosives was death, on 18 November KAL granted Thanam bail for the equivalent of one hundred thousand *baht*. This move strained Thai-Malaysian relations terribly and demonstrated that KAL's COIN support for Bangkok was weak.[337] Thai PM Chavalit ordered Foreign Minister Prachuap Chaiyasan to Malaysia to improve their relations and press for more help, such as identifying and arresting insurgent leaders hiding in Malaysia. Chavalit planned a follow-up visit in January 1997. Malaysia's Supreme Commander, General

Tan Sri Ismail, also scheduled meetings with his Thai counterparts to discuss the insurgency.[338] The talks produced no major breakthroughs, but they did keep the issue alive.

Then, in the wake of the Falling Leaves campaign in late 1997, several politicians said publicly that the insurgent problem demanded Malaysian help. An anonymous Thai source told the *Bangkok Post*, "Malaysia has repeatedly said this is our affair, but it would be impossible to end the problem without help from our southern neighbour."[339] Interior Minister Sanan Kachornprasart followed suit in a public manner, asserting boldly that insurgents, after striking in Thailand, fled for sanctuary in Malaysia and that they sometimes used Malaysia as a base from which to launch attacks into Thailand. PM Chaun asserted that southern terrorists had trained in northern Malaysia, and he lambasted their attacks on Thai policemen.[340] Such comments in the early 1990s would have been counterproductive to Thai-Malaysian relations, but in the late 1990s, the Thai were at their wits' end. Were it not for insurgent sanctuary in Malaysia, the insurgents would be virtually powerless, and both countries knew it.

Even Thai Parliament President Nor Matha, a native of Yala, said that unless Malaysia helped Thailand with the insurgency, it would not go away. He moreover said there was an economic angle to consider: "Prosperity in the southernmost region is not possible unless there is permanent peace in the area."[341] Nor Matha was referring to the Indonesia-Malaysia-Thailand Growth Triangle project, originated by Malaysian PM Mahathir Mohammad and pushed by PM Chuan, which aimed to promote trade between Thailand, Indonesia, and Malaysia.[342] In the long run, the Growth Triangle project did not evolve, but at the time, it was a major impetus for solving Thailand's southern insurgency.

Then in January 1998, Foreign Minister Surin announced he was working with Malaysia to secure increased intelligence and investigative cooperation to identify the perpetrators of the Falling Leaves campaign. "What I am expecting from Malaysia is an exchange of information and details, possibly involving the violence in the southernmost provinces of Thailand. With the intelligence information we have and that from Malaysia, we expect to identify the cause of recent events," he told *The Nation*.[343] Surin's work, past diplomatic pressure from Bangkok, and the embarrassment of the insurgents obviously being based in northern Malaysia was too much for Kuala Lumpur to bear. The result was a very sudden, fully cooperative effort by Malaysia's Special Branch and other security forces—not unlike what happened with Saudi Arabia and PULO in 1984. The end came swiftly for Thailand's southern insurgents. On the night of 12 January 1998, Malaysian police raided PULO and New PULO bases throughout northern Malaysia.[344] They made similar moves against the BRN, detaining insurgents near the border and in KAL on the thirteenth. Among them were Hayi Abdul Rohman Bazo of New PULO; Hayi Da-oh Thanam, chief of New PULO's military; and Hayi Sama-ae Thanam, military chief of PULO.[345] KAL turned them over to Thailand. In February, other top-ranking PULO leaders succumbed to the pressure and surrendered.[346]

The arrests sent shock waves though the insurgent community that had for decades relied on what it thought was a sympathetic government in KAL to look the other way as they waged war in Thailand. The insurgents had counted on northern Malaysia for decades as a friendly sanctuary. Now, it was gone.

Twelve days after the raids and arrests, insurgent leaders held several emergency meetings in Kelantan to discuss their situation, as they were essentially being overrun.[347] An anonymous source told the *Bangkok Post*, "[The insurgents] have held several meetings over the situation which has dramatically changed during the past several months. Some feel insecure, thinking it might be better for them to leave the country at the moment as they are uncertain about what happens next."[348] It was their final breaking point. Between Thai security, and political and economic pressures, the insurgents were already severely strained. With the added pressure of KAL denying them sanctuary, their organizations collapsed, and their top leadership that wasn't detained then scattered.[349] In February, the leaders of PULO, New PULO, and *Bersatu* fled to Syria, Sweden, and Saudi Arabia. These included PULO chief Tunku Bilor Kortor Nilor, ex–New PULO leader Ar-rong Mooreng, his deputy Hadi Muno, and *Bersatu* chief Wan Suleiman.[350] Scores of other insurgent leaders fled with them. Bangkok was so appreciative of Malaysia's help, the Thai ambassador to Malaysia awarded Malaysian Police Inspector General Abdul Rahim with the Knight Grand Cross of the Most Noble medal, a significant honor.[351]

Amnesty

Bangkok promoted amnesty throughout the war by rebranding it over and over again. It began in the early 1980s under *Tai Rom Yen* and the 66/2523 Plan. In October 1987, the government initiated *Muslim Santi*, a pacification program that included amnesty. Under this program, 641 insurgents surrendered and took an oath of loyalty to Thailand in January 1988.[352] The government started another new amnesty program that same year, called *Phu Ruom Pattana Chat* (Developer of the Thai Nation).[353] It was a good program on paper, but the authorities often harassed those who surrendered, and many ended up rejoining the insurgency. "We admit that in the past, some members of terrorist groups were given a hard time by some officials, while others faced extreme hardship or poverty when they · surrendered," SB-PAC Security Coordinator Thira Mindrasak told the press. "So they returned to the jungle."[354]

During General Kitti's tenure as Fourth Army commander, he designed an amnesty upgrade he called *Krong Kahn Thai Muslim Keh Ban Hah Thai Muslim*, or, approximately, "Thai Muslims Must Solve the Problem Themselves."[355] The Fourth Army funded it and CPM-43 managed it. The plan allowed insurgents to surrender so long as they joined government development programs to improve the plight of the nation's poor. Essentially, the offer was a "surrender and work for Civil Affairs" program. General Kitti thought it was a good way for insurgents to put their energies into changing the south by nonviolent means.

To join the *Krong Kahn* projects, General Kitti came up with five prerequisites. Participants had to swear to (1) be loyal to Thailand, (2) be good Muslims, (3) be loyal to the royal family, and (4) reject insurgency, and (5) be good citizens.[356] Because of the value of the development projects and these relatively soft requirements for political allegiance, General Kitti established good relationships with a wide range of southerners. "At that time," he says, "in that area, most of the Muslim leaders, they worked with me, together with me, the imams, and the political leaders, too." Unfortunately for the prospects of peace, the program never fully developed because Kitti's time as commander ended before he could fully implement it. This indicates that some programs in Thai COIN were personality-driven when they should have been policy- and strategy-driven.

Regardless, years later, the government adopted a nearly identical amnesty program.[357] In 1998, during *Pitak Tai*, the government upgraded *Phu Ruom Pattana Chat* with many *Krong Kahn* tenets to appeal to insurgents on the run from *Pitak Tai*'s security surge. This move suggested that General Kitti, with *Krong Kahn*, was ahead of his time in this war.

The new amnesty programs required legal and administrative maneuvering, however. Since past amnesty programs were based on Prem's 66/2523 plan and specifically aimed at communists, in July 1998, PM Chuan issued Order 127/2541, a new order that would apply specifically to Thai Malay Muslim insurgents. It aimed to convince them to surrender, undergo reeducation, and attend vocational job training programs to become productive citizens. SB-PAC security coordinator Thira ran the project.[358] The new program also allowed suspected insurgents who escaped Thailand to other countries to return home without legal prosecution so long as they did not have criminal records. Those with criminal records were handed over to the police.[359]

Equally important, *Phu Ruom Pattana Chat* sought to protect those who surrendered from harassment by ill-meaning government officials, a key ingredient missing from earlier amnesties. The government backed up the amnesty request with a veiled threat, however. It told insurgents to surrender by 10 March 1998, or face harsh action. The message was clear. Insurgents could rejoin the nation, or face the brunt of military action.[360]

Phu Ruom Pattana Chat followed several phases. To enter the program, the head of the MoI and a sixteen-member committee considered surrender requests. Once accepted, the surrendered persons entered the second phase, which involved orientation by CPM-43. This was much like a parole program, where former insurgents received lectures on acceptable behavior and what was expected of them—basically, a cessation of violence and support for the rebellion.

Then the SB-PAC put returnees into vocational training or development projects, or it found them full-time jobs. For vocational training, returnees and even their relatives could take three-month courses at a government facility near where they lived, or they could attend classes in their villages. The three-month courses included electronics, construction, and mechanics. The village courses lasted about forty-five days and entailed farming, dressmaking, bricklaying, and furniture making. As former insurgents got settled, the SB-PAC set up methods for them to inform on corrupt officials who were mistreating them.[361]

The government also directly appealed to some insurgents to surrender. Minister Sanan passed the word to rebels overseas and to those hiding in foreign embassies in Bangkok via the MoFA. Interestingly, one of the requests to surrender went directly to insurgent leader Amin Tomeena in Saudi Arabia, who happened to be the older brother of former Deputy Interior Minister Den Tomeena.[362] This situation was highly reminiscent of the case of General Surayud Chulanont's father, who was a CPT Central Committee member and Chief of Staff of the CPT's armed forces. The Thai did not persecute relatives of insurgents by keeping them from office. This showed high flexibility and represented a key trait that allowed amnesty programs in the first place.

Another phase of amnesty entailed SB-PAC teams at the district level serving as parole supervisors. These teams were composed of a district or deputy district head, an agricultural official, and a policeman. They visited returnees regularly to make sure they were not being harassed. Moreover, they provided medical treatment and food if necessary, and they made sure that returnees' houses were registered with the government.[363] This was a form of post conflict population control.

Overall, between 1979 and 1997, more than one thousand separatists surrendered. From the beginning of the upgraded *Phu Ruom Pattana Chat* to September 1998, fifty-eight more insurgents joined the program. An SB-PAC survey stated many returnees wanted land and scholarships for their children. Others asked for houses and livestock so they could begin farming. The SB-PAC appears to have met these needs, and the program proved successful.[364]

Eleven-year PULO member Abdul-Rohmae Durayena surrendered in 1996 and seemingly did well. "I am now growing vegetables on my rubber plantation. I hope it will give me a steady income," he said.[365] Another former PULO member, thirty-three-year-old Ma-esaw, returned to society to raise chickens. Former BRN member Mayateng Jaema spent several years as a construction worker in Malaysia, and the amnesty program allowed him to return to Thailand without fear of detention. The SB-PAC program offered him fish farm training in his native Yala.[366]

Government Corruption

Government corruption was a major problem in the far south and one of the main reasons for people's resentment against the state. The problem stemmed in part from Thailand's undercurrent of patronage and the remnants of the *sakdi na* system. Poor civil service quality, pompous attitudes of entitlement, and racism also soured the system to the point that many saw it as illegitimate.

Says Chuan, "But one must accept all organizations in the provinces have problems with human resources—personnel in the organizations. For example, there were various types of misconduct, such as using influence to extract personal interests from various civic groups in the area, or getting involved in, or having knowledge of, illegal projects in the area—organized crime. This is one of the conditions that have caused conflicts between the people in the area and the administrators. And those who do not mean well [insurgents] used this as leverage to intensify the situation. But misconduct is in all agencies."[367]

The SB-PAC was centrally involved in expelling corrupt officials. First, the SB-PAC collected intelligence on wrongdoers from civil servants and the local population. Second, it investigated the suspects' alleged misdeeds and, if the allegations were confirmed, built a case against them. Third, it submitted their names to the Fourth Army commander, who handed out punishments.[368]

In the beginning, PM Prem had a direct hand in cleaning up the south, in part based on his relationship with General Harn. They cut through the red tape and streamlined the process. Says Gothom, "Prem had a direct line to the SB-PAC, so people could directly tell him, 'Here's a bad governor, a bad policeman,' etc. It was a hotline to take care of problems. He acted immediately. He gave ears to that organization to make it more powerful than it was on paper. On paper, the SB-PAC had to go through many levels to get to the PM. In reality, the SB-PAC talked directly to Prem, so if a local complained about a local problem, there was a response."[369]

From 1981 to 1982, the SB-PAC identified seventy-two government workers guilty of malfeasance. The Fourth Army commander transferred all of them out of the south and charged fifty-one of them with criminal conduct. This action was comparable to what COIN-minded commanders did in CPT areas where officials harassed locals.

Corruption remained a major problem in the south, however, and the SB-PAC, while generally successful, was never able to eradicate the problem. Even in 1998, on the heels of the Falling Leaves campaign and in the early stages of the *Pitak Tai*, Thailand's Chief of Police met with Thai Malay Muslim leaders and promised to work harder to eject corrupt officials from the south.[370]

Doing so was not easy, especially with the rise in drug trafficking in the region. Reporting in January 1998 said police in Sungai Kolok, for example, were caught taking 5 million *baht* a month in bribes to ignore drug smuggling.[371] Such signs of ongoing police corruption indicated the gains made under Harn and Kitti with regard to improving government legitimacy had not taken root.

Psychological Operations and Public Relations

The SB-PAC was heavily involved in psychological operations. "Propaganda operations, or as you Americans call IO [Information Operations]—we called it propaganda and PR—we did it," says Chuan. (US forces as of 2013 call this

MISO, or Military Information Support Operations.) "Our messages were essentially to 'stay away from insurgents.' We had seminars at the village level, we had billboards, things like that."[372] The SB-PAC also relied on village leaders to support government psyops. "The head or subhead of the village easily approached their people—they knew them," says Chuan. "They were born there. PR was easy for them."[373]

One of the SB-PAC's first actions when it began operations was to set up a series of seminars in 1981–82 where local imams discussed Islam and local issues with the *Masjid* Committee (provincial mosque committee) and District Committees for Islamic Affairs. These were persuasive psyops based on open exchanges of information between the two sides. Not all locals were satisfied with the government's Islamic leaders' points of view, but the SB-PAC believed the fact that locals showed up was a sign they acknowledged some semblance of government authority. The meetings also opened unprecedented communication between the RTG and local Muslims. The aim here was to drive a wedge between the population and the separatists by showing the population the government cared and was truly working on RTG-Thai Malay Muslim issues, not just giving it lip service. In COIN, deeds must follow words. Not everyone saw these sessions as productive, however. Separatists and conservative imams usually refused to participate.[374]

The SB-PAC also tried to curb radical Islamism, which was not the main driver of the rebellion, but a growing one. Says Chuan, "At that time, they also set up teams of local Islamic leaders to propagate true Islamic doctrine to the people to keep them from being radicalized, and they went to every district. And these Muslims who taught true Islam were Thai Muslims."[375] Many Thai Malay Muslims, however, considered Thai Muslims racially and religiously inferior, and they rejected the latter's beliefs and political stances.

Educating Thai Malay Muslims on how the RTG worked was also important. Many locals were extremely isolated and susceptible to whatever wild rumors and accusations the insurgents could dream up. In this regard, many southern border villages in the 1980s–90s were as isolated and poorly educated as Issan villages were in the 1960s. Says Chuan, "We held meetings or seminars and took them to the other provinces of Thailand for visits to show them how the country worked and that their problems were similar to those of others in the country. We made visits to the PM and national leaders."[376] These visits exposed rural people to the whole of the nation and helped keep them from being duped by insurgent psyops.

The government had scores of other psyops designed to reduce the southern population's mistrust of the government and demonstrate that it was not trying to destroy Islam and Malay culture. For example, Channel 11 in Yala broadcast news for one hour each day in the Malay language beginning in 1996; again, vastly different from Phibun's 1930s nationalist culture policies.[377] This let the population know the government's Thai language programs were not aiming to replace Malay. The SB-PAC even helped Muslims make the *haj* to Mecca each year. In 1991, for example, it sent 471 Muslims to the holy land. "We helped them make the *haj*," says Chuan. "We held a safety orientation for them before they went overseas to study. The main points were that they were Thai people, and when you go study overseas, you must behave yourself and follow a good way of life."[378] This was designed to keep southerners from being recruited by BRN's and PULO's agents in the Middle East.

Internal Security Operations Command and Fourth Army Psyops

In the 1980s, to combat the *dawah* movement, ISOC created a countermovement, called "the official *dawah* movement." ISOC-4 ran it and staffed it with moderate Thai Malay Muslims. Their mission was to protect Islam from radical Islamists. It was parallel to the SB-PAC's moderate Islam preaching program Chuan described. "This action from the government," wrote Panomporn, "is to bring religious activities within sight and sound [of] the government's eye and ear."[379] It was also designed to collect local intelligence on insurgent ideological operations and head off propaganda and rumors that might goad the population into antigovernment demonstrations.[380]

The RTA had fewer psyops programs than during the CPT COIN. "We had some leaflet programs, but not too much," says General Kitti. "We did not need to launch a mass leaflet program because the [government's overall COIN] program was working."[381] The insurgency was not too powerful at the time, and there were significant periods of quiet and normalcy, so the urgency was less than with the communist threat in the 1960s–70s.

Economic Measures

Development programs for the 1980s–90s COIN were like those used in the communist COIN. They included improving the education system, road-building projects, bringing electricity to rural areas, agricultural projects, and job programs. The motivation behind them was also the same as in the communist COIN: to lift the population out of poverty, improve standards of living, and cultivate a grateful population that saw the government as being more legitimate than the insurgents.

The 1980s–90s COIN education programs were a continuation of what the government had begun in the late 1970s. Aside from political training, they also sought to build an economically productive southern population. State schools and state-sponsored *pondoks* continued to teach secular subject material, and quotas for Thai Malay Muslims put more than one thousand students through college, many of whom continued to help the south develop. Moreover, during these decades, most Thai Malay Muslim families stopped resisting the idea of school. According to Ornanong, by 1987, 78.1 percent of Thai Malay Muslims had finished primary school, and 89.3 percent had achieved literacy. Additionally, in the late 1980s, there were not enough high schools and colleges in the far south to accept all who had enrolled.[382]

The Private Schools Teaching Islam program excelled to such an extent that the government in 1982 categorized those that met the highest benchmarks as standard private schools and offered their students ten-thousand-*baht* subsidies.[383] By 1999, the government had closed 172 PSTIs that had not met government standards. The number of *pondoks* teaching only Islam had withered to thirty-seven. A 2000 survey of Thai Malay Muslim students in grades nine and twelve found that their Thai language abilities surpassed the national average.[384]

Bangkok carried on 1970s-era college-level reforms into the 1980s–90s as well. With the help of the Islamic Development Bank, in 1998, the government opened a private Islamic college in Yala. Bangkok also began Islamic studies programs at the Prince of Songkhla University's Pattani campus, the Teachers' College in Yala, and the Yala Islamic College.[385]

The government reduced college quotas but increased scholarships during the 1980s. SB-PAC educational programs in 1991 sent 128 Thai Malay Muslim students to universities and granted sixteen scholarships worth fifty-four thousand *baht*.[386] The *Kuruthayat* program was the biggest such program for Thai Malay Muslims, providing four-year university scholarships for prospective teachers. Upon graduation, these people became teachers in the far south. The goal was to close the culture gap between students and teachers by adding more Thai Malay Muslims to school faculties. These teachers also replaced Thai Malay Muslims who had been educated in Islamic institutions overseas and whom the government suspected of preaching rebellion. The Department of Teacher Training and the Department of Vocational Training doled out tens of millions of *baht* for scholarships since the 1990s—29 million *baht* for 1,260 scholarships between 1994 and 1996 alone.[387]

Bangkok's secular education programs seemed successful, as Thai Malay Muslim college attendance dramatically increased.[388] Ornanong writes, "One bit of evidence is the demonstration at Yala's Teacher's College in 1998, where parents and students called for an increase in the number of students admitted."[389] RTG education programs, in theory, co-opted Thai Malay Muslims into the government system, which reduced rebellion.[390]

Development

The SB-PAC carried out national-level economic plans in the far south and special projects as well. Among them was the 150-million-*baht* energy distribution plan to provide electricity to three hundred southern border villages and the 2.7-million-*baht* Bangrang Dam in Yala. This dam also provided irrigation to farms in Pattani, Yala, and Narathiwat. The SB-PAC, along with the RTA, carried out road building and other infrastructure projects, too.[391]

Regarding agriculture, the SB-PAC promoted technology to double rice crops each year, and it supported the Rubber Plantation Board in Yala to boost rubber crop yields. It also pressed forward major irrigation projects such as the Munoh irrigation project in Pattani. The government stated that these projects would allow farmers to grow two rice crops a year instead of one, thereby raising local farmers' incomes.[392]

When the government passed the Southern Border Provinces Development Plan of 1985–87, it continued the infrastructure development and agricultural programs of the early 1980s. Many programs were delayed, likely for budget reasons, and they made paltry progress.

Then a disturbing issue came to light. A 1980s SB-PAC study stated the far south remained in abject poverty. After all the early 1980s CA projects, the region remained depressed. In 1985, the per capita income there was a mere 15,449 *baht*, which was 4,814 *baht* below the national average. Limited application of technology was partly to blame for keeping the agricultural sector depressed. This problem was a major sticking point since agriculture employed 80 percent of the population. Ornanong cites the SB-PAC economic study as saying, "Most of the people are in poverty and cannot depend on themselves economically."[393] Based on the results of this study, Bangkok and the SB-PAC decided to increase investment in development projects.

The RTA did, too. In 1988, it began a major development project called *Krongkarn Puea Kuamwang Mai* (The New Hope Project), or *Harapan Baru* for short. CPM-43 carried it out. It ran concurrently with a similar project in Issan called Issan *Keaw* (Green Issan), which aimed to bring mass irrigation to the northeast to improve agricultural output.[394] The RTA also implemented scores of smaller projects, such as providing dental care.

The goals of *Harapan Baru* were to (1) improve villagers' standard of living, and (2) let the border provinces know that the government cared for them so that they would, in turn, view themselves as Thai citizens. The project budget was more than 619 million *baht*.[395] *Harapan Baru* entailed RTA troops interacting with the local population at the village level and doing small development projects villagers needed done right away.

General Kitti described RTA CA as all encompassing. "The army did psyops and civic action," he says. "It ran some medical teams, built houses for the poor, gave clothes, provided education, and awarded scholarships. The troops visited the *pondoks* and Muslim schools and talked to people about peace, citizenship, and the dangers of joining the insurgency."[396] RTA CA also included house and farm repairs, small-plot agricultural assistance, and minor road and bridge repairs.

Regarding large-scale development, the government launched the National Security Policy for the Border Provinces of 1988–92 to bring more business and industry to the far south, increase employment, and diversify the regional economy. Because of this and other programs, by 1991, vigorous business and industry had developed in the region. In that year, the border provinces had a trade surplus of 17,423.79 million *baht* that included exports of natural gas, plastics, seafood, canned food, and rubber products. Per-capita income in the far south rose to 19,389.20 *baht*, about 2,500 *baht* below the national average, but still a 4,000 *baht* improvement over 1988 levels.[397] By 1993 Yala, Narathiwat, and Pattani had an average income of 28,833.6 *baht*. Songkhla had an average income of 43,849 *baht*.[398] These latter figures were above the national average.

In 1991, the SB-PAC helped the NESDB write a new Southern Border Area Development Plan as part of Thailand's 1992 through 1996 Seventh National Economic and Social Development Plan (SNESDP). It also managed infrastructure projects totaling 370 million *baht* for the Ad Hoc Committee, a special board created to manage unique projects—in this case, the Special Infrastructure Development Project. In line with the central government's plan to turn the south into a Special Free Trade Zone, the SB-PAC helped the government generate investment privileges for far south investors. The SB-PAC also established government-backed, low-interest loans, helped to design industrial estates in Yala and Narathiwat, upgraded existing industrial estate in Pattani, promoted tourism, and spurred airport, seaport, and warehouse improvement.[399]

These initiatives were in part preparation to contribute to the Indonesia-Malaysia-Thailand Growth Triangle project (IMT-GT) proposed by Malaysian PM Mahathir Mohammad and agreed to by Indonesia and Thailand. Quelling the insurgency became a top economic priority for Thailand, as strife in the south would keep the Growth Triangle from materializing. Unfortunately, the project was ultimately abandoned, as the three nations never reached full agreement on a plan to make it happen.

Regardless, the preparations for the Growth Triangle still benefited the south, and the SB-PAC pressed forward with its economic programs, adding to progress made between the late 1980s and 1990–91. By 1992, the far south had 8,738 factories worth over 12 million *baht* and employing 53,397 workers. Many of these were very small enterprises employing a mere handful of people. Others employed more than thirty people. They processed rubber (resin and latex sheets), seafood, and palm oil, among other products. Moreover, there were 664 companies (nonfactory businesses) worth 1,238.2 million *baht*. The area had emerged as a mini economic powerhouse. Its overall population was no longer in poverty, its workers no longer unemployed on a mass scale.[400] This is one of the reasons the insurgency dwindled. The southern border population was mostly employed, largely out of the clutches of abject poverty, and therefore saw the government as legitimate.

These policies resulted in increases in the south's development budget. In 1994, it averaged 1 million *baht* a year. By 1997, it was 5 million. Most monies went into infrastructure projects. Private investment and business associations joined the effort.[401] Ornanong criticizes the degree of progress, however, by noting the 1994 economic plan focused more on business interests and less on the economic well-being of the southern population.[402]

The 1999–2003 NESDP picked up where the 1994 version left off. It aimed to continue infrastructure projects but also added a human element, seeking to improve "the potential of human resources and society," as Ornanong notes.[403]

The plan included stipulations for training locals for factory jobs and skilled labor, ensuring that incomes were adequate, and providing for the general welfare of the population. The government also sought to ensure fairness, equal opportunity, and peaceful living conditions. The latter might have been added in the wake of *Bersatu*'s 1997–98 Falling Leaves campaign. The violence had erupted after a period of relative calm, and Bangkok likely sought COIN follow-through. It had to let the population know its well-being continued to be a top government priority.

This step was vital because economic development in the far south, effective as it was, had some pitfalls. First, the industrial investment statistics that showed a reduction of abject poverty and increased incomes by an average of four thousand *baht* did not reveal that Chinese and Thai businessmen ran most businesses, and Thai Malay Muslims provided most of the labor. Some businessmen assert that most Thai Malay Muslims had not sought to become business leaders, as it was not in their perceived "sedentary culture."

Second, much of the investment in the south yielded profits for big businessmen without dramatically improving the lives of small-scale farmers and fishermen. To be sure, regional investment beginning in the late 1980s saved the far south from economic destitution, and road projects improved the lives of laborers and small businessmen through increased business traffic and access to markets. Because most big profits went to non-Thai Malay Muslims, however, some of the latter resented the economic boom, and antigovernment advocates used it as a rallying cry: "The outsiders are economically exploiting us." And as pockets of the population became mere labor pools, this created yet more resentment.

And in the labor pockets, Ornanong asserts, some poverty remained. Development and investment did not reach everyone, and rural people with no access to industry jobs remained on the fringes while the rest of Thailand became known as an "economic tiger" during the 1990s. In some areas, poverty remained because inept civil servants kept development projects from happening. In other cases, Thai Malay Muslims themselves were the obstacle, not wanting development projects of any kind, which contributed to their own economic plight.[404] Says Rotary Club official Amara Pongsapich, "Locals did not fight development in the communist counterinsurgency. But some southerners did. An anti-infrastructure movement did start in the south."[405]

Royal Initiative Projects

King Bhumibol was highly active in the southern COIN. Royal development projects were successful in helping people out of poverty and in convincing them that the state cared for them. When the king himself visited villages and personally assigned specific projects to state agencies, his politically soothing presence had a giant ripple effect on everyone who saw or heard about the project. The king had a powerful impact wherever he went because Thailand's people fervently revered him.

Whereas past royal projects were scattered and uncoordinated, for the southern COIN PM Prem organized and coordinated them via law in 1982 through a single office, the Royal Initiatives Project (RIP). Managing members of the RIP included the Minister of Defense, the Commander in Chief of the RTA, and the heads of the MoI and Agriculture, the National Economic and Social Development Board, and the National Budget Office. The Fourth Army commander managed the projects in the field. The RIP had its own budget and was not beholden to other agencies for funding, thereby streamlining its chain of command.[406]

The RIP's primary mission was to combat poverty at the village level. Its ministers could draft any civil servant, or military personnel, or police officer into any RIP project. It was the most efficiently coordinated development program in the far south, and it was by far the most successful. RIP projects were also highly prestigious, and no internal squabbling or personal power plays were involved. The mission was simply to carry out the king's orders to alleviate poverty in Thai Malay Muslim and Buddhist villages, and his subjects carried out those orders without questioning.[407]

Aside from small but numerous village improvement projects, the RIP was heavily involved in irrigation projects, which included irrigation ditches, small dams, wells, and the like to help improve agriculture. It also introduced handicrafts such as weaving, pottery, and silk growing to the far south. Fish farming, an alternative for maritime villages hit by a decreasing fisheries population, was another category of RIP project, as was road building.[408]

Narathiwat was the epicenter of RIP programs, where on 65,520 *rai* of land there were nineteen irrigation projects. The king built in Narathiwat the Pikulthong Research Center, an RIP agricultural research institution, to infuse new farming technology into the far south.[409] It remains to this day.

4

THE SECOND SOUTHERN COIN: 2004–PRESENT

Prelude

After their defeat in 1998, insurgent leaders retired to mediocrity in Europe and Malaysia, still fervent for their cause but exiled and impotent. Sometime between then and 2002, however, someone—Thai authorities are not sure who—engineered an insurgent revival in the far south. Says Professor Bhumarat: "After 2001, the separatists spurred a new chapter, a new generation, which included educated people."[1] This time around, the gangland-style overtones were gone. The new movement was steeped in radical Islamist ideology, secrecy, and terrorism. It had an operational tempo far higher than the prior southern insurgency, which made it more of an immediate threat.

Additionally, although the former insurgents had been defeated, the far south did not enjoy complete peace in the years immediately after 1998. Criminal violence continued because of a growing drug trade. Thai Malay Muslim gangs, corrupt politicians, smugglers, and crooked military officers and policemen conducted illegal activities in the border provinces, and all of them killed to protect their miniature empires.

Against this backdrop, some assert PM Thaksin Shinawatra (9 February 2001–19 September 2006) used extrajudicial killings to get rid of the far south's undesired elements in efforts to clean up the region once and for all. According to Chuan Leekpai, "The administration had the belief that the way to solve problems in the south was via violence and extrajudicial killings. This was the beginning of the use of extrajudicial killings—murders of the suspects of terror and criminal organizations beginning in year 2001. This was not the war on drugs. That came later."[2]

Here, Chuan is referring to Thaksin's nationwide antidrug sweeps of the early 2000s, which eliminated powerful drug gangs that had established de facto feudal realms within Thailand. They were keeping the nation from advancing and needed to be confronted and dealt with. Thaksin's sweeps, however, resulted in the deaths of more than one thousand gang members in just a few years. He received great criticism for what scores of observers said were extrajudicial killings. Regardless, the big drug fiefdoms were gone.

As for Thaksin's actions in the south, Chuan says the motivation behind the killings was a brutal ideology that went far beyond the scope of normal police work. "It's some form of the mentality of police who believe that to maintain order in the village is to kill all the thieves," he says.[3] Adds John Cole, former US Army defense attaché to Thailand, "A lot of those killed were former insurgents and gangsters who provided intelligence to the RTA, which helped it and the SB-PAC keep tabs on former rebels to maintain a relative peace."[4] Southern insurgents still lived in the far south, just as ex-CPT members still lived throughout Thailand. Whether they became reenergized to fight depended in part on Bangkok's handling of the peace. The killings of these ex-insurgents seem to have stoked the embers of rebellion, but it was not the single, decisive factor in renewing the insurgency. The most important component appears to have been Islamist jihad, which was experiencing a regional and international surge at the turn of the century.

Jemaah Islamiyah (the Islamic Congregation, or JI) spearheaded that regional jihad. Indonesian radical Islamists Abdullah Sungkar and Abu Bakar Bashir founded JI in 1993 while hiding in Malaysia to escape Jakarta's crackdown on religious extremists. They returned to Indonesia in 1998 and began creating terror cells and planning operations. They also established links to like-minded terrorist and insurgent organizations such as al Qaeda and Malaysia's Kumpulan Militan Malaysia (KMM). In the Philippines they established ties with the Abu Sayaaf Group (ASG) and the Moro Islamic Liberation Front (MILF).

In 2000, a flurry of activity by these groups commenced, tethered to an international radical Islamist tidal wave. From 5 to 8 January, JI's operational head, Riduan Isamuddin (a.k.a. Hambali), sponsored a meeting in Kuala Lumpur of JI, AQ, KMM, and other like-minded individuals and organizations to plan regional and global terror attacks. These included an attack against a US Navy ship in Yemen—ultimately the USS *Cole*—and the September 11 attacks in the United States. Both the CIA and Malaysian intelligence covered the meeting, but apparently only by video, and they did not prioritize following these people once their meeting ended.[5] Regardless, the overall gist of the situation was that radical Islamists had agreed to push their ideology forward regionally and internationally along a united front. The results were increased terrorism and insurgency in Southeast Asia and internationally, all in the name of jihad.

JI began the campaign that year in Jakarta with the 1 August assassination attempt via bomb against the Philippine ambassador and the 13 September Stock Exchange bombing. On 24 December 2000, JI detonated as many as thirty bombs within hours of one another against a variety of targets throughout Indonesia, including Christian churches and priests. On 30 December, JI, working with its contacts in the MILF, set off five bombs in Manila, killing twenty-two and wounding one hundred.[6] Scores of similar attacks continued in the following years, including the AQ attacks on New York and Washington on 11 September 2001 and JI's 2002 bombings in Bali.

In response, police in multiple Southeast Asian countries arrested scores of terror cells across the region. The Malaysians pressured and muted KMM activities, Philippine authorities launched offensives against jihadists there, and the RTP arrested a twenty-five-man AQ support cell, all Middle Eastern, in March 2002. Professor Zachary Abuza says they also shut down three AQ front companies.[7]

In August 2002, a man known as Assuluk Ismuljaminah, living in Kelantan, Malaysia, wrote a spiritual guidebook to inspire a jihadist insurgency in southern Thailand. He titled it *Berjihad di Pattani* (*The Fight for the Liberation of Pattani*). In it, Ismuljaminah used stanzas from the Koran mixed with Pattani myth to indoctrinate and propagandize the population into war. He asserted it was the duty of all Muslims in the area to fight in the jihad, and that if anyone tried to stop them—be they friends, relatives, or even mothers or fathers—they should be killed.[8] Years later, Thai authorities would find this book on insurgents who murdered police officers during a bloody uprising in Pattani. But the book had not yet made its highly public debut. The main terrorist trouble in Southeast Asia continued to be JI and AQ.

In May 2003, Cambodian authorities detained an AQ cell in Phnom Penh at a radical Islamist *Um al Qura* school. An Egyptian and two Thai Malay Muslims from Yala staffed it.[9] The involvement of Thai Malay Muslims was troubling for Thailand.

In August 2003, JI's Hambali was captured in Ayutthaya, Thailand, apparently through a joint Special Branch–CIA operation. He had been networking in Thailand and had dispatched an operative to Laos, all efforts to set up terror cells to bomb various targets in the region.[10] Abuza asserts that Hambali wanted to co-opt Thailand's Malay Muslims into JI's orbit. The southern border war was apparently being rejuvenated, but one of its senior clerics, Ismail Lufti Japagiya, rejected JI's terrorist strategy in favor of an insurgent strategy. The two men's revolutionary ideologies, however, were nearly identical.

Hambali also apparently contacted *Jemaah Salafiya* (the Salafist Congregation, or JS) insurgent leader Abdul Fatah (a.k.a. Muhammad Haji Jaeming) for the same purposes.[11] Fatah had participated in several JI conferences on expanding Islamist jihad throughout the region, and he had aided JI operatives with logistics services. He said no, however, to Hambali's co-opting scheme, asserting JS was but a tiny faction of the '90s era insurgency and defanged as a result of government operations and ongoing surveillance.

Abuza additionally points out Hambali spent time in Yala's Thammawittaya Foundation School. Masae Useng, a senior leader in the BRN-C, taught at this school (and Samphan Wittaya School).[12] As of 2013, Useng is one of Southeast Asia's most wanted insurgent leaders, primarily for his prolific use of terrorism against both Buddhists and Muslims in southern Thailand.

While it appears, then, that JI was unsuccessful in co-opting the southern Thai insurgency, at the very least Hambali's tour there demonstrated that jihadist personnel, jihadist ideological fervor, and a network of jihadist-minded people were present in the south. These linkages were unsettling.

Against this backdrop, a surge of organized, insurgent-like violence in Thailand's far south had begun in 2001. In June, according to authorities, alleged BRN personnel killed six people in Narathiwat. While this group had been defeated years earlier, a handful of the old BRN cadre might have tried to continue the fight, or it might actually have been a new group. At any rate, around the same time, unknown persons kidnapped and beheaded two people in Sai Buri district, Pattani.[13] The latter attack did not coincide with organized crime typical of the far south. The decapitation indicated radical Islamist overtones.

General Akanit, one of the RTA's top intelligence officers (and Chief of Staff of CPM-43 in 2002), watched the region's and Thailand's southern turmoil with alarm. "There was a rash of incidents in the late 1990s and before 2004," says Akanit. "They were not done by PULO and BRN."[14] He wrote an intelligence estimate on the violence and hypothesized a new movement was behind it, but he did not know its name.

"When I presented this report," he says, "they laughed at me. I warned the Fourth Army commander. I warned many people in the Fourth Army that it would face Islamic militants. Nobody understood what I said. 'What's the meaning of Islamic militants?' they asked. 'Now you are facing the soldiers of God,' I told them. I did not use *mujahideen* or jihad terminology. I said the struggle in the southern provinces was going to be a new paradigm."[15]

Akanit's analysis said the movement had three strategies. First was to wage low-level violence to attract media attention. Heavy violence would come later, he figured. Second was to raise the rebellion's profile to the international level and get the UN or OIC involved to leverage a third-party settlement, as had occurred with the rebellious movements in Aceh and East Timor, Indonesia. Moreover, the OIC had used its political power in conjunction with the Moro National Liberation Front's (MNLF) guerrilla warfare and terrorism to achieve some semblance of a Muslim autonomous-zone agreement for the latter in the Philippines in 1996.[16]

The third strategy was to recruit and indoctrinate children and youth and turn them into insurgents. So long as they were indoctrinated at an early age, Akanit thought, the movement would have plenty of dedicated followers. "This strategy was not of PULO, or BRN, or *Bersatu*," he says. "We did not know where it came from."[17] Akanit's warnings went unheeded.

Thaksin did not link the initial violence to terrorism. He told the press, "The people responsible for the attacks are not terrorists." Some locals blamed it on political feuds, saying many politicians were corrupt and ran criminal empires.[18] Ex-insurgents thought differently. Former PULO official Yusouf Longpi told the *New York Times*, "Certainly there is some influence here of the ideology of Al Qaeda. It is dangerous for me to say more."[19]

Amid all this, PM Thaksin decided in April 2002 to dissolve CPM-43 and the SB-PAC. Says recent former SB-PAC Director General Pranai Suwannarat, "The Interior Minister, Dr. Purachai [Piumsombun], submitted to the cabinet to close the SB-PAC [and CPM-43] on grounds that it was no longer needed since the situation was close to normal."[20] Others speculate Thaksin wanted these agencies gone because they were connected to his political rivals in the Democratic Party.[21]

Regardless of the actual reasons, these shutdowns resulted in intelligence blindness in a region that still needed to be watched. Insurgencies never end cleanly. "When Thaksin got rid of CPM, we lost our access to the villages," says Professor Bhumarat. "Our information on the separatist movements in the villages dropped off."[22]

By design or not, the new crop of insurgents took advantage of the vacuum. Violence grew in 2002. From March to November, there were multiple raids against police checkpoints and several bombings at hotels, bars, and Buddhists' wats. Many schools were burned, and more than twenty police were assassinated.[23] These activities seemed well beyond the pale of organized crime.

At the same time, security agencies in the United States, Singapore, and Malaysia said JI and jihadists in general were trying to infiltrate Thailand's far south. Professor Panitan Watanayagorn at Chulalongkorn University said Islamist terrorists might indeed have begun to base in southern Thailand. He told *Time* magazine, "Security has been tightened dramatically in Singapore, Malaysia, the

Philippines, and now Indonesia. If these guys have fled, where would they go? Thailand is the obvious choice."[24]

Bangkok launched investigations in the fall of 2002 to figure out what was behind the recent violence. In one case, authorities discovered eight sticks (or chubs) of Powergel mining explosives and extortion letters in the home of Abdul Koder Saha, a teacher at Pattani's Ban Mai Withaya School. The letters were signed by BRN member Poh Ma Su-ngaibatu. They were aiming at squeezing 1.5 million *baht* from gas stations. The letters had been written in 2001.[25] These certainly pointed toward organized crime, but not necessarily insurgency. Still, Su-ngaibatu's intentions could have been to fund insurgency.

In December, however, an obvious insurgent threat surfaced. An organization calling itself the Young Liberators of Pattani burned a Buddhist school, Wat Tantikaram School in Narathiwat, and left threat propaganda saying it would continue attacking government buildings, civil servants, and their families until it liberated Pattani.[26] The group did not ask for money. It did not steal from the school. It wanted its own government.

There was more evidence of organized resistance in 2003. On 28 April, raiders attacked RTM outposts in Narathiwat and Yala.[27] On 3 July, police arrested three Muslims and a Thai Buddhist trafficking fifteen AK-47s to the far south in Nakhon Ratchasima town, 210 kilometers northeast of Bangkok. Hours later, unknown attackers killed six people and injured three in Pattani.[28] Later that summer, police broke up a three-person JI cell in Narathiwat planning embassy bombings in Bangkok.[29] (Years later, a court acquitted the trio, but authorities insisted they were guilty and blamed inept police for not gathering enough evidence to gain a conviction.) Throughout the late summer and fall of 2003 police had shootouts with suspected Islamic militants in Pattani, and there were more raids on police outposts by unknown attackers.[30]

These incidents demonstrated a striking increase of southern border violence, seemingly insurgent-related. There were indicators of regional and domestic jihadists in southern Thailand as well. It is possible the 2000 JI/AQ meeting in Kuala Lumpur helped inspire (but not command) Thailand's southern revolt, just as it appears to have been the starting point of other regional and global terrorist campaigns.

Still, there was no solid evidence linking all of these incidents and people. It was difficult for Thai and regional authorities to discern exactly what was happening. The Fog of War was thick. Had CPM-43 and the SB-PAC been operational, the government might have been able to at least ascertain the reality of the local situation, but it did not.

When the insurgents struck overtly in 2004, it stunned Bangkok. Says Chuan, "We never believed this situation could happen in our country—that a government could make such a huge mistake. So, when the recent trouble started, we went from about ten significantly violent incidents a year to over two thousand."[31] The war was on.

Overview of the Second Southern COIN

2004

On 4 January 2004, more than thirty insurgents raided the Rajanakarin RTA camp that housed an engineer battalion in Narathiwat. They slit the throats of four Thai Buddhist soldiers, told the Muslim troops stationed there to quit the army, and stole forty pistols, three hundred M-16 rifles, four M-60 machine guns, and ammunition.[32] At the same time, arsonists burned eighteen schools, killed two police with a motorcycle bomb in Pattani, and injured another with a bomb in a park. Authorities found two more bombs at a gas station and a shopping mall. More attacks followed, and police discovered a plot by twelve Thai Malay Muslims to bomb all four provinces in the far south.[33] While Thaksin at first blamed bandits, the government later accused GMIP, BRN, and PULO of being the culprits. General Kitti hypothesized AQ might have helped them. There was no mistake, however. Thailand had an insurgency on its hands.

In response, PM Thaksin declared martial law in Pattani, Yala, and Narathiwat and sent three thousand soldiers to provide security.[34] The Fourth Army developed a COIN plan complete with security, political, and economic measures, but it never went into effect. Many blamed Thaksin's meddling with the national security chain of command for not allowing the RTA to do its work. Thaksin's supporters denied this. Regardless, the RTA "stayed behind the wire," said foreign military attachés. The government was playing defense, which was weak, and the insurgents were on the offense.

On 28 April 2004, more than one hundred insurgents attempted to start a region-wide revolt, led by a man named "*Ustaz* Soh" Rayarong, a *pondok* teacher. Multiple rebel units raided as many as fifteen RTP and RTA posts in Pattani and Yala and one in Songkhla, shouting Islamist jihadist death slogans. One raiding party, composed of thirty militants, took over Krue Se mosque in Pattani town, chasing down and stabbing to death nearby police in a bloody frenzy. Attackers declared over the mosque's loudspeaker that they would fight to the death for their rebellion and called for local civilians to join them.[35]

Armed with a few assault rifles and pistols but mostly machetes and knives, all but one of the raids failed. Raid leaders had brainwashed most attackers with mystic Islamist chants and holy water into believing they were bulletproof.[36] As an aside, the mystic chants indicate the insurgents were not Salafists, an AQ ideological trend, who are purists and believe mysticism in Islam is heresy.

At any rate, the insurgents did manage to overrun the 5th Southern Development Unit in Yala, stealing seventeen M-16 A2s and two M-203 grenade launchers. They also took an M-79 grenade launcher from the Krong Penang police station in Yala.[37] Despite the bloodshed, several raiders later captured by the police told an academic researcher they had not intended to kill anyone, just scare them.[38] As evidenced by the murdered police at Krue Se, this is a farcical assertion.

Regardless, RTA forces surrounded the insurgents in Krue Se and pressed for negotiations for several hours. The insurgents responded with assault rifle and 40 mm grenade fire, which wounded several troopers. A crowd of civilians that eventually reached one thousand gathered to protest the troops amid the shooting. They chanted not to kill Muslims after an imam walked into the melee to administer last rites to insurgents and was shot by security forces.[39] The crowd did not call for the insurgents not to kill Buddhists, nor did it urge the rebels to surrender. The insurgents inside the mosque were most likely encouraged by this loud show of support.

General Chavalit in Bangkok and General Panlop Pinmanee, who was on the scene, conferred on how to solve the crisis. Chavalit was serving as DPM and defense minister at the time. Panlop, an RTA officer with an aggressively fierce reputation, was running ISOC-4 and the Southern Peace Enhancement Center, Thaksin's answer to CPM-43 and SB-PAC.

Chavalit ordered Panlop to continue negotiations. Panlop, however, feared losing positive control of the situation. Insurgents were continuing to fire at his troops, and the large crowd increasingly surrounding the battle scene clearly was not pro-government. Accordingly, Panlop ordered the mosque cleared.[40] Two assault teams, reportedly covered by troopers firing RPG antipersonnel rounds (other reports say hand grenades) and by snipers cleared Krue Se, killing all inside.[41]

In total, the casualty report for the entire 28 April uprising was five security personnel killed and scores more wounded. Security forces killed more than one hundred insurgents. Many political activists and Thaksin's opponents condemned the action as a barbaric human rights violation, decrying the use of firearms against people armed only with knives, machetes, and the like. The insurgents had indeed used firearms, however. Regardless, relatives of the dead saw them as martyrs.[42] One of the dead insurgents wore a JI motif on his clothes and several wore green Hamas-style headbands, says Abuza.[43] Among some of the dead's belongings was the insurgents' guidebook, *The Fight for the Liberation of Patani.*

On the heels of the failed 28 April uprising, there followed a summer of assassinations, bombings, and arson against government and civilian targets. In the fall, the government committed a serious blunder at Tak Bai, Narathiwat, on 25 October 2004. More than one thousand male protesters gathered at the Tak Bai police station and demanded the release of village security personnel who had been arrested for handing their guns over to insurgents without a struggle. A handful of protesters were armed, and they had hidden a few weapons wrapped in plastic in the river next to the station.[44]

Authorities tried to get the crowd to disperse, and they asked local Muslim leaders and family members to help. Protesters booed them. Rally leaders blocked some of these people from leaving, and security forces formed a perimeter around the crowd.[45]

Then, without warning, at 3:10 p.m., protesters rushed the police station, shooting and injuring an officer. A riot ensued. Authorities fired their guns both in the air and directly at protesters. After a tense melee, security forces subdued the crowd. Security personnel had suffered fifteen wounded. Police and military arrested the protesters, handcuffed them, and stacked them like cordwood in trucks, facedown, with their hands behind their backs. There were multiple beatings, too, which caused several deaths. More, a total of seventy-eight protesters died while being transported to the RTA's Ingkayuth camp in Pattani. Medical examiners said fasting for Ramadan had made detainees more susceptible to harsh treatment. The army reportedly provided halal food and water to those that survived the journey.[46]

Official reporting says insurgents organized the protest to goad authorities into harsh action in order to enrage the local population. This has happened in scores of insurgencies throughout history, such as the Bogside riots in Northern Ireland in August 1969. If this assertion is true, it worked.[47] While the police and military rightfully defended their station and arrested those who refused to leave, they blundered in killing eighty-five of the protestors. Opponents of the government, including insurgents, have successfully used this human rights violation as a PR trump card. Insurgents have also used it as a highly effective recruiting tool, the general message being, "The Siamese are slaughtering us 'defenseless Malay Muslims' like cattle—so join us, and fight back!"

2005

Violence increased in 2005, but the government took no significant offensive or defensive action to stem it. Insurgents doubled the number of bombings and arson attacks. Assassination attempts statistically averaged about one a day. The insurgents began to carry out raids and ambushes as well. Authorities say the injection of light infantry power came from a unit called *Runda Kumpulan Kecil* (Small Unit Tactics, or RKK), which allegedly trained in Indonesia in irregular warfare. Some security personnel assert RKK is the military wing of the BRN-C, resurrected in name to spearhead the current war.

Regardless of what organization was behind all this, violence grew. On 17 February 2005, insurgents set off a hundred-kilogram car bomb next to the Pikul Restaurant and Marina Hotel in Narathiwat. Authorities said it was Thailand's first car bomb. It killed six and wounded fifty.[48]

On 3 April 2005, insurgents set off three bombs in Songkhla at the Hat Yai International Airport, the French-owned Carrefour department store in Hat Yai, and the beachfront Green World Palace Hotel in Songkhla town. The bombings killed two and wounded sixty-five, including Thai, French, British, American, Malaysian, and Brunei citizens.[49]

On 15 July 2005, insurgents raided downtown Yala in a well-coordinated attack. Witnesses said the raid consisted of at least sixty insurgents divided into three groups, each with specific missions. One group pinned down *Thahan Phran* at a railroad station, preventing them from responding to the attack. The other two groups bombed and shot up the town's hotels, businesses, and a movie theater.[50] It was the largest infantry action of the war at the time, and it demonstrated professional training, rehearsals, and intelligence gathering on behalf of the insurgents.

On 21 September in Narathiwat, over one hundred locals from Tanyong Limo village took two Marines hostage for supposedly executing a drive-by shooting on a teashop. Intending to show their innocence to the villagers, the Marines voluntarily gave up their arms. Women and children blocked politicians, police, and military from entering the village to conduct hostage negotiations. They demanded to tell their story to the Malaysian press because they did not trust the Thai media. Twenty hours later, as the Malaysian press was arriving, authorities discovered the insurgents had tortured, beaten, and stabbed the Marines to death. Torture included carving on the Marines with knives and sprinkling biting black ants on them. Bangkok issued twenty-nine arrest warrants shortly thereafter and apprehended numerous suspects.[51] Tak Bai organizers were among them.[52]

On 16 October, twenty insurgents raided Wat Promprasith in Pattani, where they murdered and mutilated a monk, killed two temple workers, and desecrated the *wat*'s interior.[53] Thailand's chief Crime Scene Investigator (CSI), Dr. Pornthip Rajanasanun, and her team deployed to Pattani and solved the case by analyzing key evidence, including a torch cut from a tree from the front yard of one of the attackers. While a heinous incident, human rights watchers who decried Krue Se and Tak Bai remained largely silent on this attack and others like it. Bangkok was losing the information war to the insurgents and government opponents, and violence only got worse the next year.

Insurgent violence increased dramatically in 2006, with nearly ninety raids and ambushes, three times as many bombings as in 2004, scores of arson campaigns, and statistically more than one assassination attempt per day. Some insurgency watchers contend that up to 20 percent of the assassinations might have been due to personal conflicts. This could indeed be true, but no hard evidence has been presented to support this supposition.

On 15 June, insurgents detonated sixty-nine bombs, including a car bomb, in Pattani, Narathiwat, and Yala. Targets included Pattani City Hall, an education office in Pattani, rail and ferry facilities in Narathiwat, karaoke bars, and other civilian targets. The attacks killed two and wounded twenty-three.[54]

Insurgents demonstrated their growing tenacity and light infantry abilities on 28 June when, after ambushing a column of local forces, they broke cover, entered the kill zone, and executed all the wounded. It was the first time militants decisively cleared a kill zone in an ambush.[55]

As for the COIN campaign, Thaksin had given newly appointed RTA Commander General Sonthi Boonyaratglin, a Thai Muslim, complete power over all government agencies involved in the war. After a few weeks, however, it seemed to many that Sonthi's power was in name only. Rumors claimed the general's lofty authority was a ruse and designed to cause Sonthi's failure, which would then allow Thaksin to seize more national security power as the only person who could solve the unrest.[56] Some also believed Thaksin wanted to put his classmate and ally, Assistant Army Chief of Staff General Pornchai Kranlert, in charge of the army.[57] Defense Minister General Thammarak Issarangkura said on 25 July the government still did not have a cohesive COIN strategy, and the existing command structure lacked unity. He told the press that "certain people in high places" had denied Sonthi full command to wage COIN, and the result was turmoil.[58] Thammarak was no stranger to effective COIN. He had served as the Fourth Army's intelligence chief during the *Tai Rom Yen* era.

Thaksin and his supporters wholly denied these accusations. They said the RTA did not have the brain trust to deal with the southern violence. They also accused the RTA of making trouble for the PM because he wanted to decrease the army's traditional political power.

Amid the political wrangling, on 16 September, insurgents detonated six bombs in downtown Hat Yai's tourist district, killing four and injuring as many as seventy. All bombs went off nearly simultaneously at 9:15 pm. The targets were the Big C department store, the Lee Gardens Hotel, the Monkey Pub, the Odeon Shopping Mall, and a cinema toilet near the Diana department store.[59] So brazen was the attack on Hat Yai that security officials thought insurgents might make similar strikes on other resort areas, such as Phuket, that contribute to Thailand's $10-billion-USD-a-year tourist sector.[60]

It was the last straw for the RTA. The government's inaction on the insurgency, Thaksin's alleged politico-military intrigue, and his purportedly illegal business affairs caused General Sonthi to lead a coup against PM Thaksin on 19 September 2006, while he was in New York at a UN meeting. Backing Sonthi was a consortium of RTA personalities via the Council for Democratic Reform under Constitutional Monarchy (CDRM). The CDRM was rumored to have the blessing of the king and the Privy Council, of which Prem was a member. Sonthi's forces arrested the cabinet and established an interim government under the Council for National Security.

From that point on, the RTA began the COIN campaign it had designed two years earlier. The army was playing catch-up, however. From 2004 through 2006 the insurgency had killed nineteen hundred people.[61] Quelling it became the new government's top national security priority. As a first step, retired RTA General Surayud Chulanont took over as PM and apologized to Thai Malay Muslims for decades of ill treatment and for the deaths at Tak Bai.[62] In the meantime, the RTA planned its COIN campaign to begin in early 2007.

The year ended with nine bombings throughout Bangkok on New Year's Eve, killing three and wounding forty-two. The explosive devices and targets mimicked those in the far south, and some intelligence officials suspected the work of JI. The Department of Special Investigation (DSI), an FBI-like investigative agency created in 2002, alleged a "possible link" to the insurgency based on technical aspects such as the timing devices used: Casio watches.[63] Vocal pundits, however, pointed to the coup and convincingly blamed the military and/or Thaksin's followers.[64] The whole episode was murky. No culprits were ever caught.

2007

Before PM Surayud and General Sonthi could put their COIN plan into action, the insurgents staged the biggest bombing campaign of the war up to that point on Sunday, 18 February. For the first time, they struck all four southern provinces at once, beginning at 7:00 p.m. and lasting into the next day. There were about fifty bombings along with multiple acts of arson and scores of assassinations.[65] The insurgents tried to bomb a 7-Eleven with a large device, but it was discovered in a freezer box and defused.

From 27 to 29 May, insurgents targeted Songkhla, mostly Hat Yai, in yet another bombing campaign. On day one they detonated seven bombs in Hat Yai at hotels and other tourist venues, killing one and wounding thirteen. The next day they set off a massive bomb at a market in Saba Yoi district, killing four and wounding twenty-six.[66]

Meanwhile, the RTA's COIN campaign began by applying the king's advice of understanding the population's needs, interfacing—or at least trying to interface—with the people regularly, and executing development projects. The government also overhauled ISOC and focused most of its resources on the insurgency. The RTA revived CPM-43, now simply called CPM, and the SB-PAC.

For security operations, the RTA increased its intelligence capabilities and began receiving more tips from villagers, resulting in scores of arrests and weapons cache raids. On many occasions the RTA and BPP attempted arrests only to be met with hasty ambushes—proof their intelligence was accurate, but also that insurgents had an effective early warning system.

On 29 July, a battalion-sized CPM force of five hundred raided *tambon* Tapoyor in Narathiwat's Yingo district. They arrested fifty suspects, including alleged RKK officer Abdulromae Pereesee. The force also discovered a cache of four pistols, two M-16s, ammunition, PVC piping and fertilizer (insurgents use fertilizer to make bombs and PVC piping as bomb casings), camouflage uniforms, and medical supplies. Overall, the new government's COIN campaign resulted in nearly two thousand detentions. The government said that about three hundred were rank-and-file fighters or organizers, while the rest were auxiliary support personnel. [67] Government opponents and some NGOs, however, contended that many were innocent villagers caught up in overly harsh government dragnets.

As CPM carried out its missions, the SB-PAC infused cash into the border provinces and assembled advisory boards of local imams, village leaders, and businessmen to develop solutions for the south's socioeconomic woes. Diplomatically, the government engaged Malaysia to try and resurrect a 1998-style working relationship, but progress was slow. Internationally, Bangkok deployed both diplomats and senior military officers to halt Middle East and OIC support for the insurgency.

Security operations began to show some results. Authorities discovered and stopped a plot to bomb Hat Yai on 5 October. They found as many as seventeen bombs hidden near Prince of Songkhla University and twelve near a restaurant owned by the RTN. [68] At the same time, in Narathiwat, they discovered and shut down a ten-person terrorist cell—including two women—that had communications equipment, ammunition, Molotov cocktails, bomb material such as electronic circuits, and fake license plates. [69] (Insurgents frequently place fake license plates on cars and motorcycles used as bombs. In other cases they remove the plates.) Additionally, multiple bombings failed because of poor device placement and faulty construction. In a more dramatic case in December, two insurgents in Pattani were killed when the device they were transporting exploded prematurely. [70]

While these setbacks demonstrated the insurgency was certainly down, it was by no means out. It proved this on New Year's Eve by bombing two celebrations in Narathiwat. It struck the Riviera Hotel and, for the second time, the Marina Hotel. Bombers exploded two devices hidden behind speakers in the Riviera's ballroom, causing panicked revelers to flee into the parking lot, a prearranged kill zone where a motorcycle bomb awaited. The Marina was struck in similar fashion. In total, both attacks injured thirty-one.[71] By the end of 2007, 2,848 people had died as a result of the insurgency.[72]

2008–2009

In early December, the Constitutional Court of Thailand removed Thaksin ally and brother-in-law Somchai Wongsawat from the PM's office (18 September 2008–2 December 2008) for alleged political violations. Parliament voted in Abhisit Vejjajiva as PM on 15 December 2008 (17 December 2008–5 August 2011). Despite the political instability, the RTA, led by General Anupong Paochinda, who assumed command on 1 October 2007, managed to decrease insurgent violence by nearly half.[73]

The RTA's security increase showed its effects in several different ways. On 3 August 2008, for example, insurgents launched a bombing campaign in Songkhla. Their usual urban focal point in this province was Hat Yai town, and they typically struck major civilian entertainment targets there. This time, however, insurgents struck but a few small targets in Hat Yai and concentrated most of their bombings in Songkhla town, north of Hat Yai on the coast.[74] It seems they could not penetrate Hat Yai.

By early to mid-2009, the government had managed to institute a new village security program, *Pattana Santi* (Development and Peace), combining village security forces coupled with specially CA-trained *Thahan Phran*. RTP and RTA forces reinforced them. While not decisive, they showed positive effects. Violence had not gone away, but it had decreased, and intelligence tips on insurgent activities had increased. Government spokesman Panitan said the number of insurgent-controlled villages, though still more than four hundred, had decreased by nearly half.

Insurgent violence, however, increased slightly in the spring of 2009. Then on 8 June, gunmen in Narathiwat fired into al-Pukon Mosque in Joh I Rong district, massacring ten people during prayers. By the fall of 2009 the government had identified a suspect: a former local force trooper apparently incensed at the recent insurgent murder of a pregnant Thai Buddhist woman.[75] This episode illustrated the growing Muslim-versus-Buddhist violence that had characterized the war since 2004. Human rights groups and NGOs lambasted the government for the mosque killings, but not the murder of the pregnant woman.

2010–Present

By August 2011, the government said of the two hundred thousand Buddhists living in the far south, only sixty thousand remained. NGOs alternatively said 30 percent of Buddhists in the far south had been forced from their homes.[76] Whichever was correct, despite the government's degree of success in reducing violence, it was not enough to halt ethnic cleansing. No one was officially using this term, however.

Insurgent death squads continued operations unabated. On 16 September 2011, four insurgents stormed into a mosque in *tambon* Budi in Yala's Muang district and shot Police Sergeant Major Arong Malaya and defense volunteer Mahama Yama as they prayed. A hundred people witnessed the assassinations, and some nearby were wounded.[77] Human rights groups and NGOs were largely silent on this *takfiri* mosque murder.

Adding to the tension, in November 2012 the OIC issued a statement heavily criticizing the RTG for its treatment of the war. It issued insurgent-friendly remedies such as removing all military and local force troops from the war zone and allowing Islamic law to prevail there. In doing this, the OIC gave the insurgency the international Islamic recognition and leverage it had sought for decades.

As the war in the south carried on, politics in Bangkok became so divisive that it distracted the government from effectively working on COIN. This is not to say that the RTG halted operations. The RTA was on the case, as was the SB-PAC, and there were new programs being developed and fielded. Bangkok's political rancor, however, prevented a whole-of-government effort and distracted key players from their duties.

It was quite a complicated tryst, but basically it involved the Democrats' network of supporters versus Thaksin's network of supporters. The former had on its side the People's Alliance for Democracy, otherwise known as the Yellow Shirts, and similar groups. They mostly consisted of the upper and middle class, central and southern peoples, a majority of Bangkok, and most of the RTA. Their political bonding element was being anti-Thaksin. The latter had various support groups, namely the *Pheu Thai* Party and the United Front for Democracy Against Dictatorship, also known as the Red Shirts. They mostly consisted of Issan people, the poor, socialists and former CPT, anti–status quo cliques, a minority of Bangkok, and scores in the RTP and RTN. Their political bonding element was being pro-Thaksin.

While none of these descriptions are 100 percent rigid—there were pro-Reds in the RTA and pro-Yellows in the RTP, for example—each side staged major, economically debilitating protests at various times from post-coup 2006 onward, culminating in the Red Shirt protests and riots in Bangkok and elsewhere in the country. These resulted in an RTA crackdown, more than eighty killed, and multitudes of buildings torched by the Reds, including some skyscrapers in the business district in Bangkok. The Reds bore the brunt of the crackdown and from then on saw themselves as martyrs.

In the wake of the turmoil, the Thaksin clique elected Thaksin's sister, Yingluck, into the PM's position in 2011 (5 August 2011–present.) This was Thailand's first ever female PM. While Yingluck thereafter tried to assert order over an incredibly delicate and potentially volatile national political climate, Thailand remains a powder keg as of February 2014. A central point of contention is Yingluck's attempts to change the Constitution to, among other things, allow Thaksin back into the country a free man, coup charges against him dropped, and seized tens of millions of dollars returned to him. Protests numbers by the opposition in November reached into the hundreds of thousands, the biggest protests ever to hit the capital, some say. The anti-Thaksin clique boycotted elections on 2 February that were supposed to solve the impasse, and the country is at risk of widespread political violence. Because of this, the RTG has had trouble focusing its full resources on the southern COIN—shades of the early to mid-1970s.

At the same time, PM Yingluck did make the southern COIN a priority. On 8 August 2012, she announced that while the government's COIN strategy was generally correct, coordination was not. She authorized a new body, nicknamed "Pentagon II," to improve coordination. General Panlop, the new head of ISOC, was put in charge of it.[78] The new head of the NSC, the very efficient Lieutenant General Paradorn Pattanatabut, had a new task as well; namely, improving coordination between the SB-PAC and the military.[79] PM Yingluck also released her "Strategic Plan for Southern Border Provinces Development, 2012–2014," which was essentially a policy statement on her administration's track for the war.[80]

The Yingluck administration also made some progress in lifting the emergency decree that established martial law in the southern provinces in 2004 and replacing it with the Internal Security Act (ISA). The National Assembly passed the first ISA on 7 November 2007, and then another in February 2008, but it was not widely applied.[81] Some pundits say the ISA is "less draconian" than the emergency decree, but it still grants the government wide arrest and detention powers. To date, the government has applied the ISA to four districts of Songkhla (Na Thawee, Saba Yoi, Thepha, and Chana) and one district of Pattani (Mae Lan).[82] The RTG judges these districts as less violent than the rest of the far south, which remains under the emergency decree.

On 13 February 2013, the RTG experienced its biggest battlefield victory of the war. Authorities came across detailed intelligence on an insurgent night raid to be carried out on a Marine base in Bacho, Narathiwat. Commanders removed the RTM conscripts manning the base and replaced them with Reconnaissance Marines and RTN SEALs. These elite forces then ambushed sixty insurgents as they attacked the base, killing sixteen within twenty minutes. More insurgents died of their wounds later. Security forces followed blood trails and searched hospitals the next day, hunting for the wounded.[83]

The insurgency had meant this raid to be a major victory. Its fighters had made significant preparations for it, including reconnaissance, training, and special equipping. The fighters had assault vests, lights attached to their weapons, body armor, and flex cuffs for taking prisoners. Moreover, they sent a forward strike element to the target base well in advance of the main force. Despite their highly professional preparations, the operation turned out to be their biggest blunder. Because of this humiliating loss, the insurgents intensified terror attacks shortly thereafter with multiple bombings and assassinations, some in Pattani town, which had not been heavily bombed for some time. They could not allow morale to suffer.

The loss also meant the insurgents did not have prisoners for upcoming formal peace talks with the government, publically announced on 28 February. General Paradorn spearheaded talks for the RTG, and Hassan Taib, apparently an old BRN leader with wide influence—or a current insurgent leader, pundits are not too sure—was primary spokesman for the current insurgency.

Taib is a mystery to the public. It could be that he has little true authority and the government is on a fishing expedition, or it could be he is indeed entrenched in the current movement and the government is talking to the right people.[84] Some sources say Taib is the administrative head of an organization called, among other names, the *Dewan Pembabasan Pattani* (DPP), and indeed the leader of the entire insurgency. In the murky world of insurgency and COIN, especially in Thailand, the present truth is hard to see.

Either way, little if any progress has been made since then, and fighting has not waned, despite both sides calling for a halt to the violence. As a case in point, on 1 May 2013, four insurgents on two motorcycles rode up to a group of Buddhists and their Muslim friend having dinner outside a grocery store in Ban Khok Muang, a small hamlet in Pattani. They got off their bikes, leveled their M-16s at the group, and gunned them all down in a hail of one hundred bullets. They also shot the victims in the head as they lay bleeding. There were six killed, including the Muslim and a two-year-old baby.[85] Again, human rights groups, NGOs, and the OIC were largely silent.

Then on 22 December, an alarming chain of events happened that indicate increased and widespread insurgent attacks unless Bangkok fixes its domestic political mess and refocuses on COIN. Insurgents bombed three locations in Sadao district of southern Songkhla province, areas they had never struck before. The first two targets were the police stations in Padang Besar and Sadao town. Here, they used bombs hidden in motorcycles. Damage was minimal, and no one was injured.

The third target was the Oliver Hotel in Danok. Reporting is sketchy, but two to four people might have been killed, and at least 27 were wounded. The blast here was from a bomb hidden in a pickup truck. Damage to the hotel amounted to $2 million USD, twenty nearby stores destroyed, and nine cars incinerated. Authorities also defused bombs set to explode at a Lotus Express and a McDonald's. These attacks aimed to kill and maim Thai and Malaysian tourists in Danok, a popular Christmas holiday destination.

Shocked, the RTP scrambled to increase vigilance at scores of police stations throughout the entire south, including 160 miles north in Phuket. Here, police at the main Phuket station decided to inspect a pickup truck that was parked nearby, abandoned since August. In it, they found a bomb big enough to destroy a ten-story building. It had been set to explode on 1 August, nearly five months prior. A faulty timer had kept it from detonating. A background check revealed the truck belonged to a Pattani man, earlier murdered by the insurgents. On top of this, Phuket police suddenly realized that a bomb that had exploded at their local Provincial Administrative Organization on 1 August had not been due to local mafia action after all. The insurgents had done it.

The implications were obvious. Frustrated at the lack of progress in their war and at the peace table, the insurgents—or possibly a radical breakaway faction—decided to expand their target list and geographic reach to police and civilian targets well outside the established insurgency zone. Whether they have the clandestine networks to continue such far-reaching action remains to be seen, but it seems they do. At any rate, these attacks demonstrate Thailand's war has reached a new level of violence, which could have catastrophic results if not kept in check.

The Insurgents

The current southern insurgency is much more centralized than its predecessor, though it still appears to be made up of scores of different groups. The BRN-C seems to be its centralized core, however, and in part driven by Islamist jihad. Its prolific use of terrorism indicates its fervor, and its political warfare is exceptionally effective. The recent bombings in Sadao and Phuket clearly indicate the insurgency has the potential to cause severe damage to Thailand writ large. The longer the problem festers, the worse it will get.

Strategy

Numerous pundits, reporters, and national security commentators say Thailand's current insurgency has yet to state its strategic end goals. This is untrue. Insurgents regularly state their objectives through propaganda leaflets, indoctrination, PR, and their violent deeds. Prisoners of war have also described the insurgency's ambitions.

The insurgency's end goal is to separate Yala, Narathiwat, Pattani, and Songkhla provinces (or parts of Songkhla) from Thailand and establish *Pattani Raya* (or *Pattani Darussalam*), a Malay Muslim Islamist republic based on sharia law (*syariat* in Malay). In 2004, PULO also laid claim to Satun province, but neither it nor any other group has done so since. Some strategists, such as retired RTA General Watanachai Chaimuanwong, also an advisor to former PM Surayud, assert the insurgents want "a pure Islamic state" that encompasses not only Thailand's Malay Muslim provinces, but also Malaysia's two northern states.[86] Regardless, as in other Islamist insurgencies, political and religious goals are the same. Copious insurgent propaganda has asserted *Pattani Raya* is to be just for Malays, which demonstrates the movement's racist tendencies and explains why it seeks to drive Thai Buddhists out of the provinces. The insurgents' guidebook, *The Fight for the Liberation of Pattani*, asserts this end goal in several places. At the same time, it also says non-Malays living in this state must submit to *dhimmi* laws, or special rules for non-Muslims living in Islamic-run states. *Dhimmi* can amount to apartheid-like, third-class citizenry status for non-Muslims, along with extra taxes. Few outside hushed Thai security circles call this war what it truly is—ethnic cleansing.

The Fight for the Liberation of Pattani touts end goals inspired by Taliban- and AQ-like ideologies.[87] On the other hand, the insurgents' mystic adherence to rituals and magic, such as making fighters bulletproof with holy water and Islamist chants, is considered impure in AQ circles, so the movement cannot be considered *Salafist*, a form of Islam that adheres to religious goals and an austere lifestyle harking back to Muhammad the Prophet's immediate disciples. It is important to note here one can be a *Salafist* and not a jihadist.

To achieve its ends, the insurgency uses Islamist political operations, guerrilla warfare, and terrorism to exhaust the RTG to the point it can harness the OIC, UN, or a like international organization to mediate an East Timor or Aceh-type settlement.[88] In 2012, the insurgency partly achieved this goal when the OIC endorsed its rebellion. Insurgent operations also make war on the south's economy, which has been partly successful.

Organizational Structure

Unlike the highly fractured southern insurgency of the 1980s–90s, the current movement is more centralized. While it appears to encompass multiple organizations, it is unified in cause, ideology, and operational capabilities. Authorities suspect its coordinating authority is the *Dewan Pembabasan Pattani* (Pattani Liberation Council, or DPP). The name *Dewan Pimpinan* Party has also been used in this regard, and they might be one and the same. There looks to be several groups under this senior authority, such as a new version of the BRN-C, and maybe some semblance of the former PULO, although some insurgents insist the movement has no formal name.

The insurgency seems to have a pyramid structure, with a leadership hierarchy commanding field lieutenants who manage clandestine fighter units and auxiliary support forces in the war zone. Its high operational security has insulated the movement's leadership, and its compartmentalized cell structure reflects professional planning designed to protect the movement when individual cells are compromised. This is similar to the 1950s Algerian insurgent organizational model.[89]

In 2009, Marc Askew interviewed a rebel field commander named Abdul who knew only the names and locations of his twenty-four fighters. He understood, however, that other cells existed, and he knew his operations and theirs coincided. Hamad, another insurgent, told Askew, "I often wondered just what the structure of the organization was like. But I was told that it wasn't necessary. It was enough just to do my job."[90] These comments reflect blind faith in the movement's upper leadership and high motivation among cell members.

The Police Operation Center Forward Command in Yala says the insurgents operate under a five-tiered structure of groups. Group one consists of Islamist leaders and *ustaz* who propagandize, recruit, and indoctrinate people to hate the state and join the movement. It also initiates new recruits via ceremonies designed to solidify groupthink and loyalty. The *ulama* are part of this top tier. They study the RTG's activities, world events, and formulate strategy.[91] Group two consists of the movement's administrative body. It manages the rebellion through a shadow government that parallels the state at provincial, district, and village levels. Che Man, *Bersatu's* former leader (who insists he and his former organization have nothing to do with the current war), alleges the insurgents also have agents inside the Thai government.[92]

Group three is the rebels' financial wing. It raises and distributes money. Group four, say the RTP, is the military wing, which consists of the RKK and its many trainees. Authorities discovered the RKK in November during an investigation into the 16 October 2005 insurgent raid on Wat Phromprasit in Pattani.[93]

Interestingly, Askew found that captured insurgent combatants he interviewed do not call themselves RKK. They say that the military has given them this label. They call themselves simply jihadists. This could be the truth, it could be denial and deception on behalf of the prisoners, or it could be that these prisoners were fighters but not members of the RKK. At any rate, they also told Askew their fighting formations consist of squads, platoons, and companies.[94]

Some reporting says the insurgents call themselves *juwae* or *pejuang*.[95] A July 2011 article in *The Nation* asserted *juwae* was not a name for insurgents, but an entirely different insurgent group.[96]

Group five is *Pemuda* (or *Permudor*). It consists of teenage and younger trainees that provide auxiliary support such as intelligence gathering on the routines of state officials. They also conduct harassment operations such as laying spikes on roads. These types of activities prepare them to become full-fledged fighters.[97] Few rights organizations outside Human Rights Watch criticize the insurgents for their use of child soldiers.

Southern Insurgent Numbers

In the early years of the war, the RTG estimated the insurgents numbered three thousand fighters. General Sonthi said in a November 2005 press conference that the auxiliary force numbered about five thousand.[98] Others claim it was as high as seventy thousand. In July 2009, the police said there were between seven thousand and nine thousand insurgents, that they had the staunch support of fifty thousand villagers, and that they controlled 274 of the twenty-two hundred villages in the far south.[99]

Logistics and Sanctuary

Insurgents rely on local sources and Malaysia for logistics, and they have sanctuary in Malaysia as well, just like the insurgents of the 1980s–90s. Local source logistics means securing weapons from dead army, police, and local forces. It also means stealing them from local forces insurgents manage to intimidate. Since insurgents mostly live in the villages and serve as part-time fighters, they depend on the population for food, shelter, information, etc. The few units that coagulate in the field do not seem to have problems acquiring provisions from friendly or intimidated villagers.

Some insurgents smuggle weapons from within Thailand. For example, on 19 October 2005, police seized a container truck in Phetchaburi, headed for Pattani with one AK-47, two M-16s, and two hundred rounds of ammunition. Police arrested three Pattani natives in the truck, and one confessed to having smuggled weapons to his brother in the far south on eight previous occasions.[100]

Insurgents carried out an audacious weapons theft operation on 26 October 2005. Between 7:00 and 9:00 p.m., they raided defense volunteers at sixty locations in Narathiwat, Yala, and Pattani, stealing ninety-two firearms, eighty-five of which were shotguns. Police recovered only three. Insurgents struck while the volunteers were either at home or on guard duty, demonstrating their local intelligence prowess.[101] Some volunteers gave up their weapons without a struggle, and militants killed those who resisted. The raids took place a day after the one-year anniversary of the Tak Bai protest.[102]

War materiel coming in from Malaysia is commonplace. One notable incident occurred on 9 March 2005, when Malaysian police arrested five insurgents at Sentral Station in KAL, the city's main rail station. The five in question were aiming to secure weapons from a JI arms cache. All were armed at the time of arrest. Ironically, the cache the insurgents were accessing was reportedly the result of arms smuggling operations out of Thailand and into Indonesia. JI had been using this particular overland trafficking route since at least 2000.[103]

In another weapons smuggling case on 3 June 2005, customs officials seized six hundred kilograms of sodium chlorate just outside Thung Lung Market in Hat Yai. Intelligence indicated the material was headed for insurgents. It came from Zunhuad Company in Panang, Malaysia. Farmers use sodium chlorate as an herbicide, and it can also be used to make explosives, just like ammonium nitrate and urea. Sodium chlorate is a similar compound to potassium chlorate, the main ingredient used in JI's 2002 Bali bombing.[104]

Regarding pistols, insurgents use 9 mms, .38 caliber revolvers, and .45 caliber semiautomatics. For long guns, they use twelve-gauge shotguns and several types of assault rifles such as HK 33s, AK-47s, and M-16s. They also use 40 mm grenade launchers and hand grenades. They have, on occasion, used belt-fed .30 caliber machine guns stolen from the RTA. Regarding explosives, they make compounds out of ammonium nitrate and similar agricultural materials, and they

254

also use commercial explosives including dynamite, Semtex, PETN, and Powergel, a commercial mining explosive acquired both locally and regionally.

Concerning border sanctuary, Bangkok has, since the war began, asked KAL for increased border security to halt insurgent infiltration from northern Malaysia. Evidence demonstrates insurgents regularly use Malaysia as a base and headquarters area. For example, captured rebels who participated in a large raid on Yala town on 14 July 2005 reportedly confessed to have planned the operation on 28 June in Kelantan, Malaysia.[105] In August the same year, police captured Masaki Ma, a thirty-eight-year-old accused bomber who crossed between Thailand and Malaysia regularly, further indicating the insurgents' use of Malaysia as sanctuary.[106] Such happenings are commonplace.

Insurgents train inside and outside Thailand. Within Thailand they undertake light training in small, remote areas and at *pondoks* where they study ideology, undergo weapons familiarity, and learn intelligence gathering. Trainees partake in calisthenics to instill discipline and unit integrity.[107] Insurgents obtain knowledge on guerrilla warfare tactics from manuals and the Internet, a common, global jihadist trend. On 20 January 2008, 15th Infantry Division Commander Major General Jamlong Khunsong said rebels were studying terrorist tactics such as how to build bombs and set up ambushes from jihadist websites.[108]

Police have uncovered multiple local training facilities since the war started. In May 2004, a joint RTA-RTP task force raided several Islamic schools in Pattani and found not only written and audiovisual instructional materials on weapons handling, explosives, and surveillance authored by AQ, but also a makeshift shooting range. The range was near the dormitories of Jihad Witthaya School in Ban Taloh Kapo village. Four students acknowledged that *ustaz* had given attendees firearms training and taught them how to make bombs. Authorities found bullet holes in coconut trees and cans. Some documents found there contained indoctrination and propaganda material urging students to revolt against Thailand.[109]

Additionally, the RTA says some *ustaz* claim rebel-minded students have undergone tactical training in Indonesia and Malaysia. They also say female insurgents have taken medical classes in Kedah, Malaysia.[110] Kuala Lumpur has not publically commented on these accusations. The RKK supposedly began training in Indonesia, years before the current violence erupted.[111] Scores of Thai Malay Muslims are suspected of having undergone ideological training in Pakistan's tribal areas, and they may have received weapons training there as well.[112]

Regarding financing, authorities have discovered evidence of insurgent reliance on drug money, Islamic charities, and cash smuggling. Interior Minister Kongsak Wanthana linked drug dealers, caught in November 2005, moving $3 million in narcotics from Malaysia to Thai Malay Muslim insurgents.[113] Days later, DPM and Justice Minister Police General Chidchai Vanasatidya named more than ten drug gangs providing insurgents with millions of dollars from illicit narcotics sales. He moreover pinpointed twenty locations in Thailand targeted for counternarcotics operations, many within the insurgents' battle space. Antinarcotics officials said the main drug involved was methamphetamines, colloquially known as *yaba*.[114]

As with the insurgency of the 1980s–90s, *zakat* is another form of insurgent financing. In August 2005, Nimu Makaje, Vice President of the Yala Islamic Committee, asserted the government needed to regulate Islamic charities more tightly because militants were siphoning money from them to fund their operations.[115] In December 2005, Anti-Money Laundering Office (AMLO) Police Major General Peeraphan Prempooti said police had arrested several insurgents after tracking their illegal financial activities through *zakat* networks. The accused had also abused charity funds to purchase personal vehicles and homes and to send their children to foreign schools.[116] Apparently, for some insurgent leaders, the "cause" is about milking the poor of Thailand's south, not independence.

In November 2005, police staged a series of raids that netted fifteen insurgents who had in their possession six bank deposit passbooks, indicating militants spread their financing activities across multiple accounts to camouflage it.[117] In the same month General Peeraphan said anti-money laundering operations had forced the insurgents to rely mostly on cash smuggling. General Peeraphan also said his officers had evidence from 1997 to 2003 revealing Middle Eastern financial transfers into the accounts of organizations linked to the insurgency.[118] Closer to the far south, Malaysian officials asserted in December 2004 that the Malaysia Islamic Welfare Organization, a.k.a. PERKIM, donated tens of thousands of dollars to Thailand's southern insurgents through Malaysia's PAS party.[119]

Tax collecting is another fund-raising scheme. A former insurgent tax collector told the press in 2009, "They told me to collect one *baht* from a person daily, as a monthly payment. For annual payment, 360 *baht* would be collected from everyone. And they could pay more than that if they wanted. Every tenth of a month, members would have to get the collected money to me. After that, another member would take it from me. I did not know what the organization did with the money."[120]

Political Operations

The southern insurgency's political message, indoctrination, propaganda, and recruiting are all intertwined. The movement's political-religious goal is to convince as much of the southern border population as possible that the Thai government is illegitimate and that they should embrace an independent Pattani state—by Malays, of Malays, and for Malays—with ultraconservative Islamism and sharia law as its governing principles.

Insurgents rely on imams to indoctrinate and recruit the masses. This is the *dawah* tactic authorities discovered in the 1980s. At that time, this tactic seemed to be used only somewhat because Islamist jihad was not the movement's central rallying cry. Now, it is. In October 2004 in the far south, *Time* reporter Simon Elegant witnessed an imam preach for two hours to fifty men, women, and children about Thailand's social evils, its history of cruelty, how Muslims were not allowed to worship freely, and the West's "war on Islam." He spliced his message with verses from the Koran and concluded by appealing to his audience to stand up for their rights, join the insurgency, and liberate the south.[121] Elegant says the imam said to the crowd, "Will you join hands with me to fight? Fight the army that tortures and kills our people? The army that has caused the disappearance of many Muslims?"[122] The sermon ended with cries of "Allahu akbar!"[123]

Agents of the insurgency also propagandize people one-on-one, relying on trickery and group pressure to convince people to join the movement. A former insurgent of four years describes an *ayah*, or a village religious leader, talking to him for several years in casual conversations about the history of Pattani and Thailand's transgressions against it. The ex-rebel told the press, "He never talked about the good side of the Thai government. No one thought of asking him either."[124]

Over an extended period of time, the *ayah* told villagers the insurgent movement was powerful, that it could be successful. He would talk to villagers individually, telling them everyone else in the village had joined the movement, which he called jihad, and that they needed to as well. By doing so, the *ayah* convinced the entire village to join the movement.[125] Scenarios such as this signify expert messaging and intricate study of the target audience to ensure that it will be receptive and susceptible to core political-religious rhetoric.

Key to this rhetoric are several themes. One is Thailand is a colonial conqueror, so insurgents call it "Siam" to associate it with its pre-1932 name and the annexation of Pattani. The overall message is Thailand unlawfully invaded and subjugated Pattani centuries ago. In the process, insurgents say Thai troops burned southerners' homes, took their water and land, and stole their women and children. Preaching this establishes a legacy of victimization of Thai Malay Muslims, justifying revenge through guerrilla war and terrorism against an "inhuman" enemy.

Building on that theme, insurgents insist Bangkok's present goal is to kill all southern Muslims, or breed them out, so it can establish more effective control of the far south and its rich natural resources—yet more victimization. Insurgents also draw an ethnic dividing line to ensure political and material reparations cannot assuage the harm done to them. Specifically, they assert the south is made up of Malay people who despise being called Thai and have nothing in common with Thai people—not religion, not language, not history, and not culture. Insurgents say they and Thai people cannot live together because of these differences and historical "bad blood." For these reasons, insurgents claim their revolt is legal.[126]

The Fight for the Liberation of Pattani contains some of the most forceful political-religious themes of the movement. As with the CPT where not all rebels could quote Mao—especially the uneducated—not all insurgents in the far south can quote this guidebook. Top insurgent imams likely use it as guidance to tell fighters and supporters what they need to know. The book calls on southern Muslims to unite and defend Islam against *infidels*, meaning Thai Buddhists. It declares the religious duty of all Muslims to fight and die to liberate "Patani" from Thailand. It also says if they shed blood for this mystical and heroic state, history will remember their glorious feats forever.[127]

One of the book's more poignant quotes declares, "It is known that all Muslims who have faith in God and his prophets have warriors' blood."[128] This is meant to lift the Thai Malay Muslim "victim" out of the ashes of despair and fill him or her with the resolve of a heroic fighter. The book further states, "If any Muslim betrays Islamic principles, even though he is a father or friend, you should kill him. They are enemies of those who have true faith in religion."[129] This makes all members of the insurgency part of a special, elite movement and responsible for its operational security. It also justifies *takfir* behavior.

Perhaps the book's most revealing statement is, "Let us go and spark this fire and look for them everywhere, night and day, and kill those *infidels* to show nonbelievers that Muslims are strong while living in this world."[130] This statement again capitalizes on Thai Malay Muslim victimology, urging southerners to correct past "wrongs" and prove Muslim strength by hunting down non-Muslims. It is a revenge fantasy brought to life by the insurgency. It moreover speaks to the temporary nature of this life and that the afterlife waits for true believers, a place of reward for those who fight for the cause. This is supposed to induce fighters to die for the movement.

As mentioned in the previous chapter, *The Fight for the Liberation of Pattani* also uses a popular AQ tool from the Koran to justify murdering civilians: VIII:

60. It tells the jihadist fighter to prepare for war to the maximum extent possible. It also instructs to "strike terror" not only into the hearts of one's enemies and God's enemies, but of "others besides, whom ye may not know." From a targeting perspective, these are bystanders and random civilians. The same stanza forgives the jihadist for killing these people, because despite the fact that the fighter does not know them, God knows them, indicating the Almighty will sort out the guilty from the innocent in heaven. The final part of VIII: 60 states, "Whatever ye shall spend in the Cause of God shall be repaid unto you, and ye shall not be treated unjustly." Appropriately justified and forgiven, Thai Malay Muslim fighters can murder civilians at will. And they do.

Another political theme of the insurgency is antigovernment propaganda. In July 2005, for example, insurgent leaflets found in Yala said not to cooperate with government work and aid programs, stating "Those who cooperate are merely loyal dogs to their rulers," and "You are not the enemy of *Mujahidin* fighters for Pattani, but if you still cooperate and support Siamese rulers who invaded our sovereignty, it is the equivalent of declaring war against us."[131] This is meant to keep the population ideologically insulated from government aid programs so they will not see Bangkok in a favorable light. As an aside, dogs (and pigs) in ultraconservative Islam are filthy animals to be shunned. Labeling RTG collaborators as dogs helps dehumanize them, making them easier to kill.

Threat propaganda is another common political tool insurgents use. In August 2005, assassins murdered a husband and wife in Narathiwat and left four threat propaganda leaflets behind, saying it was revenge for the government's killing and arrests of "innocent people."[132] In a beheading in Yala in June, militants placed the head of the deceased in a box along a road with a note stating, "We want to get Pattani State back. You arrest innocents, we'll kill innocents."[133] This particular incident happened while six representatives from the OIC were visiting the region. Observers of the conflict say such violence is an insurgent attempt to reach out to the OIC and enlist its support in wrestling the south away from Thailand.[134] To date, the OIC has not publicly addressed the Islamist jihadist violence in the far south.

In several cases, insurgents have used threat propaganda to force civilians to "rebel," thereby giving the appearance of mass support. For example, in July and August 2005, militants distributed leaflets throughout Yala, Pattani, and Narathiwat threatening violence against merchants who did not close their businesses on Friday, the weekly Muslim day of worship. Thousands obeyed. In Yala, more than 90 percent of businesses closed. Across the south, many street vendors stayed indoors. Some buses stopped running their routes.[135] This gave the illusion that southern Thailand was an ultraconservative Islamist area whose people supported the rebellion. Since then, southern businesses have remained open on Fridays.

Sometimes, assassinations of public figures serve as magnified threat propaganda that not only scare the population, but also telegraph the insurgency's ideology and goals. For example, on 12 March 2009, insurgents in Yala murdered a well-known women's rights activist, Laila Paaitae Daoh. It was an example of their disdain for her high status as a woman in society, her peace efforts, and her development work in tandem with the government. Insurgents had threatened her and her family for years, branding her a *munafik*.[136] Killing her was therefore justified under *takfir* regulations.

Military Operations

Insurgents have five main lines of violent operations: assassinations, bombings, arson, raids, and ambushes. Their operational tempo is high. They carry out violent operations on a weekly basis. From 2004 to 2012, the war has resulted in the deaths of five thousand people. (While most of these deaths are attributed to the insurgents, some have been at the hands of the government, pro-government militias, and criminals.) In October 2006, former Yala Governor Boonyasit Suwanrat said that the insurgency's tactics were not like those of the past. Instead of living in jungle bases, fighters masqueraded as civilians and lived among the population, making them harder to decouple from the population.[137]

The tempo of insurgent operations peaked between 2005 and 2006. These were excessively violent years, and security forces and PM Thaksin appeared helpless to stop them, one of the several reasons for the 2006 coup. In mid-2007, however, the RTP and RTA increased their intelligence activities, resulting in scores of arrests and successful raids against arms caches. These actions severely decreased militant attacks for the next two years. Attacks in 2008 decreased by 47 percent compared to early 2007. Insurgents killed about 546 people and wounded 1,075 in 2008. In 2007 insurgents killed approximately 866.[138] Since mid-2009, however, insurgents have slightly increased their attack tempo, indicating they have learned to circumvent some state security measures.

Analysts such as Srisompob estimate insurgents commit at least 80 percent of assassinations. The rest, he says, are probably executed by criminals. Statistically, in 2004, there were approximately 1.04 assassinations attempts a day. (This means assassins went operational this many times that year. It does not mean they successfully killed or wounded their victims.) In 2005, there were 1.09 assassinations attempts per day, while in 2006 there were 1.22 per day.[139] These patterns have largely held steady since then. Assassinations are the one line of operation hardly impacted by RTG security activities. Assassins mostly kill at close range with pistols, and they seem to prefer to strike victims in transit. They occasionally attack people with assault rifles, knives, and machetes. Postmortem mutilation, such as beheadings or hacking off arms, is common.

Bombings grew from 6.3 a month in 2004 to 18.8 a month in 2005. They were 24.5 a month in 2006. The rate began to decrease in the second half of 2007 and has since declined back to 2004 levels. Insurgents usually set off one or two bombs at a time, but in 2006, they carried out nine bombing campaigns that involved detonating scores of bombs at multiple locations almost simultaneously. Their preferred delivery methods change from year to year. They relied heavily on motorcycle bombs in 2004. In 2005, they began using more car bombs. In 2006, they still used car bombs but overwhelmingly relied more on motorcycle bombs. Frequency of arson incidents followed a pattern similar to bombings.

Regarding light infantry operations, insurgents executed a mere six raids in 2004, none of them too professional. With the advent of the RKK in 2005, however, raids increased to forty-three for the year. In 2006, there were forty.

Ambushes followed a similar pattern. In 2004, there were no classic ambushes. In 2005, there were forty-five; in 2006, thirty-one. These operations meant the insurgents had transformed from a band of saboteurs to a light infantry force in less than a year. With these operations, insurgents mostly target the military and police, but they use them on civilians, too.

Insurgents use a robust information network to produce rapid, actionable intelligence. Compartmentalized auxiliary forces case targets, conduct surveillance, and carry out vulnerability assessments without detection. Militants would never have been able to bomb so many high-value targets—police teacher escort convoys and military patrols, etc.—if they did not know when and where these targets were on the move. Likewise, insurgents could not assassinate so many local leaders in transit without knowing their daily habits. As proof of their intelligence prowess, in May 2005, police raided several Islamic boarding schools in Pattani and found bombing materials along with notebooks containing the habits of military and police personnel and maps of several security posts.[140] In one case in May 2005, nineteen rebels surrendered and told authorities they had been paid to collect intelligence and/or assassinate people.[141] Similarly, in December 2005 in Narathiwat, police arrested forty-six villagers accused of collecting intelligence on security forces for militants. They apparently passed their information to their handlers at clandestine meetings, basic tradecraft for spies.[142]

While these cases reflect standard population-guerrilla intelligence activities, the insurgents showed excellent spy craft prowess with their infiltration of the RTA's joint intelligence center at Sirindhorn camp in Pattani. Authorities discovered this network in late December 2007 after finding a laptop belonging to an insurgent; it contained classified information that the RTA traced to government intelligence personnel. Police investigators accused ten Thai Malay Muslims of espionage, including three RTA intelligence officials—among them a lieutenant colonel—and seven police officers. Authorities said that these spies had provided insurgents with information on security tactics, techniques, and procedures, including checkpoint locations, troop rotation schedules, and the timing of missions. The insurgents then acted on the intelligence via a series of deadly ambushes and bombings that killed and wounded scores of Thai military and police.[143]

The militants' target sets include civilians, civil servants, and security forces. They tend more toward attacking civilians, however, which makes the movement terrorist in nature. For example, militants in 2005 directed assassinations against about ninety security personnel and more than three hundred civilians. The largest subgroup among these civilians was local village government officials, followed by education personnel, including students, teachers, and school administrative officials. In July 2005, authorities captured teenage insurgents who confessed to having targeted teachers and school administrators.[144] Insurgents know their war is mainly an ideological one, and government teachers teaching secular subjects can expand the minds of the south's youth, so insurgents target them frequently. The insurgents need a population that is inward-looking, racist, and radically Islamist for their movement to succeed.

In 2009, the government released statistics showing that most of those killed in the insurgency from previous years were Thai Malay Muslims—some 1,788 people. The violence had killed 1,384 Thai Buddhists. The number of wounded included 3,224 Thai Buddhists and 1,633 Thai Malay Muslims.[145]

Insurgents target big businesses and major infrastructure in attempts to injure the far south's economy and scare tourists away. Many of these attacks are bombing campaigns such as the 3 April 2005 triple bombing in Hat Yai, Songkhla.[146] This campaign began a period of slowed tourism in Hat Yai that severely hurt the town's usually bustling economy. Hotel occupancy, for example, dropped by more than 80 percent.[147]

Another type of operation used frequently in 2005–07 but less often since is insurgent mob violence, which co-opts villagers into group kidnappings, beatings, and murders. On 21 September 2005, for example, insurgents induced Thai Malay Muslim women and children to shield them from authorities while they murdered two kidnapped Marines.[148] As such, these women and children aided and abetted premeditated torture and murder.

In another case, on 19 May 2006, one hundred villagers led by a Thai Malay Muslim woman (the wife of an insurgent leader) seized Kuding Rupa School in Narathiwat. With help from the schoolchildren, they separated the Buddhist teachers from the Muslim teachers and locked the Buddhists in a closet. At the same time, men surrounded the perimeter of the area wielding axes, knives, and machetes. Other villagers scattered spikes on nearby roads to inhibit security forces from accessing the site. Then the captors pulled the Buddhist teachers from the closet and proceeded to club two females, Sirinart Tavornsuk and Julin Kampongmoon, into unconsciousness. Children were present during the beatings. A woman helping lead the violence encouraged villagers to join in via a mosque's loudspeaker. Both victims sustained broken bones and internal bleeding. Julin died from her wounds.[149]

Mobilizing villagers into the fight makes combatants out of everyday people. The insurgents, through expert psyops, have convinced these people that terrorism and lynching are justified. To do this, the victims must first be dehumanized. These scenarios also create an environment where ordinary villagers—men, women, and children—pit themselves against soldiers and police, which is an explosively dynamic problem. If the insurgents can get security units to apply force to these mob operations, it will produce the image of a civilian massacre and promulgate the insurgent fantasy that the government aims to exterminate all Muslims. This would empower organizations such as the OIC to outwardly aid the insurgents, which would feed insurgent strategy and energize the conflict.

Insurgent Groups

As earlier stated, a number of groups have been mentioned in relation to the current insurgency. Old BRN-C and PULO leaders assert they have nothing to do with the current generation of insurgents. The new rebels do not appear to consort with the older generation, but this could be a ruse. Having said this, current insurgents may have adopted the names of older organizations, or they might be using them as denial and deception efforts to confuse RTG intelligence.

According to Askew, some captured insurgents assert they belong to no specific organization, and their fight is simply called jihad.

Whatever the case, aside from the DPP, new versions of the BRN-C (plus its RKK and *Pemuda* units) and PULO have been associated with the current movement. Others include, but are not limited to, *Pejuang Kemerdekaan Patani*, GMIP, *Bersatu*, *Tarikah*, and *Persatuan Mahasiswa Islam Patani*.[150]

Dewan Pembabasan Pattani (Pattani Liberation Council)

The DPP appears to be the insurgent command and control organization for the whole war. Its alleged founder, Sapae-ing Basor, is the former rector of Yala's Thammawitthaya School, which has as many as ten thousand students. Thaksin's administration at one time suspected Basor of being a top leader of the insurgency, if not its most senior leader. Basor has also been suspected of being chief of the BRN-C.[151] A man named Masae Useng is also said to be a top leader of the BRN-C. Other sources say Basor is the spiritual leader of the DPP, and Masae Useng is its operational head. It could be that the DPP is a board of trustees–like organization for the insurgency, and that the head of the BRN-C has a dual leadership role. Others assert the man presently spearheading talks for the insurgents, Taib, might be head of the DPP and/or the BRN-C. The exact truth about DPP, its connection with the BRN-C, and its leadership remains elusive to the public.

BRN-Coordinate, *Runda Kumpulan Kecil* (Small Unit Tactics), and *Pemuda* (Youth)

General Anupong announced in 2007 that the BRN-C and its military wing, the RKK, was the main threat in the far south. The BRN-C of present seems to be an incarnation of the same organization from the 1980s–90s in name only. It has much stronger radical Islamist overtones. To form RKK, BRN-C allegedly recruited Thai college students attending school in Jakarta, Yogyakarta, and Bandung, Indonesia. It supposedly trained them there with assistance from JI and Indonesia's Free Aceh Movement.[152] General Anupong told the press, "This group is very influential. But the RKK is not the real brains behind the unrest. It is a militant wing of the BRN-Coordinate, the main group causing all the problems in Narathiwat, Pattani, Yala, and part of Songkhla since 2004."[153] A captured RKK member in 2009, however, said he had never heard of RKK. Some pundits assume RKK might be an RTG term. *Pemuda* appears to be the BRN-C's youth wing. These young teens, and perhaps younger, receive heavy indoctrination and participate in nonkinetic operations such as laying spikes on roads, felling trees, and intelligence collection of targets to be bombed and persons to be assassinated. These activities prep them to be fighters as they get older.

Pattani United Liberation Organization

It is not clear whether PULO has fighters in the far south or if it is a support group that conducts propaganda for the movement. Then again, it might be sitting on the sidelines, simply cheering on the fight. Perhaps some ex-PULO insurgents have joined the movement and are identified by their previous affiliation. Zachary Abuza, who has done extensive research on the insurgent groups in the far south, says PULO seems to be a hanger-on and little involved in operational planning and execution.[154]

Regardless, PULO has set up several websites on the current war. PULO claims to be active in the insurgency and to speak for at least parts of it. For example, in January 2009 Kasturi Mahkota, PULO's Chief of Foreign Affairs, wrote on one of its websites the "Patani Malay Movement" was ready to establish a formal dialogue group with Bangkok in order to end the fighting in the far south.[155]

Pejuang Kemerdekaan Patani (Patani Liberation Fighters)

Human Rights Watch (HRW) said in June 2009 the *Pejuang Kemerdekaan Patani* was responsible for killing 115 teachers and wounding one hundred more. HRW specifically linked *Pejuang* to the killing of five teachers in May 2009 and the arson of over two hundred schools.[156] According to HRW, *Pejuang* are village militants under the BRN-C and the "backbone" of the movement.[157] It is possible *Pejuang* and RKK are one and the same.

Gerakan Mujahideen Islam Patani (Pattani Islamic Mujahideen Movement)

Abuza's research contends GMIP is active in the south. It might be an organization independent of BRN-C but working in tandem with it. It retains its radical Islamist mind-set. In fact, says Abuza, after the September 11 attacks against the United States, GMIP disseminated propaganda leaflets supporting Osama bin Laden and his jihad.[158]

Bersatu

In November 2008, an anonymous intelligence official told the press that *Bersatu* worked for the insurgency collecting money, weapons, and perhaps vehicles for car bomb attacks.[159] In April 2009, another such official stated after a Thai-Malaysian security meeting that *Bersatu* was responsible for attacks in the far south. The official said *Bersatu* was based in northern Malaysia and infiltrated fighters into Thailand via Sungai Kolok and Waeng districts in Narathiwat and at seaports where there was little security.[160] Abuza says insurgents talk of *Bersatu* not as an organization, but as a sign of their cohesiveness.[161] Che Man, now living in Malaysia, denies being involved.

Tarikah (Truth)

In January 2008, police arrested twenty-two-year-old Waeumeng Dueramae and twenty-six-year-old Kari Mahman for the murder of Buddhist schoolteacher Suwit Bunsanit. The pair was apparently involved in the failed 28 April 2004 uprising and said they were now part of a splinter group, *Tarikah*. *Tarikah* typically means "way" or "path" in Arabic, but in the more mystic-leaning Sufism it means "truth." Since the 28 April fighters believed mystic rituals and Islamic chants would make them bulletproof, *Tarikah* in this case likely refers to the Sufi meaning. Interestingly, however, pure *Salafist* jihadists despise Sufism, but this does not mean they do not cooperate. Regardless, Dueramae and Mahman wanted to leave *Tarikah*, and their leader told them they could so long as they murdered Suwit. Accordingly, they collected their pistols during morning prayers at a mosque and shot Suwit dead.[162]

Additional Insurgent Groups

The RTA says the DPP aids another group, the *Perjuangan Merdeka Patani* (Independence Struggle of Pattani) with economic, diplomatic, recruiting, and psyops services. [163] The RTA also says *Persatuan Mahasiswa Islam Patani* (Association of Islamic Graduates of Pattani) handles finances for the insurgency writ large. It is allegedly made up of Thai Malay Muslim students schooling in Indonesia.[164] The names of other groups continue to surface seemingly every six months, including "AQ in Southeast Asia." There does not seem to be a firm grasp on exactly who they are. They might be independent and acting in concert with the BRN-C, or small units directly tied to a central leadership body, or outsiders simply rooting on the insurgency with political warfare material.

The At-Risk Population

The population involved in the current insurgency is largely the same as that from the 1980s–90s. The basics of their culture, ethnicity, and religion have not changed. Malay ethnicity and Islam remain their core identity, and they are still a largely rural, agricultural, and impoverished people. Crime remains prevalent, too. Still, as more researchers have infiltrated the region, more nuanced information has evolved on this unique population, revealing greater diversity. Also, the people there have evolved since the 1980s–90s, in part due to government education and language programs. The region is also more tightly connected to the rest of Thailand because of improved communications, commerce, and travel.

Marc Askew, who spent four years in the far south, has discovered details about Thai Malay Muslims that debunk some common misperceptions. For one, he is not convinced that the south in general wants to force Bangkok to recognize Malay Muslim culture. Nor does he think this sentiment is a mainstay of the insurgency. He writes, "For every Malay nationalist who regards the Thai state as the perpetrator of injustice there is another who resents insurgent groups and affirms the claim to belong to an entity called 'Thailand.'"[165] This is perhaps one reason of many the insurgency has yet to attract a majority of the southern population. This, in turn, is a key reason the movement uses terrorism, which punishes the people for their lack of support.

Askew discredits oversimplifications of Thai Malay Muslims and their politics:

> Ordinary Malay Muslims (i.e., non-elite Muslims) are not the apathetic or unthinking mass of peasants depicted by Surin Pitsuwan in his elite-centered account of Islam and Malay nationalism over twenty years ago. They are a highly mobile population with a diverse range of occupations and experiences, and their orientations towards the different Islamic movements that compete in the region are also diverse. The essentializing anecdote, "Scratch a Malay Muslim and you find a separatist

underneath" [sic], marginalizes a host of variant views and positions. It is just as common to scratch a Malay Muslim and hear one using the expression "Rak Chart" (love the country/Thailand) and happy to identify as Thai, yet conducting most of his/her daily life in the local Malay dialect.[166]

Askew's conclusions, while cutting against common perceptions, are nevertheless penetrating and impossible to ignore.

More, Askew knows pure Muslim districts in Yala and Pattani where locals have organized their own security forces to kill insurgents. He also discovered that southerners do not blindly follow their local and religious leaders. In fact, some villagers Askew met said they did not trust their village headmen and imams. Others had never heard of some of the most outspoken Thai Malay Muslim leaders on the subject of Malay Muslim identity in Thailand.[167]

Srisompob Jitpiromsri purports a more traditional view of the population, arguing that many Malay Muslims want "political space for their own cultural and religious identity."[168] Pattani National Assembly member Nimukta Waba (*Puea Pandin* Party) suggested yet another interpretation in February 2008 by saying PULO was out of touch with the political goals of the far south. He told the press, "The local people are only demanding justice, fair treatment, and equal rights. I think at least 90 percent of people here do not want autonomy."[169]

Medical statistics show a region with serious health and sanitation problems. The maternal mortality rate in the far south is higher than in the rest of Thailand. The Ministry of Health (MoH) found the mortality rate in the five southernmost provinces was 42.4 per 100,000 births in 2008, rising from 39.5 per 100,000 in 2007. The national average is 17.7 per 100,000. Aside from poor access to medical care, Professor Banchong Withayametha of Sinidhorn College of Public Health in Yala told the press it also had to do with a high degree of unwanted pregnancies, a direct result of a lack of contraceptive usage. "We can't tell them to stop getting pregnant. It contradicts their culture and they won't do it," he said.[170] As a result, many Thai Malay Muslims do not engage in family planning.

Banchong is working with the UN to find culturally sensitive solutions, a difficult proposition in an ultrasensitive Thai Malay Muslim culture that needs help but does not want outsiders to force change upon them.[171]

Far from being a puritanical Islamist society, AIDS is on the increase in the far south, mostly from heroin use and promiscuous sexual behavior by married men who then spread it to their wives.[172] Drug use is so widespread, ISOC antinarcotics personnel believe as much as 70 percent of the far south's youth use, or have been exposed to, illegal drugs. Aside from *yaba*, the region is replete with heroin, marijuana, and a homemade narcotic composed of cough syrup, boiled *kratom* leaves, soft drinks, and mosquito repellent. Locals call it "4 x 100."[173]

Some southerners embrace Islam to the extent that it shapes government policy. In March 2005, *Ustaz* Abdulroni Kahama criticized a government-proposed lottery to raise money for scholarships for the far south. He said gambling was against Islam, and Malay Muslims would not accept money from it.[174] While these beliefs and rules are understandable, they inhibit development projects and limit options for regional problem solving.

Some Thai Malay Muslims blame the government for the insurgency and want Bangkok out of their lives. They have garrison mentalities and reject state aid. One Pattani villager told the press, "Money can't change what's happening. No one can buy an end to the problems here."[175] He said government policies caused the war and added, "They have to understand that our way of life is different [from that of] other Thais."[176] Another villager had a cynical view of government development funding. "It could end up in the hands of the militant groups," he said.[177] "Investment won't stop the violence. Corrupt officials will keep the money for themselves. This is a useless idea."[178] While these men may have exaggerated their objections for media consumption, the problem of corruption certainly remains a factor in southern perceptions of government. It takes place among the police, the military, and Malay Muslim TAO officials, and to other locals sympathetic to the rebellion. Such corruption makes the government appear illegitimate, regardless of which side a villager might be on.

The combination of violence in the far south and locals' penchant for superstition and rumormongering sometimes results in mayhem. According to *New York Times* reporter Seth Mydans, in May 2003, when a mysterious wave of either insurgent or criminal violence swept the south, people in Narathiwat attributed it to "black ninjas." When two police not local to the area stopped in Tam Nob village to have coffee and ask for directions, a mob of three thousand villagers descended on them, accusing them of contributing to the rise in crime. The village headman was unable to protect them; the mob stabbed and beat them to death in an orgy of violence. As this incident graphically illustrates, many in the far south are highly susceptible to manipulation and easily incited.[179]

In May 2009, Professor Srisompob spearheaded a poll on southern attitudes toward the insurgency and socioeconomic issues for the Deep South Watch Center and the Prince of Songkhla University's Study of Conflict and Cultural Diversity. Srisompob and his team interviewed 1,878 people in four districts of Songkhla, plus the whole of Yala, Narathiwat, and Pattani. The government's National Research Council supported the project.[180]

Regarding economics, the study found a majority of participants said their incomes were adequate, and a minority said they were inadequate. Ninety-one percent said unemployment was the most critical issue confronting the region, while illicit narcotics ranked second, and the insurgency was third. Srisompob concluded:

> These opinions show that locals seem to perceive that the current problems confronting communities in the deep south are largely economic and social. Such perceptions are reflective of the alarming rates of unemployment and drug abuse—particularly among young men—plaguing the region....Hence, though the current conflict and violence are viewed by locals as a key problem, more pressing issues are economic and social, specifically the often related problems of unemployment and drug abuse.[181]

Abuza quotes statistics citing the far south had two of the poorest provinces in Thailand. Narathiwat, he says, was Thailand's poorest province in 2002, with a poverty rate of 45.6 percent. Yala's poverty rate was 37.9 percent. The national average was 13 percent. This clearly indicates the economic progress made by these provinces in the 1990s did not endure. They have fallen back below the national poverty average.[182]

Regarding the insurgency, the Srisompob poll asserted 23.6 percent said "unequal treatment by state officials" was the main driver of the violence. Nearly the same amount, 23 percent, said insurgent groups were driving the conflict. Some 16.1 percent blamed injustice, 13.5 percent blamed state-sponsored violence, 8.5 percent pointed at poverty, and 8.5 percent blamed poor education and an excessive population "resulting from large Muslim families." Only 4.5 percent said the insurgency was driven by the quest for autonomy.[183]

Who, then, joins the insurgency? Obviously, it is the politically and economically dispossessed who see the government as illegitimate. Racists who believe Malays cannot live with Thais are also candidates for the insurgency. But politics, economics, and race are not always enough to get people to join a movement and kill for it. Usually, it takes an ideology to rally these grievances. In the case of the current southern insurgency, that ideology is Islamist jihad. Most Muslims simply do not become radical on their own, however. They are taught to behave this way by insurgent indoctrination and propaganda.

As previously stated, radical Islamist teachers and their students appear to make up the bulk of insurgent membership. Teachers are continually caught leading insurgent operations, and their students often serve as fighters. This trend is troubling because the numerous *pondoks* in the south are one of the centers of Thai Malay Muslim life.[184]

There are scores of examples of the south's Islamic educational community being intricately involved in the insurgency. One comes from the infamous 14 July 2005 raid on Yala town.[185] While they relied on Malaysia as a planning base for the operation, insurgent imams also used Yala's Thammawithaya Foundation

School to facilitate this operation and others.[186] Additional Islamic schools that have served as planning sites include Jihad Witthaya School and Porming School, both in Pattani.[187]

Insurgent fighters are not always the urchins of society, either. Police assert the RKK is composed of "devout Muslim students who are clever, well-behaved, and disciplined."[188] To fill the ranks of the RKK, recruiters look for achievers, not losers.

Everyday villagers join, too, if they have been indoctrinated. The 19 May 2006 attack on Kuding Rupa School in Narathiwat displayed that, on occasion, the entire population of villages joins the insurgency as fighters. This pattern appears only in certain pockets of the south, not in every area.

Strategy

As with past insurgencies, Thailand has gone through a series of strategy changes in the current war in the south. The first strategy was PM Thaksin's, which lasted from 2004 until his overthrow in the fall of 2006. The second strategy, developed by the military coup government of Generals Surayud and Sonthi, has been applied from 2006 to 2011. General Anupong, however, added significantly to that strategy in 2007 with specific tenets designed to counter security problems. PM Abhisit continued these latter two strategies during his tenure, and PM Yingluck has also largely adhered to them as well.

Thaksin's COIN Plan

The government decided from the beginning to fight the insurgency and not simply give up the far south. Says former diplomat Arun Bhunupong, "How can we accept those provinces as a different part of our country? Our constitution says we are a unitary state. Secondly, we have about at least twenty percent of Thai Buddhist people in that area. What are we going to do? Change their status? And what about Islam? We have Muslims in other areas that are not ethnically Malay. Do we change their status, too? It's impossible."[189]

PM Thaksin developed a strategy three months after insurgents struck on 4 January 2004. It was called "The Policy to Promote Peace and Happiness in the Three Southern Border Provinces" and was sanctioned by PM Order 68/2547. It did not include Songkhla, and it is not clear why. Thaksin and his advisors might have assumed Songkhla was not under threat. But it was.

General Chavalit is rumored to have helped draft the plan. It included socioeconomic and good-governance measures. A Thai government PR announcement said the plan "will promote cultural and traditional identities of the region, as well as their religions and languages. The government will promote the education of people in the localities, and will respect their cultures, traditions and religious faiths. Everybody will be given freedom to hold any religion, faith and lifestyle." [190] As this was already the case for some time, this PR announcement was curious. The RTG might have felt the need to reiterate that the Thai Constitution had recognized all these issues for a while. At any rate, the core of the strategy was political and cultural.

Order 68/2547 also included the king's COIN guidance, issued in February 2004, citing *khao jai* (understanding), *khao tueng* (reaching out), and *pattana* (development).[191] It meant understanding the people and culture with which you are dealing, interfacing with them, and providing the assistance they need.

Despite all these measures, however, PM Order 68/2547 does not appear to have been a cohesive COIN plan. It did not define a decisive end state, nor did it indicate the security, political, and economic operations and assets required to achieve it. Ends, ways, and means were not clearly defined. It was more a series of general statements on how Bangkok wanted southerners to behave. Only the king's advice provided even general guidelines on what to do.

The faults of the 68/2547 plan are odd. After all, General Chavalit was brilliant at COIN and had the track record to prove it. Perhaps Chavalit did not see the insurgency as the threat it truly was. Since he had spent considerable time dealing with the southern insurgency in the 1980s–90s, this is unlikely. A more probable scenario is that bureaucrats close to PM Thaksin, or Thaksin himself, kept the venerable Chavalit from implementing a proven and effective COIN plan, maybe because it would have put the RTA in the center of things. This is all just speculation, however.

Regardless, while the civilian government floundered, the RTA developed a COIN strategy on its own. The RTA's Southern Border Provinces Peace-building Command (SBPPC)—the COIN coordination center in the south—designed it. It embraced the king's guidance and built a specific plan of action based on the sentiment behind 68/2547. The RTA's overall strategy had five tenets and aimed "to build peace by using psychological operations together with social and economic development leading political and military operations. Organizations with unity will be established by government officials and the patriotic community leadership (local people), to terminate violence, and to quickly establish order, peace and stability in the southern areas."[192] It was a broad copy of Prem and Harn's strategies from the 1980s, but by this point in history, it is evident this was more or less the overall Thai way of COIN.

One interesting aspect of the strategy was the phrase "social and economic development leading political and military operations." The intonation was that CA was to lead, and politics and the military were to follow. It is not clear if this was a mistranslation from Thai to English or if the SBPPC truly meant it. Regardless, this specific issue never came to the fore. Social and economic development, while important, has never spearheaded strategy in the current COIN.

The RTA's five tenets were:

1. Promoting peace and protecting resources.
2. Building trust and economic and social strength.
3. Developing the potential of people, communities, and society.
4. Developing cooperation with neighboring countries.
5. Exercising good and sound administration and management.[193]

This appeared to be a good start, but it never was enacted. It is not clear why. Some rumors say Thaksin blocked the RTA from carrying out its plan. He had the power to do so since he maintained control over all national security issues. It also might have been that, because of RTA-Thaksin tension, army commanders simply did not engage, but this seems less likely. Whatever the reason, without RTA expertise, Thaksin's COIN efforts sputtered on as an uncoordinated patchwork of programs and ideas.

Without RTA input, then, it was Thaksin's 2004–2006 strategy at the fore. It did not unfold well, however, because of five main inadequacies: (1) Thaksin did not accurately explain to the public that his strategy included politics and economic development, (2) he did not put enough actual effort into politics and economic development, (3) in press conferences, he overemphasized both force and his personal control over the troubles, (4) he failed to establish an adequate coordination system to drive strategy (weak though it was) in the field, and (5) he never gave the RTA full authority to apply the ways and means to make his strategy happen.

Interestingly, Thaksin wisely instituted martial law in the affected areas, demonstrating that he understood the basics of population control. He gave the police and the military wide arrest and detention powers and also declared an evening-to-dawn curfew to cut down on insurgent mobility. The curfew was not strictly enforced, however, and he let his detractors inaccurately portray martial law as an excessive hardship that stripped the population's freedoms, which it did not. The people of the south could travel freely during the daytime and could speak and worship as they wished. The only real force impinging on their freedom was the insurgency, which raged out of control with wanton violence.

Overall, despite some genuine COIN efforts, Thaksin's attitude sent the wrong message about his strategy. It was a major PR failure. His callous reaction to the 28 April 2004 uprising (erroneously called the "Krue Se Mosque massacre"), his equally dismissive attitude toward those killed at Tak Bai, and his hard-hearted remarks to the press about the rebellion in general suggested he was taking a purely force-oriented approach to the insurgency. For example, in November 2004 Thaksin told the press he was ordering "a crackdown" and would use an iron fist "to sweep out these people." His reference to taking a soft approach in the same speech fell on deaf ears.[194] He claimed, "We will decisively prosecute the separatists who wanted a separate territory…Don't worry, if there is a separatist war, I will be on the front line."[195] He additionally instructed the police and military to be more decisive in dealing with southern militants who wanted a religious war in the south.[196]

Thaksin's softer ways were multifaceted. In May 2004, he authorized the RTA to deploy former East Timor peacekeepers to the border provinces. The peacekeepers excelled at political and CA development tasks.[197] Thaksin also sought dialogue with the former leader of *Bersatu*. He met at least twice with Malaysian PM Abdullah Ahmad Badawi over Tak Bai and enhancing border control. He also requested that PM Badawi send Malaysian imams to southern Thailand to counter radical Islamist propaganda spread by insurgents.[198]

Despite these moves, Thaksin received heavy criticism for using only force to quell the insurgency, indicating he had lost control of the information sphere.

This was a critical mistake in COIN, especially so early in the war. Accordingly, he made five strategic changes to soften his war rhetoric. First, he announced he was curtailing the use of the military. "Our forces need to focus on investigation and prevention instead of heavily armed troops," he told the press in 2005.[199]

Second, he announced DPM and Interior Minister Police General Chidchai was taking over the COIN effort, and he would be using the RTP as its main COIN tool, a sound decision if the police were up to the task. Thaksin even said in this announcement that using military force was "pointless." Third, until the government could generate a cohesive COIN plan, which would take about a year, Thaksin said he would deal with the insurgency on a day-to-day basis.[200] This indicated he had rejected the SBPPC's COIN plan.

Fourth, on 28 March 2005, by PM Order 104/2548, Thaksin sanctioned an insurgency study group called the National Reconciliation Committee (NRC). He put the highly respected former PM Anand Panyarachun in charge of the committee, which had at least forty-eight members.[201] The NRC's insurgency solutions, published in 2006, were nearly all cultural and economic. It gave little credence to security measures, save for a proposed unarmed security force to maintain law and order in the face of regular bombings and assassinations.

The government adopted only one of the NRC's strategies, which was replacing martial law with an emergency decree, which Thaksin embraced. And this was his fifth strategic change. Parliament passed the decree into law on 30 August 2005.[202] The emergency decree was supposed to reflect a strategy of crime prevention, as proposed by the NRC's Anand, UN crime prevention officials, and DPM Chidchai. It was generally the same as martial law, however. It restricted the sale of items that could be used for bomb components, it required people to register SIM cards because insurgents were using cell phones to trigger bombs, and it restricted public gatherings. The law also allowed the detention of suspects for thirty days without cause, and it gave immunity to government personnel involved in the death, injury, and/or property damage of civilians if they were involved in an insurgent-related incident.[203] This latter tenet was necessary from the government point of view because insurgents are the population, or at least part of it. Traditional COIN philosophy says the government must protect a population from the insurgents, which is true, but it must also go to war with the part of the population that takes up violence against the people and the state.

In any event, getting rid of martial law was supposed to alleviate locals' concerns that the military was "too fierce." The press, pundits, foreign observers, and some Thai politicians believed the army's deployment had somehow made the situation "more tense." This was curious because the military had not launched a single offensive against the insurgents.[204] The only major instances of force had been Krue Se and Tak Bai, and the former was to quell a violent uprising that began with the horrific murder of police officers. The latter was a huge mistake, however, and it took center stage.

The government's molested logic, then, was self-defeating. It appeared Bangkok's strategy was all or nothing. Either deploy the military and have it widely exert haphazard force—which it had not done—or redeploy back to barracks and have unarmed units provide security while the police investigated bombings and murders after they happened. There was no flexibility. There was no innovation regarding retraining military units to switch from a conventional to a COIN role. Neither Thaksin nor the NRC had any creative options. Moreover, no one in the government—not Thaksin, Chidchai, or Anand—had a realistic strategy to protect the southern population from insurgency.[205] This was a critical misstep. The southern population was left unprotected from insurgent violence and indoctrination. Unchecked, the war raced forward.

The Sonthi-Surayud COIN Plan

General Sonthi Boonyaratglin took over as RTA Commander-in-Chief in October 2005. A Special Forces commander, Sonthi had experience with small wars and contingencies. Though unafraid to use force, he was a proponent of winning hearts and minds via CA—as Prem, Harn, Chavalit, Kitti, and Somkiat had done before him.[206] Sonthi's strategic view of the war was: (1) it had to be fought and won at the village level, (2) the government still did not understand

Thai Malay Muslim culture to an effective degree, and (3) separating the insurgents from the population was critical.[207]

After the 2006 coup, General Sonthi retained his post as Commander-in-Chief. He and General Surayud developed a new COIN plan, and their cohorts contributed. They included, but were not limited to, Fourth Army Commander Lieutenant General Ongkorn Thongprasom (and his replacement who arrived in November), and MoI Chief Aree Wong-araya and his deputy, Banyat Jansena.[208]

Sonthi and Surayud set out to apply their COIN strategy by December 2006 or the New Year. They had two core aims: (1) to win the support of the alienated Malay Muslim population, and (2) to engage with and defeat insurgent forces. The title of their strategy was "Policy for Peace-building the Southern Border Provinces." Administratively, it was known as PM Order 206/2549.[209]

The new COIN strategy had four core tenets and twelve underlying principles. The four tenets were:

1. Apply King Bhumibol's strategy of "understand, approach, and development" and add to it His Majesty's "Sufficiency Economy" philosophy.
2. Apply the rule of law via the nation's justice system to restore authority.
3. Involve local people in developing the region and promoting peace.
4. Communicate with the domestic and international sectors to ensure they understand the truth about the conflict and realize the state promotes harmony, diversity, and multiculturalism.[210]

The twelve principles were:

1. The political offensive is supreme and "ensure[s] justice in society." The latter includes law enforcement adhering to the rule of law, building up robust intelligence and counterintelligence capabilities, and protecting the population, which will increase their trust in the state.

2. Foster understanding between the at-risk population and the government by exchanging "views among the government, leaders, religious teachers, community leaders and the private sector" to increase cooperation in stabilizing the area.

3. Purge the conditions causing the at-risk population to feel inferior and isolated. Treat the people as dignified Thai citizens with a unique and valuable culture.

4. Disseminate accurate, timely, and truthful information on events in the affected area and counter rumors and disinformation, so as to instill popular confidence in the government's problem-solving abilities.

5. Uniformly increase communication with insurgent leaders, field personnel, and their auxiliary forces.

6. Instill popular confidence in the judicial system by revamping it, eliminating all forms of injustice, dispensing justice "in an integrated manner," creating laws that adhere to local culture, encouraging popular participation in the judicial system to protect people's rights, and developing a "community judicial system" and "alternative judicial system" based on local customs.

7. Strengthen society, families, and communities and build peace via "social development," including embracing different cultures, bolstering "interreligion relations," advancing nonradical religious teachings, and fostering cultural exchanges between the region's many ethnicities and religions.

8. Upgrade the region's education sector rapidly, with advice from the region's religious leaders and scholars in order to adhere to local customs.

9. Create an economy capable of sustaining itself, improve standards of living, and fight poverty using the king's principles of Sufficiency Economy and local resources while adhering to local customs.

10. Rely on state and private PR, including education and religious sectors and "public forums," to keep the people informed of government programs and garner their support in problem solving. The king's guidance of "understand, reach out, and develop" is key here.

11. Inform regional countries and global organizations about the truth of the insurgency in the far south and make sure they understand the state guarantees the rights of all its citizens, regardless of race or religion.

12. Train government personnel in the far south to appreciate and adhere to local customs and to enact good governance. Deploy only competent officials to the area. Punish civil servants and government personnel who abuse their power and make the insurgency worse. [211]

This was a detailed plan that covered multiple facets of security, politics, and economics. While similar to the *Tai Rom Yen* Plan and the societal retooling goals of the 1980s–90s, Order 206/2549 was tailored to fit the south's current problems—witness principle three, for example, regarding treating Thai Malay Muslims with respect and celebrating their culture. As with Thailand's past COIN strategies, the Sonthi-Surayud strategy mentioned little about force application, but it was indeed policy. Martial law and military operations would remain as population control and insurgent suppression tools.[212]

Indeed, a top priority of the new strategy was to stop the daily violence, per core tenet two regarding restoring authority.[213] Pressuring insurgents offensively to the point at which they could not freely operate was another top goal. Restraint was pivotal, Sonthi said, so as not to isolate the population through civilian deaths.[214]

As with many past Thai COIN strategies, the new strategy said nothing about amnesty, though it did evolve as a government line of operation. Amnesty tied in with several points, including principles two, five, and six. For example, one of the reasons why Bangkok sought close relations with teachers and Islamic leaders was to motivate these community pillars to convince insurgents to turn themselves in.[215]

Along with security, General Sonthi believed in continual contact with the people. He told the press, "Our strategy to tackle the unrest is to stay close to local people and keep a close eye on violence-prone areas and suspected insurgents."[216] Consistent with this strategy, Sonthi invested heavily in local forces, stating that the government aimed to "win the hearts of local residents through their participation in community defense and local activities, which will also create better understanding between the local villagers and state officers [and] lead to the end of the spate of violent unrest."[217]

Regarding politics, Sonthi believed the government needed to relate to, and understand, Thai Malay Muslims.[218] He told one COIN planning conference that diversity in society was good, which represented "flowers of various colors."[219] Gaining trust and cooperation from diverse social groups was a cornerstone of his COIN beliefs.[220] Justice and fairness were imperative in order to win over the population and separate them from the insurgents.[221]

At the same time, Sonthi and Surayud emphasized integrating Thai Malay Muslims into Thai society. They sought to befriend government-friendly Muslims as a way of segregating antigovernment forces. They aimed to convert the skeptical via political means such as exposing the far south's youth to the rest of Thailand, modernizing *pondoks*, and carrying out CA projects to improve rural standards of living.[222]

Surayud and Sonthi said politics must lead the military—a nod to the strategies of past Thai COINs. They believed heavy suppression created more insurgents and negated cooperation between locals and the government.[223] Consistent with previous Thai COIN approaches, Surayud and Sonthi supported amnesty and peace talks with rebels, but they did not know what rebel leaders to speak to because none had stepped forward, at least not publicly.[224]

Anupong's Strategic Additions

In 2007, the Thai COIN chain of command changed, most notably with the ascension of General Anupong to Commander-in-Chief of the RTA on 1 October. On 28 November, General Anupong, upon returning from a tour of the south, wrote a sixteen-page report describing his additions to the Sonthi-Surayud strategy. He likened COIN to treating a cancer patient and cautioned that quelling the southern insurgency would take a long time.[225] More, while he agreed with the Sonthi-Surayud strategy, he recommended additions, including the deployment of elements of all of Thailand's Army Regional Commands to the far south to increase security and to carry out more offensive operations. These deployments began in the summer of 2007 as Operation Southern Protection.[226] Anupong's strategic objectives were:

1. Gain the trust of Malay Muslims.
2. Instill Malay Muslim confidence in the security forces.
3. Provide security for the southern border population.
4. Streamline the chain of command and coordination regimen.
5. Deploy troops from every RTA Region in the far south to enforce security.
6. Take the offensive against the insurgents, as being on the defensive allowed insurgents, who live in the villages, to intimidate villagers into whatever political funnel they wanted them in.
7. Increase the police, BPP, and military presence in and around the villages through visits and nearby kiosks, so that the people will have confidence in the government and reject the insurgents.[227]

General Anupong's main additions to the original strategy were coordination and security. Without coordination, strategy and political-military-economic operations were meaningless. Although the government had brought back the proven-effective trinity of ISOC, CPM, and the SB-PAC, Anupong understood that, even with these institutions in place, Thai political wrangling could infiltrate and muddle things. Furthermore, although the 2006 COIN strategy did include security, it mentioned the subject only once. With almost daily assassinations, weekly bombings, and monthly raids and ambushes happening, Anupong likely believed that greater emphasis on security was necessary. In fact, under Anupong, a new village security program, *Pattana Santi*, evolved. An anonymous Thai security official said the program aimed to "put government-friendly fish into the water of the villages" instead of merely separating the "insurgent fish" from the "village waters."[228] This followed a Village Scout–type concept.

By 2008, the new Thai COIN strategy had been applied throughout the whole south. General Vaipot Srinual, Director-General of the RTA's Office of Policy and Planning, explained the overall strategy: "The priority now [2008] is to stop the killing. The second priority is to quell the insurgent ideas and propaganda and indoctrination. So you talk about initiative, you talk about poverty, you talk about economic development. This you have to address and implement, but it takes time. But you have to stop the daily killings first. That is what we are trying to do."[229]

COIN Strategy under Abhisit and Yingluck

By 2009, PM Abhisit's administration had assumed power and decided to keep the RTA strategy as it was. He told the press, "My government has made it a clear policy that the key to peace in the south is justice." Abhisit further explained, "It may be the aim [of the insurgency to demand a separate state], but my government will prove that the people living in the five provinces are treated fairly, that they will have opportunities, and that they are valued by the Thai government."[230]

When Yingluck Shinawat took over as PM in 2011, she also announced that the overall COIN strategy for the far south insurgency was sound, indicating she would adhere to what was in place when she arrived in office. She made no major changes, as demonstrated by the release of her Southern Border Provinces Development Policy for 2012–2014. The Secretary General of the Office of the NSC, Police General Vichean Potephosree, made this public in February 2013. In broad strokes, General Vichean said the policy entailed a security component and a development component. He said three main tenets were: (1) apply His Majesty the King's "understand, reach out, and develop" concept, (2) reduce all insurgency-inducing conditions, and (3) apply the king's Sufficiency Economy concept, which calls on society to produce more of its own consumer goods and food.

General Vichean provided additional detail regarding tenet two. He said the government would use peaceful means to quell the insurgency, decentralize the southern government, apply rule of law, and respect human rights. It is important to point out that these are political initiatives. Finally, Vichean said RTG coordination would have to increase if the war was to be dealt with correctly—but he left it up to the various agencies to iron out—and that amnesty programs that included reeducation were certainly appropriate.[231]

In the larger scheme of things, then, this seemed to be the Yingluck administration's way of officially announcing it was addressing the insurgency. But it was a general and nebulous announcement. Leaving the various agencies to coordinate with each other on their own was a major weak point. More, Vichean's statement seemed to steer away from protecting villages and quelling the increasing violence, two critical issues that have not been adequately addressed by any Thai PM since the beginning of the war.

Coordination

Coordination for the current COIN has gone through multiple changes, just like strategy. Some of these changes have been clumsy and counterproductive. Regardless, the Thai, as demonstrated in past COINs, place heavy emphasis on coordination, and their struggle to achieve Prem-like, 1980s efficiency seems never-ending.

COIN Coordination under Thaksin

Thaksin constructed a three-tiered chain of command to coordinate the more than forty thousand RTA, RTP, and civilians involved in the southern COIN. The most senior agency was the Committee on Southern Provinces Peace-building Policy (CSPPP), based in Bangkok. Next in line was the Southern Provinces Administrative Committee (SPAC), also in Bangkok. On the ground in the far south was the RTA's SBPPC. It is not clear where the NSC fit into this model.

The SBPPC's mission was to wage COIN in the far south by military, social, and political means. Its motto was the king's strategy: "understand, reach out, and develop."[232] The CSPPP's primary tasks were to formulate COIN strategy and policy. PM Thaksin supervised it, and DPM Chidchai managed it.[233] The SPAC's mission was to coordinate with the SBPPC, see that Bangkok's new COIN policies were carried out, and advise the military.[234] General Sonthi headed it, and Supreme Commander General Ruengroj Mahasaranond served as an advisor.[235]

This chain of command was cumbersome, unnecessary, and violated basic military logic—keep it simple. There was no need to have so many senior layers of bureaucracy to manage the war. These multiple organizations may have reflected the competing camps within the RTG, with Thaksin and his forces on one side and the RTA on the other.

Regardless, as Bangkok was formulating these agencies, it further refined the coordination effort with one major organizational and one leadership change. Regarding organization, in February 2005 the RTA clarified the coordination effort by color-coding the insurgency zone into red, yellow, and green areas. Green was friendly to the state and low violence—permissive to government operations. Yellow was neutral to the state and had medium levels of violence—

semipermissive to government operations. Red was hostile to the state and had high levels of violence—nonpermissive to government operations.[236] As for leadership, Thaksin handed over management of the war to DPM Chidchai on 13 March 2005. Chidchai then assumed control over all coordinating agencies, plus the MoD, MoI, NSC, and NIA.[237] This was a highly appropriate measure that was supposed to assert discipline throughout the chain of command. On the other hand, per the wrangling that happened between Thaksin and the RTA over the south, it is not clear if Chidchai himself ever truly ran things.

COIN Coordination under Sonthi and Surayud

When the 2006 coup group reformulated strategy, it also reformulated coordination. Almost without hesitation, it brought back the familiar and effective SB-PAC and CPM-43 (calling the latter simply CPM). Upon the advice of the NSC, it also reinserted ISOC back into the chain of command. The color-coded identification system remained. It was an effective metrics tool to gauge the expanse of insurgent versus pro-government territory to better allocate resources.

General Vaipot says coordination was critical to the fight. "The political view of the government or the lead organization needs to be one hundred percent, not only the government or lead agency, but all the agencies," he says.[238] "The lead organization needs to have a program to make sure all agencies involved understand the strategy. They must have the same objective. They must have the same picture of the strategy. And we try to encourage everyone to accept the strategy."[239]

Internal Security Operations Command

The government retooled ISOC via PM Order 205/2549 on 30 October 2006. It became operational on 1 January 2007.[240] It expanded to all seventy-six provinces. It was previously just in forty. ISOC's COIN mission was to help coordinate ending the insurgency. It also had other missions, including combating money laundering, drug trafficking, and political "undercurrents"—such as Thaksin and his clique that were trying to stage a comeback from exile. General Sonthi commanded ISOC. Army Regional Commanders took command of regional ISOCs in their respective areas.[241]

Under Sonthi, General Saiyud's son managed ISOC operations as of the spring of 2008. "One of the reasons they do this [put relatives in leadership positions]," says Professor Bhumarat, "is so the younger brother or son can consult the brother or dad. And the Muslim community looks favorably upon this, so some of their fears are relieved."[242]

Under ISOC-4 in the far south were the SB-PAC and CPM. Lieutenant General Wiroj Buacharun was Fourth Army commander when ISOC began and therefore was ISOC-4 commander, too.[243] ISOC's new structure incorporated personnel from twenty-five government bodies, specifically, five agencies and twenty ministries. The agencies were the RTP, DSI, AMLO, the Department of Immigration, and the Office of Narcotics Control Board. ISOC also coordinated with provincial governors of the far south and the MoJ.[244]

Civilian Police Military Program

On 30 October 2006, PM Surayud revived CPM and the SB-PAC by PM Order 207/2549, the same day as it resurrected ISOC.[245] Order 207/2549 moreover nullified seven previous coordinating legal orders issued by Thaksin and one by the coup group. This paved the way for CPM and the SB-PAC to essentially begin Bangkok's COIN anew. It also ordered the budgetary authorities of the RTA, the Comptroller General's Department, and the Budget Bureau to transfer all funding from previous coordinating bodies to the new coordinating structure within two months.[246] This was a mammoth undertaking, and the fact that Surayud wanted it done in such a short time indicates how serious the RTG was about turning the tide of insurgency. CPM's tasks were to:

1. Implement the government's policies in solving the southern unrest while also coordinating with the SB-PAC.
2. Supervise all civilian, police, and military assets involved in preventing and resolving violence and promoting understanding.

3. Generate CPM plans and projects and administer their finances, submitting all such plans to ISOC-4 for approval; track and evaluate progress of projects.

4. Improve intelligence capacity across all relevant civilian, police, and military agencies; establish local forces to aid in protecting the population.

5. Establish task forces as needed to help in carrying out projects.

6. Carry out other tasks assigned by ISOC-4.[247]

Also part of CPM was the Intelligence Operations Center. It was an RTA-run intelligence fusion center that collated and distributed intelligence to units in the field. It additionally disseminated intelligence to the RTP in Region 9 and its operations center, run by Police Lieutenant General Adun Saengsingkaeo.[248]

Southern Border Provinces Administrative Command

General Sonthi met with advisors to discuss reinstating SB-PAC on 16 October.[249] The PM and the Ministers of Defense and Interior met on 23 October to discuss the same issue.[250] Having received positive feedback, PM Surayud revived the SB-PAC on 30 October 2006, by the same order that brought back CPM.[251]

While the SB-PAC and CPM still had to pass legislative muster to become wholly legal via ISA law, they began operations nonetheless. Of the legality of the organization, SB-PAC Director General Pranai Sawannarat said in March 2008, "The last page of the new security law said the SB-PAC would be under a special office of the ISA. So there's no need to have a specific law for SB-PAC. It's under ISOC and operates under the Fourth Army Area."[252] The SB-PAC began preliminary operations on 1 November 2006.[253] The Interior Minister was its temporary chief. Pranai, former governor of Nonthaburi, was its first permanent director.[254] PM Order 207/2549 granted all SB-PAC chiefs status as Deputy Permanent Secretaries of the MoI.[255]

Says Pranai, "I was a governor of the best province in Thailand at that time, Nonthaburi. I was approached, and it seemed like it was very hard to deny the posting. It was a chance to pay back the country." He had excellent experience for the position. "I was in the south fifteen years ago," Pranai explains, "three years in Pattani as a Deputy District official, or 'DO.' Also, my brother was the old SB-PAC director. He was in Pattani province for four years before getting the post."[256]

With the renewal of SB-PAC came a familiar mission, which is to "Restore peace and reconciliation to the five southern provinces."[257] As in the past, the current SB-PAC consists of multiple government agencies, including the Ministries of Justice, Agriculture and Cooperatives, Commerce, Interior, Education, Public Health, and Industry, just to name seven. Pranai explains SB-PAC this way: "We have [multiple] areas we cover. They include education, health, psychological operations, how to win hearts and minds. The best way to get things done is to spend money on these types of programs, so it's war without bullets."[258]

Top security officials welcomed the return of SB-PAC. Says an anonymous senior Thai official, "In the past, during the communist COIN, many other government ministries came and went from the field, and some of their projects were sustainable, and some were not. But under the SB-PAC, the other organizations worked under the governors, so it's a clearinghouse of ministries, so they can quickly support their work in each province. This makes it flexible and fast, easy for them to operate and respond."[259]

The SB-PAC's seven main tasks are to:

1. Supervise all civilian government agencies related to justice, development, local grievances, and cultural understanding; coordinate activities with CPM to prevent and resolve unrest.

2. Recommend, manage, and execute all SB-PAC projects, manage project funding, and finance all participating government agencies; submit budgets to ISOC-4 for approval; monitor and evaluate the progress of all projects.

293

3. Monitor all justice ministry activities and developments to ensure local people are treated fairly in the eyes of the law, including processing citizens' complaints about corrupt officials and seeking punishment of the guilty.

4. Improve civil servants' abilities to operate according to local cultural, social, and economic conditions.

5. Widen participation in security and development problem solving to "all parties concerned."

6. Establish advisory boards as needed to help in carrying out projects.

7. Carry out other tasks assigned by ISOC-4.[260]

The SB-PAC has an Advisory Council for Peace consisting of thirty-five personnel from the government, private, journalism, and religious sectors. The government authorized this council in PM Order 207/2549 and established it on 16 March 2007. Its job is to advise the Director General of SB-PAC on what types of community-friendly projects to carry out. In addition to focusing on education, social, cultural, and development issues, one of its main assignments is to arrange forums where people in the far south can talk about their experiences and views while encouraging equity and liberty.

The SB-PAC has seven committees:

- Education, Religion, and Culture
- Socioeconomic Development
- Justice, Equality, and Security
- Environment and Natural Resources
- Communication and Society
- Cross-cultural Participation
- Southern Border Provinces Study, Analysis, and Solutions

Shortly after the SB-PAC began operations, the government identified four problems that needed to be addressed. First, because it was a war zone and insurgents targeted government employees, working at the SB-PAC was none too desirable. Says Pranai, "It's hard to get people in there to work in the south. It's hard to attract people. There is a threat of being killed because these workers must go out into the field and work in red zones and in remote areas, and the insurgents don't want these projects to work."[261]

Second, the SB-PAC had a "lack of clear-cut vision" to shepherd the organization.[262] Third, it had yet to establish effective communications with red-zone villages because of the unstable situation, yet its people still ventured into these areas on occasion. Fourth, the SB-PAC lacked support from local government and Islamic leaders, which impeded support from the people.[263] To help solve these issues, on 13 September 2007, the PM passed Order 229/2550, which established the Committee on Special Administrative Development Zone (CSD). The CSD's mission was to develop a framework that would more effectively focus the SB-PAC's resources, but not command it.[264] It was an advisory board of sorts.

Corruption within the SB-PAC might be an issue as well. Though there have been no public charges of wrongdoing levied against the otherwise well-respected organization, in March 2011, Sukarno Matha, MP from Yala, complained in Parliament about "suspected irregularities in projects by the SB-PAC." Until such charges are made formal, they will remain, like so many suppositions regarding the south, political rhetoric.[265]

COIN Coordination under Anupong

In November 2007, General Anupong adjusted COIN coordination by deploying elements of all Army Regional Commands to the far south. The First Army deployed assets to Narathiwat, the Second Army did so in Pattani, the Third in Yala, and the Fourth put troops in the four at-risk districts in Songkhla.[266] As stated in the strategy section, the goal was to increase security. Anupong's design was a decentralized system where Army Regional Commanders and their staffs used national strategic guidance working within coordination guidelines—including the existing color code system—to plan and implement operations as they saw fit.[267]

COIN Coordination under Samak

Though PM Samak Sundaravej (29 January 2008–9 September 2008) was only in power for a short time, the cabinet, under his auspices, undertook critically needed and innovative police coordination reform. Accusations of corruption and the poor performance of some of the RTP in the field was obviously not helping the situation in the far south, so the cabinet on 19 August 2008 agreed to create a southern COIN police coordination unit, the Southern Border Provinces Police Operation Center in Yala (also referred to as the Police Operation Center Forward Command, or SBPPOC). Its job was to plan and execute police COIN operations. This center is fully functional, with personnel, logistics, intelligence, and communications functions.[268] Unlike Thailand's regular police forces, the SBPPOC focuses exclusively on COIN, and it recruits and trains its own members. It is equal in authority to, and independent of, Police Region 9 HQ.[269] This is a new concept in Thailand, and a sorely needed one. The organization appears to be much more than just a fancy titled unit. In 2011, when insurgents set off a car bomb at an RTP apartment building in Narathiwat's Si Sakhon district, the SBPPOC fired the Narathiwat Police Chief from his post for dereliction of duty.[270] The organization seems to herald quality and professionalism, which could signify greatly improved COIN operations.

COIN Coordination under Abhisit

While PM Abhisit recognized the strategy for the war was adequate, he figured coordination was not. Based on advice from his advisors of the Southern Border Provinces Development Strategy Committee (not a command), Abhisit devised changes in January and February 2011. First, he asserted that COIN was largely a police and civilian problem and that the military should reinforce these two entities instead of leading the fight so prevalently. Despite Thaksin's attempts to increase the RTP's role in the south, this classic COIN operational theory had never been wholly applied in Thailand before. But even many in the military had complained that the fight in the south had too much of an RTA stamp on it—that it needed more of a civilian touch—so switching to an RTP over an RTA lead seemed possible.

But how to do this? Simple, thought Abhisit. Since the SB-PAC had both the RTP and Special Branch attached to it, he needed to take control of SB-PAC, and task it to be the vanguard of the southern COIN. Abhisit then successfully pushed legislation through Parliament that moved the SB-PAC directly under his command. Prem had the same arrangement in the 1980s. Abhisit's move streamlined the chain of command in the south, and his personal involvement gave the SB-PAC power it had not previously possessed. More, under Abhisit, the SB-PAC no longer had to go through the RTA and ISOC for funding, and it made it possible, over time, for the SB-PAC—and specifically, Special Branch—to assume a greater role in the war.

Second, Abhisit aimed to have the RTP mostly, but not exclusively, assert security in towns, and have the military mostly, but not exclusively, secure rural areas. Up to this point in the war, the RTA had taken the lead in both rural and urban areas. The theory was that the civilian-friendly police belonged in towns, and the heavier army belonged in the countryside. There would be exceptions, however. Where the police did not have the manpower to provide enough physical security for urban infrastructure, the army would be necessary. And the BPP, which specialized in rural operations, would continue its classic role.[271]

These bold steps demonstrated real leadership by Abhisit and reflected the classic COIN coordination model that the British had used successfully in Malaya in the 1950s. Here, the police and civilians, headed by Special Branch, managed the war. The military, though intricately integrated into the chain of command—including intelligence and strategy-making entities—supported the civilian-police command with physical security, light infantry, and DA missions. It is possible Abhisit and his staff got these ideas from Sir Robert Thompson's COIN theories.

Regardless, Abhisit's coordination scheme bucked Thai tradition where the RTA commanded nearly all organizations in the insurgency zone, except under

Prem's model where the PM commanded the SB-PAC. Abhisit maneuvered masterfully to get the RTA to agree to his idea while moving elements of the RTP, a Thaksin-leaning organization, closer to him. Abhisit could have continued with the status quo, but instead he took a major career risk to improve Thailand's national security, a move not fully appreciated by his detractors.

COIN Coordination under Yingluck

Since taking office, Yingluck and her subordinates have wrestled intensely over coordination. Her key people include Defense Minister Sukumpol Suwanatat and DPM Yutthasak Sasiprapa. Yutthasak oversees security matters. Yingluck scrapped Abhisit's scheme for another that has yet to fully take shape. One thing is clear, however. She has authorized another coordination center in Bangkok that is reminiscent of her brother's arrangement with its multiple layers of bureaucracy.

The cabinet approved this new center in April 2012, when it became apparent that the national command authority leadership did not have a full handle on the war. Violence had increased through a series of high-profile bombings, which caught Yingluck unawares. The new center therefore suggests Yingluck is unhappy with the lack of progress being made by the traditional coordinators of the war. It also indicates the new center might be a mechanism for upper leadership to better grasp the strategic view of the conflict, so it can issue more effective guidance to ISOC, the RTA, and the SB-PAC for fulfilling strategy with optimal ways and means. Only time will tell if this is the case.

At any rate, DPM Chalerm Yubamrung initially nicknamed the new center "Pentagon II." Its official name is the Operations Centre for the Implementation of Policy and Strategy to Resolve Problems of the Southern Border Provinces (OC-IPSRPSBP). Its mission is to coordinate the war and increase intelligence flow. General Paradorn of the NSC runs it. He supervises four lieutenants that run three distinct portfolios: Defense Minister Sukumpol Suwanathat (security), DPM Chalerm Yubamrung and Interior Minister Charupong Ruangsuwan (development), and DPM and Education Minister Pongthep Thepkanchana (justice).

Establishing the OC-IPSRPSBP was not easy, and its future is unsure. Scores of powerful personalities and entities involved in the southern COIN rallied to radically alter the coordination of the war after the election, and they eventually might get their say. The RTA is not happy about the SB-PAC being moved out from under its authority. The new national police chief, General Adul Saengsingkaew, said ISOC should control the SB-PAC, whose chair technically outranks the Fourth Army commander under Abhisit's policies.

Adding to the confusion, the SB-PAC's entire advisory council nearly resigned in protest in 2012 over the possibility of the Pentagon II seizing control over the SB-PAC and the Fourth Army. They said a Bangkok-based center had less knowledge of day-to-day operations in the far south and therefore was less capable of effective leadership. General Paradorn, however, has guaranteed outside influence over the SB-PAC's operations will be minimal.[272]

The Three Pillars of the Second Southern COIN

Security, political, and economic ways and means for the current war do not differ too much from Thailand's past COINs. There are some key differences here and there, however. One major difference in the political realm, for example, entails deradicalization programs for those indoctrinated by Islamist jihadi ideology. As indicated in the previous section, however, coordination of these three pillars has been lacking for nearly the duration of the war, and internal government bickering has kept the Thai from waging a more effective fight.

Security Measures

Security programs in the current southern COIN consist mostly of intelligence, patrols, physical security, population control, village protection, investigations, QRF, and DA. Regarding assets, the Thai use the same type forces used in past wars—the military, police, intelligence units/agencies, and local forces. In the current war, however, the number of personnel deployed far exceeds the effort applied in the previous southern COIN. The current insurgents strike far more often than their predecessors, and they are more destructive as well. This requires a stronger government response. Bangkok has deployed more than sixty thousand security personnel to the south, covering one thousand villages and thirty-three districts.[273] RTA troops serve in the far south for six months to a year.[274]

The Royal Thai Military

RTA forces in the current COIN are in the lead and come from the First, Second, Third, and Fourth Army Regional Commands, plus the newly formed 15th Division. The 15th, part of the Fourth Army, is composed largely of personnel from the far south and is meant to be a permanent force in the border provinces.[275]

SF contributes as well, as do the RTN, RTM, and RTAF. All these forces supply CPM with the units that it needs. Most operations are battalion-size or smaller.[276] The RTM in particular have a long-standing presence in Narathiwat and carry out operations at a brisk pace.

The RTA relies heavily on SF troops for DA and CA missions. The RTM and RTN carry out DA as well, as demonstrated by the brilliantly executed 13 February 2013 Marine base ambush in Narathiwat by Recon Marines and Navy SEALs. Their missions are classified, tied to well-placed intelligence assets, and rarely make the news.

In an effort to professionalize and better motivate the forces, in March 2009, PM Abhisit ordered an increase of pay for units in the insurgency zone. In some cases, this was by about a thousand *baht*. For example, rank-and-file troops' pay increased from an average of fifteen hundred to twenty-five hundred *baht* a month.[277]

The RTA carries out the same kinds of security missions as it did in the 1980s–90s, just at a much higher tempo. General Anupong said in 2008 that the RTA's main mission was to raid "suspected separatist shelters," meaning separatist hideouts, sanctuaries, and arms caches. These types of missions depend heavily on actionable intelligence.[278]

The RTA, via CPM, works jointly with the RTP. An RTA official explains the relationship: "The south still has the normal police in their regular areas at police stations, etc. Everything operates as normal, but CPM helps the police do their job of investigation, checkpoints, arrests, maintaining order, etc. But if the police find an insurgent or group of insurgents they can't handle, then they can request help from CPM. It can feed more forces into the operation. And if the army wants to capture an insurgent, then it must coordinate with the police."[279]

As for RTA training and doctrine, a high-ranking RTA general says the Thai military trains its officers to value locals and work with them, which is key in COIN. "This is the knowledge that has passed through generations of officers," he says. "We learned this in Staff College as well. They [officer trainees] are aware of the significance of this—it's our way."[280] He stressed it was not doctrine for Thai officers to "go around kicking doors," but of course, kinetic operations do literally require some door kicking.[281] Another senior military official stressed that the king's philosophy of "understand, access, and develop" was indeed RTA doctrine. "That's the king's philosophy, and it's proper, and we follow it," he asserts.[282]

All RTA troopers receive predeployment briefings on Malay Muslim culture, the basic problems of the far south that contribute to the insurgency, and insurgent tactics. The RTA's Intelligence Command published a 408-page guidebook on the south to educate troops for their deployments there. The guidebook provides background on the origins of the war and the groups involved. It also lists by name more than one thousand auxiliary force personnel.[283] The RTA also has a COIN manual, *FM 100-20*, which is similar to a US COIN manual from the 1980s, but not all forces are familiar with it.

While many RTA troopers train in COIN theory and know it well, others do not. It is not clear why this happens. In 2008 in Pattani, an RTA colonel thoroughly described COIN theory as expressed by David Galula and the Prem-Harn clique and how it was applied in his area of operations. In 2011, however, a captain said his company had received no substantive COIN education. His unit had CA, physical security, and patrol duties near a village that was deemed hostile, and they were not properly trained for all these missions. He also said they were undermanned for their high operational tempo. The young captain confessed to having searched for COIN strategies on the Internet and found the teachings of Sir Robert Thompson, which he had enthusiastically embraced and tried to apply in the field.[284]

Various human rights groups have accused the RTA and other security forces of extrajudicial killings in the far south. Abuza cites an operation he says smacked of government involvement on 21 June 2005. In this case, a small group of shooters armed with silenced pistols killed three *ustaz*.[285] The speculation is, since they were silenced weapons and the operation was swift and effective, it had to be the military. While this may be true—Abuza is a respected expert in his field—more than tactical considerations are necessary to indict the military. Insurgent assassins have proven highly effective in their own right. At the same time, Bangkok's critics often ignore the fact that, in war, governments are indeed sanctioned to assassinate enemy personnel despite how distasteful this tactic might sound. In COIN, the assassination of a handful of insurgent leaders can collapse entire cells, prevent violent operations, shorten wars, and save lives. Additionally, if insurgents use assassinations, chances are a government will use them, too. This is especially true in Thailand.

COIN Operations in the Field

As previously stated, security missions in the current southern COIN are the same type carried out in past wars. Of these, teacher escort duty is one of the most common and dangerous, because teachers are one of the insurgents' main target sets. Says reporter Nick Nostiz, "All security forces do teacher escort duties, but it's dangerous, because it's regular and predictable. They hit the pickup point, the drop-off point, the same road to and from the schools, etc. Teachers own the cars they convoy in, and they usually have an escort in front and back, and sometimes just in front if there's not enough people to cover their six [rear]."[286]

Some government entities, such as SB-PAC, do not always want security. "CPM can provide security for SB-PAC, but mostly *Or Sor* does physical security of SB-PAC buildings and places like that," says an RTA soldier. "In the field, normally, the SB-PAC does not need security. Mostly, if it looks good for the villagers, they can work the projects with no violent incidents. But if it's Thai language instruction, then they must have security. SB-PAC usually tries to avoid military escorts. For example, the health department workers usually do not want to ride with military that has weapons in the vehicle."[287] The SB-PAC, however, seldom carries out operations in red zones where it would certainly need security. Operating in yellow and green zones requires less protection, if any.

Ambulance crews in hostile districts in Songkhla, however, report if they do not carry guns with them and demonstrate to insurgent road sentries that they are armed, they will surely be attacked.[288] In February 2012, insurgents set off a forty-pound car bomb at the Pattani Health Department, killing one and injuring thirteen. This demonstrates providing CA-type help to the population does not guarantee safety from insurgent violence.

Apart from traditional security, the RTA has introduced a unique COIN tool to the field: police forensics. Gathering evidence against insurgents is vital, as neither the military nor the police are supposed to detain suspects without sufficient evidence. To help identify insurgents, General Sonthi in 2006 tapped CSI Chief Dr. Pornthip to deploy to the far south with her team to collect and process evidence at attack sites. She has helped to identify and arrest scores of insurgents through painstaking investigative work, including building a massive DNA database of thousands of samples taken from bombings, assassinations, raids, and ambushes.

In January 2009, Fourth Army Commander General Phichet Visaichorn announced DNA evidence had confirmed the army had killed insurgent leader Imran Binma-eng in a firefight. Authorities had his DNA on record from multiple bombings in Narathiwat. Accordingly, the government was able to prove he was indeed an insurgent and not simply an innocent bystander murdered by authorities, as antigovernment human rights organizations and insurgents often assert.[289]

Security forces have sometimes carried out illegitimate killings, however, and this sullies government legitimacy. Some accusers have presented convincing evidence of torture as well, though many such claims are also denial and deception operations by insurgents. Claiming torture upon capture is an excellent tactic to discredit one's captors and harness NGOs in one's defense. Such is the deceptive nature of insurgency and terrorism.

RTA-run operations, while generally effective, have several flaws, according to army personnel. First, some officers complain that poor information management impedes effective operations and planning. They say, for example, the CPM staff will not discuss the strategy of the war—the end goal of the campaign and how to get there—at the staff level. This smacks of poor flexibility and leadership at the theater operational planning level.

Second, many CPM forces lack basic COIN soldiering skills. For example, on 18 December 2010 in Yala, insurgents hidden in a pickup truck slowly approached an RTA monk protection detail and sprang up at the last minute, killing the soldiers and the monk. CCTV footage showed the whole episode. The troopers were casually walking their route, completely oblivious to the approaching threat. Better-trained troops would have had weapons at the ready during the entire detail, and they would have addressed the pickup truck in question well before it came within ambush range.

Third, insiders say CPM needs to include more civilians in operations to make the combined nature of the organization more effective. While the CPM structure is generally effectual, even some military personnel complain it is too influenced by the army.[290]

Fourth, communications in joint operations could be better. Says an RTA trooper, "The security sweeps are sometimes effective, sometimes not. Some units train poorly and then deploy poorly. Sometimes their communications are ineffective, and hammer and anvil units are not in position when the hammer force strikes. This allows the insurgents to escape." Here, the trooper is referring to hammer and anvil tactics where the "hammer" force finds, fixes, and engages a guerrilla unit, and the "anvil" force sits in ambush for it as it tries to move away from the hammer.

The trooper additionally notes, "Also, in many sweeps, it's the army, the police, and the *Thahan Phran* combined on one operation, and they are not coordinated."[291] The high number of caches discovered, arrests made, and the decline in insurgent operations since 2008, however, demonstrates some measure of success, but not a stellar record.

At the same time, security operations are having an impact on the insurgency. Askew interviewed one insurgent, an apprentice bombmaker named Hamad, who described how security forces chipped away at his cell by arresting his cohorts one by one. (The RTA was a part of these investigations and actually made his arrest.) He explained how authorities, through their 2007–08 security sweeps, had captured his supervisor, an *ustaz*. Investigators also found bomb-making equipment at Islamburapha School and promptly shut it down, which cut Hamad off from his bomb-making base. When the government arrested other insurgents in his circle, he was reduced to making bombs at home, alone. His expertise was shallow, however, and he made numerous faulty devices. This angered his insurgent comrades, which put him in danger. "I was starting to get scared of this pressure," he told Askew.[292]

Eventually, the civilian casualties caused by his bombs forced Hamad to reconsider his activities. When he accidentally blew up a bomb at his home that shredded his hand, authorities arrested him. Askew writes, "When Hamad was arrested by soldiers outside his parents' home in January 2009, he was already tired, depressed, and disillusioned with the insurgency. He admits that he was relieved to be captured, though also anxious in case the soldiers mistreated him. Fortunately, he was not treated roughly."[293] The arresting officer laughed at his long quest to capture Hamad, joking about the several pairs of boots he wore out tracking the young man all over the south. He offered Hamad cigarettes. In turn, Hamad provided them with intelligence on the movement.[294] It is worth noting that fervent jihadis do not respond to this kind of treatment.

The Royal Thai Police

The officers of the SBPPOC, Police Region 9's PP, the BPP, and Special Branch make up the bulk of police forces in the southern COIN. The RTP's mission is the same as in past COINs. It conducts regular police duties, investigates violent attacks, builds cases, arrests suspects, and provides physical security for checkpoints, government facilities, infrastructure, monks, and teachers. As in the past, the RTP also works with village security forces. The BPP are especially active in rural areas and carry out COIN missions such as patrols, raids on caches, and arrests—especially high-risk arrests where the subjects might be armed. The BPP also carries out CA missions as they did in the communist COIN. The police are highly active and have tracked down and arrested more than one hundred insurgent suspects. Most of these are hardened fighters, not just part-time village auxiliary forces. RTP "wanted" posters appear all over the far south in hotels and restaurants, on billboards, and in common areas. People who provide information that leads to arrests can earn rewards of twenty thousand *baht*.[295]

Police CPM duties require interaction with the military. There are rivalries between the two entities, and they have not nearly achieved seamless cooperation. Says a Thai officer, "The police-army relationship is up and down. It's caused a lot of problems in the south because they don't coordinate strategy together. It's been rough."[296] In one case, both the police and the army deployed to arrest the same suspects without coordinating with each other. When they arrived on the scene, the insurgents opened fire, and chaos resulted since neither government force knew what the other was doing.[297]

In other cases the police and army have worked work well together. The 2 January 2006 beheading case of an SF trooper, Sergeant Somjit Lorsaeng of the First SF Battalion, provides a good example.[298] Says a military officer, "Last year, an SF team was ambushed, and one of the insurgents cut off an NCO's head. Afterwards, the police, with the army in tow, launched an operation to find the insurgents who executed the ambush. SF went with a police team on its investigation, but as liaison only. The police were in charge of the investigation. However, they requested the military stand by as QRF to aid in the apprehension of the suspects if needed. The police in this case had a great intelligence network, and in seven days they found all the insurgents involved. Their investigation found the SF NCO's head, his red beret, and his GPS [Global Positioning System unit]. And they tracked the insurgents to their houses, including the head insurgent, and they all lived in different areas. The operation was over in two or three months, and it was integrated between the police and military. The police were a huge help."[299]

Despite successes such as this, the bad reputation that plagued the RTP in times past remains a major impediment to effective COIN. This negativity is primarily directed against the Provincial Police and not the BPP or Special Branch. Some accuse the PP of being corrupt and abusive, and in some instances, the accusations are justified. Since the police directly represent the state and have power over the population, such abuse, both real and perceived, feeds the insurgency by delegitimizing the government. Some observers add that the police are neither properly staffed nor trained to fight the insurgents. Says Nostiz, "The police, they can't properly work. There are lots of deaths—too many to investigate properly—so they all get filed away as being part of the insurgency. And they don't collect evidence. Plus, they are underpaid and corrupt."[300] This was one of the main reasons the government established the SBPPOC.

As with the CPT and the first Thai Malay Muslim COINs, it is important to note that scores of police officers have died in the line of duty in the far south, and it would be unobjective and false to say they were all corrupt. They are not. Scores of them are dedicated professionals. Without their investigative work, the southern COIN would have experienced much less success, and insurgents might well have made more headway.

Local Forces

Local forces are a significant part of the equation in Thailand's current COIN, especially the *Pattana Santi* program. The RTG believes they are prudent, effective, and the best way to drive a wedge between guerrillas and the people. The government in 2006 took steps to increase the efficiency and professionalism of local forces by reinforcing doctrine and increasing training of *Or Lor Bor* (Buddhist Security Units), *Chor Ror Bor* (Village Security Units), the *Or Sor*/VDC, and the *Thahan Phran*. The *Pattana Santi* program makes extensive use of these forces, especially the *Thahan Phran*.

A senior Thai military officer describes why the RTG continues to rely on local forces in COIN. He says, "Regarding the government use of local forces, they have many advantages over some standard government forces. They know the local areas. They know the local language. They know the local people. Soldiers from other parts of the country will have difficulty operating smoothly in these areas regarding intelligence and operations that require contact with villagers. Also, the community has the natural propensity to look out for its own safety, and again, local forces are highly motivated to do this because it's their families, friends, and property they are protecting."[301]

Or Lor Bor

Or Lor Bor is an exclusively Buddhist self-defense group. It began at the behest of Buddhists that were continually under attack from radical Islamists bent on genocide and/or forcing their removal from the southern border provinces. Lacking protection, Buddhists petitioned Queen Sirikit to sponsor their training, and she agreed. The mission of *Or Lor Bor* is to protect Buddhist personnel and places. In 2008, it operated only at night, however. A Yala government official said at that time, "The Queen's *Or Lor Bor* is only a partial solution. They work in the day and provide security only at night. We want to have a full-time security force."[302]

The program's royal ties are supposed to ensure its high quality. The exact number of *Or Lor Bor* members is elusive. Estimates have been as high as thirty thousand. They were originally armed only with shotguns, but their training and armaments have increased as insurgents killed more and more Buddhists. Srisompob says, "They are very strong and well armed, better armed than the village security groups."[303] They are increasingly toting assault rifles such as AK-47s and M-16s.[304] The exodus of tens of thousands of Buddhists from the insurgency zone, however, indicates the *Or Lor Bor* have not been decisive enough to prevent ethnic cleansing.[305]

Chor Ror Bor

Chor Ror Bor are village protection units composed of both Thai Malay Muslims and Thai Buddhists. They also carry out some village development projects. They are approximately fifty thousand strong and are affiliated with the MoI. Members initially carried shotguns but are expanding their arsenals with assault rifles.[306] *Chor Ror Bor* exercise population control by manning checkpoints at village entry and exit points. Says Srisompob, "The village head is leader of the *Chor Ror Bor*. They are an armed militia of about twenty. The village headman secures the money to pay them twenty thousand *baht* a month for the whole group."[307] This pay is quite low and violates a lesson learned during the CPT COIN era— namely, that poorly paid and poorly trained local forces perform poorly.

Or Sor

Or Sor are the same Volunteer Defense Corps forces used in past COINs. A few years into the current war, the government increased their training and gave them new uniforms—distinctive American desert camouflage uniforms from the early 1990s informally known as "chocolate chip." *Or Sor* duties include physical security of government buildings such as the SB-PAC building in Yala, and they are increasingly deploying for teacher protection duties, close protection for government officials, and urban patrol. Sometimes they augment village defense forces.[308] They carry M-16s and other light infantry weapons. *Or Sor* remains a joint MoI-RTA program, but the MoI commands the force.[309] Srisompob says the *Or Sor* are professional and effective, but their ever-expanding role puts them more and more into harm's way, and their casualty rates have risen.

Thahan Phran

Thahan Phran remain a staple in the Thai COIN arsenal. General Sonthi announced in August 2006 that he was deploying thirty new *Thahan Phran* companies (along with twenty regular RTA companies) to the far south at a cost of 800 million *baht*.[310] These included a multitude of Thai Malay Muslim *Thahan Phran*. Their mission remains intelligence and DA. One reason for their deployment was that some poorly trained local militias have been timid and in some cases have handed over their weapons to insurgents too easily—the exact scenario that led to the Tak Bai riot.[311]

In March 2009, PM Abhisit deployed four thousand more *Thahan Phran* to the far south.[312] Most of these were specially trained CA *Thahan Phran* participating in the *Pattana Santi* program. While Abhisit said they were deploying in a noncombat role, the *Thahan Phran* are combat-capable and will likely be used in battle when the need arises.[313] Says Srisompob, "The new *Thahan Phran* are better and more professional than the older *Thahan Phran*. They don't rape and commit atrocities, but that bad image is still there."[314]

One aspect of upgrading the *Thahan Phran* has involved indoctrination, especially regarding the Thai royal family.[315] Thailand has taken some motivational concepts from the Village Scouts and transferred them to the *Thahan Phran*. This approach also helps to discourage barbarism, as the *Thahan Phran* realize that behaving badly or committing atrocities will sully the honor of the king.

Another aspect of upgrading the *Thahan Phran* is increased pay. On 1 October 2009, the government announced they will be paid fifty-five *baht* a day instead of a mere ten.[316] Increased pay levels and training indicate that Bangkok is relying more heavily on these forces.

Thahan Phran go through three months of training conducted by RTA SF, and regular RTA forces command them in the field.[317] They carry M-16s and AK-47s but prefer the latter because they are more durable and the round is heavier. *Thahan Phran* continue on-the-job training after completing their basic training.[318]

Critics decry the *Thahan Phran* as ineffective. Some say they do the "dirty work," the hard jobs the RTA does not want to do or cannot do.[319] The Thai defend their use of *Thahan Phran* vigorously, however. Says one civil servant in Yala, "People who criticize them don't understand this about guerrilla war, how gangster-like it is. The *Thahan Phran* can do things the army can't always do well at the local level, and that is getting intelligence and killing insurgents."[320] He continues, "We can't put a tank on the street to fight a gangster. So we put a *Thahan Phran* on a motorcycle to fight the gangsters. And the *Thahan Phran* sometimes has the gangster mentality. We use the gangster to fight the gangster. This is guerrilla war, and the normal rules don't apply. If we fight by all the normal rules, then we will lose. The state will lose."[321]

Pattana Santi

By 2008, the ever-resilient Chavalit, back inside the government as DPM in charge of national security, developed a village security system similar to the CPM units deployed during the communist COIN. Initially, it was a trial program in six districts that began on 11 October, with the exact locations kept secret.[322] After the trial's success, Bangkok standardized the program throughout the entire insurgency zone in February 2009, calling it *Pattana Santi* (Development and Peace) program. *Pattana Santi* seeks to professionalize local forces by integrating them with government kinetic and CA assets. More than just a security-CA program, however, it also aims to enlist locals into development and job programs, and it has a psyops and PR component that reinforces the program's ultimate goal. The end goal, according to Chavalit, is "to engender a sense of shared national and local pride in all the races, religions, and cultures present in Thailand"—again, shades of the Village Scouts combined with almost amnesty-like work programs along the lines of General Kitti's.[323]

Pattana Santi has deployed forces in 217 red-zone villages.[324] Each *Pattana Santi* unit ideally has thirty-one personnel made up of RTA, *Thahan Phran*, RTP, and local defense volunteers. An RTA spokesperson said the units' mission is to "stay in the villages and promote better understanding, extend a helping hand and provide mobile medical services."[325] It injects government forces directly into the red-zone villages to counter the presence of guerrillas and auxiliary forces.[326] The full impact of the program has yet to be gauged.

Border Security

Since Thai Malay Muslim insurgents use Malaysia as sanctuary, Bangkok has increased security along the border. The results so far have been less effective, however, than the joint Malaysian-Thai operations of the 1980s–90s. In 2011, the two countries were deep in talks to solve this problem. General Akanit, General Kitti's aide from the 1980s, is a key leader in that effort, but progress has been slow.

Colonel Ghazali says of the southern border population, "[Locals] don't respect the borders, because they are artificial. They shop, visit relatives. In some places they can wade over the river border. There is smuggling, but it's not serious smuggling. It's fuel, flour, bread, rice. Rice is cheaper in Thailand. Back-and-forth smuggling is common."[327] Colonel Ghazali also believes, however, that the insurgents might be using northern Malaysia as sanctuary. "Kelantan is the only state ruled by the PAS [Pan-Malaysian Islamic Party] and Nik Aziz, and they are more sympathetic to those people, the Thai separatists. My gut tells me that they might be connected. They have more sympathies with their cross-border friends. This is not so in Kedah."[328]

A leading RTG official says, "Border control is a big part of this conflict. We must find ways to secure the border to make sure the insurgents cannot get away after hit-and-run operations or escape our dragnet operations of targeted personnel. We've been working with Malaysians on this. In the old days, Malaysia was facing the CPM [Communist Party of Malaysia], which is why they put emphasis on border control. But now they don't have the challenge that they used to have, so there is less urgency, but we still cooperate."[329]

In April 2009, Bangkok and Kuala Lumpur announced they were increasing border security and intelligence sharing. Thai Supreme Commander General Songkitti Chakkabhat and Malaysian Defense Forces Chief General bin Haji Zainal met to confer on the insurgents' use of Malaysia as sanctuary. On their agenda were specific insurgent border crossing points, such as where Narathiwat's Sungai Kolok and Waeng districts adjoin Malaysia's Kelantan state, and certain maritime ports. General Zainal said he agreed with getting rid of dual Thai-Malaysian citizenship that made insurgency easier.

Zainal also announced the return of eighty-nine Thai Malay Muslims—Narathiwat natives—from Malaysia. They were among the 131 people from Tak Bai, Sungai Kolok, and Sungai Padi districts who fled to Kelantan in 2005, citing fear of annihilation by Thai authorities.[330] Both the Malaysian government and the UN investigated the matter and found no credence in their assertions. Malaysia branded their entry into Kelantan as illegal.[331] A suspected insurgent officer led the group, and authorities saw it as a propaganda ploy to gain international sympathy.

Intelligence

The intelligence agencies involved in the current COIN are essentially the same as in past COINs: Special Branch, the RTP, the RTA, the NIA, and the DSI. The NIA sees the southern COIN and terrorism as two of its top priorities. The DSI, originally tasked mainly with economic crimes, uses its mandate to investigate complex crime to engage in the south.[332]

As for the RTA's intelligence apparatus, organic intelligence units—both reconnaissance and human intelligence—collect information, and upper echelons process and disseminate it. Deputy Permanent Secretary of Justice Charnchao Chaiyanukij says the RTA's intelligence prowess is nearly autonomous. "Most of the time," he says, "the military has its own intelligence and investigative network, and it uses the police sparingly."[333]

The best information sources for the RTA (and other intelligence assets) continue to be the population. Security forces look for opportunities to reward and build relations with people who volunteer information. After all, insurgency is of, by, and for the people—at least the rebellious people. Says an RTA officer, "If the villagers provide intelligence information, then the troops try to help, and when doctors give away drugs and help with medical things the villagers don't have, it helps to build a trustful relationship with the villagers."[334] He adds, "Success most often happens when there is information from a hunter, local villagers, and our spies." The officer says that local defense forces also provide good intelligence.[335]

Another RTA officer says that local forces "can be used to set up a centralized system to watch the villages, as in intelligence and reconnaissance. Not everyone needs to be shooting. Sometimes, they can just watch and report. Headquarters expects local forces to report on enemy activities."[336]

At other times, CA generates intelligence sources. "We can get intelligence from walk-ins or when the army does community relations," says an RTA field officer, "but if the insurgents can easily strike back at the village or the information source, then the military might not act on it."[337] This is a clear indication that the government does not always have enough security personnel to protect the population, a critical weakness that can cause COIN failure.

A Thai official says teachers also provide information on suspected students. In this regard, they act similarly to American teachers who provide information to truancy police on wayward teens. "The Ministry of Education is trying to work closely with the teachers to make sure the insurgents don't come to the schools and recruit," he says.[338]

As in COINs past, the RTA also uses *Thahan Phran* to collect intelligence at the village level. Nick Nostiz has seen them in action. "*Thahan Phran* try to get good intelligence," he says. "The *Thahan Phran* and RTA get phone call tips, and they do reconnaissance, and take photos. They talk to the village heads, and the village heads might be one hundred percent legitimate, or they might also be *mafia*, but also an RTA supporter, so it's always a bit difficult to deal with these types."[339] Such are the perils of human intelligence work in an insurgency zone.

In other cases, *Thahan Phran* set up observation posts in critical areas. Says Nostiz, "They will also pull an operation on a road that gets bombed a lot. They will watch, wait, and see who the bomber is. They can see at night, some of them, through night-vision goggles, but they complain a lot about them. They say they are too old."[340]

By late 2007, the RTG's intelligence system was proving effective. "At the present time," says Professor Bhumarat, "there are many insurgent defectors. Things are working very well. The government has information on the separatists. The RTA has a good intelligence network. It gets a lot of intelligence, and can send it to other units and organizations to exploit."[341] By 2008, intelligence on insurgent activities, personnel, and arms caches had helped reduce levels of violence by nearly half of what they were in 2005–06.

Thailand's southern intelligence apparatus is not without its problems, however. As Somchai Rakwijit observes, "The situation in the south today is much more difficult than getting information from northeast Thailand during the communist insurgency because here you have the cultural gap, the language gap, and the religious gap."[342]

A senior officer expands on the impact of culture on intelligence: "At *pondoks* we have no control, no eyes and ears, but slowly we are reaching out to local Islamic leaders. They are always there among the people, and they know the people well, and so our troops have to contact them, work with them, and intermingle, doing good things with the community. We also work with community leaders. The teachers and imams are but two of the groups we contact."[343]

General Phichet of the Fourth Army began a new intelligence program in June 2009 called "Pineapple Eye." The pineapple aspect refers to having eyes everywhere, since the eyes of the pineapple face all directions. The network mimics what insurgents do by providing local people—businessmen, concerned citizens, and local forces—with an armed, early warning communications network. In addition to enhancing protection, the program is also politically oriented in that it connects the people to the state.[344]

Pineapple Eye volunteers are organized in a network of static and roving observers who report potential preattack behaviors via walkie-talkies. They look for people reconnoitering targets, placing motorcycle bombs, and doing similar threatening activities. Volunteers also report violent incidents to medical and security forces to improve response times. Pineapple Eye volunteers provide security at targets that insurgents traditionally strike, such as government buildings, markets, stores, and banks. The program is low-cost. The radios cost a mere thirty-two hundred *baht* each.[345]

Pineapple Eye began in Hat Yai, Songkhla, with one hundred volunteers and the hope of expanding to other provinces. After General Phichet pitched the program to local leaders and businessmen, it expanded to 576 people. He discussed spreading it to Yala, depending on its success in Songkhla.[346] In August 2009, the program was reportedly having success in Betong, Yala.[347]

Political Measures

The political programs the RTG is using in the current COIN are in many cases identical to those used in the 1980s–90s. However, the RTG is retooling some programs because the insurgents are using them to their own advantage. Current political measures include, but are not limited to, revamping grassroots-level political programs, hiring SB-PAC advisors from the local community, upgrading the education system, engaging in international diplomacy, offering amnesty, running a complaint department at SB-PAC, and implementing psyops and PR.

Political Reform at the Grassroots Level

The question of Thai Malay Muslim political participation is no longer a real issue in the far south, thanks to the success of 1980s–90s era programs. In the December 2008 legislative elections, 75 percent of the far south's population voted. The increased number of lower-level officials that must be elected, however, gave an opening to the insurgents. They inserted their agents into the electoral process. As a result, some of them won, allowing them to subvert the government from within. This is not to say all Thai Malay Muslims that vote are manipulating the system, but it is an issue. Says Srisompob, "Many of the Ministry of Interior officers don't trust the leaders of TAO. They believe that most of the presidents of the TAO are supporters of the insurgents, that they are a front group of the separatists."[348] As a result, the SB-PAC and TAO officials often do not work together.

"Many of the presidents of TAO," says Srisompob, "are not [insurgents], because they themselves are targets of assassinations and bombs. Many of them get killed." But he admits, "Maybe the insurgents have infiltrated some TAOs." Srisompob says scores of TAO leaders are caught between the government and the insurgents. "They are pressed by the military and the governors," he says, "and at the same time they are threatened by the separatists in the villages, so they have to be careful. They are sitting on the fence."

Accordingly, many Thai believe that increased democracy—offered too quickly to a population that was not prepared for it—has added to the insurgent turmoil and allowed it to flourish. For example, Srisompob explains that, under the 1997 Constitution, "the village head was elected by locals, the villagers, to serve a five-year term. It became messy. You had an election for the *tambon* administrator and an election for the village headman, and also the imam—they were elected from the members of the mosque. This is why local people complain that there are too many elections. Local leaders became more politicians than leaders. They have local parliament elections, senate elections, provincial administrative elections. It's a lot for the locals to handle."

Too much democracy manifested itself most evidently in the mosque. According to Niran Pantharakit, Director of the Chularatchamontri's Office, the election of imams caused competition and power struggles, which in turn contributed to the insurgency. (The Chularatchamontri is the RTG's national Muslim advisor, a position ordained in 1997.) Some imams, in their zeal to obtain power, strived to become "more Islamic" than their rivals, often leaning toward radical Islamism. The situation opened the door for insurgents to manipulate imams and, indirectly, to manipulate the people. One of Niran's solutions to the problem was to meticulously screen Islamic leaders before they entered government service, a proposition the government began considering in 2007.[349]

To relieve local "election pressure," PM Surayud in 2006 reinstated the appointing of imams and village heads.[350] As Srisompob explained in 2008, "Now we have three local leaders in the south. One is an elected leader, the president of the TAO. You have the village headman, now appointed by the governor. And you have the imam, now appointed by the central Islamic committee in Bangkok and through the provincial Islamic committee." Village heads now serve sixty-year terms, which is the traditional Thai way.[351] Free from elections, Bangkok now believes village headmen and imams can serve everyone, concentrate on leadership, disseminate state-friendly information, and make hard decisions instead of catering to niche power cliques and insurgents.

Aside from these national and local programs, governors have their own grassroots political initiatives under ISOC-4. For example, Yala Governor Thira Mintrasak has the *Yala Santisuk* (Peaceful Yala) program. It established a local council of ten advisors in every district where villagers can seek advice, lodge complaints, and ask for justice in cases of wrongdoing against them. Councils also advise villagers on their legal rights and encourage them to work with the state to solve problems. In this regard, the government is essentially teaching Thai Malay Muslims, often for the first time in their lives, what it means to be a citizen of Thailand. This instruction addresses the isolation and fringe mentality of the dispossessed.[352]

Despite all the local politics and empowerment at the grassroots level, some politicians contend that good governance is the real key to fixing the far south. As long as local politicians are corrupt, the people will not trust Bangkok, they say. Pattani Senator Anusart Suwanmongkol has said, "What we need is not autonomy but good governance and transparency. Even Muslims are clamoring for good governance. There is already decentralization—60 to 70 percent of the budget is in the hands of local officials—but that is meaningless without good governance."[353] It is unclear if there are good governance training programs in the current southern war. And as an aside, Senator Anusart himself was injured in a car bomb attack on the CS Pattani Hotel, which he owns, in March 2008.

Southern Border Provinces Administrative Command Advisors

In April 2007, the SB-PAC established an advisory board of thirty-five locals to guide its projects. The board's purpose is to help the SB-PAC identify and solve problems plaguing villagers at the local level. Chairing the council was Aziz Benhawan, President of the Yala PAO. His deputies were Kraisorn Sritrairat, the rector of Yala Rajabhat University; Vichai Ruangroengkulrit, National Legislative Assembly member; and Prince of Songkhla University's Worawit Baru, a Pattani senator. The head provincial Buddhist monks and their imam counterparts also serve on the board. Other members included academics, journalists, and businesspersons. Their span of service is two years.[354]

Local Education Reform

Ministry of Education inspector Prasert Kaewphet, in charge of education in the far south, submitted a *pondok* upgrade plan to Education Minister Wijit Srisa-arn (also chair of the Southern Education Board, or SEB) on 23 July 2007 in Narathiwat. It was in many respects similar to the Private Schools Teaching Islam program that the government ended in the late 1990s. The new plan standardizes *pondok* curriculum, checks the backgrounds of *pondok* executives and teachers, and establishes benchmarks to judge schools' progress. Specific aspects of the program include standardizing correct teaching of Islam, nullifying radical

Islamism, providing vocational training, and upgrading teachers' training. The SEB, staffed by Muslim scholars, local leaders, and southern Ministry of Education personnel, supervises the program.[355]

Yet another *pondok* reform program surfaced in August 2008, known as Curriculum *Pondok* Reform (CPR). The Secretary General of the Office of the Higher Education Commission (OHEC), Sumeth Yamnoon, explained that CPR was attempting to empower *pondoks* to reform themselves but could not force them to do so. He urged them to work with Bangkok in developing curricula that prepared students for the real world. Secretary Sumeth said OHEC linked Prince of Songkhla, Ratjabhat, and Thaksin Universities with *pondoks* to help them modernize. CPR has a diploma program enabling *ustaz* to attend math and science classes so that they can teach these secular subjects to their students.[356]

A similar program in April 2008 focused on training teachers at *tadikas* (private Islamic schools for children ages five to twelve) to prevent them from teaching children radical Islamism. Justice Secretary Charnchao started this effort after *tadika* teachers directly requested the training from him on one of his many fact-finding missions to the far south. They also wanted to learn about Thai state law.

All these education programs directly address the teacher-insurgent nexus, a major enabler of the movement. Pattani *tadika* teacher Nisit Nirano told the press that some teachers joined the insurgency out of "ignorance, lack of education and in-depth knowledge of Islam."[357] He said others joined to earn additional money to supplement their meager salaries. Some feared both the insurgency and the authorities because the latter frequently suspected *tadika* and *pondok* teachers of being insurgents.[358]

The Thai royal family is involved in *pondok* reform, too. Via the Privy Council, it runs a program called *San Jai Thai Su Jai Tai* (Uniting Thai Hearts for the South). It is designed to expose *pondok* students to the rest of Thailand and provide them with vocational training, which is supposed to imbue them with a sense of confidence. Princess Maha Chakri Sirindhorn sponsors it. Through *San Jai Thai*, many southern border youth have lived with host families in Bangkok, and others have learned carpentry and welding skills that they then used to repair their own schools. In 2008, the program had enrolled 295 students of Yala's Darussalam *pondok* in Muang district. [359] The RTA, the southern border governors, and the MoI chose the participants.[360] Says Professor Bhumarat, "I think the program works very well. After one or two months, before they return home, many of them cry and say they were treated very well by the other Muslim families in the central part of the country, and that life, and the lives of Muslims, are more than what they originally thought."[361]

ASEAN Secretary General Surin Pitsuwan, a *pondok* student himself, praised Bangkok's efforts to reform the *pondok* system. At an April 2008 educational reform conference in Pattani titled "Educational Systems in Majority and Minority Muslim Societies: Strategies and Perspectives," he said no government should force *pondoks* to change. "We are entitled to learn any subject Allah could offer," he said.[362] At the same time, he urged *ustaz* to take the initiative to boost their teaching skills and widen their curriculum to teach students more than just Islam. "But are we ready to do that? I'm not sure," Surin told the conference. He said it was time for Muslims to shed their "long-held siege mentality" and become better equipped "to interact with the outside."

Diplomacy

As in the past, Bangkok has put significant diplomatic effort into its current COIN. It has sought peace talks with southern insurgents hiding in Asia, Switzerland, and Egypt. It has strived to block Middle Eastern support for the insurgency through the OIC. Bangkok has also secured votes of confidence from Arabic countries for its conciliatory approach to its southern COIN and for its religious tolerance. This support is specifically designed to counter insurgent propaganda that says Bangkok does not let Muslims worship freely.

Peace Talks

Peace talks have been difficult to arrange. Says General Perapong, "In the past, we could negotiate because PULO and the other groups wanted political access. But in this current war, they have merged nationalism and Islam together and latched on to an international movement, the jihadists."[363] To the radicals, this makes negotiating a moot point, he says.

The government attempted talks with current insurgent leaders on Langkawi, off the northwest coast of Malaysia, during the Thaksin administration. The secret talks, supposedly brokered by former Malaysian PM Mahathir Mohammad, went nowhere. Says a Thai general, "We are always open for dialogue, and we'll talk. There are many occasions that there was an approach about dialogue, but nothing came out of it. The insurgent leaders are still reluctant to show their presence. So they remain in the dark, in the shadows, waiting to see how their war will play out. Most of our dialogue has been with the older insurgent groups, PULO and the like. We went to them, and they also came to us."[364]

PULO Foreign Affairs Chief Kasturi Mahkuta said talks with the government began in June 2005 with Thaksin and continued into the Samak administration.[365] In 2007, Thai academics held talks in Geneva and Jeddah with insurgents.[366] As an aside, the rebels' location all over the world reflects their considerable international connections.

In any case, in September 2008, additional talks took place in Bogor, Indonesia. Moderators included Indonesian Vice President Jusuf Kalla; Anis Baswedan, rector of Paramadina University; and Muhammad Hatta, Indonesian ambassador to Thailand. Five representatives from Thailand attended, headed by Lieutenant General Khwanchart Klahan, former Fourth Army commander. Eleven insurgent representatives led by a man named Wahyuddin Mohammad attended as the "Pattani Malay Consultative Congress." This might have been the *Dewan Pembabasan Pattani*, the group supposedly supervising the insurgency. Regardless, after the talks, Indonesian President Susilo Bambang Yudhoyono greeted the insurgents at his palace on 22 September. However, it is not clear if the proceedings were official RTG policy or not. It is possible they were supposed to have been kept secret and that, when they were exposed to the press, Bangkok claimed they were unofficial. Some insurgent circles derided the talks for engaging the wrong insurgents. Regardless, they ended without achieving peace.[367]

Official and highly public peace talks began in February 2013, rumored to have been jump-started by Thaksin working behind the scenes in Malaysia with the help of its Special Branch. This is not surprising, however. Thaksin, though far from perfect, made multiple peace overtures from the war's beginning, despite heavy criticism from his detractors saying all he offered the opposition was a haphazardly applied iron fist.

At any rate, General Paradorn of the NSC began meeting with an alleged insurgent intermediary or senior leader, Hassan Taib, in talks brokered by the Malaysian government. Regardless of Taib's true position, he asserted multiple precursor demands in order for talks to proceed:

- Malaysia serves as mediator, not just an intermediary
- All insurgent prisoners be released immediately
- Acknowledgment of the BRN-C as the vanguard of the insurgency, that the movement officially be referred to as a liberation movement, and that Thailand be referred to as "colonialist Siam"
- ASEAN member states participate in the talks
- The OIC and other NGOs witness the talks

General Paradorn did not initially agree to these. Regarding point one, the RTG did not want a third party making decisions for either of the two sides. That would mean giving up national sovereignty in negotiations to a country where insurgents had sanctuary. As for point two, many insurgent prisoners were facing terrorism charges for mass murdering civilians, crimes that could not go unpunished. Per point three, Bangkok was never going to elevate the insurgency to "liberation" status and insultingly refer to itself as pre-1932 "Siam." These were labels that would give the insurgents propaganda victories. In Bangkok's view, point four was wholly unnecessary. It would merely confuse the issue with too many commentators and "regionalize" the war, PR-wise—and maybe internationalize it. Finally, point five would allow pro-insurgent front groups into the process and increase political warfare against the RTG.

Regardless of these concerns, meetings between the two sides continued into March. Then, on 30 May, Taib and another insurgent spokesperson, Adulkareem Kalib, described as a top insurgent leader of the BRN, published a statement on YouTube asserting that the RTG was killing Malay Muslim civilians as part of its official strategy. This angered many in the government, especially Defense Minister Sukumpol, who publically fired back, calling Taib and Abdulkareem liars and saying the insurgents were the actual civilian-killers.[368]

Insurgents pressed even harder after that, making additional demands that the RTP:

- Drop all warrants for suspected insurgents
- Stop hunting suspect insurgents
- Grant all insurgent negotiators diplomatic immunity[369]

Coupled with the original five demands, Taib was essentially asking Bangkok for a "time-out"; that it stop the war while negotiations proceeded. At the time, Bangkok declined.

When Ramadan arrived (8 July–7 August 2013), both sides agreed on a cease-fire, and the insurgents requested the RTG remove all security forces from the far south. As a show of faith, the government initially redeployed the RTA back to barracks, but police and local forces maintained their posts and continued their missions.[370] Taib then seemed to back away from the cease-fire, however, and it never materialized. Violence increased, and while peace talks continued administratively, in reality they were crumbling.[371] To accentuate this final point, in August three hooded insurgents gave a statement on YouTube asserting that if the RTG did not adhere to the insurgency's original five precursor demands, then peace talks were off and violence would intensify.[372]

As a result of these developments, negotiations faltered as summer turned to fall. In February 2014, the RTG announced it would continue talks with insurgents despite setbacks, but the timing has not been set. At the same time, in a masterful counter to Taib's challenging political gamesmanship, General Paradorn envited a host of older insurgent groups such as *Bersatu* to join the peace talk process, thereby muddying the water on the insurgent side, diluting the BRN's authority, and softening its Islamist jihadi goals. Whether the government will acquiesce to insurgent demands as a precursor to genuine peace talks remains an open issue.

Regional Diplomacy

COIN cooperation with Malaysia continues to be one of Bangkok's top priorities, but to date, progress has been slow. General Akanit is working on this issue, but rarely do bilateral negotiations in Southeast Asia happen quickly. Says Professor Arun, "Diplomacy…first we give notice to our neighbor [Malaysia]. No separatist movement in the world is located far from the border from which it fights. Movements in Ceylon, Africa, the Middle East, in other areas—most of them rely on other countries."[373]

Says General Vaipot, "Malaysia is an ASEAN country, so it won't agree with Islamist extremism, and they've been a great help to us so far. Malaysia's new policy is a modernized, new Islam. They are creating a 'modern Muslim' and are expanding the 'modern Muslim' community, and that is something we are keenly interested in."[374]

Bangkok has engaged Malaysia on a continual basis since the war began. It has held at least five major meetings with Kuala Lumpur on the war between August 2007 and April 2009, and there may have been more secret meetings, too. One of the more public talks was in April 2008 when PM Samak went to Kuala Lumpur on a two-day visit. He was specifically interested in Malaysia arresting and extraditing two insurgent suspects who allegedly staged terrorist attacks in Thailand and then fled to Malaysia for sanctuary. Samak met with both PM Abdullah Badawi and Foreign Minister Rais Yatim. Pattani Senator Worarit Baru indicated the trip was useless because Malaysia was not harboring any insurgent suspects. [375] His comments are curious because plentiful evidence, even statements from the Malaysian government, says otherwise.

In April 2009, in tandem with the diplomacy between the RTA and Malaysian Defense Forces, PM Abhisit met with newly elected Malaysian PM Najib Razak during the ASEAN summit in Pattaya, Thailand, to discuss COIN cooperation. Abhisit and Razak discussed reinvigorating cooperation between the two countries, COIN security, and restarting the IMT-GT, not only to combat insurgency but also to financially benefit Thailand, Malaysia, and Indonesia.[376]

Professor Arun believes Thailand's diplomatic efforts to stifle outside support for the insurgents have been effective. "And now I think we are successful in the diplomatic effort with the OIC," he continued. "No country has given overt support to those movements. Some material support, yes. Only from some areas in the name of Islamic donations, so…we think they seek to internationalize the issue. That is why our policy is to manage it. If we cannot solve it, we can manage it."[377]

Bangkok's diplomatic efforts with Middle Eastern countries have been Herculean. In April 2007, Foreign Affairs Minister Nitya Pibulsonggram visited Bahrain and the United Arab Emirates (UAE) to shore up support for Thai COIN efforts and to demonstrate that Thailand was not slaughtering Muslims, as insurgent propaganda had claimed. Both countries had provided education and mosque building assistance to Thailand, and thousands of Thai worked in and/or visited Bahrain and UAE. Thammasat University political science professor Charan Malureem, who was an advisor to PM Surayud, said Thailand saw Bahrain as a "gateway through which Thailand connects with the Muslim world."[378] The UAE, he told the press, was "the region's biggest investment powerhouse."[379] As such, it was a natural choice for the government to court for its COIN efforts.

The Organization of the Islamic Conference

In another diplomatic case, Thailand successfully prevented the OIC, at its thirty-fourth ministerial meeting on 17 May 2007 in Islamabad, Pakistan, from calling for an independent Malay Muslim state within Thailand. Interestingly, had the declaration happened, it would have been a de facto declaration of war on Thailand by a nonstate actor, in that the OIC would be recognizing and supporting an insurgent group trying to separate territory from Thailand. This would have been somewhat similar to 1953, when Beijing set up the Thai Autonomous People's Government in China and proclaimed it the rightful governing power of Thailand. Bangkok did not want another foreign power aiding yet another internal rebel group.

More, if the OIC had been successful, it would have encouraged the rebellion and triggered higher levels of violence. It would have demonstrated that terrorism and guerrilla warfare were working. The OIC supporting the insurgent cause with a political declaration was 80 percent of what the insurgents wanted. All that remained was for the OIC to apply political pressure to make secession a reality, and it nearly happened in 2007 through a complex, snowballing chain of events.[380]

First, the coordinator for Yala's Civil Society Empowerment Project, Mansour Saleh, said in May 2007 that Thai Malay Muslims wanted more control over their own governance. He told the press, "They do not want an advisory role. They want to have their own path of doing things."[381] Then the OIC inserted itself into the melee. According to Saleh, the secretary general of the OIC, Ekmeleddin Ihsanoglu, "promised the Muslim *ummahs* in the South that he would cooperate with the government in finding a way for the locals to lead their own lives with dignity, peace and prosperity."[382]

Second, that same month, several Muslim scholars told a visiting OIC delegation headed by Secretary General Ihsanoglu that Thai Malay Muslims needed an autonomous zone within Thailand. Their language, however, leaned more toward a separate state than autonomy. In this regard, insurgents and some in the OIC might have believed the scholars really meant that the OIC should have aided the insurgents in gaining independence, something Surin Pitsuwan warned against.[383]

When it appeared that the OIC might actually make a pro-insurgent declaration, General Sonthi himself hurriedly applied diplomatic efforts to stave off such a maneuver. The OIC, he said, based on "information from someplace else," was set to demand that Thailand establish autonomous zones for Thai Malay Muslims because it believed Bangkok denied them religious freedom. Secretary General Ihsanoglu changed his mind after visiting Thailand and speaking to General Sonthi, a fellow Muslim, who convinced him the complaint was, in fact, a propaganda ploy by insurgents.[384]

The OIC's efforts did not end there, however. At the thirty-fourth session of the OIC, the Thai discovered a plot to make an end run around Sonthi and approve a pro-insurgent announcement. Thai Foreign Minister Nitya scrambled to block the measure. He and his staff made their way to the OIC session, and from his room at the Serena Hotel, he lobbied the OIC not to support the insurgents with what was effectively a psychological operation. Minister Nitya secured a draft of the OIC proclamation and was aghast at what it called for: an "elected Muslim representative[s] and elected governors" for a Malay Muslim "southern state" in Thailand.[385] OIC ambassador Sayyed Kaseem El-Masry, special envoy of Ihsanoglu, coined these pro-insurgent terms. The Thai delegation was incensed because the OIC had previously told General Sonthi it would not use such terms in its report on the matter.[386] As an aside, in its statement, the OIC also was calling for the RTG to violate its own constitution—the MoI appoints governors. They are not elected.

Luckily for Bangkok, Thai diplomacy prevailed in this case. The OIC's final statement on the war said it approved of how Thailand was handling the southern unrest via a "conciliatory approach." It acknowledged the insurgency was not about religion, but about political, economic, and cultural issues. It praised PM Surayud for apologizing for past wrongs done to Thai Malay Muslims by the state. The OIC applauded Thailand's efforts to adjust the local governing system to recognize and embrace the cultural uniqueness of the southern border population. It also demanded an immediate halt to the violence and said people of different faiths living there should exist peacefully side by side.[387] Additionally, both Thailand and the OIC declared they would work together to end the conflict. These proclamations were entirely different from the pro-insurgent track the OIC was previously planning to take.

In November 2012, however, the OIC made a complete about-face. In effect, it politically attacked Thailand at its annual meeting in Djibouti from 15 to 17 November. The OIC passed a resolution castigating the RTG's policies in the far south. The OIC began by saying Thailand had made mere "meager" progress in solving the southern war, which was not untrue or particularly damning. It was its five specific criticisms, however, that drove home the political dagger:

- The emergency decree was too draconian and should be discarded
- Too much military presence was pressuring the everyday life of the population
- Too many "undisciplined" paramilitary troopers were deployed to the south, which might exacerbate the situation
- The far south's youth were not spending enough time studying the Malay language in schools
- Not enough Islamic rights were recognized, and the RTG should hold talks with Islamic leaders to resolve this issue[388]

Points one, two, and three assailed RTG security ways and means, exactly in accordance with insurgent propaganda. It appears the OIC wanted most government security programs halted and those forces removed from the theater. Interestingly, the OIC did not—in any way, shape, or form—criticize insurgent death squads, the ethnic cleansing of Buddhists, and *takfiri* murders.

Points four and five made it seem as if the RTG was still clinging to Phibun's 1939 National Culture Act, which was not the case. Thai Malay Muslims do indeed study Malay in classrooms throughout the far south. They also study Thai. Much of the youth population is bilingual. More, the government certainly recognizes Islamic rights, and no restrictions on Islamic worship are imposed. Thai laws on civil and criminal matters, however, do not follow sharia law as they do in Saudi Arabia, Pakistan, Iran, and other Islamist, theocratic-run governments. It appears the OIC, in arguing these points, was lobbying for a "separate but equal" style of territory for the insurgents, a cultural wedge that they could use to force progress for their ultimate end goal of an independent *Pattani Raya*.

None of these statements reflected the OIC working *with* Bangkok as both sides had declared to do in 2007. For that reason, Vice Foreign Minister

Jullapong Nonsrichai, who attended OIC meeting as an observer, offered a retort. He said, "If the OIC wants to continue cooperating with Thailand, it should realise the fact that Thailand has made a lot of progress in the South. Otherwise we might not cooperate with it in the future."[389] Regardless of this polite response, one thing was certain: while the OIC had not openly sanctioned the insurgency, it surely supported it by condemning the RTG. More, it was now officially lobbying for the southern insurgency as part of its de facto front group, which raised the stakes of this conflict to an international level.

Amnesty

Amnesty is once again a major component of Thai COIN strategy. Says an RTA officer, "[We have] big campaigns on TV requesting insurgents and their supporters join the amnesty program and surrender. The message of this initiative is to stop fighting and help develop the south together."[390] As of 2009, amnesty was available for low-level operatives and auxiliary forces only.

Bangkok began to develop amnesty as an official policy in April–May 2007. Fourth Army Commander Ongkorn Thongprasom and his staff developed the core concepts. Defense Minister General Boonrawd Somtas said he would support it if it brought peace to the far south.[391]

On 1 May, PM Surayud announced a general amnesty "to all persons involved in the ongoing violence" that had not violated Thailand's criminal code. In 2008, the National Assembly passed the measure. Surayud said ISOC-4 and the Fourth Army commander would work out the details of how to implement it.[392]

In the meantime, in March 2008, Yala provincial authorities, including Governor Thira and Deputy Governor Gissada Boonraj, established their own amnesty program with ISOC's blessing. Called the Peace Outreach Center (POC), it grants amnesty to insurgents and auxiliary personnel. More than a simple surrender offer, however, POC provides security, job training, and job placement, much like General Kitti's program in the 1990s.[393]

ISOC General Akara Thiproj told the press in March 2008, "[Insurgent sympathizers] see others who have turned themselves in are able to lead normal lives and I guess they're wanting that too. Most separatist sympathizers joined the separatist movement not knowing any better. If they wish to turn themselves in, our priority is to change their past beliefs about the southern situation instead of punishing them. We will then support them in their career development to ensure they are able to lead a happy life."[394] Deputy Governor Gissada said many militants surrendered because the conflict "didn't seem to have an end game."[395]

ISOC announced in April 2008 that the POC was experiencing success. On 7 March, for example, seventy-seven auxiliary support personnel surrendered to authorities, along with three insurgent leaders. Yala Governor Thira oversaw their surrender ceremony, administered by the Yala Islamic Committee. It undid the radical Islamist oath the insurgents had taken upon joining the movement.[396]

By March 2011, the government had set up the *Sanjai su Santi* (Uniting Hearts for Peace) amnesty program. It is identical to past "turn yourself in and join a work program" schemes. It has had modest success. On 24 March 2011, twenty-one insurgents and village support personnel surrendered under this program to the Bacho District Chief in Narathiwat. Reminiscent of Special Branch Commissioner Somkiat's amnesty ceremonies in 1998 under *Pitak Tai*, Muslim clerics and local government personnel attended the event.

Alleged RKK unit leader Sopian Sadeng was one that decided to quit the fight. He was apparently tired of living on the run, hinting that pressure from security forces might be having an impact. He told the press, "From now on I will be a good person, helping the authorities to develop Bacho City to be peaceful." Time will tell if *Sanjai su Santi* can achieve more successes.[397]

Southern Border Provinces Administrative Command Complaint Department

The SB-PAC resurrected its complaint department for the current COIN. Says Charnchao, "The complaint unit is run by MoI and MoJ, and supervised by Pranai. But the problem is, when we found something wrong—a human rights violation, for example—we could not do much about it because we had little power."[398] Charnchao says the Fourth Army commander is backing the program, which now gives it teeth.[399] Adds Pranai, "Concerning local officials' abuses, we have measures to deal with them that are the strongest of anywhere in Thailand. We have a law that says the SB-PAC can report any bad doings by the army or police directly to the PM. If we take it seriously, as SB-PAC did in the past, then we can expect changes soon."[400]

Psychological Operations and Public Relations

The RTG has a wide array of information operation-related COIN programs in the far south, such as education, promoting moderate Islam, airing grievances, PR, and psyops. Most of these overlap in some way. Psyops are the most prolific, and the RTA is one of the biggest proponents of it. Scores of government agencies carry out these programs, too.

Regarding education, the SB-PAC runs a series of conferences and workshops to spread moderate Islam, air and reconcile local grievances, and address gross misperceptions of Thai and Pattani histories. These programs are akin to "population repair" where the government seeks to mend the deep government-population divide caused by decades of maligned historical perceptions and propaganda.

As for promoting moderate Islam, the SB-PAC invites learned and mainstream Muslims from countries such as Jordan to visit rank-and-file civilians, local Muslim leaders, and even captured insurgents to teach them proper Islam as opposed to the radical view proposed by Islamist and poorly educated imams and ustaz. "We try to keep the RKK from getting too radical, partly by talking them out of it," says Pranai. "We get them to un-commit to their religious insurgent commitment, and we do it with the help of nonradical Muslims."[401]

Adds Professor Bhumarat, "In southern Thailand, some try to say they are fighting for jihad. But it's actually not jihad. Jihad is simply an excuse to get some youngsters to fight. So we bring the Muslim teachers from Saudi Arabia and Indonesia to tell southerners they are not fighting jihad...that their war has nothing to do with religion. We try to bring the youngsters who walk in the wrong way to come back to society."[402]

Regarding airing of grievances, the SB-PAC hosts workshops for locals, imams, and *ustaz* so they can vent their frustrations about southern border inadequacies, injustices they have suffered, and changes they would like to see in the region. During these sessions, the SB-PAC corrects misperceived wrongs. Not all Thai Malay Muslim accusations of state wrongdoing are factual. "We work with religious teachers and make all gray religious and ethnic issues clear," explains Pranai. He continues:

> We do this via workshops. Seven-day and fifteen-day workshops. For these gray area people, we have Muslims come in from Bangkok and tell them about being a Muslim in other parts of Thailand and how the government is not out to destroy Islam or kill Muslims, as insurgent indoctrination says. We have dialogue day in and day out about their beliefs and history. They exercise their frustrations and their views of the government, and we try to tell them what is and is not true. They even write their views down. We start with ten people, and if two change their minds it can be a good model. We've had this program for a long time, quietly. We print books for them on what true Islam discusses. We get experts in like the Great Imam of Cairo, rector of one of the most famous universities in Cairo. The Muslim League, represented by al-Turki [Dr. Abdullah al-Turki], helps out with this program, too.[403]

Many Thai Malay Muslims have vented genuine concerns, such as police corruption, which Bangkok must curb if it is serious about COIN. Others harbor erroneous grievances rooted in exceptionally narrow-minded or limited thinking. Pranai explains, "One asked, 'I am a Muslim in a city of sin, surrounded by prostitutes, karaoke, whiskey. What can I do? How am I supposed to live here? I have to do something [i.e., join the war].' So a Muslim advisor said, 'Look, you are a Muslim born in a non-Muslim country, so don't participate in sinful activities and teach your children to do the same.' This helps to clear the air," says Pranai.

Concerning historical distortions, the SB-PAC has a program to counter not just specific insurgent propaganda, but general misperceptions of Thai and Malay Muslim histories that provide the foundation for propaganda and hatred toward the state. Says Pranai, "One [captured insurgent] said his parents were taken to Bangkok with chains through their ankle tendons as slaves to dig a canal. It's just illogical. It's impossible."

Indeed, Thai rulers in the 1800s had canals dug throughout Bangkok for transportation. The most famous is the Khlong Saen Saeb, which connects the Chao Phraya River to Prachin Buri and Chachoengsao provinces. King Rama III had it built between 1837 and 1840. Some rulers used slaves to dig the canals, and many Thai Malay Muslims assert they provided the bulk of the forced labor— even in recent decades.

The SB-PAC patiently explained to the young insurgent it was biologically impossible for his middle-aged parents to have been slaves 160 years ago. Moreover, being cut and chained through the Achilles tendon and not dying shortly thereafter from gangrene on a several-hundred-mile forced march in tepid, tropical Southeast Asia is yet another improbability. This is the perceived history Bangkok must contend with, however, and it demonstrates just how powerful insurgent propaganda can be, even when spun from fantasy. With this type of politicking, insurgents successfully persuade Thai Malay Muslims to murder other human beings. "So we try to work the truth into people like this," says Pranai, "but this type of propaganda uses material from two hundred years ago, so we work with academics to fix this. We try to forget the bad past, look to the future, and fix it."

Fixing historical misperceptions has to date entailed Thai Malay Muslim and Thai historians working together to try to wash out both ultranationalist aspects of state history and fantasized aspects of Thai Malay Muslim history. Powerful issues of race, religion, and culture are at loggerheads. Says Pranai, "We try to work on clearing up our historical differences…we are talking to clear up misconceptions by people who use history improperly. And it's not easy, because everyone has real differences in historical views. Historians, even from the universities, have real differences regarding the history of Thailand and southern Thailand, and that's proven to be a sticking point. So our job is more difficult, but we know where we must go now."

Regarding psyops, says an RTA trooper, "Psyops—we try to do that all the time. Psyops are very important because, in this style of war, the main factor is the people. They decide who will win and lose, and we can't win the hearts of the people by killing. This is a reasonable way to think. This is also an army policy."[404]

The Psychological Affairs section of CPM is responsible for carrying out most psyops in the far south. Special Forces runs it, but regular RTA units also have their own combination CA-psyops teams.[405] The SF units are called Peace Teams, just like the *Santi Nimit* units deployed in 1980.[406] Their message is simple, says an RTA soldier. "Psyops mainly try to tell the locals that the government, and police, and troops don't want to harm them," he says.[407] A combat medic says the RTA also tries to explain to locals, "There are insurgents in your village, in your homeland. Even though you have another religion, everyone thinks you are Thai [a Thai citizen], and we must work together to push out the bad people."[408] Other army messages are that "Buddhists and Muslims can work and live together" and that "the war does no good—both sides die."[409] Two of the government's unifying messages are that "people living in the southern border provinces are part of the nation, not outcasts" and that "the king wants everyone to live in peace."[410]

The Thai do not restrict psyops to just psyops units. "Every soldier in the south helps with psyops," says an RTA officer. "They do this by being friendly with people, talking to the villagers, asking what they need, and fostering community relations."[411] In this regard, the Thai have tried to capitalize on the idea of the "strategic corporal," but this requires specialized training for all units deployed, and it is not evident such training has occurred.

CPM gets its message out via leaflets in both Jawi and Thai. It distributes these when touring villages and towns, during village medical visits (via Medical Mobile Units), and when visiting local leaders in their districts.[412] Radio is also a common information outlet in the far south. CPM psyops units recruit villagers as disc jockeys to spread their message. "But once you become a DJ, you get targeted," says Nick Nostiz.[413] The RTA also uses its own television channel, Channel 5, as a psyops platform on a regular basis.[414]

In other cases, Thai forces enter villages to explore their options. An RTA CA officer describes this as a two-phase process. "In Phase one, we initiate contact with a person we can rely on, such as a village leader. We don't go in with a big force. We assess the problems of an area and gather information on the insurgents and the people." This is what many COIN experts call "human terrain mapping." The CA officer continues:

> We don't talk about the war or fighting or anything like that.
> We just make contact. In Phase two we find the best
> application by which to access the village. Sometimes we want
> to go a village where the Thai forces and medical people are
> not well received. So we look for an "in." For example, in one
> case in a denied area, a Peace Team found an elderly man who
> had a leg injury, and it had become severely infected, and they
> could not move him. So the psyops unit visited him every day
> and talked to him. They also spoke to a lot of villagers about
> him and eventually got to know everyone.[415]

In this way the team achieved situational awareness.

> On the fourth visit they were able to bring in a doctor. The old
> man still would not let them look at him, but the fifth time was

the charm and he allowed it. It took about a month, but in the end they took him to a care unit. Each subdistrict has a small building where they can clean wounds and do sutures, basic medical procedures, and first aid. The moral of the story was they won the confidence of the village over this.[416]

An RTA reeducation program for suspected insurgents caused controversy in 2006 and 2007. The MoJ's Charnchao says it had the right goal but was executed incorrectly. Under this program, the police and military arrested or detained multitudes of Thai Malay Muslim males at risk of joining the insurgency and put them in job training camps against their will. The camps did not involve hard labor or rigors of imprisonment, but they did have loyalty and citizenship indoctrination classes.[417] Charnchao explains, "A local NGO run by the wife of missing lawyer Somchai Neelaphaijit filed a complaint in the Thai court system, saying the program was illegal. The court agreed in part, saying persons attending the program could not be forced to do so. They had to attend on a voluntary basis. So the military approached the MoJ, asking if they could work together on the project, and the MoJ agreed."[418]

Somchai Neelaphaijit had been Chair of the Muslim Lawyers Association and Vice-Chair of the Human Rights Committee of the Lawyers Association of Thailand. His supporters say he was a "human rights lawyer," but he was actually a lawyer for New PULO. He successfully defended two New PULO fighters in court but lost three other cases in 2002, in which his clients received life sentences for terrorism and treason against the state.[419] Government critics accuse the police of abducting and murdering Somchai in 2004 over his suspected ties to insurgent activities. Some accuse his wife, Angkhana Wongrachen, and her NGO, Working Group of Justice and Peace, of supporting the insurgency, though no evidence of this supposition has surfaced. Regardless, Somchai's death has given the RTG a major black eye from the view of the international community and many citizens of southern Thailand.

At any rate, regarding the RTA's insurgent reeducation camp, Thai courts ordered the release of its eighty-five detainees in October 2007. MoJ-RTA cooperation reestablished it as a voluntary program under which the RTA invited Thai Malay Muslims to the camp for one or several days to attend vocational and citizenship classes. Diana Sarosi of the Working Group on Justice for Peace told the press, "People are too scared to turn down these invitations."[420] The RTA insists it is open and public about the camps and no one is forced or coerced to go.[421]

As for counterpropaganda, an RTA soldier says, "Counterpropaganda...in the communist war era, this was possible. But now, the villagers are not all innocent. They have already been indoctrinated by the RKK, and government psyops are less effective. Bad government officials and police have helped to bolster this indoctrination."[422] Billboards and posters are the government's main means of counterpropaganda.[423] Says Chuan Leekpai, "One of our billboards reads, 'Killing one innocent person means to kill the whole world.'"[424] As an RTA medic reports:

> Insurgents tell villagers they are not Thai, that they are *"Patani Darussalam* people"...They say the Thai will always refuse you and take your jobs...the Thai will take everything from you and take advantage of you. The government tells the villagers the government would never do these bad things to them. "You are Thai" is the message. You have all the same rights as other Thai despite having a different religion, but you have to do your duty. If you want something in your village to be fixed, or if there is a situation we can fix, you cannot kill over it or organize a mob. There is a way to go through channels. [425]

The SB-PAC carries out psyops through its Office of Public Relations. Normally, civilian psyops or PR is left to the central government's Department of Public Relations, but warfare requires a more nuanced effort.[426] "Like the army," says an RTA trooper, "the SB-PAC sets up posters that encourage peace and togetherness. Its workers will put up a big poster of the Koran that says, 'peace, not war,' and things like that."[427]

Thailand has adopted mass PR to help refurbish its not wholly deserved tarnished reputation regarding its current southern COIN. In May 2009, for example, Foreign Minister Kasit Pimromya led a host of European Union (EU) diplomats on a tour of the far south. Kasit took the delegation to the Islamic College in Yala to talk to students. He also introduced them to Muslim Women for Peace, an NGO in Yala that had received complaints about torture and disappearances. Kasit even took the delegation to the Working Group of Justice and Peace, where they heard Mrs. Wongrachen's version of the 8 February 2009 raid on her office by authorities looking for links to insurgents. In granting such access to opponents of the regime, Kasit wanted to prove to the EU that the wild assertions that Thailand was harming Muslims with reckless abandon were patently false. He also wanted to demonstrate Thailand was not trying to hide what was happening in the insurgency zone and that there was no NGO or press blackout concealing alleged government atrocities.[428]

ISOC also runs psyops. Its counternarcotics section runs a dual-purpose national security program aimed at both getting southern border teens off drugs and building trust between villagers and the government. (The latter is a psyop.) RTA Colonel Suwan Chirdshai, who holds the title of Chief of the Office of Coordination for Mass Strategies to Solve the Problem of Narcotics in the Three Southern Border Provinces, ran the program in 2008. Colonel Suwan says drugs have become rampant in the far south and are interconnected with the insurgency. He estimates 70 percent of southern youngsters have been exposed to drugs such as marijuana, *yaba*, ecstasy, ice, and *kratom*. The last of these is a naturally growing narcotic in Thailand, and insurgents mix it with cough medicine and give it to teens to inebriate them for certain missions so as to remove their fear. This is the "4 x 100" homemade drug mentioned earlier. Insurgents and noninsurgents alike grow marijuana in red zones because authorities infrequently patrol many of them. Drug use has increased because teens are bored, restless, and living in a stressful environment.[429]

ISOC uses RTA CA units to implement the program. "So it's a campaign to teach people about the negative side effects of the drugs and how bad it is for the local people. The output here is trust. They'll trust this operational unit as a result. And they don't suspect we are up to no good."

The antinarcotics teams focus on the parents of the drug addicts, who frequently resist the program at first because, Suwan says, no parents want to admit their children use drugs. The ISOC teams say to the parents, "Agree with us. We must solve the drug problems of the children together." They also work with the community leaders and religious leaders. Says Suwan, "They need to support us so that we can work with the parents and drug users."

The teams then meet with the children, parents, and community and religious leaders all at once. "We make sure they understand that we want to help them help themselves to keep away from drugs," says Suwan. "We tell the kids they are not on any list of suspects." After the kids understand the program, ISOC takes them to an educational camp in Songkhla called *Yalanan Baru*, a Malay phrase for "New Road." It means "to adopt a new way of life."[430] The program's unstated goal is to steal youths back from the insurgents who get them hooked on drugs and then use them as auxiliary forces and fighters.

At the antidrug camps, for six days youngsters run through light military boot camp training and learn about the military and citizenship. They also learn about life's journey and how a person develops good and bad decision-making skills. Srisompob and his team conduct surveys to analyze participant attitudes and determine whether their outlooks are changing. The camps have been in operation since June 2007 and can take sixty youths at a time. As of the spring of 2008, three thousand had completed the program. ISOC-4 has enough personnel and space to run ten camps at once.[431]

The results so far have been positive. Says Suwan, "Before this project, the local communities did not trust the army, did not trust the officers who are working on the ground. But right now, in many areas where the military has worked with kids on this antidrug program, the kids went back to the villages and now organized youth groups to help the soldiers. They have become informants and supporters of the army. Before, the army could not penetrate into the communities, but right now they have the contacts, and the imam, and the leaders of the village, the head man too, and many realize this is a good project for the Muslim youth."

Economic Measures

The development programs currently applied in the far south are none too different from those of past COINs, especially the 1980s–90s. All government ministries, the SB-PAC, and the military engage in development, ranging from small village projects to large industrial concerns. As in the past, education is also part of the government's strategy to integrate isolated Malay Muslims into the state, creating productive citizens who study more than just Islam. The royal family remains intricately involved in developing the far south, too.

Far South Development Plans

Administrations from Thaksin to Abhisit have all submitted development plans for the far south. As there have been six turnovers in Thai governmental leadership since 2004 (technically seven, since Chaovarat Chanweerakul served fifteen days between Somchai Wongsawat and Abhisit via a Constitutional Court ruling), not all the plans have been carried out. Some administrations borrowed from their predecessors, and others developed wholly new plans. The frequent changes in leadership have been confusing, to say the least. It is noteworthy that the RTA's SBPPC had the first actionable development plan for the south.

Thaksin wanted all government agencies to have their COIN development plans finalized by December 2005, yet more proof that his COIN plan, shallow though it was, was not simply based on violence. Initiatives under his watch included the Board of Investment of Thailand (BOI) sponsoring the "Promotion Years," which was a "fire sale" of sorts tendering advantageous, three-year investment terms in the southern border provinces. These measures were also aimed at protecting businesses in the south that were floundering because of the violence.[432] Additionally, the Ministry of Industry began planning to expand fishing businesses and create a halal food industry, the latter of which has continued every year into 2013.[433]

Another project the government has continued year after year is transforming the far south into a Special Economic Zone, which began on 1 January 2007 under the tenure of PM Samak. The goal was to attract investment to the war zone by lowering taxes and improving infrastructure. For example, the RTG lowered corporate taxes in the region from 30 to 3 percent, cut interest rates, eased restrictions on importing laborers from outside the south, and compensated businesses for higher insurance premiums.[434]

In March 2008, the Samak government gave the SB-PAC and its associated agencies forty-five days to write the far south's economic COIN plan.[435] In early April 2008, the SB-PAC submitted, and the cabinet thereafter approved, a more detailed COIN plan for the far south than what it began with in 2006. This plan more or less remained intact through the Abhisit administration.

The SB-PAC's plan was essentially a restatement of its 2006 goals, but with more precise implementation tasks. The government planned for Pattani to become an international Islamic educational and halal food center. Yala was to become the region's agricultural hub. Narathiwat was slated to become an export-processing zone for goods destined for Malaysia's East Coast Economic Region. Songkhla was chosen to become a global center for rubber farms, sports, education, and tourism. The SB-PAC included Satun in the plan as well. It was to become a major international and domestic cargo transport center. The National Economic and Social Development Board approved this plan on 8 April 2008.[436]

Abhisit's administration tried to make these projects more permanent. Abhisit says the basics of his economic development strategy focused on education, entrepreneurship, and employment—the "three Es." The "three Es" program actually began under the Surayud government. Abhisit simply expanded it.[437]

In March 2009, Abhisit said he wanted to downsize military forces in the far south by ten thousand troops in 2010 "to rid the region of its frightening image and boost tourism and investment."[438] But this did not happen. The security situation was highly unstable, and the government could not withdraw military. Regardless, under Abhisit, Bangkok's top economic specialists began planning 605 major industrial development projects with a price tag of over eighty billion *baht*. Projects included industrial parks and special economic zones for export.[439]

Educational Development

In April 2007, Deputy Foreign Minister Sawanit Kongsiri went to Egypt to visit Thai students at al-Azad University, where approximately fifteen hundred Thai were enrolled. Sawanit gave 1 million *baht* to the university and reached an agreement with Dean Sheik Tantawi that Thai students should study secular as well as Islamic subjects such as "engineering, finance and rural development."[440] The reason was economic. Said Sawanit to the press, "Thai students studying religion overseas often find difficulty landing jobs when they return to Thailand. It is because there are already too many religion teachers. If they study other subjects, with their experience and education background they could find other jobs."[441]

Pranai heralds education as the government's most important COIN instrument. He says, "On March 21st [of 2008], we submitted to the PM that the Education Ministry must [do] its job under this new strategy as fast as possible. If we don't tackle education in the south, things are going to go on like this for some time."[442] He told the press, "Through education, people will have more hope, which is very important in this region. The SB-PAC will provide more educational opportunities for Muslim students in the provinces to enable them to achieve their dream."[443]

This program faces an uphill battle. Some current statistics say over 70 percent of Thai Malay Muslim students attend six thousand *pondoks* in the far south. The remaining 30 percent attend public schools. As a result of the heavy *pondok* attendance, fewer Thai Malay Muslims make it to universities than any other ethnicity in all of Thailand. This is why scholarships are one of the SB-PAC's largest programs. In 2008, it provided one thousand scholarships for southern border youth to study in the Middle East, Indonesia, and Malaysia.[444] Scholarships for Thai Malay Muslims are not a new program, however. Says Pranai, "Since forty-six years ago, the MoI has had scholarships for southerners."[445]

In July 2008, the Office of the Basic Education Commission in the South announced it was increasing the amount of study time devoted to Islam in public schools. Primary schools would increase from two to ten hours a week. High schools would increase to twelve hours a week. It began as a test project in 2006 in a few schools and is being expanded because it was achieving its goal. That goal was to increase Thai Malay Muslim enrollment in public schools where secular subjects are taught in abundance. The new Islamic curriculum covers Islamic history and culture, and the increased hours of study allow students to receive Islamic studies certificates. About 274 public schools had adopted the program in July 2008.[446]

In 2006, Bangkok sanctioned an experimental program where public school teachers used Jawi and Malay in the first two years of new students' schooling to help in explaining their lessons. After two years, teachers weaned students off Jawi and Malay and onto Thai. The RTG believes speaking Thai is necessary for students to succeed in Thailand's job market after graduation, but Jawi and Malay are necessary to lure Thai Malay Muslims into public school in the first place.[447] The overall government sentiment is, "keep and maintain Malay culture, but train students to work effectively within the Thai system." This project began at twelve primary schools and expanded to twenty-four by October 2007 in response to high parent demand.[448]

Business Development and Employment Programs

Government agencies, the SB-PAC, and the RTA have launched scores of programs aimed at improving the far south's economic plight. These initiatives range from jobs and investment programs to agriculture support, import-export initiatives, and cash payments to victims of the fighting. It is too early to tell if these programs are having an effect. COIN development programs are rarely if ever decisive, but they provide the long-term foundation that can lift a population out of poverty and keep it from backsliding into mediocrity where it is vulnerable to insurgent propaganda.

Concerning investments, on 15 June 2007, the BoI said existing business in the far south would pay no taxes, and new projects applied for by 31 December 2007 would have an eight-year tax holiday regardless of the value of the company. The new investment rules were supposed to spur new investments. But from 2003 to 2006, a mere eight companies worth 2.42 million *baht* applied for BoI investment incentives in Pattani, Yala, and Narathiwat.[449]

Pranai says, "We asked the government to instruct the Finance Ministry to facilitate tax incentives for the very wealthy to invest in the south, like for the top-ten richest bracket, so they can get a reduced tax rate if they invest. We just submitted the plan to the government [March 2008], and the PM told the Finance Ministry to work it out."[450]

The government continually talks about the Indonesia-Malaysia-Thailand Growth Triangle project as a way to expand the far south's economic prowess and economically link it to similar cultures. General Surayud in January 2007 attended the second annual IMT-GT meeting in the Philippines. Surayud and Indonesian and Malaysian leaders agreed to a five-year road map and initial "flagship projects" to begin the project but provided no details.[451] Despite all the talk, forward movement has been slow, the projects small. In May 2008, Thai representatives attended an IMT-GT conference in Bangka Belitung, Indonesia, on ensuring the authenticity of halal food products via labeling and the potential to expand halal food manufacturing between the three countries.[452]

Employment programs are yet another focus of government development projects. "Job programs," says Pranai, "yes, as far as the economy in the area is concerned, in the past four years, five years ago, there was no investment, not one real plan, no existing one, really. The services industry down there is the hotel and restaurant business. GDP in the south has dropped, purchasing power has fallen."[453] These woes demonstrate how successful the insurgents' war on the far south's economy has been. Explains Pranai:

> So this caused a lot of problems, especially for those in need of jobs. So what the government did in the past two to three years was hire those people who've been unemployed. We have almost three thousand jobs that pay about four thousand five hundred *baht* a month, carried out through various channels, like the Labor Department, the army, ISOC, etc. And we have other job programs, too, such as those in the rubber tapping industry, which is a part-time job for a lot of people. They might also do security as their other part-time job, and in that way, they can help protect the rubber plantations where so many have been killed. [454]

SB-PAC pays particular attention to the south's sometimes-neglected fishermen. Says Pranai:

> Small fishermen…maybe there are three hundred thousand from Narathiwat to Songkhla. We are talking about the way to empower them to help themselves. We talk about underemployment during the monsoon season when they cannot go out to sea and fish—it's a seasonal industry. We figured out some local jobs that they can do when they are not employed during monsoon. They can make a secondary product from the sea like crispy snacks. We are trying to upgrade to a higher quality so we can export these things to the Middle East as halal food. We talk a lot about this. [455]

Pranai also says it is hard to get people to invest in a war zone to create jobs:

We have to go out looking for jobs. We've tried a program in the Middle East where we've trained a lot of people in Songkhla in the oil service industry—pipeline welding and things like that. We've sent them to Oman, Bahrain, etc....We've also talked with Malaysia and worked out a cross-border jobs program. Yesterday, in fact [27 March 2008], we finished a training program where such people can go to Malaysia with grace and work professionally and not underground. [456]

In May 2008, the SB-PAC announced it was recruiting for two hundred jobs as pipe fitters at twenty thousand *baht* a month plus benefits in Qatar, Kuwait, UAE, and Oman.[457]

Another critical economic COIN initiative is agriculture support. The SB-PAC's May 2008 program to help farmers transition from rubber to rice resulted in the harvesting of 424 tonnes of rice and enough income to keep those in the program out of poverty.[458] Since the insurgency had prevented many farmers from cultivating rubber, their incomes were suffering and their plantations were failing from lack of care. Rice, on the other hand, is easier to grow and was in high demand in 2007–08, resulting in good profits. As a result, the SB-PAC provided funding and expertise to help farmers in five districts in Narathiwat transform nine hundred *rai* of abandoned rubber farms into rice paddies. It aimed to transform seven thousand nine hundred *rai* by August 2008.[459]

The health sector is another COIN area of importance and focus. While the SB-PAC has MoH personnel on its roster, the MoH also has it own independent project called the Health Center Administration of the South. It provides medical outreach to locals who in the past needed health assistance but did not know the state could provide it. The MoH also provides universities with money and research to deepen its reach into the at-risk population.[460]

There are also numerous scattered, smaller programs throughout the south. Says a Thai soldier:

Every branch of government will have a development project. They are not forced to set up a development project, but they try to apply the king's concept. For example, teachers and educational departments set up local educational programs, or they teach people how to grow vegetables at the schools they attend so they can eat them there for lunch and things like that. They also do things like set up fish ponds, take care of the fish, they feed the fish, and so then they can then feed the school. Gardening and farming programs are done by the Department of Agriculture and at lower levels through the district governor's local agriculture departments. The Health Department uses lots of local volunteers to work for it and to try and combat, for example, dengue fever. They spray ponds and jars of water to kill mosquitoes.[461]

Royal Thai Army Civil Affairs

RTA CA was one of the government's first responses when the war began. In fact, the SBPPC's development program was perhaps the first cohesive government COIN plan of the war. In March 2005, SBPPC spokesman Lieutenant Colonel Sanirote Thammayos announced that a 250-*tambon*, 250-million-*baht* development project was in full swing. It had an eleven-person advisory board composed of local leaders, including imams, to help propose needed projects such as irrigation.[462]

The RTA's projects are usually small-scale and impact villagers immediately. The army has the resources and personnel to do this on a wide scale. Each battalion, for example, has twenty CA personnel, including medics and doctors.[463] Says an RTA general, "We send medical teams into the villages, and we send some advisors to go out to help with their day-to-day living, some construction teams, some agricultural and animal husbandry experts to teach things like cattle and goat herding, fruit and vegetable farming."[464] He hopes by reaching out to locals, the government will demonstrate it wants Thai Malay Muslims to have better standards of living, and that it understands their culture.

RTA Special Forces has CA programs, too. It works through the RTA's Civil Military Operations Center. An SF CA officer says, "If a TF [Task Force] wants to operate in an area, it goes in and coordinates with district managers and police, and other district leaders, and it asks what the problems are of the whole group, sort of a mini-conference or roundtable, and then they set up small centers to execute problem solving. It's worked well. For example, in Betong, Yala, the police, civilians, and army work well together."[465]

In 2009, General Phichet Visaichorn had put so much effort into development that many in the south began to call him the "EM General"—EM meaning "effective microorganisms." EM is a fertilizer that Phichet's community center encouraged southerners to use on their crops. Located across from the Fourth Army and CPM headquarters at the Sirindhorn RTA camp in Yarang district, Pattani, the center hosts locals each day who come to learn how to raise fish in homemade ponds, grow vegetables, and raise livestock. Phichet's experience as Second Army commander helping Issan farmers provided him with the expertise to support the center. It also doubles as a drug treatment center, and auxiliary force insurgents can turn themselves in there, undergo rehabilitation, and reintegrate into society. The center focuses on positive reinforcement and does not prosecute insurgents, as long as they have not committed major crimes.[466]

An army medical technician says the RTA deploys Mobile Medical Teams into villages to provide health services to rural villagers who cannot travel to hospitals. He says, "We set up a medical clinic by working together with the local district and hospital staff and army staff. We have nurses, dentists, etc., and a place to print and give out ID cards."[467] Other government administrative personnel participate and run side programs. "The villagers can get local paperwork done there," says the medical technician. "The agriculture department brings good seeds to the villages. Animal husbandry people teach people how to improve local fruit and garden production."[468]

The RTA also tells villagers to contact nearby army camps for development assistance. In one case, swarms of mosquitoes made villagers sick with malaria, and they sent a nearby RTA medical unit a letter requesting help. Says a medic, "Villagers used to not do this at all, but now they do because of the new approach the army has taken in the south. If the army can solve it, then it does. If not, then it gets another government office to do it."[469] In this case, army medics could not eradicate the mosquitoes, so they asked a malaria control unit of the MoH to spray the village and provide medicine. The army also coupled this initiative with PR. It kept the villagers informed of its actions every step of the way, which improved its image in the eyes of locals, especially when the problem was solved.[470]

The villagers sometimes do not always appreciate government help, however. An RTA medic says, "Some Muslim villagers come and say thank you for helping the kids, or for helping with drugs. In these cases, they might give a glass of water and say thanks. Before, they said nothing. There is always a mix. Some take the medicine and then leave quickly. Some programs, such as free food distribution, attract villagers. But when the army doctors come, everyone shows up. People like the doctors."[471]

There are indications development is making an impact in the far south. A former insurgent says for him, the war eventually began to take its toll, and he felt "only chaos and strain." In 2008, government development personnel came to his village and, according to him, "showed their sincerity" through development projects. The combination of pressure from war and government aid convinced him and antistate villagers to give the government a chance and reject the insurgency, which is what happened.[472] In 2009, General Phichet told the press that security and CA forces had been so successful that insurgents were beginning to attack them while they were working in the villages, previously a rare event.[473]

Royal Development Programs

King Bhumibol's development programs are as prolific now as in past COINs. One of many is the *Kampung Janda*, or Widow Village, for women whose husbands were killed in the insurgency. There are a few poor couples living there, too. The queen also had a major hand in this. Some Malay speakers also call it *Kampung Bujang* (Unmarried Widow). The *Kampung Janda* is located in Narathiwat near Kampung Rotan Batu. It consists of 124 homes inhabited by three hundred women and children on twenty-four hectares of land. The government did not want the far south's widows to succumb to poverty and immoral occupations to make a living—hence, the farm. The army guards it.[474]

The women's occupational choices include pottery, growing fruits, vegetables, rice, and/or mushrooms, and raising farm animals. The government buses their children to school. Women living there stay in improved housing, and some make enough money to send their children to overseas schools. They also are provided with technology to turn cooking and other oils into motorcycle fuel—a popular bio-diesel project in Thailand.[475] A widow told the press, "I had nobody to turn to after my husband died five years ago. So when the authorities here asked me whether I wanted to stay here, I immediately agreed and I'm glad that I made that decision."[476]

After parsing the particulars of all three Thai COINs, what, then, are the patterns? What are the trends according to each section of the COIN Pantheon? Even though the current COIN's outcome has yet to be determined, and the war is waning back and forth between the government's and the insurgents' favor, the nine years it has been fought still offers fodder for the final analysis. Additionally, there are further insights to be learned by filtering Thai COIN trends through the lenses of David Galula and Robert Thompson's core tenets, which were mentioned briefly in the introduction. This final section addresses these issues and, in the end, reveals the Thai way of COIN.[1]

Strategy

There are several patterns regarding Thai COIN strategy. First, the Thai adjust strategy while waging COIN. While not uncommon in warfare, the fact that the Thai do this demonstrates a degree of flexibility. The Thai typically adjust strategy for three reasons: (1) they gain a better understanding of the enemy as a war progresses, (2) the status of a war changes, requiring a different approach—less force and more economics, for example, or (3) they adjust ends, ways, and means that are not working and adopt those that more sharply address a war that lingers too long or grows beyond the government's control. Some nations never learn to adjust to ever-changing irregular threat environments. The Thai do, albeit sometimes slowly.

Second, Thailand has applied most of the principles of the RTA-driven 66/2523 Plan to its insurgency problems since 1980. This was an RMA initiated by the RTA's critical thinking clique of Prem, Harn, Chavalit, Saiyud, and others. It has had a significant and long-lasting impact on Thailand's entire national security community.

Third, in league with point two, the Thai believe in order for COIN to be effective, politics must lead the military. This means they will use negotiations, political concessions, amnesty, psyops, PR, and like ways over heavy suppression. The RTA is responsible for generating and applying this concept, which is not unusual since it is both a political and military entity combined. While politics leads the military is Thai COIN doctrine, it sometimes happens slowly, and it is the most difficult strategic concept for them to apply, especially early in an insurgency, when shocking insurgent violence escalates.

Fourth, the Thai usually require an informal consensus of generals and senior national security officials to agree on a strategy for it to be cleanly implemented through government agencies and the security forces. Even if a strategy is law or official policy ordained by both a sitting PM and the National Assembly, the Thai bureaucracy usually will not effectively implement it unless this consensus has occurred. The application of Thai strategy, then, is seemingly personality-driven and social network–driven. This might be because of a long-standing tradition of patronage networks.

Fifth, the Thai believe in harnessing the population in COIN. They do not believe COIN is exclusively a government affair. The Thai understand insurgency is the people's war, that it infiltrates and infects villages, neighborhoods, households, and families. Accordingly, the Thai establish ends, ways, and means to "weaponize the citizenry" in security, political, and economic realms to use against insurgents. To the Thai, this is natural. After all, insurgents "weaponize the citizenry" for their benefit. The Thai have used several practical phrases to illustrate their thinking on this subject, such as "the villages surrounding the jungle," which is the direct opposite of Mao's "villages surrounding the cities," and also "adding good fish to the water" (local forces) to neutralize the "bad fish" (insurgents) that "swim" (operate) in the "water" (the population).

Sixth, and finally, there are ten strategic end goals common to Thai COINs over the last fifty years. They are:

1. The enemy's military forces destroyed or disbanded.

2. The population uplifted from poverty.

3. The population and insurgency politically placated.

4. The population protected/isolated militarily from insurgent force application and military recruitment.

5. The population protected/isolated ideologically from insurgent political manipulation.

6. A population that sees the government as legitimate, or at least more legitimate than the insurgents.

7. A safe and secure monarchy.

8. An empowered and productive population along political, economic, and educational lines.

9. A pluralistic society accepting of various religions and ethnicities within the Thai construct.

10. Territorial integrity secured.

Again, these are end goals. Just because they are end goals does not mean they are all met. For example, poverty reduction has always been a strategic end goal in the far south, and while it has been met from time to time, pockets there remain exceedingly poor. It is one of many drivers of the current war.

Coordination

The Thai firmly believe in coordinating COIN. They have a thorough understanding of the criticality of making strategy happen through a controlling body—or individual—specifically tasked with parsing out manpower, finances, and material resources. It is their doctrine. Witness the alphabet soup of coordinating authorities the RTG has used over the past fifty years: CSOC, ISOC, the CC, CPM-43, the SB-PAC, the SBPPC, CPM, etc. The RTA and the Fourth Army in the far south have been key coordinators of COIN as well. Most of the time, they have been the de facto epicenter of Thailand's COIN efforts.

Thai COIN is best coordinated when a central leadership figure has taken control over all subordinate groups. Prem did this as PM, and General Kitti did this as Fourth Army commander, for example. In the present war, Sonthi and Anupong appeared to achieve this for a short while, and PM Abhisit tried to achieve this partially by moving the SB-PAC and its Special Branch/RTP assets under his control. PM Yingluck appears to be centralizing COIN authority under a new regime, the "Pentagon II."

Having said this, there is also a pattern of excessive coordination problems in Thailand, proving that a well-designed management scheme on paper does not necessarily translate to efficiency in the field. Coordination problems have come from prime minister, military, police, and government agency turf battles, patronage squabbles, and inflated egos. This, in turn, has prolonged warfare and contributed to civilian, military, and police deaths. A glaring example comes from early in the communist COIN, when Army Area Commanders ignored CSOC's authority and its strategy. Another example comes from the Thaksin era, where multiple coordination authorities muddled an already hazy COIN policy. If the Thai could overcome these problems, their COIN effectiveness might be 50 percent higher.

Security

The Thai use nearly identical security assets and programs in COIN. They have used the same military, police, intelligence agencies, and local forces in each war discussed here, and they have used them in nearly identical ways. The Thai aim to pressure guerrillas with myriad security programs—physical security, patrolling, village security, etc.—while using DA units to decisively neutralize them. Police investigations, especially those by Special Branch, have been critical to quashing insurgent movements.

Similarly, the Thai strive to achieve intelligence dominance regarding understanding insurgent capabilities and intentions, and key personnel. Once achieved, they then use this prowess to interrupt their planning cycles, and/or arrest, turn, or neutralize them. While the Thai have indeed achieved this, in some cases it has happened at a slow pace because "Thainess" clouded their objectivity. In other words, it seems the Thai have had some issues seeing an insurgency from the perspective of their opponents. When the Thai achieve intelligence dominance, however, they exploit it with impressive skill in both kinetic and political realms.

Some Thai COIN forces suffer from a lack of quality control. The RTP in particular has had a reputation for corruption and COIN inability. As a result, in many cases it has had to restructure, retrain, and reconstitute to achieve effectiveness. This was especially true in the communist COIN and in the present war. Witness the establishment of the SBPPOC. It represents a reinvigorated police approach to COIN with upgraded staff and mission parameters. In order for Thailand to prevail in the current COIN, this new RTP force will have to perform at exemplary levels or transfer its duties to the RTA, especially if the war intensifies to an intolerable level.

Some local forces have also suffered from a lack of quality control. It took years to achieve a successful formula for village defense units during the communist COIN, and their cousin units in the far south have had marginal results in some instances. Similarly, when *Thahan Phran* have demonstrated criminal behavior, it has wrecked government legitimacy and hurt COIN efforts. The Thai usually learn from their local force mistakes, however. They understand that for units of this type to be successful, high-quality training, good pay, and strong leadership are essential. This is one reason for the current COIN's new iteration of the *Thahan Phran*.

These criticisms, on the other hand, do not detract from the fact that local forces, including village security forces and the *Thahan Phran*, have been decisive in Thai COIN. Village security has been present in every COIN. The Thai know armed men loyal to the state are necessary to maintain security at the village and hamlet level twenty-four hours a day, seven days a week. This has not happened to an optimal level in the current war, however.

Regarding the *Thahan Phran*, when they have been effective, and they have been effective most of the time, they have proven to be one of the best counterguerrilla forces the Thai have ever deployed. They are also Thailand's de facto admission about the dirty little secret of insurgency and COIN—that insurgents do not play by established rules of state-versus-state warfare. The Thai government gives insurgents a dose of their own medicine with this force. For that reason, the *Thahan Phran* are a linchpin of Thailand's security approach, and it is a correct one.

Politics

In keeping with the strategy "politics leads the military," the Thai use a wide array of political assets and programs in COIN, each one tailored to fit a unique political, social, or religious problem. There are distinct patterns, however. The top four commonly applied Thai political programs are psyops and PR, diplomacy, amnesty, and good governance.

Regarding psyops and PR, the Thai try diligently to persuade insurgents that their core ideology is wrong and that their decision to use violence as an instrument of change is incorrect. They use prolific influence operations to counter insurgent propaganda, and they seek to deprogram insurgents steeped in indoctrination. The Thai moreover endeavor to keep the citizenry informed of government COIN initiatives—to a reasonable extent—to educate the population on the dangers imposed by insurgency and to advertise the government as an effective problem solver.

The Thai used their considerable diplomatic skills in the communist COIN and the 1980s–90s southern COIN to isolate and cut off insurgents from their outside support and sanctuary. In both cases, there were dramatic political fissures the Thai exploited. In the first case, it was the collapse of the Chinese-Vietnamese relationship. In the second, it was a crescendo of embarrassing publicity that revealed the heavy extent of Thai Malay Muslim insurgent sanctuary inside Malaysia. In the current war, Thai officials have fanned out across Southeast Asia and the Middle East, lobbying to end support for Islamist jihadist rebels.

They have also suffered a few diplomatic setbacks. After keeping the OIC from recognizing the insurgency in 2007, a major feat, they failed to do so in 2012. It could very well be that Islamism, in its dedicated and relentless march to spread its ultraconservative version of Islam around the globe via political deception and warfare, is naturally insulated from diplomacy. It could also be the OIC acquiesced to the RTG's 2007 engagement, knowing it would betray this promise later on in a premeditated maneuver harnessing *taqiya*, the duty to lie during jihad.

Amnesty has been used to great effect in the first two wars, and to good effect in the current war. The Thai would much rather persuade its rebellious citizens to cease and desist fighting and rejoin society as productive citizens rather than war with them. As Denny Lane and Jeffrey Race said, this has to do with the Buddhist penchant for compassion and the ability to accept the moral capacity of others. At the same time, the Thai are under no illusions that insurgents simply take amnesty because it is offered. Insurgents take amnesty because they are being pressured kinetically coupled with offers of socioeconomic and/or political rewards.

Regarding better governance programs, the Thai aim to increase government legitimacy over the insurgents. While many of these programs have worked, others have not penetrated deep enough into problem areas, nor have they lasted. For example, good governance in the south in the 1980s–90s was not enough to help preclude a second war there. Additionally, better governance certainly improved Bangkok's legitimacy in the communist COIN, but corruption and substandard government services persisted after the war's end to a degree that large pockets of Issan remained impoverished, or at least lagged behind the rest of Thailand. And this was one of several reasons for the rise of the Red Shirt movement that politically and violently challenged the government in 2010.

Peace talks are a Thai political COIN pattern, but a lesser one. Formal and public peace talks between senior government and CPT officials did not happen, but the Thai did indeed have direct lines of communications with top communists in efforts to persuade them to surrender or change their ways. The Thai have attempted talks with insurgents in both southern wars, but none of them were decisively productive. As of December 2013, it looks as if current peace talks have not achieved much, but the future remains wide open.

Another lesser political pattern is education. The Thai applied education improvement programs in the communist COIN, but these had more to do with general school improvement, which had a political impact regarding gaining popular support for the government. In the far south, the education system has been, and remains, one of the central ideological battlegrounds between the government and the insurgents. The main efforts there are citizenship training and reduction of cultural isolation.

Nearly every government agency and security service has engaged in political programs. At the very least, these have involved PR where the agency in question spread awareness about its particular effort to increase government legitimacy. More concerted and complex efforts to widen political participation and influence the mind-set of the population, insurgent groups, and their foreign supporters have been carried out by the PM's office, the MoI, the MoFA, the RTP, and the RTA. The RTA has been a lead organization, if not the central lead, in all of these efforts.

As an aside, in the current war it sometimes seems as if Bangkok has lost control of the information sphere. It has been slow to react to insurgent propaganda labeling the government as Muslim-haters and civilian-killers. The government has yet to call the insurgents what they truly are: *takfiri* Islamist jihadists—"Patani" and locally focused for sure (and so far), but *takfiri* jihadists just the same.

Economics

Thailand, in every COIN, has used economic programs to nation-build to a certain degree. The most common Thai economic COIN programs are village-level antipoverty, agricultural, road/infrastructure building, health, education, and job creation projects. Every RTG agency and all security forces engage in economic development projects. The royal family does likewise. Curiously, despite Thailand's modern amenities and highly functional national system, it seems to have chronic pockets of poverty scattered throughout the country. One would assume they would disappear with so many agencies involved.

Just as with political COIN, the Thai have tailored economic programs to meet the realities of each conflict. For example, education in the far south has meant more than just increasing opportunities for schooling, as it did in the communist COIN. It has urged the population to embrace secular as well as Islamic studies, so it can earn a living and simultaneously retain its unique culture. More, job creation in the current COIN is more than employing people through enterprise investment. The government has established job programs at the local, regional, and international levels, too, for people, not just companies.

A continual pattern of Thai economic COIN is the RTA's lead role in CA. This is natural because it has constant contact with villages, can protect itself while on CA missions, and has the manpower and material to carry out the mission. Additionally, the RTA perceives itself as protectors of the Thai people, and it follows the strategic intent of the king, part of which is philanthropy for the poor.

Insurgent Capabilities and Intentions

Guerrilla warfare is common to all insurgent groups in Thailand. They have all targeted and attacked government security forces. They have all used terrorism, too, but not in the same volume. The CPT used it sparingly, the southern insurgents of the 1980s–90s used it semiregularly, and the current insurgency uses it almost weekly.

Insurgency in Thailand has always had outside sponsorship and/or foreign ideological impetus. The CPT had PRC and North Vietnamese communist influences. Thai Malay Muslims of the first southern COIN had extremist Islamist influences from the Middle East—including socialist Libya—and Malaysia. The current insurgency has ideological linkages with radical elements in Malaysia, Indonesia, and seemingly, the Middle East. This is not to say these insurgencies were 100 percent born of foreign intrigue. They were not. It is clear that certain unhealthy domestic issues in all insurgency cases covered here were key causes of these wars, but it is also clear that foreign influences rallied these grievances around ideologies that were not thoroughly germane to Thailand.

In a similar vein, all of Thailand's insurgencies have relied on cross-border sanctuary. The CPT relied on China, North Vietnam, Laos, and to a certain extent, Cambodia. The first southern insurgency relied heavily on Malaysia and the Middle East. PULO in particular deeply depended on Saudi Arabia for sanctuary. In the current insurgency, it is painfully obvious Malaysia is yet again a sanctuary for the movement, and it appears Indonesia has been used as well. More, the Middle East is, again, suspect as a southern insurgent sanctuary.

While their ideologies have differed from each other, all Thai insurgent groups have used powerful political campaigns to delegitimize the RTG and sway the population to their causes. They have all been exceptionally effective at rallying popular grievances, too. Overall, each movement's political effectiveness has been proven by the fact that they have carried enough of the population to wage wars lasting more than ten years.

There are other areas where Thailand's rebel groups share only slight similarities, but they are worth noting. For example, the CPT and the current insurgency share high operational tempos, whereas the 1980s–90s insurgent tempo was sporadic. The CPT and the current insurgency was/is more centralized in command and control and united in cause. The 1980s–90s insurgency was a scattering of multiple groups with varied political and gangland goals. Islamist jihad here was a minor but growing issue. Both Thai Malay Muslim movements are largely, but not exclusively, restricted to the far south, but the CPT's war spanned the entire country. The 1980s–90s southern insurgents did indeed strike Bangkok with a series of bombings in the 1980s, but nothing more. And while the current insurgency certainly has the capabilities and ideological motivations to strike the capital, it has not done so yet, unless one chalks up the 2006 New Year's Eve bombings to them, and there is nowhere near enough evidence to do so.

The At-Risk Population

Thailand's at-risk populations share several traits. Rebellions have begun in populations ethnically different from the central Thai, they have been exceedingly poor, they have had substandard education systems, they all were at least slightly rebellious of Bangkok to begin with, and they were all initially politically marginalized by the RTG. Regarding this latter point, Bangkok did not deny these populations political representation by design (except for the Hmong, who at the time were not citizens). They all had the right to vote. Here, Bangkok failed to prioritize their political well-being, which translated to underrepresentation, poor government services, and de facto second-class citizenship. In short, these populations seemed to matter less than those in other sections of Thailand. Thai nationalist laws requiring outlying minorities to adopt central Thai cultural habits, short-lived though they were, exacerbated this sentiment. It should be noted, however, that the CPT's rebellion eventually spread to all ethnic groups, and not all of Thailand's insurgents came from society's downtrodden classes. Many were intellectually and politically elite—student leaders, for example. Many of these people had economic security as well.

Another trend common among at-risk populations is tyrannical treatment by the government. Tyrannical actions, particularly in the 1960s–70s, pushed thousands into the arms of the communists, especially the Hmong, student groups, and eventually, rank-and-file citizens suffering from adverse economic conditions and restrictions of basic freedoms common to all Thai. In the far south in the 1970s, the government used heavy suppression against Thai Malay Muslims, which cast the government in such a bad light that it never fully recovered. Thailand has not been universally tyrannical in the far south since 1980, however. Still, even in the present day, if there is a violent incident that smacks of heavy-handedness—true or not—there are cries of heavy suppression and heinous government abuse attributed to the policies of yesteryear.

Thai COIN Compared to Galula's Theory of COIN

The Thai have indeed followed most of Galula's COIN concepts, especially regarding strategy and operations.[2] Galula said, from a strategic approach, the population is the prize in COIN because insurgency is largely political. He also said ideology in COIN is more powerful than weaponry, and analyzing the political, economic, and cultural aspects of conflict was vital to understand the nexus between the enemy and the people. Galula moreover said isolating the insurgent from outside political and military support was critical to victory. All this was imbedded in his axiom, "A revolutionary war is 20 percent military action and 80 percent political."

The Thai have applied all of these, but not readily. It took them nearly fifteen years to use the 20/80 percent approach in the communist COIN, for example, a direct result of commanders applying enemy-centric methods over the protests of COIN-minded strategists. When the Thai finally did follow these Galula ideals, their COIN campaigns proved effective. The Thai made the population the prize to win in their 66/2523 Plan to defeat the CPT and in their *Tai Rom Yen* Plan for the far south. The current COIN also has the population as the prize, even to the point that population control—checkpoints, for example—have been left a little lax so as not to pressure the people too much.

As for ideology, the Thai fully understand its usefulness as a primary COIN tool. The Thai have created space for the politically disenfranchised—political parties in the far south, for example—and they have created counterinsurgent political movements such as the Village Scouts. In the present southern COIN, there is anti-jihad counseling at the local level, among scores of other programs.

The Thai apply ways and means to understand local populations and their cultures in order to comprehend the population-insurgent nexuses. Against the CPT, they deployed Somchai Rakwijit's village intelligence program to meet this end. For the 1980s–90s COIN in the south, they did this through the SB-PAC, RTA human intelligence, and like outreach programs. In the current war, it is again the SB-PAC.

The Thai have also used Galula's four laws of COIN. The first law is *realizing the importance of the population and tapping its support.* The Thai have done this. Witness their wide-ranging political programs meant to bring the population to the government's side in each war, and also their extensive use of local forces.

Galula's second law is to *seek support from an active minority* and build on it in order to attack insurgent areas of strength. The Thai have done this. Their village security programs, for instance, have been applied in friendly areas first or lightly in contested areas before branching out and/or expanding to more difficult areas. The Thai moreover seek linkages with pro-government citizenry to use as leverage against antigovernment citizenry. Far south college graduates serving as government civil servants are a prime example.

Galula's third law warns that *support from the population is conditional.* The Thai have learned this the hard way. In the CPT COIN, for example, scores of villages rejected RTA CA assistance until troops helped harvest crops and the like, which proved their sincerity, but it took months. In the south in the 1990s, insurgents who surrendered and became civilians were harassed by corrupt police and resumed rebel activities until the advent of effective amnesty through the *Pitak Tai* Plan. In the current war, entire villages have attacked and killed Thai Buddhist teachers and Royal Thai Marines, and they have also provided intelligence that led to the swift demise of insurgents.

Galula's fourth law is *applying intensity and vastness of means,* indicating a whole of government and country effort. Thai have done this once they have achieved effective strategy and coordination. For the CPT COIN, both Kriangsak and Prem applied intensity and vastness of means, not just by using all the state's resources, but by expanding them—building the twelve-thousand-strong *Thahan Phran,* for example. Other examples include surging of democracy and easing harsh domestic conditions such as poor wages, punitive political laws, and freedom of the press. In the first southern insurgency, most of the Fourth Army was involved, along with the SB-PAC and a multitude of government agencies, a vast effort. In the current southern insurgency, the Thai have done the same by applying all regional assets to the fight—all army commands, the entirety of Police Region 9, and the all-encompassing political-economic and security entities of the SB-PAC.

Regarding Galula's pacification strategy, the Thai have generally followed his eight-step program: (1) destruction or expulsion of the insurgent forces, (2) deployment of the static unit, (3) contact with and control of the population, (4) destruction of the insurgent political organization, (5) local elections, (6) testing the local leaders, (7) organizing a party, and (8) winning over or suppressing the last guerrillas.

The Thai have followed this regimen more or less in every war via the combination of the CPM program, the RTA, and political operations. While the Thai have not completed each of Galula's steps with 100 percent success, they have nevertheless applied them toward victory in two wars. The third is a fluctuating work in progress. Problems among these eight steps in the current war revolve around not knowing the local culture well enough to establish more effective village security and political programs, particularly regarding counterpolitical warfare. This, in turn, hinders steps three and four.

Another one of Galula's basic tenets is that a combination of military, police, and civil servants need to collaborate in COIN to achieve a balance of security, sociopolitical, and antipoverty and economic programs. The Thai do this. All aspects of the RTG have been involved in all its COIN efforts, including the military, which has traditionally led these affairs. This approach was wholly embodied in the CSOC concept. Galula prescribes all these efforts should be coordinated under a unified command, which the Thai do. Under Prem in the 1980s, however, was perhaps the only time when Thailand's COINs were 100 percent centralized under a single senior authority.

Galula's "adaptation of minds" concept, which means unity of purpose and agreement of strategy and new ideas across the government, is another concept the Thai have tried to follow. CSOC, CPM, politics leading the military, the *Thahan Phran*, *Pitak Tai*, and Anupong's deployment of all Army Commands to the far south were six major adaptations, but it took total leadership domination for these strategies and programs to germinate, proliferate, and succeed.

Galula recommended that security operations entail mobile strike forces and static occupying forces to work in tandem to continually pressure insurgent forces. The Thai have done this in every war. Witness the RTA and RTP implementing population control while using *Thahan Phran* and Special Forces in DA roles in each COIN demonstrated here. Likewise, the Thai have applied PR and psyops along with force application operations, as Galula recommended, to convince insurgents to give up while simultaneously assuring the population that the government was there to uplift and protect them.

Thai COIN strategy and Galula differ on two major points. First, Galula advised not to mimic insurgents. He said it is a trap and a formula for failure. Taking into account the Thai's winning COIN schematics on a wide scale, however, it appears they do indeed mirror their enemies. For example, when the Thai fought the CPT using conventional methods, they failed, which is typical in COIN. In contrast, when the Thai met the CPT's guerrilla tactics with SF and *Thahan Phran* guerrilla tactics, they succeeded. When they countered the CPT's political organization and infiltration with the Village Scouts—a program that directly mimicked the CPT—they succeeded. When they opposed CPT village infiltration with their own village infiltration—village security programs—they succeeded. Similar patterns emerge from the war in the south in the 1980s–90s regarding force application and the government's political inclusion programs that mirrored insurgent exclusion initiatives based on racism and religious intolerance. Similar scenarios are happening in the current insurgency.

Second, Galula asserts that civilians should lead and control COIN. By and large, the Thai do not adhere to this concept. Thai civilians did not fare well running COIN in the 1970s, nor did they perform in the late 1990s in the far south via the MoI. Thaksin's COIN leadership did not stop or even slow the war. In fact, it grew under his command. It was the RTA that successfully managed Thailand to victory in the first two COINs, and it managed to decrease violence in the far south by approximately 40 percent in the current war. Having said this, the old-school faction of the RTA ran a shoddy anticommunist COIN in the 1960s, ignoring their subordinate and innovative COIN-minded thinkers to the country's severe detriment. In the current war, the RTA has managed to blunt insurgent efforts, but little else. Things seem to be at a stalemate. Civilians, however, have yet to come up with better ways and means than the military. SB-PAC civilians and police, on the other hand, seem to be functioning effectively, especially since it moved out from under military control, something PM Abhisit did in 2011. How this plays out in the field under PM Yingluck might be another story.

Thai COIN Compared to Thompson's Theory of COIN

Regarding Sir Robert Thompson, his COIN advice is more detailed than Galula's, and it is evident the Thai have followed much of it. Once they have achieved winning strategies, for example, the Thai clearly adhered to Thompson's five leading principles stating what a government must do in COIN: 1) have clear political aims, 2) function according to the law, 3) have overall COIN plans, 4) give priority to defeating political subversion, and 5) secure government-controlled areas first and systematically move into guerrilla-controlled areas thereafter. Thai compliance with principles one, three, four, and five were made clear under the Galula section, but principle two needs flushing out.

Principal two, functioning according to the law, is a key Thai approach. The Thai are keenly aware of the procedural formalities of a constitutional nation-state, and they do see laws as a way of achieving either perceived or genuine government legitimacy. For example, to make operations against communist guerrillas illegal, the government passed multiple Anti-Communist Acts in 1933, 1952, 1969, and 1979. These spurred other legal acts such as PM Order 219/2508 for example, which made CSOC legal.

From the 1980s–90s COIN in the south, there are several examples of the Thai using the law in COIN such as the TAO Act of 1997 and the *Pitak Tai* Plan via PM Order 127/2541. Similarly, in the current war, the government passed versions of the ISA in 2007 and 2008 to make legal Bangkok's flexibility in applying security methods in the insurgency zone.

The Thai surely follow Thompson's theory of harnessing the three key influences on a population: "nationalism and national policies, religion and customs, material well-being and progress." The Thai have used these concepts to rally the nation and undercut insurgent sentiments, such as when Kriangsak discarded oppressive political policies, pardoned rebellious students, and increased the minimum wage. Prem followed by rallying the nation with Harn's democracy surge. Even the *Thahan Phran* used the motto "Nation, Religion, King, and Citizens." The Village Scouts were the embodiment of the political aspect of Thompson's sentiments.

In the 1980s–90s COIN in the far south, the Thai used Thompson's three key influences by forming political parties, teaching secular subjects at *pondoks*, incorporating Malay Muslims into advisory positions at SB-PAC, and like programs. Similar programs are being applied in the current war where the Thai are paying more attention to religion and customs, in part because these are key issues the insurgents are using to separate the population and the state.

Thompson advised that good governance was pivotal to strengthen state legitimacy, and the Thai have attempted this in all their COINs. They have had programs in each war that identified and dismissed corrupt civil servants, and they have increased training for COIN forces and government civilians in each war, too. Prime examples are village administrative training during the communist COIN, cultural training for civil servants working in the south under Kriangsak and Harn, and both an improved police command and upgraded *Thahan Phran* training in the current war. Corruption was, and still is, an issue that hinders good Thai governance, however.

Thompson stressed that intelligence and psyops/PR were critical to waging successful COIN. As previously explained, the Thai agree. In every COIN presented here, the Thai have placed a premium on intelligence and psyops/PR. They have never been easy or quick for the Thai to achieve, however.

The Thai have also generally followed Thompson's operational concepts, which are similar, if not the same, as Galula's. Thompson describes them as "clear, hold, winning, and won." For certain, the Thai have sent military forces into enemy-held areas to clear them of main force insurgent units, then established CA, and then followed with substantial economic and political programs to integrate disaffected populations. The Khao Kho campaigns of the 1980s typify this concept.

Thompson was a major proponent of village security, and the Thai are, too. Thompson called it the "strategic hamlet method," where village defense forces cleared insurgents from their own village and then policed it to keep them out, which is exactly what the Thai have done in each COIN mentioned here, though it has not been a stellar success in the far south due to a lack of RTG cultural understanding. In a similar vein, Thompson recommended the state establish antiguerrilla units to identify, locate, and neutralize stubborn pockets of insurgents and rebellious individuals that persisted. He described them as the state's fiercer tomcat going after the guerrillas' tomcat. The Thai describe it as getting a gangster to go after a gangster—hence, the *Thahan Phran*.

The Thai disagree with Thompson in two areas. First, like Galula, Thompson says COIN should be a civilian-run affair by a war council or cabinet headed by a civilian who understands COIN and the military-civilian nexus of it all. While there are Thai civilians that have well understood COIN—PM Chuan Leekpai, for example—the RTA has decisively run all of Thailand's COINs. This includes stipulating strategy and playing a lead role not just in security programs, but in political and economic programs as well. As for the civilian-run SB-PAC, while it has indeed experienced multiple successes, it is neither staffed nor trained to supervise a COIN effort. PM Abhisit placing the SB-PAC directly under the PM's office in 2011 and infusing it with Special Branch leadership was a partial attempt to change that.

Second, the Thai disagree with Thompson regarding his concept of balance of forces. Thompson says COIN is largely a police affair and that the military should be subordinate to both it and civilian leadership, unless the security situation is too unstable and the terrain inhospitable to police forces. In Thailand, however, the RTA has always been the largest COIN force in the field. The RTP has not traditionally seen COIN as its mission, and it has taken on this role with reluctance. When the RTP has effectively engaged in COIN, however, it has proved decisive, especially Special Branch.

The Thai Way of COIN

In the final analysis, it appears the Thai followed about three-fifths of what Galula and Thompson prescribed. Certainly, the Thai are steeped in classical COIN theories. Does this mean the Thai way of COIN offers nothing unique? Not quite. Most any successful COIN campaign follows Galula and Thompson regarding strategic and even operational design—separate the insurgents from the people, attain legitimacy over the enemy, rely on local people to provide insight into local problems, allow politics to lead, clear main force insurgents from areas before political and economic operations begin in earnest, etc.

These, however, are mere concepts to apply in COIN. They are not specific solutions to specific problems. COIN requires a combination of both—using general COIN concepts to help create tailor-made solutions to specific security, political, and economic problems unique to the conflict at hand. The same applies to strategy. It is this "tailoring" that triggers deviation from, or creative adaptation of, the most prominent COIN theories and methods. This has happened in Thailand in several instances.

Most of Thailand's COIN innovations are ways or methods, but there was one instance where the Thai generated an innovative COIN strategy wholly apart from classical and modern prescriptions. This was when, in 1994, the Thai designated economics as its primary COIN weapon. In the face of massive poverty, Bangkok injected copious funds into the far south via industrial and business projects. As a result, and for a few short years only, the government changed its COIN strategy to "economics leads, public relations follows, peace and order supports." This is not in line with any of Galula or Thompson's theories. Interestingly, it also is not in line with traditional Thai strategy of "politics leads." Nor has it ever been repeated. This COIN strategy seems to be an anomaly in Thai history, but it was nevertheless significant. Accordingly, it is a unique "Thai way of COIN."

There are several methods or concepts the Thai have applied in their COINs that were never directed by Galula or Thompson. For example, the Thai application of *Thahan Phran* is indeed a local force, as many COIN theorists such as Thompson suggested be used, but the Thai took it much further than Thompson intended. Instead of a small, elite hunter-killer unit of locals to apply sparingly, the Thai made the *Thahan Phran* a massive antiguerrilla force, especially as the People's Army of Vietnam sat poised near the Cambodian border, ready to drive on Bangkok. The specter of invasion kept the RTA focused on border defense, and the *Thahan Phran* grew into a much larger force than perhaps intended. At the same time, since Thai believe insurgency is people's war, they push people's solutions, which could also explain why the *Thahan Phran* expanded to such a prominent role. Even in the current COIN, the *Thahan Phran* are a main counterinsurgent and CA force. This makes the *Thahan Phran* a unique "Thai way of COIN."

Yet another Thai method that deviates from COIN theory norms is amnesty. Instead of selective amnesty, as Thompson suggested, the Thai applied it massively across the board once they achieved the initiative in their COINs. Witness Kriangsak's pardoning of three thousand students with the stroke of a pen in 1978, Prem's massive rehabilitation programs for CPT in the 1980s that resulted in thousands of surrenders, and the BRN's capitulation in 1984 under the *Tai Rom Yen* strategy. In the current war, amnesty has yet to take wide root, but it is a program in the works. Pardoning swaths of a guerrilla movement with the proverbial wave of a hand is rare in the field of irregular warfare, and yet another unique "Thai way of COIN."

The same can be said about the Village Scouts. It was never listed as a method to follow by any COIN theorist. While Galula said to counter the guerrillas' political movement, he also said not to mimic guerrillas. With the Village Scouts, the Thai both countered and mimicked CPT political organization and infiltration. Specifically, the Thai inserted three Scouts into as many villages as possible. These three then proselytized the benefits of the Scout program and the legitimacy of the government. Recruitment and expansion of the Scout cell followed, which is exactly what the CPT did to turn villages communist. The Thai simply reversed the process, a unique "Thai way of COIN."

In the same vein, the Thai mimicked the radical Islamist aspect of the *da-wah* movement in the far south in the 1980s–90s with a counterprogram, the "official *da-wah* movement." In the current war in the south, the Thai have similarly applied deradicalization programs to reeducate persons warped by intolerant and murderous *takfiri* Islamist tenets. Reeducation of radical Islamist persons, however, is not too unique. It is also done in Kuwait, Saudi Arabia, Jordan, Singapore, and Indonesia.

Diplomacy is a unique "Thai way of COIN" as well. True, all major COIN theorists say to separate the insurgent from sanctuary and outside aid. No classic COIN theorist stressed using diplomacy as a primary COIN tool, however. Because of the decisive success of Thailand's use of diplomacy in COIN, it is impossible to ignore. Thai diplomats, military officers, and PMs have maneuvered to counter outside support for insurgents by engaging China, Malaysia, Saudi Arabia, Egypt, the Gulf Cooperation Council countries, Indonesia, and organizations such as the OIC. It is a definite pattern and an effective COIN method.

What, then, is the Thai way of COIN? The Thai way of COIN largely follows Galula and Thompson's key tenets, save for civilian control and police leadership where the RTA reigns. The Thai way of COIN is also, unfortunately, self-hindering due to turf battles, rivalries, corruption, and egos. On the other hand, the Thai way of COIN is also innovative and practical in security, political, and economic realms. The Thai generate new and edgy COIN methods, they mirror the enemy when necessary, and they match each insurgent line of effort with counterstrikes until achieving the upper hand. Then they deal a decisive series of blows. The learning curve to achieve that upper hand, however, is sometimes lengthy because some in the Thai national security chain of command have difficulty seeing past the political and cultural status quo. The Thai way of COIN, then, can be clumsy and messy, and it can be sleek and elegant. On the whole, however, the Thai way of COIN is largely effective.

AQ	al Qaeda
ARD	Accelerated Rural Development Program
ARPA	The US Advanced Research Projects Agency
ASG	Abu Sayaaf Group
Bersatu	United, The United Front for the Independence of Pattani
BIPP	*Barisan Islam Pembebasan Patani* (Islamic Liberation Front of Pattani)
BNPP	*Barisan Nasional Pembebasan Patani* (National Liberation Front of Pattani)
BPP	Border Patrol Police
BRN	*Barisan Revolusi Nasional* (National Revolutionary Front)
BRN-C	BRN-Coordinate
CA	Civil Affairs
CC	Coordination Center
CCPDF	Coordinating Committee for Patriotic and Democratic Forces
CCPT	Communist Party of China in Thailand
CD	Community Development
CDRM	Council for Democratic Reform under Constitutional Monarchy
COIN	Counterinsurgency
COMINTERN	Communist International
CPC	Communist Party of China
CPM	Civilian Police Military program
CPM-43	Civilian-Police-Military Unit 43
CPR	Curriculum *Pondok* Reform
CPS	Communist Party of Siam
CPT	Communist Party of Thailand
CSD	Committee on Special Administrative Development Zone
CSOC	Communist Suppression Operations Command
CSPPP	Committee on Southern Provinces Peace-building Policy
CTO	Communist Terrorist Organization
DA	Direct Action
DoD	US Department of Defense
DoLA	Department of Local Administration
DPM	Deputy Prime Minister
DPP	*Dewan Pembabasan Pattani* (Pattani Liberation Council)
DSI	Department of Special Investigations
FFT	Farmers' Federation of Thailand
GBC	General Border Committee
GMIP	*Gerakan Mujahideen Islam Patani* (Pattani Islamic Mujahideen Movement)
ICG	International Crisis Group
ISOC	Internal Security Operations Command
JI	*Jemaah Islamiyah* (the Islamic Congregation)
JS	*Jemaah Salafiya* (the Salafist Congregation)
JSC	Joint Security Center
KMM	*Kumpulan Militan Malaysia*
KMT	Kuomintang
MAVU	Modular Audio-Visual Unit
MDU	Mobile Development Unit
MILF	Moro Islamic Liberation Front
MIST	Mobile Information Service Teams
MoE	Ministry of Education
MoFA	Ministry of Foreign Affairs

MoI	Ministry of Interior
NESDB	National Economic and Social Development Board
NIA	National Intelligence Agency
NRC	National Reconciliation Committee
NSC	National Security Command/National Security Council
OC-IPSRPSBP	Operations Centre for the Implementation of Policy and Strategy to Resolve Problems of the Southern Border Provinces
OHEC	Office of the Higher Education Commission
OIC	Organization of the Islamic Conference
PAO	Provincial Administrative Organization
PERKIM	Malaysia Islamic Welfare Organization
PI	*Parti Islam*
POC	Peace Outreach Center
PP	Provincial Police
PR	Public Relations
PSTI	Private Schools Teaching Islam program
Psyops	Psychological Operations
PULO	Pattani United Liberation Organization
QRF	Quick Reaction Force
RCT	Regimental Combat Team
RIP	Royal Initiatives Project
RKK	*Runda Kumpulan Kecil* (Small Unit Tactics)
RMA	Revolution in Military Affairs
RTA	Royal Thai Army
RTAF	Royal Thai Air Force
RTG	Royal Thai Government
SB-PAC	Southern Border Provinces Administrative Command
SBPPC	Southern Border Provinces Peace-building Command
SDV	Self-Defense Volunteers
SEB	Southern Education Board
SF	Special Forces
SPAC	Southern Provinces Administrative Committee
SSC	South Seas Committee
TAO	Tambon Administration Organization
TAPG	Thai Autonomous People's Government
TCP	Thai Communist Party
TF	Task Force
TIM	Thai Independence Movement
TPF	Thai Patriotic Front
TPLAF	Thai People's Liberation Armed Forces
UDT	Union of Democratic Thais
VDC	Volunteer Defense Corps
VOPT	Voice of the People of Thailand
VPU	Village Protection Unit
VST	Village Security Team

amart: the upper ranks of Thai society, typically the rich, upper and middle classes, and royalty

amphoe: districts

aya: Malay village Muslim cleric

changwat: provinces

chao pho: organized crime heads (a.k.a. godfathers)

Chularatchamontri: the national Muslim advisor and administrator on all Islamic affairs, appointed by the king upon advice of the prime minister

dawah: in Islam, inviting to Islam, a roving preaching method for Islam and Islamism

enemy-centric: military dictum that calls for the destruction of the enemy's fighting units

farang: Thai word for foreigners

haj: in Islam, the Islamic pilgrimage to Mecca and one of the five requirements of Islam

human terrain: the schematics of a local population's economic, political, social, and anthropological makeup

insurgency: an organized movement to overthrow a government through subversion and armed conflict (US DoD definition)

Islamist: in Islam, Muslims who believe in the forceful global spread of an ultraconservative and intolerant version of Islam via preaching, politics, manipulation, and violence

Issan: the Thai people (and their region) of northeast Thailand

jihad: in Islam, defined as war to Islamist jihadists, and as utmost effort to moderate Muslims

kafir: in Islam, an infidel or nonbeliever

kamnans: village headman

khao jai: understanding

khao tueng: reaching out

khek: a controversial term technically meaning guest, also a racial slur denoting Thai Malay Muslims and other nonethnic Thai peoples living in Thailand

kratom: a naturally growing narcotic in Thailand, used to make a drug ingested by southern insurgents called "4 x 100"

kwam-pen Thai: what it means to be Thai, or Thai culturalism

makkh-thayok: a hamlet/village religious layman who is the link between the village and the nearby Buddhist monastery

munafik: in Islam, a hypocrite or one pretending to be Muslim, a label often used by Islamist jihadists to brand their enemies, including other Muslims

pattana: development

Pattani Raya (or *Pattani Darussalam*): a Thai Malay Muslim Islamist republic based on sharia law that current southern border insurgents aim to establish

phuyai baan: hamlet headman

pondoks: private Thai Malay Muslim religious schools for high-school-level students

population-centric: a COIN term meaning focusing on protecting the population from insurgents

sakdi na: Thailand's pre-1932 feudal class and rank system

Salafists: in Islam, followers of an ultraconservative sect that believe in tenets promulgated by Muhammad the Prophet's successors

sangha: the community of Buddhist monks

Shahada: in Islam, the declaration "There is no God but God, and Muhammad is his messenger," also one of the five requirements of Islam *takfir*: in Islam, when a Muslim excommunicates another Muslim from Islam for being a *munafik*, technically an illegal action but frequently used by al Qaeda and other Islamist jihadists when setting up another Muslim for assassination

tambon: subdistrict

taqiya: in Islamism, the duty to lie to spread Islamist jihad; lying in self-defense in moderate Islam

Thahan Phran: literally "soldier hunters," local force troops trained and deployed to "out-guerrilla" the guerrillas

prai: the lower ranks of Thai society

to-kru: headmasters at private religious schools

ummah: the global community of Muslims

wat: Buddhist monastery

yaba: methamphetamines

zakat: in Islam, charitable giving, and one of the five requirements of Islam

Introduction

1 *The U.S. Army Marine Corps Counterinsurgency Field Manual, FM 3–24 and 3–33.5* (Chicago: University of Chicago Press, 2007), 385.

2 Thomas A. Marks, Sebastian L. V. Gorka, and Bob Sharp, "Getting the Next War Right; Beyond Population Centric Warfare," *PRISM* 1/3 (June 2010): 79–98.

3 Joint Publication 3-07.2, *Antiterrorism*, http://www.fas.org/irp/doddir/dod/jp3_07_2.pdf.

4 *Marine Corps Counterinsurgency Field Manual,* 383.

1. Thailand in Historical Context

1 Donald E. Nuechterlein, *Thailand and the Struggle for Southeast Asia* (Ithaca, NY: Cornell University Press, 1966), 28–37; Tom Marks, *Making Revolution: The Insurgency of the Communist Party of Thailand in Structural Perspective* (Bangkok: White Lotus, 1994), 21.

2 Barbara Leitch LePoer, ed., *Thailand, A Country Study* (Washington, DC: Federal Research Division, Library of Congress, 1987), http://lcweb2.loc.gov/frd/cs/thtoc.html.

3 Nuechterlein, 19–27; LePoer.

4 Thanet Aphornsuvan, *Origins of Malay Muslim "Separatism" in Southern Thailand,* Working Paper Series No. 32 (Singapore: Asia Research Institute, National University of Singapore), 24–25.

2. The Communist COIN: 1965–1985

1 Gawin Chutima, "The Rise and Fall of the Communist Party of Thailand, 1973–1987," Occasional Paper No. 12 (Canterbury, UK: The University of Kent, Centre of Southeast Asian Studies, 1988), viii, 7–8. According to the Marxist Internet Archive, a site maintained by self-proclaimed "workers," there were two "first" COMINTERN meetings: the founding of the congress in Moscow in March 1919, and the second congress in Moscow and Petrograd in July and August 1920. The 1919 meeting was more of a foundry meeting, a statement of intent, and the 1920 gathering was more of a working congress and considered by some as the first COMINTERN congress. For the Marxist Internet Archive see http://www.marxists.org/history/usa/eam/ci/comintern.html.

2 Chutima, 7–9; Cheah Boon Kheng, ed., *From PKI to the Comintern, 1924–1941: The Apprenticeship of the Malayan Communist Party,* Southeast Asia Program Series No. 8 (Ithaca, NY: Cornell University Press, 1992), 92.

3 Thomas Marks, *Making Revolution: The Insurgency of the Communist Party of Thailand in Structural Perspective* (Bangkok, Thailand: White Lotus Press, 1994), 31.

4 Chutima, 10–12.

5 Nuechterlein, 36–37.

6 Chutima, 9; Cheah Boon Kheng, 92.

7 Nuechterlein, 101, 110–111; "Thailand: Minister for Scrapping Anti-Communism Act," *Bangkok Post,* 30 April 1998.

8 Marks, 94; Char Karnchanapee, "Thai Politics and Foreign Aid in Rural Issan Development and Modernization in 1990's," Rutgers University paper, http://www.rci.rutgers.edu/~karnchan/thai_isa.txt. Char Karnchanapee is an analyst and researcher at Rutgers University in New Jersey.

9 Nuechterlein, 101, 110–111; "Thailand: Minister for Scrapping Anti-Communism Act, *Bangkok Post,* 30 April 1998.

10 Robert Service, *Comrades! A History of World Communism* (Boston: Harvard University Press, 2007), 321.

11 Nuechterlein, 57.

12 Ibid., 112.

13 Ibid., 111–113.

14 Marks, 32.

15 Saiyud Kerdphol, *The Struggle for Thailand: Counterinsurgency 1965–1985* (Bangkok: S Research Center, 1986), 23–24, 33; William McLaughlin, "Thailand: Target for Tomorrow," *Radio Free Europe,* 8 June 1965, http://www.osa.ceu.hu/files/holdings/300/8/3/text/11-2-108.shtml.

16 Saiyud, 5.

17 Arun Bhunupong, Thai Ministry of Foreign Affairs (retired), author interview, Thamassat University, Bangkok, Thailand, 28 March 2008. Dr. Arun previously served in Washington, Moscow, and Paris.

18 Professor Bhumarat Taksadipong, former Director of National Intelligence Agency, author interview, Bangkok, Thailand, 1 February 2008.

19 Saiyud, 48. Information for this section also came from the timeline in Saiyud's book, 179–185.

20 Ibid., 115.

21 Ibid., 116. Not all American operations in Vietnam were of the search-and-destroy type. In I Corps in the north, the North Vietnamese Army (NVA) typically fought maneuver warfare with battalion- and regiment-size formations, and the US Marines deployed likewise. In lieu of NVA operations in other areas, Viet Cong insurgents and main forces carried out hit-and-run operations, ambushes, and sabotage. Americans conducted search-and-destroy missions against these forces and also small unit harassment. General Saiyud's assertion comes from a prevalent idea in the US military that breaking the enemy's ability to make war by attacking his forces was the key to victory, but it was not the only strategy applied.

22 Saiyud, 115–117; George K. Tanham, *Trial in Thailand* (New York: Crane, Russak & Company, 1974), 88.

23 Saiyud, 49.

24 Ibid., 48–49.

25 Ibid., 117–118.

26 Ibid.

27 *New York Times,* page 6, column 1, 15 October 1973.

28 Saiyud, 118.

29 Tanham, 112.

30 Saiyud, 117–118; Chai-Anan Samudavanija and Sukhumbhand Paribatra, "In Search of Balance: Prospects for Stability in Thailand during the Post-CPT Era," in *Durable Stability in Southeast Asia*, ed. by Kusuma Snitwongse and Sukhumbhand Paribatra (Singapore: Institute for Southeast Asian Studies, 1987), 188.

31 Samudavanija and Paribatra, 188.

32 Saiyud, 118.

33 Saiyud, 119.

34 Ibid., 119 (see footnote comment), 120.

35 Ibid., 179–185.

36 Ibid.

37 Chai-Anan Samudavanija, Kusuma Snitwongse, and Suchit Bunbongkarn, *From Armed Suppression to Political Offensive* (Bangkok: Aksornsiam Press, 1990), 67–68.

38 Ibid., 67.

39 LePoer, "Internal Security System" section.

40 General Prem Tinsulanonda, "Thai Experience in Combating Insurgency," 4 March 1995, available on General Prem's website, http://www.generalprem.com/ranks.html.

41 Ibid.

42 Ibid.

43 Ibid.

44 Desmond Ball and David Scott Mathieson, *Militia Redux: Or Sor and the Revival of Paramilitarism in Thailand* (Bangkok: White Lotus Press, 2007), 33.

45 Saiyud, 179–185.

46 Ibid.

47 Ibid., 161.

48 Ball and Mathieson, 33.

49 Saiyud, 179–185.

50 Prem website, http://www.generalprem.com/ranks.html.

51 William R. Heaton and Richard MacLeod, "People's War in Thailand," in *Insurgency in the Modern World*, ed. by Bard E. O'Neil, William Heaton, and Donald J. Roberts (Boulder, CO: Westview Press, 1980), 91.

52 Ibid., 95; Marks, 42–43.

53 Institute for Defense Analyses, *Counterinsurgency in Thailand*, Report R-146, volume 1, Summary and Evaluation (Washington, DC: US Government Printing Office, June 1968), 4.

54 Alexandra Ferry, "The Laotian Crisis of 1960–62: Birth of the Rusk-Thanat Joint Communique," *International Affairs Journal*, 1/1 (Winter 2005), http://davisiaj.com/content/view/378/86/.

55 Samudavanija, Snitwongse, and Bunbongkarn, 97; LePoer.; John Schlight, *The United States Air Force in Southeast Asia: The War in South Vietnam, The Years of the Offensive: 1965–1968* (Washington, DC: Office of Air Force History, 1988), 7–8, 54, 76.

56 Marks, 88.

57 Ibid.

58 Ibid.

59 Chutima, 53.

60 Professor Bhumarat, author interview, 3 March 2008.

61 Ibid.

62 Ibid.

63 LePoer, "The Highland, or Hill Peoples" section.

64 Marks, 97.

65 Chutima, xi, 60–61.

66 Marks, 97.

67 Ibid.

68 Saiyud, 34.

69 Marks, 202.

70 Tanham, 48–65.

71 Marks, 99.

72 Merrill L. Bartlett, "The Communist Insurgency in Thailand," *Marine Corps Gazette*, 11 May 2011 (originally published March 1973).

73 Professor Bhumarat, author interview, 3 March 2008.

74 General Harn Pathai, Special Army Advisory General (retired), author interview, Bangkok, Thailand, 1 April 2008; Saiyud, 124.

75 Tanham, 56.

76 Chutima, 46; Marks, 100 (map).

77 Chutima, 46.

78 Tanham, 47–48, 61, 69.

79 Central Intelligence Agency, *Intelligence Report: Peking's Support of Insurgencies in Southeast Asia Reference Title: POLO LIII* (Washington, DC: CIA, 1973), 74–75.

80 Yuangrat Wedel, *The Thai Radicals and the Communist Party: Interaction of Ideology and Nationalism in the Forest, 1975–1980*, Occasional Paper No. 72 (Singapore: Maruzen Asia [issued under the auspices of the ISEAS], 1983), 25.

81 Institute for Defense Analyses, vol. 1, 34.

82 Harn, author interview.

83 Ibid.

84 Central Intelligence Agency, 5, 65, 72.

85 Tanham, 61.

86 Harn, author interview.

87 Chutima, 47.

88 Jeffrey Race, "The War in Northern Thailand," in *Modern Asian Studies*, 8 (University of Cambridge, January 1974), 106.

89 Central Intelligence Agency, 78.

90 Saiyud, 124.

91 Chutima, 16, note 35.

92 Ibid., 45.

93 Institute for Defense Analyses, vol. 1, 34.

94 Tanham, 48.

95 Chutima, 54.

96 Ibid., 54.

97 Ibid., 25.

98 Ibid.

99 Ibid.

100 Ibid.

101 Union of Democratic Thais, "Thailand: Songs for Life Sung by Caravan: Songs of the Peasant, Student and Worker Struggle for Democratic Rights." (Brooklyn, NY: Paredon Records, 1978), 1, 5.

102 Union of Democratic Thais, 2.

103 Ibid.

104 Ibid.

105 Ibid.

106 Ibid.

107 Chutima, 56.

108 Ibid., 55.

109 Union of Democratic Thais, 1, 5.

110 Ibid., 5.

111 Ibid.

112 Smithsonian Folkways, http://www.folkways.si.edu/albumdetails.aspx?itemid=257; http://www.folkways.si.edu/albumdetails.aspx?itemid=242; http://www.barbaradane.net/Home.html, accessed 8 January 2011.

113 Union of Democratic Thais, 1, 5.

114 Chutima, 58.

115 Ibid.

116 Ibid.

117 Ibid., 59.

118 Ibid., 58–59.

119 Ibid.

120 Wedel, 8–9.

121 Marks, 90.

122 Ahmed Ghazali, Colonel, Malaysian Army (retired), author interview, Malaysia, 26 February 2008.

123 Bartlett, "The Communist Insurgency in Thailand."

124 Srisompob Jitpiromsri, author interview, Hat Yai, Songkhla, Thailand, 22 March 2008; Tanham, 52.

125 Tanham, 51.

126 Ibid., 60.

127 Tanham, 50; Chutima, 25.

128 Saiyud, 128–129.

129 Ibid., 153.

130 Tanham, 50.

131 Ibid.

132 Ibid.

133 Union of Democratic Thais, 3.

134 Ibid.

135 Tanham, 43.

136 Marks, 159.

137 Tanham, 51.

138 Union of Democratic Thais, 3.

139 Tanham, 59.

140 Marks, 106.

141 Ibid., 241–245.

142 Ibid., 241.

143 Ibid., 244.

144 Samudavanija, Snitwongse, and Bunbongkarn, 67.

145 Harn, author interview.

146 Ibid.

147 "Former Communists Receive Land, Cows under 1980 Program," *Pattaya Mail*, 13 May 2011, http://www.pattayamail.com/localnews/former-communists-receive-land-cows-under-1980-program-3383, accessed 6 January 2012. This article comments that the CPT had set up a "state within a state" in Thailand.

148 Tanham, 53–56.

149 Race, "War in Northern Thailand," 107.

150 Tanham, 55–56.

151 Ibid., 56.

152 Tanham, 55–56.

153 Marks, 93.

154 Race, "War in Northern Thailand," 107.

155 Ibid., 109.

156 Ibid., 110.

157 Saiyud, 152.

158 Institute for Defense Analyses, vol. 1., 4–7.

159 Tanham, 5; Paul M. Handley, *The King Never Smiles: A Biography of Thailand's Bhumibol Adulyadej* (New Haven, CT: Yale University Press, 2006), 127.

160 Prem website, http://www.generalprem.com/ranks.html.

161 Tanham, 7.

162 Saiyud, 55.

163 Tanham, 6–8; Saiyud, 55.

164 Race, "War in Northern Thailand," 89–100.

165 Marks, 103–105; Race, "War in Northern Thailand," 106; Saiyud, 55.

166 Tanham, 9.

167 Ibid., 10–11.

168 Handley, 217–218, 229; Wedel, 3–5.

169 Chutima, viii, 12–13.

170 Ibid.

171 Saiyud, 95, 128.

172 Tyrell Caroline Haberkorn, "States of Transgression: Politics, Violence, and Agrarian Transformation in Northern Thailand," (PhD dissertation, Cornell University, 2007), 5, 90, 133.

173 Ibid.

174 Institute for Defense Analyses, vol. 1, 40–41.

175 Haberkorn, 5–6, 137–138, 140–142, 150, 173, 204–208, 218–221.

176 Ibid.

177 Ibid., 174.

178 Mark Urban, *Big Boy's Rules: The SAS and the Secret Struggle Against the IRA* (London: Faber and Faber, 1998).

179 Saiyud, 81, 84–85, 89–95, 128, 153.

180 Ibid., 94.

181 Ibid., 128.

182 Chutima, 55.

183 Ibid., 49.

184 Prem website, http://www.generalprem.com/ranks.html.

185 Saiyud, 37.

186 Race, "War in Northern Thailand," 90–96; see also Alfred W. McCoy, *The Politics of Heroin in Southeast Asia.*

187 Race, "War in Northern Thailand," 89.

188 Ibid., 98–99.

189 Wedel, 3.

190 Denny Lane, former US Defense Attaché to Thailand, author interview, Bangkok, Thailand, 26 January 2008.

191 Ibid.

192 Ibid.

193 Kanok Wongtrangan, "Change and Persistence in Thai Counter-Insurgency Policy," *Occasional Paper No. 1* (Bangkok: Institute of Security and International Studies, Chulalongkorn University, 1983), 10.

194 LePoer, "Table 14. Prime Ministers, 1932–87," http://lcweb2.loc.gov/frd/cs/thailand/th_appen.html. M.R.W., or Mom Rajawongse, is a formal Royal Thai title meaning "Honorable."

195 Samudavanija, Snitwongse, and Bunbongkarn, 57, 143.

196 Institute for Defense Analyses, vol. 1, 46–47, 52; Tanham, 115–150.

197 Samudavanija, Snitwongse, and Bunbongkarn, 144.

198 Professor Bhumarat, author interview, 1 February 2008.

199 Institute for Defense Analyses, vol. 1, 68–70, 73, 75.

200 Kanok, 6.

201 Institute for Defense Analyses, vol. 1, 68–70, 73, 75.

202 Kanok, 6.

203 Ibid., 7.

204 Kanok, 8–9; Samudavanija, Snitwongse, and Bunbongkarn, 60.

205 Glenn Ettinger, "Thailand's Defeat of Its Communist Party," *International Journal of Intelligence and Counterintelligence*, 20/4 (2007): 663–664, 666–668.

206 Ibid.

207 Kanok, 8–9.

208 Saiyud, 69.

209 Samudavanija, Snitwongse, and Bunbongkarn, 61.

210 Ibid., 67–68.

211 "Kriangsak Chamanand, Thai General, Dies at 86," *New York Times*, 25 December 2003, http://query.nytimes.com/gst/fullpage.html?res=9E05E5D71F3FF936A15751C1A9659C8B63\; LePoer.

212 Samudavanija, Snitwongse, and Bunbongkarn, 67–68.

213 LePoer, "Internal Security System" section.

214 Prem website, http://www.generalprem.com/ranks.html.

215 Ibid.

216 Ibid.

217 Samudavanija, Snitwongse, and Bunbongkarn, 73.

218 Kanok, 18–19.

219 Ibid., 18.

220 Ibid.

221 Ibid., 13.

222 Ibid.

223 Ibid., 20.

224 Ibid., 13, 18–19.

225 Ibid., 19.

226 Ibid., 20.

227 Ibid., 22.

228 Prem website, http://www.generalprem.com/ranks.html; Samudavanija, Snitwongse, and Bunbongkarn, 72–73.

229 Samudavanija, Snitwongse, and Bunbongkarn, 72–73.

230 Kanok, 22–23.

231 Samudavanija, Snitwongse, and Bunbongkarn, 149.

232 Ibid., 120.

233 Saiyud, 6.

234 Ibid.

235 Ibid., 74–82.

236 John Cole, (Colonel, US Army, retired), former US Army defense attaché, author interview, Bangkok, Thailand, 14 March 2008.

237 Samudavanija, Snitwongse, and Bunbongkarn, 78; Marks, 197.

238 Samudavanija, Snitwongse, and Bunbongkarn, 82–83, 122.

239 Ibid., 70–71, 144–145.

240 Somchai Rakwijit, former intelligence officer and advisor to PM General Prem, author interview, Bangkok, Thailand, 24 February 2008.

241 Ibid.

242 Somchai, author interview, Bangkok, Thailand, 27 January 2008.

243 Tanham, 116–117, 122, 145–146.

244 Papers of Major General Richard Clutterbuck website, http://janus.lib.cam.ac.uk/db/node.xsp?id=EAD%2FGBR%2F0014%2FCLBK.

245 Saiyud, 19 (footnote) and foreword; Papers of Major General Richard Clutterbuck, http://janus.lib.cam.ac.uk/db/node.xsp?id=EAD%2FGBR%2F0014%2FCLBK.

246 Tanham, 116–117, 122, 145–146.

247 Katherine A. Bowie, *Rituals of National Loyalty: An Anthropology of the State and the Village Scout Movement in Thailand* (New York: Columbia University Press, 1997), 82.

248 Samudavanija, Snitwongse, and Bunbongkarn, 68–69.

249 Suria Saniwa, "Democracy and Elections: A Case Study of the Malay-Muslims in Southern Thailand," http://gotoknow.org/blog/niksof/101398.

250 Samudavanija, Snitwongse, and Bunbongkarn, 69.

251 Kanok, 24.

252 Ibid., Appendix I.

253 Saiyud, 186.

254 Samudavanija, Snitwongse, and Bunbongkarn, 52–53, 57, 101; Marks, 99.

255 Samudavanija, Snitwongse, and Bunbongkarn, 52–53, 57, 101; Marks, 99.

256 Marks, 102; Institute for Defense Analyses, for the Joint Chiefs of Staff, US Department of Defense, volume 4, *Appendixes: The Insurgent Threat and the RTG Counterinsurgency Effort* (Arlington, VA: US Department of Defense, 1968), 68.

257 Samudavanija, Snitwongse, and Bunbongkarn, 99; Tanham, 85–86, 89; Institute for Defense Analyses, vol. 4, 68.

258 Samudavanija, Snitwongse, and Bunbongkarn, 99; Tanham, 85–86, 89; Saiyud, 29.

259 Samudavanija, Snitwongse, and Bunbongkarn, 99; Tanham, 85.

260 Major General Perapong Manakit, Thai National Security Council, author interview, Bangkok, Thailand, 24 March 2008.

261 Samudavanija, Snitwongse, and Bunbongkarn, 99; Tanham, 85.

262 Perapong, author interview.

263 Samudavanija, Snitwongse, and Bunbongkarn, 99; Tanham, 85.

264 Saiyud, 29–30.

265 Marks, 102.

266 Saiyud, 29–30.

267 Ibid., 69.

268 Ibid., 70–71.

269 Ibid., 42–43.

270 Ibid., 43–44.

271 Ibid.

272 Ibid., 44.

273 Ibid., 44–46.

274 Ibid., 46–47.

275 Ibid.

276 Institute for Defense Analyses, vol. 4, 78–79.

277 Somchai, author interview, 24 February 2008.

278 Samudavanija, Snitwongse, and Bunbongkarn, 101–103; Institute for Defense Analyses, vol. 4, 81 and fig. 4.

279 Institute for Defense Analyses, vol. 4; Samudavanija, Snitwongse, and Bunbongkarn, 101.

280 Tanham, 88.

281 Marks, 141.

282 Saiyud, 14.

283 Samudavanija, Snitwongse, and Bunbongkarn, 103–104; Kanok, 10.

284 Saiyud, 81–85, 154.

285 Ibid., 85.

286 Ibid., 85–86.

287 Ibid., 86–87 (footnotes).

288 Samudavanija, Snitwongse, and Bunbongkarn, 110.

289 Ibid., 110–111.

290 Saiyud, 165.

291 Institute for Defense Analyses, vol. 4, 102–105, 114.

292 Institute for Defense Analyses, vol. 4, 91–96; Harn, author interview.

293 Ibid., 96.

294 Harn, author interview.

295 Institute for Defense Analyses, vol. 4, 96; Samudavanija, Snitwongse, and Bunbongkarn, 59–60.

296 Harn, author interview.

297 Institute for Defense Analyses, vol. 4, 98.

298 Ibid., 96–98.

299 Ibid., 171.

300 Ibid., 96–97.

301 Harn, author interview.

302 Institute for Defense Analyses, vol. 4, 96.

303 Srisompob, author interview, 22 March 2008.

304 Institute for Defense Analyses, vol. 4, 171–172.

305 Ibid., 173.

306 Harn, author interview.

307 Ibid.

308 Official RTG documents on the battle for Khao Kho: "History of The Royal Keg Basin Development Project (Rom Krao, Khao Kho, Phetchabun)," and "Pha Muang Phadejsuk Operation," no date, provided by General Harn, translated by May Jeerajit, Bangkok, Thailand, April 2008.

309 Ibid.

310 Desmond Ball, *The Boys in Black: The Thahan Phran (Rangers), Thailand's Para-military Border Guards* (Bangkok: White Lotus Press, 2004), 14. Ball writes that the *Thahan Phran* tried to assault the stronghold but was forced to stop because of heavy fire from 57 mm recoilless rifles and 60 mm mortars ten kilometers from their target. These weapons, however, have a range of only about three kilometers. In all likelihood, the *Thahan Phran* closed with and fixed the enemy while the KMT flanked them, a classic infantry maneuver.

311 Ball, 26.

312 Harn, author interview; Saiyud, 160.

313 Institute for Defense Analyses, vol. 4, 201–207.

314 Ibid., 204–205.

315 Ibid.

316 Ibid., 205.

317 Richard Clutterbuck, *The Long, Long War: The Emergency in Malaya, 1948–1960* (Singapore: Cultured Lotus, 2005), 36–41.

318 Institute for Defense Analyses, vol. 4, 206.

319 Ibid., 201–203.

320 Institute for Defense Analyses, vol. 4, 201–202, 203; personal observations by author over a four-month stay in Thailand. Merchants, students, professionals, hotel and restaurant

employees, professors, the military, and people on the street all decried the police over corruption and perceived ineptitude. The author was witness to a traffic violation where a police officer instructed the violator how to offer and extend a bribe in lieu of receiving a ticket. It is important to note, however, that other police, such as BPP units and police on patrol in southern Thailand, an active insurgency zone, were exceptional, competent, and professional. Many dedicated police have died fighting southern insurgents.

321 Institute for Defense Analyses, vol. 4, 195.

322 Ibid., 209.

323 Samudavanija, Snitwongse, and Bunbongkarn, 80–81.

324 Ball and Mathieson, xxvii, 1.

325 Ibid., 9.

326 Institute for Defense Analyses, vol. 4, 211–212.

327 Tanham, 86–87; Saiyud, 31; Institute for Defense Analyses, vol. 4, 212.

328 Tanham, 86–87.

329 Saiyud, 43, 80; Institute for Defense Analyses, vol. 4, 215–218.

330 Saiyud, 31.

331 Prem website, http://www.generalprem.com/ranks.html.

332 Saiyud, 154.

333 Ibid.

334 Ball and Mathieson, 41–42.

335 Prem website, http://www.generalprem.com/ranks.html.

336 Ibid.

337 Harn, author interview.

338 Marks, 109.

339 Ibid., 203.

340 Ball, *Boys in Black*, 9–11.

341 Ibid., 22.

342 Ibid., 9.

343 Ibid., 5.

344 Cole, author interview.

345 Ball, 10.

346 Lane, author interview.

347 General Kitti Rattanachaya, *The Last Role of Chin Peng; The Communist Party of Malaya, Malaysia, and Thailand* (Sahadhammika, Thailand, 2007), 17.

348 Ibid., 18–26.

349 Ibid., 31–32, 45–47.

350 Ghazali, author interview.

351 Institute for Defense Analyses, vol. 4, 343.

352 Ibid., 347, 349 (diagram).

353 Ibid., 73–75, 346, 347, 351.

354 Ibid., 346, 347, 351.

355 Ibid., 350.

356 Somchai, author interview, 24 February 2008.

357 Ibid.

358 Ibid.

359 Professor Bhumarat, author interview, 1 February 2008.

360 Institute for Defense Analyses, vol. 4, 68–75; Srisompob, author interview, 7 April 2008.

361 Institute for Defense Analyses, vol. 4, 74, 106, 162 (chart).

362 Tanham, 104–105.

363 Samudavanija, Snitwongse, and Bunbongkarn, 60.

364 Tanham, 77.

365 Ibid., 105.

366 Tanham, 104–105.

367 Samudavanija, Snitwongse, and Bunbongkarn, 73, 74; Saiyud, 170 (footnote).

368 Samudavanija, Snitwongse, and Bunbongkarn, 73, 74; Saiyud, 170.

369 Samudavanija, Snitwongse, and Bunbongkarn, 74.

370 Tanham, 77, 82–83, 105–106.

371 Saiyud, 83.

372 Institute for Defense Analyses, vol. 4, 263–265.

373 Ibid., quotation on 73, supporting material on 74, 103, 157–158, 177.

374 Ibid.

375 Somchai, author interview, 24 February 2008.

376 Samudavanija, Snitwongse, and Bunbongkarn, 110–111.

377 Saiyud, 94.

378 Institute for Defense Analyses, vol. 4, 292.

379 Bowie, 1, 56–59, 191.

380 Ibid.

381 William Hillcourt, *The Official Boy Scout Handbook*, Boy Scouts of America, 1979.

382 Bowie, 22–23.

383 Ibid., 1, 119–120, 124, 182–201, 190, 229.

384 Ibid., see also Table A.4, 289.

385 Ibid.

386 Somchai, author interview, 24 February 2008.

387 Professor Bhumarat, author interview, 3 March 2008.

388 Tanham, 77.

389 Institute for Defense Analyses, vol. 1, 52.

390 Samudavanija, Snitwongse, and Bunbongkarn, 77.

391 Lane, author interview.

392 Amara Pongsapich, Chair, Thai Rotary Club, Chulalongkorn University, Rotary Peace and Conflict Studies Program, author interview, Bangkok, Thailand, 29 February 2008.

393 Jeffrey Race, contractor during the communist COIN in Thailand, author interview, Bangkok, Thailand, 29 February 2008.

394 Race, author interview.

395 Lane, author interview.

396 Perapong, author interview.

397 Lane, author interview.

398 Gothom Arya, Director, Mahidol University Research Centre on Peace Building and Chairman of the Second National Economic and Social Advisory Council, author interview, Bangkok, Thailand, 4 January 2008.

399 LePoer, "Thailand, Insurgency" section.

400 Saiyud, 182–185; Gothom, author interview.

401 Lane, author interview.

402 Thailand Elections 2006: Thaksin Shinawatra Vs. People website: http://thaksin2006.blogspot.com/2006_03_01_archive.html.

403 Race, author interview.

404 Professor Bhumarat, author interview, 1 February 2008.

405 Professor Bhumarat, author interview, 1 February 2008; see also John B. Haseman, "Thailand and the Realities of Southeast Asia," Military Review (May 1977): 83–84, http://calldp.leavenworth.army.mil/eng_mr/txts/VOL57/00000005/art10.pdf.

406 Vasana Chinvarakorn and Supara Janchitfah, "The Long Road Ahead," http://www.thaiworld.org/en/thailand_monitor/answer.php?question_id=263.

407 Professor Bhumarat, author interview, 1 February 2008; see also Douglas Pike, PAVN: People's Army of Vietnam (Novato, CA: Presidio Press), 83, note 20.

408 Professor Bhumarat, author interview, 1 February 2008; Samudavanija and Paribatra, 190.

409 Professor Bhumarat, author interview, 1 February 2008.

410 Professor Bhumarat, author interview, 1 February 2008. Chinvarakorn and Janchitfah explain it differently, saying that Kukrit feared a Vietnamese invasion of Thailand in 1975, but that Vietnam did not invade Cambodia until 1978. The story that these journalists tell and that of Professor Bhumarat are similar, however.

411 Professor Bhumarat, author interview, 1 February 2008.

412 Ibid.

413 "Cambodian Rebels Fight Vietnamese at Camp," *United Press International*, 7 January 1985, http://query.nytimes.com/gst/fullpage.html?res=9B01E1D71F38F934A35752C0A963948260; "3 Cambodian Rebel Forces Unite over Vietnam Talks," *New York Times*, 2 July 1988, http://query.nytimes.com/gst/fullpage.html?res=940DE1D61F3CF931A35754C0A96E948260.

414 Professor Bhumarat, author interview, 1 February 2008.

415 Samudavanija, Snitwongse, and Bunbongkarn, 78.

416 Handley, 258–261, 265–266; "Thanom Kittikachorn: Tyrannical Soldier-Strongman Who Ruled Thailand with an Iron Fist," *The Guardian*, 21 June 2004, http://www.guardian.co.uk/news/2004/jun/21/guardianobituaries.johnaglionby; LePoer, sections on "November 1971 Coup," "Thailand in Transition," and "Military Rule and Limited Parliamentary Government, 1976–83"; Somchai Rakwijit, "Problems of Thai Internal Security," in *Southeast Asian Affairs* 1978 (Singapore: Institute of Southeast Asian Studies, Heinmann Educational Books, 1977), 286.

417 Somchai, 295–297.

418 Ibid., 298–300.

419 Samudavanija, Snitwongse, and Bunbongkarn, 67–68.

420 "Kriangsak Chamanand, Thai General, Dies at 86," *New York Times*, 25 December 2003, http://query.nytimes.com/gst/fullpage.html?res=9E05E5D71F3FF936A15751C1A9659C8B63; Somchai, 299.

421 LePoer, sections on "Military Rule and Limited Parliamentary Government, 1976–83" and "Internal Security System."

422 Saiyud, 38–39.

423 Harn, author interview.

424 Perapong, author interview.

425 LePoer, "Irrigation" section.

426 Ibid.

427 Amara, author interview.

428 Ibid.

429 Mahidol University, "The Modern Monarchy," http://www.mahidol.ac.th/thailand/monarchy.html; Royal Project Foundation, http://www.royalprojectthailand.com/general/english/index.html; "Principles of Royally Initiated Projects," in *Inside Thailand Review*,

http://thailand.prd.go.th/ebook/review/content.php?chapterID=35&PHPSESSID=1c5e22987e66
5e511bf6059fb9be3680.

430 Tanham, 74–75; Institute for Defense Analyses, vol. 4, 274; see also
http://www.cabinet.thaigov.go.th/eng/bb2_main11.htm for a list of positions held by Prasong.

431 Tanham, 74–75; Institute for Defense Analyses, vol. 4, 274, 282 (chart).

432 Ibid.

433 Tanham, 73; Marks, 110.

434 Tanham, 74.

435 Institute for Defense Analyses, vol. 4, 278.

436 Ibid., 282 (chart).

437 Perapong, author interview.

438 Prem website, http://www.generalprem.com/ranks.html.

439 Ibid.

440 Ibid.

441 Harn, author interview, 1 April 2008.

442 George Tanham, foreword to Saiyud Kerdphol, *The Struggle for Thailand: Counterinsurgency 1965–1985* (Bangkok: S. Research Center, 1986), 6.

443 Official Rotary Club of Thailand website, "Brief histories of the first clubs of each geographic region, Rotary Club of Bangkok, the First Club of Thailand, 28 Nov 1930, Rotary International District 3350, Rotary International Convention host: 2012," http://www.rotaryfirst100.org/global/countries/thailand/index.htm.

444 Tanham in Saiyud, 6.

445 Marks, 116–117.

446 Ibid.

447 Saiyud, 91.

448 Professor Bhumarat, author interview, 1 February 2008.

449 Amara, author interview.

450 Saiyud, 53–65, 89–96.

451 Ibid., 57.

452 Srisompob, author interview, 22 March 2008.

453 Lane, author interview.

454 Ibid.

3. The First Southern COIN: 1980–1998

1 Michel Gilquin, *The Muslims of Thailand*, trans. by Michael Smithies (Bangkok: Silkworm Books, 2002), 64–66; Surin Pitsuwan, "Islam and Malay Nationalism: A Case Study of the Malay-Muslims of

Southern Thailand" (PhD dissertation, Harvard University, 1982), 213; https://www.einaudi.cornell.edu/SouthEastAsia/outreach/resources/history_and_politics.pdf; Aphornsuvan, *Origins of Malay Muslim "Separatism" in Southern Thailand*, 24–25.

2 Chuan Leekpai, twice former prime minister of Thailand, author interview, Bangkok, Thailand, 3 April 2008.

3 Professor Bhumarat, author interview, 1 February 2008.

4 Panompom Anurugsa, "Political Integration Policy in Thailand: The Case of the Malay Muslim Minority" (PhD dissertation, University of Texas at Austin, 1984), 213.

5 Farish A. Noor, Raja Amin, and Badrul Hisham, "Betrayal after Betrayal," *The New Nation*, 9 April 2005; Surin, 238; Ornanong Noiwong, "Political Integration Policies and Strategies of the Thai Government Toward the Malay-Muslims of Southernmost Thailand (1973–2000)" (PhD dissertation, Northern Illinois University, 2001), 148–149; Anurugsa, 220–223.

6 Surin, 237–238.

7 Ibid.

8 Ibid., 238.

9 Anurugsa, 220–223, 427; Noiwong, 148–149.

10 Wan Kadir Che Man, "Muslim Separatism: The Moros of Southern Philippines and the Malays of Southern Thailand," (Manila: Ateneo de Manila University Press, 1990), 101.

11 Anurugsa, 220–223, 427; Noiwong, 148–149.

12 Che Man, 101.

13 Anurugsa, 220–223, 427; Noiwong, 148–149.

14 Surin, 239–240.

15 Surin, 240–241, 256; Global Security.org commentary on Thai insurgents, http://www.globalsecurity.org/military/world/para/gmip.htm; Anurugsa, 430–432.

16 Chaiwat Satha-Anand, *Islam and Violence: A Case Study of Violent Events in the Four Southern Provinces, Thailand, 1976–1981*, USF Monographs in Religion and Public Policy, No. 2 (Tampa, FL: University of South Florida, 1987), 13.

17 M. Ladd Thomas, "Thai Muslim Separatism in South Thailand," in *The Muslims of Thailand, volume 2: Politics of the Malay-Speaking South*, ed. by Andrew D. W. Forbes (Bihar, India: Centre for Southeast Asian Studies, 1989), 24; Che Man, 107.

18 M. Ladd Thomas, "Political Violence in the Muslim Provinces of Southern Thailand," Occasional Paper No. 28 (Singapore: Institute of Southeast Asian Studies, 1975), 23.

19 M. Ladd Thomas, "Political Violence in the Muslim Provinces," 23–24; *Thai Muslims* (Bangkok: Royal Thai Ministry of Foreign Affairs, 1979), 15–16; Noiwong, 137; Utai Dulyakasem and Lertchai Sirichai, eds., *Knowledge and Conflict Resolution: The Crisis of the Border Region of Southern Thailand* (Bangkok: School of Liberal Arts, Walailak University, Thailand, 2005), 86.

20 Anurugsa, 168–169, 170–171, 173.

21 Ibid.

22 *Thai Muslims*, 12; Surin, 194.

23 Surin, 189–190; International Crisis Group (ICG), "Southern Thailand: Insurgency, Not Jihad," *Asia Report No. 98* (Jakarta/Brussels: 18 May 2005), 7.

24 Anurugsa, 179–180; the quotation is on 179.

25 M. Ladd Thomas, "Political Violence in the Muslim Provinces," 24; Noiwong, 139–143.

26 Noiwong, 138–141.

27 Ibid., 138–143; *Thai Muslims*, 15; Surin, 173, 205–210.

28 Noiwong, 140–143.

29 *Thai Muslims*, 12.

30 Ibid.

31 Anurugsa, 209.

32 Surin, 214.

33 Ibid., 212.

34 Surin, 213; Pranai Suwannarat, Director, SB-PAC, author interview, Bangkok, Thailand, 28 March 2008.

35 Somchai, author interview, 24 February 2008.

36 Noiwong, 173–174.

37 Anurugsa, 158–163.

38 Samacha Potavorn, former Deputy Director of SB-PAC in Buddhist calendar years 2544–2546, author interview, Bangkok, Thailand, 4 April 2008.

39 Chuan, author interview.

40 Anurugsa, 235–236.

41 Samacha, author interview.

42 *Thai Muslims*, 13.

43 Ibid., 20.

44 Ibid.

45 "Pattani Separatists Claim Responsibility for Bangkok Bombings," *Bangkok Post*, 23 July 1980.

46 Gilquin, 83–84.

47 Ibid.

48 Noiwong, 160.

49 Ibid.

50 Official Thai Government website on the cabinet: http://www.cabinet.thaigov.go.th/eng/pm_20.htm.

51 Rodney Tasker, "Southern Discomfort," *Far Eastern Economic Review*, 2 September 1993, 21.

52 D. Abhiradee, "Adhammic Society," *Business Review* (June 1994): 105.

53 Gordon Fairclough, "Hidden Hands; Politicians and Army Blamed for Bombings in the South," *Far Eastern Economic Review*, 9 June 1994, 20.

54 "Security in Southern Thailand Tightened After Bombings," *Bangkok Post*, 12 November 1997.

55 "Army Chief Notes Lack of Unity among Officials in South," *Bangkok Post*, 4 May 1997.

56 "Prime Minister Urges Soldiers To Restore Peace in South," *Bangkok Post*, 19 January 1997.

57 "Southern Thai Separatists Said Getting Little Support," *Bangkok Post*, 19 January 1998. This piece merely describes the early attacks during Falling Leaves.

58 "Reports Lists 4 Terrorist Groups Operating in South," *Bangkok Post*, 14 July 1997.

59 "Report Suggests Way to End Violence in Thailand's South," *The Nation*, 8 January 1998.

60 Ibid.

61 Anurugsa, 425.

62 "50 Bandits Operating in South," *Bangkok Post*, 14 July 1997.

63 Iik A Mansurnoor, "Muslims in Modern Southeast Asia: Radicalism in Historical Perspectives," *Taiwan Journal of Southeast Asian Studies*, 2/2 (2005): 3–54, http://www.cseas.ncnu.edu.tw/journal/v02_no2/pp3–54.pdf.

64 Professor Bhumarat, author interview, 1 February 2008.

65 Arun, author interview.

66 Ibid.

67 Police Major General Tritot Ronnaritivichai, Deputy Commissioner, Special Branch, author interview, Bangkok, Thailand, 13 March 2008.

68 Che Man, 106.

69 Arun, author interview.

70 Andrew Tian Huat Tan, *Handbook of Terrorism and Insurgency in Southeast Asia: The Emergence of Postmodern Terrorism* (University of New South Wales: Edward Elgar Publishing, 2007), 57.

71 M. Ladd Thomas, "Thai Muslim Separatism," 29; University of Maryland, "Minorities at Risk," http://www.cidcm.umd.edu/mar/chronology.asp?groupId=80002.

72 Angel Rabasa and Peter Chalk, "Muslim Separatist Movements in the Philippines and Thailand," in *Indonesia's Transformation and the Stability of Southeast Asia* (RAND, 2001), 97; Che Man, 101.

73 Anurugsa, 431.

74 A BRN-sympathetic website detailing the life and times of Iskandar: http://members.fortunecity.com/barisanrevolusinasional/brnagree.html, accessed 29 January 2012.

75 Che Man, 104–105.

76 Chuan, author interview.

77 "Bandit Shot Dead in Southern Clash," *Bangkok Post*, 5 April 1998.

78 Che Man, 104–105.

79 Ibid., 104–105; Surin, 265.

80 General Kitti Rattanachaya, *Thailand's Southern Insurgency, Creation of Pattani State* (Bangkok: Sor. Pichit Publication Company, 2004), 115–116.

81 Surin, 171–172.

82 *Thai Muslims*, 10.

83 Anurugsa, 433–434.

84 Unattributed comment by an ISOC official, National Defense University, Washington, DC, 3 September 2009.

85 Surin, 223.

86 Ibid., 245.

87 Ibid.

88 Anurugsa, 285.

89 Surin, 248–251.

90 Rattanachaya, *Thailand's Southern Insurgency*, 126–128.

91 Che Man, 109–110, 160.

92 Ibid., 110.

93 "Lessons in Jihad as Secret Terror Manual Translated by Mi-5 Is Made Public by America," *The Daily Mail*, 15 March 2008; Al-Qaeda, "Declaration of Jihad (Holy War) Against the Country's Tyrants, Military Series," UK/BM-8; "US under Fire over al-Qaeda Guide," BBC, 27 July 2005.

94 Rohan Gunaratna, Arabinda Acharya, and Sabrina Chua, *Conflict and Terrorism in Southern Thailand* (Singapore: Marshall Cavendish Academic, 2006), 123.

95 Kitti, author interview; "Report Lists 4 Terrorists Groups Operating in South," *Bangkok Post*, 14 July 1997.

96 University of Maryland, "Minorities at Risk"; "Inside Politics: Confession—No Surprise," *Bangkok Post*, 19 February 1998.

97 Anurugsa, 211–213.

98 "Journey into the Separatist Domain," *Bangkok Post*, 6 July 1994, 29–30.

99 Ibid.

100 Professor Bhumarat, author interview, 1 February 2008.

101 Much of the information in this section comes from Rattanachaya, *Thailand's Southern Insurgency*, 126–128.

102 M. Ladd Thomas, "Thai Muslim Separatism," 24.

103 Mansurnoor, 36.

104 Che Man, 99–100, 106.

105 Surin, 228–230.

106 Angelo Carlo Valsesia, "Thailand: Insurgency in the South," Equilibri.net (19 May 2007), 6, http://uk.equilibri.net/article/6794/Thailand__insurgency_in_the_South.

107 Surin, 228–230.

108 PULO website: http://puloinfo.net/?Show=Sejarah.

109 Che Man, 104–105.

110 Rattanachaya, *Thailand's Southern Insurgency*, 81; Che Man, 106; M. Ladd Thomas, "Thai Muslim Separatism," 24–25.

111 Surin, 235–236; quote found in Chaiwat, 15–16.

112 Mansurnoor, 36.

113 Chaiwat, 16.

114 Ibid., 32.

115 Che Man, 108; Surin, 223, 234; Chaiwat, 15; "Abolition of Crucial Law 'Is Sensitive,'" *Bangkok Post*, 14 February 1998; Moshe Yegar, *Between Integration and Secession: The Muslim Communities of the Southern Philippines, Southern Thailand, and Western Burma/Myanmar*, (Lanham, MD: Lexington Books, 2002), 146.

116 University of Maryland, "Minorities at Risk."

117 Chaiwat, 15–16.

118 Che Man, 110.

119 Chaiwat, 44–45, footnote 6.

120 Surin, 217, 262, 263; Che Man, 161–162.

121 Chaiwat, 13.

122 Ibid., 10–12.

123 2bangkok.com website, Thai terror incidents: http://www.2bangkok.com/thai-terror-incidents.shtml.

124 Rattanachaya, *Thailand's Southern Insurgency*, 64; Peter Chalk, "The Malay-Muslim Insurgency in Southern Thailand Understanding the Conflict's Evolving Dynamic," (RAND Santa Monica, CA, 2008) 7, http://www.rand.org/pubs/occasional_papers/2008/RAND_OP198.pdf.

125 Stephen Brown, "Thailand's Rising Terrorism Problem," Front Page Magazine.com, 17 July 2003.

126 University of Maryland, "Minorities at Risk."

127 "Malaysia To Be Asked To Help Trace Killers," *Bangkok Post*, 26 April 1997.

128 "Abolition of Crucial Law 'Is Sensitive,'" *Bangkok Post*, 14 February 1998.

129 Rattanachaya, *Thailand's Southern Insurgency*, 45; Che Man, 106; "Amin Urged To Return from Exile," *Bangkok Post*, 9 March 1998.

130 Che Man, 108.

131 Chaiwat, 10–12.

132 University of Maryland, "Minorities at Risk."

133 Ibid.

134 Ibid.

135 "Security Beefed Up in South after Bomb Attacks," *Bangkok Post*, 12 November 1997.

136 University of Maryland, "Minorities at Risk."

137 Rattanachaya, *Thailand's Southern Insurgency*, 46.

138 Rattanachaya, *Thailand's Southern Insurgency*, 46; Zachary Abuza, "A Breakdown of Southern Thailand's Insurgent Groups," in *Terrorism Monitor* (Jamestown Foundation), 4/17 (8 September 2006), http://www.jamestown.org/single/?no_cache=1&tx_ttnews%5Btt_news%5D=893.

139 "3 Armed Separatist Leaders Surrender to Yala Police," *Bangkok Post*, 24 February 1998.

140 Rattanachaya, *Thailand's Southern Insurgency*, 66–67; Storey, "Ethnic Separatism."

141 M. Ladd Thomas, "Political Violence in the Muslim Provinces," 18. Ladd referred to this organization as "Black 1902."

142 Anurugsa, 427–428.

143 Anurugsa, 428; he writes that this occurred in July 1977.

144 Chaiwat, 16; Anurugsa, 427–428.

145 International Crisis Group (ICG), "Southern Thailand: Insurgency, Not Jihad," *Asia Report* No. 98 (Jakarta/Brussels, 18 May 2005), footnote 118.

146 Che Man, 109; ICG, "Southern Thailand: Insurgency, Not Jihad," 14; Human Rights Watch, "No One Is Safe" (New York: Human Rights Watch, 27 August 2007), http://www.hrw.org/en/reports/2007/08/27/no-one-safe; Virtual Information Center, "Primer: Muslim Separatism in Southern Thailand," a paper provided for the US Commander in Chief, Pacific, 29 July 2002.

147 Che Man, 111.

148 Michael Vatikiotis, "Resolving Internal Conflicts in Southeast Asia: Domestic Challenges and Regional Perspectives," in *Contemporary Southeast Asia*, 28/1 (Singapore: Institute for Southeast Asian Studies, 2006), 27–47.

149 "Southern Centre Director To Decide on Personnel Changes," *Bangkok Post*, 8 January 1998.

150 "Bomb Blast at School Fair Kills Two, Injures 13 in Yala," *The Nation*, 30 December 1997.

151 Zachary Abuza, *Conspiracy of Silence: The Insurgency in Southern Thailand* (Washington, DC: United States Institute of Peace Press, 2009), 28.

152 Gilquin, 52. Gilquin's book consisted of research from the 1990s and before, and was published in French in 2002, and later published in English in 2005.

153 Ibid., 59.

154 Ibid., 38–42.

155 Omar Farouk Bajunid, "Islam, Nationalism, and the Thai State," in *Dynamic Diversity in Southern Thailand*, ed. by Wattana Sungunnasil (Pattani, Thailand: Prince of Songkhla University, 2005), 5.

156 Dulyakasem and Sirichai, 70, 81.

157 Gilquin, 34–35.

158 Bajunid, 4.

159 Gilquin, 52–54, 93.

160 Ibid., 57.

161 Andrew Cornish, *Whose Place Is This? Malay Rubber Producers and Thai Government Officials in Yala* (Bangkok: White Lotus, 1997), 2, (Cornish calls this a "fundamentalist social Islamic movement"); Gilquin, 94.

162 Gilquin, 94.

163 Ibid.

164 Professor Bhumarat, author interview, 1 February 2008.

165 *Thai Muslims*, 6–7.

166 Piya Kittaworn, "Voices from the Grassroots," in *Dynamic Diversity in Southern Thailand*, ed. by Wattana Sungunnasil (Pattani, Thailand: Prince of Songkhla University, 2005), 38.

167 Gilquin, 61–62.

168 Bajunid, 4.

169 Gilquin, 51.

170 Cornish, 10–13.

171 Gilquin, 56.

172 Ibid., 57.

173 Ibid., 93.

174 Duncan McCargo, "Southern Thai Politics," in *Dynamic Diversity in Southern Thailand*, ed. by Wattana Sungunnasil (Pattani, Thailand: Prince of Songkhla University, 2005), 28.

175 Ibid., 29.

176 Ibid., 33.

177 Gilquin, 56.

178 Cornish, 5, 9–10; Gilquin, 63–64. See also Ibrahim Syukri, *History of The Malay Kingdom of Pattani*, trans. by Conner Bailey and John N. Miksic (Bangkok: Silkworm Books, 1985); Bajunid, 7.

179 Author's personal observations from "Panel on the Violence in the Thai South," Thai Studies Conference, Thammasat University, Bangkok, Thailand, 11–13 January 2008.

180 Che Man, 134.

181 Anonymous Thai security official, September 2008.

182 Kanok, 25.

183 Perapong, author interview.

184 Anurugsa, 420–425; Kanok, 24.

185 Noiwong, 135.

186 Kanok, 25.

187 Chuan, author interview.

188 Cole, author interview.

189 Anurugsa, 305(quotation), 435; Che Man, 131.

190 Arun, author interview.

191 General Akanit Munsewat, Royal Thai Army intelligence official and liaison to Malaysia, author interview, Bangkok, Thailand, 21 April 2008.

192 Arun, author interview.

193 Akanit, author interview.

194 Kitti, author interview.

195 Ibid.

196 Noiwong, 176–177.

197 "Thai Army Okays Repeal of Anticommunism Act," *Bangkok Post*, 27 February 1998; "Minister for Scrapping Anti-Communism Act," *Bangkok Post*, 30 April 1998.

198 "It's Time for Peace—Not Violence," *Bangkok Post*, 25 October 1998.

199 Ibid.

200 Ibid.

201 Anurugsa, 306.

202 Royal Thai Government, "Southern Border Provinces Administrative Centre (SB-PAC)," 1991, 12–13; anonymous.

203 Royal Thai Government, *SB-PAC Report*, 12–13.

204 Kitti, author interview.

205 Ball and Mathieson, 102.

206 Chuan, author interview.

207 Kitti, author interview.

208 Anurugsa, 334–335.

209 Ibid., 317–320, 323.

210 Gothom, author interview.

211 Royal Thai Government, *SB-PAC Report*, 12–13; anonymous; Chuan, author interview.

212 Anurugsa, 326; anonymous.

213 Anonymous; Royal Thai Government, *SB-PAC Report*, 12–13.

214 Anonymous.

215 Chuan, author interview.

216 Anurugsa, 347.

217 Royal Thai Government, *SB-PAC Report*, 12–13.

218 Anurugsa, 352.

219 Royal Thai Government, *SB-PAC Report*, 12–14; Anurugsa, 346–348.

220 Ibid., 14–15; Anurugsa, 392.

221 Royal Thai Government, *SB-PAC Report*, 25–26.

222 Ibid., 17; anonymous.

223 Royal Thai Government, *SB-PAC Report*, 22–23.

224 Anurugsa, 327.

225 Chuan, author interview.

226 Ibid.

227 Royal Thai Government, *SB-PAC Report*, 19; Anurugsa, 345–347.

228 Anurugsa, 332.

229 Ibid., 332–333.

230 Pranai, author interview.

231 "Security in Southern Thailand Tightened after Bombings," *Bangkok Post*, 12 November 1997.

232 "Army Chief Notes Lack of Unity among Officials in South," *Bangkok Post*, 4 May 1997.

233 Ibid.

234 "Minister Wants Military To Secure Southern Zone," *The Nation*, 28 December 1997; "Sanan Ready To Disband Border Centre," *Bangkok Post*, 29 December 1997; "Southern Thai Separatists Said Getting Little Support," *Bangkok Post*, 19 January 1998.

235 "Another Policeman Shot Dead," *Bangkok Post*, 23 December 1997; "Fourth Army To Take Full Charge of South Security," *Bangkok Post*, 31 December 1997; "Sanan Ready to Disban Border Center," *Bangkok Post*, 29 December 1997.

236 Ibid.

237 "Thailand: Army Commander Backs Chuan Order on Southern Separatists," *Bangkok Post*, 24 July 1998; "Surin Against Deploying Forces in the South," *Bangkok Post*, 7 January 1998.

238 "Minister Wants Military To Secure Southern Zone," *The Nation*, 28 December 1997.

239 "Surin Against Deploying Forces in the South," *Bangkok Post*, 7 January 1998.

240 "Troops To Stay in South as Separatist Movements Remain," *Bangkok Post*, 5 July 1998.

241 Dulyakasem and Sirichai, 25.

242 Chuan, author interview.

243 Kitti, author interview.

244 Ibid.

245 "Malaysia Arrests Four Muslim Thai Separatists," *The Nation*, 27 October 1996.

246 University of Maryland, "Minorities at Risk." The website has both 1993 and 1994 as the dates for this attack.

247 "Thailand: Situation Seen Improving after Key Terrorist's Death," *Bangkok Post*, 8 April 1997.

248 Ibid.

249 Kitti, author interview.

250 "Bomb Blast at School Fair Kills Two, Injures 13 in Yala," *The Nation*, 30 December 1997; "Army Chief Considers Deployment in South," *Bangkok Post*, 5 January 1998; "Thai Government Gives Separatists One Month To Surrender," *Bangkok Post*, 27 January 1998.

251 Perapong, author interview.

252 Chuan, author interview.

253 Professor Bhumarat, author interview, 3 March 2008.

254 University of Maryland, "Minorities at Risk."

255 "Bomb Blast at School Fair Kills Two, Injures 13 in Yala," *The Nation*, 30 December 1997.

256 "Muslim Separatists Surrender to Thai Police," *Bangkok Post*, 2 July 1998.

257 Perapong, author interview.

258 "Another Policeman Shot Dead," *Bangkok Post*, 23 December 1997.

259 Chuan, author interview.

260 "It's Time for Peace—Not Violence," *Bangkok Post*, 25 October 1998.

261 Ibid.

262 Ibid.

263 ICG, "Southern Thailand: The Problem with Paramilitaries" (Jakarta/Brussels: 23 October 2007), 15.

264 Gilquin, 58.

265 Chuan, author interview.

266 Srisompob, author interview, 7 April 2008.

267 Kitti, author interview.

268 Ball, 101.

269 Ibid., 101, 103.

270 Ibid., 98–99.

271 ICG, "Southern Thailand: The Problem with Paramilitaries," 4.

272 Ball, 105.

273 ICG, "Southern Thailand: The Problem with Paramilitaries," 5.

274 Ball, 106.

275 "Rangers Seize Explosives, Ammunition in Separatist's House," *The Nation*, 15 August 1997.

276 "Thailand: Thai Rangers Clash with Southern Separatists," *Bangkok Post*, 2 April 1998; Ball, 106.

277 Tritot, author interview.

278 Akanit, author interview.

279 Chuan, author interview.

280 Kitti, author interview.

281 Ibid.

282 Chuan, author interview.

283 "Anti-Terrorism Force Launched," *Bangkok Post*, 16 January 1998.

284 Chuan, author interview.

285 Anurugsa, 339–340.

286 Ibid., 340.

287 Noiwong, 127.

288 Bajunid, 11; Surin, 239–240.

289 Bajunid, 11.

290 Royal Thai Government Cabinet website on Wan Muhammad: http://www.cabinet.thaigov.go.th/eng/WanMuhamadNoor47_1.htm.

291 ASEAN website, biography of Minister Surin: http://www.aseansec.org/drsurin-biodata.pdf.

292 Saniwa, "Democracy and Elections."

293 Ibid.

294 Bertil Lintner, "Peace Stays Far Away in Southern Thailand," *Asia Times*, 15 March 2006, http://www.atimes.com/atimes/Southeast_Asia/HC15Ae02.html.

295 Patrick Jory, "Multiculturism in Thailand? Cultural and Regional Resurgence in a Diverse Kingdom," *Harvard Asia Pacific Review* (2002), http://www.hcs.harvard.edu/~hapr/winter00_millenium/Thailand.html.

296 University of Maryland, "Minorities at Risk" (website has election as 1991 but it was 1992); Saniwa, "Democracy and Elections."

297 University of Maryland, "Minorities at Risk."

298 Noiwong, 134.

299 *Thai Muslims*, 14.

300 Noiwong, 159.

301 Bajunid, 12.

302 "It's Time for Peace—Not Violence," *Bangkok Post*, 25 October 1998.

303 "Participatory Approach to Transport Infrastructure Development," Economic and Social Commission for Asia and the Pacific, *Transport and Communications Bulletin for Asia and the Pacific* (New York: United Nations, 1999), 34, http://www.unescap.org/TTDW/Publications/TPTS_pubs/bulletin69_fulltext.pdf.

304 Fumio Nagai, Nakharin Mektrairat, and Tsuruyo Funatsu, "Local Government in Thailand: Analysis of the Local Administrative Organization Survey," JRP Series 147 (Wakaba Mihama-ku

Chiba-s, Japan: Institute of Developing Economies, 2008), chapter 3, page 51, http://www.ide jetro.jp/English/Publish/Download/Jrp/147.html.

305 Narumol Thapthim, "The Roles of Tambon Administrative Organization (TAO) in Coastal Fishery Resource Management," thesis abstract, Asian institute of Technology; Participatory Approach to Transport Infrastructure Development, 30–36.

306 "It's Time for Peace—Not Violence," *Bangkok Post*, 25 October 1998.

307 Gilquin, 52.

308 Chuan, author interview.

309 Tritot, author interview.

310 Gothom, author interview.

311 Chuan, author interview.

312 Anurugsa, 266–268.

313 Anurugsa, 259.

314 *Thai Muslims*, 9.

315 Anurugsa, 268–269.

316 Noiwong, 166; Tritot, author interview.

317 Anurugsa, 254–255.

318 Dulyakasem and Sirichai, 73; Anurugsa, 255–256, 258.

319 Anurugsa, 255–256, 258.

320 Ibid., 260.

321 Ibid., 289–293.

322 Ibid.

323 Royal Thai Government, *SB-PAC Report*, 31; Anurugsa, 252–258.

324 Anurugsa, 295–296.

325 Perapong, author interview.

326 Professor Bhumarat, author interview, 1 February 2008.

327 Akanit, author interview.

328 Kitti, author interview.

329 Akanit, author interview.

330 Ibid.

331 Che Man, 108.

332 Ibid.

333 Akanit, author interview.

334 University of Maryland, "Minorities at Risk." The website has this date as 1995 as well.

335 Akanit, author interview. Parnthep, aka Puwanartnurak, commanded the Fourth Army from October 1994–30 April 1996.

336 "Malaysia Arrests Four Muslim Thai Separatists," *The Nation*, 27 October 1996; "Army Given Approval To Divert Funds to South for Security," *Bangkok Post*, 20 December 1996; "Malaysia's Release of PULO 'Terrorist' May Harm Cooperation," *Bangkok Post*, 23 November 1996.

337 "Malaysia Arrests Four Muslim Thai Separatists," *The Nation*, 27 October 1996; "Army Given Approval To Divert Funds to South for Security," *Bangkok Post*, 20 December 1996; "Malaysia's Release of PULO 'Terrorist' May Harm Cooperation," *Bangkok Post*, 23 November 1996.

338 "PULO Men Said To Be Behind 'Bomb Blasts' in South," *Bangkok Post*, 2 December 1996.

339 "Malaysia Arrests, Detains Three Thai Separatists," *Bangkok Post*, 20 January 1998.

340 "Separatists Arrested in Malaysia: Operation against Pulo to Expand," *Bangkok Post*, 20 January 1998; "Kuala Lumpur Police Deny Malaysia Used as Rebel Training Base," *South China Morning Post*, 5 January 1998.

341 "Thailand: Malaysia Arrests, Detains Three Thai Separatists," *Bangkok Post*, 20 January 1998; "Separatists Arrested in Malaysia: Operation against Pulo to Expand," *Bangkok* Post; "PM: Peace in South Vital to Growth Triangle," *Bangkok Post*, 21 January 1998; Akanit, author interview; Kitti, author interview.

342 "PM: Peace in South Vital to Growth Triangle," *Bangkok Post*, 21 January 1998; "Separatists arrested in Malaysia: Operation against Pulo to expand," *Bangkok Post*, 20 January 1998.

343 "Surin: Malaysian Terrorism Data To Help Thai Police," *The Nation*, 10 January 1998.

344 "Arrest of 4 Southern Separatists Viewed," *Bangkok Post*, 5 February 1998.

345 "Malaysia Arrests, Detains Three Thai Separatists," *The Nation*, 27 October 1998.

346 Abuza, *Conspiracy of Silence*, 28.

347 "Southern Separatists Hold Urgent Talks in Kelantan," *Bangkok Post*, 24 January 1998.

348 "Border Separatists Flee Abroad," *Bangkok Post*, 22 February 1998.

349 "Pulo Net Closing in on Rebels in Malaysia," *Bangkok Post*, 12 February 1998.

350 "Border Separatists Flee Abroad," *Bangkok Post*, 22 February 1998.

351 "Border Separatists Flee Abroad," *Bangkok Post*, 22 February 1998; "Separatists in Malaysia Flee Abroad," *Bangkok Post*, 22 February 1998.

352 Noiwong, 160.

353 Ibid., 161.

354 "From the Jungle, Separatists Turn Over a New Leaf," *Bangkok Post*, 27 September 1998; "Thailand: Thai Official Confident of Achieving Peace in South," *Bangkok Post*, 20 July 1998.

355 Kitti, author interview.

356 Ibid.

357 Ibid.

358 "From the Jungle, Separatists Turn Over a New Leaf," *Bangkok Post*.

359 "From the Jungle, Separatists Turn Over a New Leaf," *Bangkok Post*; "Thailand: Thai Official Confident of Achieving Peace in South," *Bangkok Post*, 20 July 1998.

360 "Anti-Terrorism Force Launched" *Bangkok Post*; "Thailand: Army Commander Backs Chuan Order on Southern Separatists" *Bangkok Post*; "Ultimatum to top Pulo leaders," *Bangkok Post*, 27 January 1998; "Net closing on rebels in Malaysia," *Bangkok Post*, 12 February 1998; "A Storm in a Teacup?" *Bangkok Post*, 27 September 1998; "Separatist Groups Face Crackdown," *Bangkok Post*, 27 February 1998.

361 "From the Jungle, Separatists Turn Over a New Leaf," *Bangkok Post*.

362 "Thai Official Confident of Achieving Peace in South," *Bangkok Post*, 20 July 1998.

363 "From the Jungle, Separatists Turn Over a New Leaf," *Bangkok Post*.

364 Ibid.

365 Ibid.

366 Ibid.

367 Chuan, author interview.

368 Anurugsa, 340–344.

369 Gothom, author interview.

370 University of Maryland, "Minorities at Risk."

371 "Southern Thai Separatists Said Getting Little Support," *Bangkok Post*, 19 January 1998.

372 Chuan, author interview.

373 Ibid.

374 Anurugsa, 336–338.

375 Chuan, author interview.

376 Ibid.

377 Noiwong, 141.

378 Chuan, author interview.

379 Anurugsa, 287.

380 Ibid.

381 Kitti, author interview.

382 Noiwong, 163.

383 Ibid., 163–166.

384 Ibid., 167.

385 Ibid., 171–172.

386 Royal Thai Government, *SB-PAC Report*, 31.

387 Noiwong, 171–172.

388 Ibid., 163.

389 Ibid., 172–173.

390 Ibid.

391 *Thai Muslims*, 17; Noiwong, 174.

392 *Thai Muslims*, 17.

393 Noiwong, 175.

394 Ibid., 128.

395 Ibid., 175.

396 Kitti, author interview.

397 Noiwong, 175–176.

398 Dulyakasem and Sirichai, 168.

399 Royal Thai Government, *SB-PAC Report*, 34.

400 Noiwong, 176–177; Dulyakasem and Sirichai, 166–167.

401 Noiwong, 177.

402 Ibid.

403 Noiwong, 178.

404 Ibid., 180–181.

405 Amara, author interview.

406 Anurugsa, 392–393.

407 Ibid., 393–395.

408 Ibid., 396–399.

409 Ibid., 399–401.

4. The Second Southern COIN: 2004–Present

1 Professor Bhumarat, author interview, 3 March 2008.

2 Chuan, author interview.

3 Ibid.

4 Cole, author interview.

5 "Malaysia Arrests Alleged Allies of '20th Hijacker' Moussaoui," *The Independent*, 5 January 2002; "Mabuhay, Bem-vindo, Bienvenue, Welcome to Malaysia," *Malaysian Insider*, 16 July 2009; *The 9/11 Commission Report* (New York: W.W. Norton & Company, 2004), 156–160, 181–182, 190–191, 215, 266–269, 353–354.

6 "CA Affirms Conviction of Rizal Day Bombers," *Philippine Star*, 27 January 2012; "Arrests Follow Church Bombings," BBC, 26 December 2000; "Jakarta Bomb Targeted Manila Envoy—Blast Kills Two; Philippine Ambassador Escapes Serious Injury," *Wall Street Journal*, 2 August 2000; "15 Die in Bomb Blast at Jakarta Stock Exchange," *The Daily Telegraph*, 14 September 2000.

7 Abuza, *Conspiracy of Silence*, 37.

8 Gunaratna, Acharya, and Chua, 118–145; Zachary Abuza, "The Islamist Insurgency in Thailand," *Current Trends in Islamist Ideology*, 4/1 (November 2006).

9 "Al-Qaeda Supporters in Thailand Inactive, Says Premier," International, *The News*, Jang Group online editions, 30 May 2003; "Cambodia Arrests 'JI members,'" BBC, 28 May 2003; "Cambodia Court Upholds Life Sentences," *Radio Australia*, 14 March 2008.

10 Wayne Turnbull, "A Tangled Web of Southeast Asian Islamic Terrorism: The Jemaah Islamiyah Terrorist Network," *Monterey Institute of International Studies*, Monterey, California, 31 July 2003.

11 Abuza, *Conspiracy of Silence*, 49–51.

12 Ibid., 151.

13 "Thailand: Muslims Rally Rejecting Violence," *Islam Online*, 22 June 2001.

14 Akanit, author interview.

15 Ibid.

16 "MNLF Vows Support to Gov't," *Philippine Star*, 16 March 2012.

17 Akanit, author interview.

18 "Thai Bomb Blasts Fuel Terror Fears," *CNN*, 30 October 2002; Seth Mydans, "Threats and Responses: Southeast Asia"; "Warnings of Terrorism Along a Porous Border In Southern Thailand," *New York Times*, 16 November 2002.

19 Mydans, "Threats and Responses."

20 Pranai, author interview.

21 Peter Chalk, Angel Rabasa, William Rosenau, and Leanne Piggott, "The Evolving Terrorist Threat to Southeast Asia: A Net Assessment," (Washington, DC: RAND Corporation, prepared for the Office of the Secretary of Defense, 2009), 11, footnote 15.

22 Professor Bhumarat, author interview, 3 March 2008.

23 "Bomb Explodes in Southern Province Before Thai Interior Minister Arrives," *People's Daily Online*, 16 March 2002; "Primer: Muslim Separatism in Southern Thailand," USCINCPAC Virtual Information Center (VIC), an open source intelligence report provided by the Virtual Information Center for US Pacific Command, Honolulu, Hawaii, 3 July 2002; "Silent Witness: Has Thailand's Muslim-Dominated South Served as a Training and Staging Base for Jihadi Terrorists?" *Time*, 17 November 2002.

24 "Silent Witness," *Time*.

25 "Thai Teacher Arrested for Suspected Involvement in Bomb Attack," *Xinhuanet*, 4 November 2002.

26 "Temple School in Southern Thailand Burnt Down by Separatists," *Xinhuanet*, 6 December 2002; University of Maryland's National Consortium for the Study of Terrorism and the Responses to Terrorism (START), Terrorist Organization Profile: Young Liberators of Pattani, http://www.start.umd.edu/start/data/tops/terrorist_organization_profile.asp?id=4522.

27 Seth Mydans, "Tales of Black Ninjas Are Spreading Fear in Rural Thailand," *New York Times*, 25 May 2003.

28 "Large Weapons Cache Seized in South Thailand," *Associated Press*, 4 July 2003.

29 Global Security.org, "Thai Islamic Insurgency,"
http://www.globalsecurity.org/military/world/war/thailand2.htm.

30 "Give Info on Hired Killer, Thai Cops Told," *The Star*, 31 August 2003; "Thai Police Gun Down Hired Killer," *The Star*, 11 September 2003 (these two articles mentioned both Pattani and Satun, but it was likely in Pattani); "Police Kill Most Wanted Muslim Gunman in Southern Thailand," *Xinhuanet*, 28 August 2003; "Army on Trail of Attackers," *The Nation*, 27 October 2003.

31 Chuan, author interview.

32 "Blast Hits Southern Thailand," BBC, 5 January 2004; "Armed Raids in Southern Thailand," BBC, 4 January 2004; "Militants Face Treason Charges," *The Nation*, 15 January 2004; "Barrack Raided, 20 Schools Torched in South," *The Nation*, 5 January 2004; "Two More Suspects Held in Swoop on Pattani Village," *The Nation*, 9 January 2004; Conference on Thailand's Southern Violence, Johns Hopkins University, School of Advanced International Studies, Washington, DC, comments by Don Pathon, journalist for *The Nation*; Kelly Mark, "Special Press Summary: Unrest in Southern Thailand," 9 January 2004, VIC for US Pacific Command, Honolulu, Hawaii, 3.

33 Kelly Mark, "Special Press Summary," 3.

34 Ibid.

35 Royal Thai Government, *Krue Se* report. Translated by *The Nation*.
http://www.nationmultimedia.com/specials/takbai/p2.htm.

36 Duncan McCargo, *Tearing Apart the Land: Islam and Legitimacy in Southern Thailand* (Ithaca, NY: Cornell University Press, 2008), 135–142.

37 Thai military press conference web page, "The Royal Thai Army (RTA) Organic Units Meeting 4/2003," http://armysecretary.rta.mi.th/pressconferencee.htm (link no longer active); "The South Erupts as Never Before," *The Nation*, 29 April 2004.

38 McCargo, *Tearing Apart the Land*, 135–142.

39 Royal Thai Government, *Krue Se* report. Translated by *The Nation*.

40 Dana R. Dillon, "Insurgency in Thailand: The U.S. Should Support the Government," Heritage Foundation, Executive Memorandum 936, 10 June 2004,
http://www.heritage.org/research/asiaandthepacific/upload/64842_1.pdf; "Southern Carnage: Kingdom Shaken," *The Nation*, 29 April 2004.

41 Royal Thai Government, *Krue Se* report. Translated by *The Nation*.

42 "The New Face of Militancy in the South," *The Nation*, 19 May 2004; Royal Thai Government, *Krue Se* report. Translated by *The Nation*.

43 Abuza, *Conspiracy of Silence*, 61.

44 Royal Thai Government, *Tak Bai* report. Translated by *The Nation*.
http://www.nationmultimedia.com/specials/takbai/p1.htm.

45 Ibid.

46 Ibid.

47 Ibid.

48 "Rebels' Response: Car Bomb Blast in Narathiwat," *The Nation*, 18 February 2005; "Phones To Be Cut after Bomb Blasts," *Bangkok Post*, 19 February 2005; "Police Hold Bomb Maker for Blast," *The Nation*, 20 February 2005.

49 "Three Bomb Blasts in Hat Yai Kill Two," *Thai News Agency*, 3 April 2005; "Two Dead, 40 Wounded as Bombs Rock Airport, Cities in Thai South: Police," *Agence France-Presse*, 3 April 2005; "Emergency Security Meeting Following Latest Bomb Attacks in South," *The Nation*, 4 April 2005; "Full Alert at Airports in the South after Bomb Attacks," *The Nation*, 4 April 2005; "Public Announcement, U.S. Department of State, Office of the Spokesman," 4 April 2005; "Police Announce Name of Suspect in Hotel Bombing," *The Nation*, 6 April 2005; "Bombs Kill Two, Wound Dozens in Thailand," Associated Press, 3 April 2005; "Lone Bomber Suspected," *The Nation*, 4 April 2005; "Two Die in Triple Hat Yai blasts," *Bangkok Post*, 4 April 2005; "Terror in Hat Yai: Blasts Hit Airport, Hotel and Carrefour," *Bangkok Post*, 4 April 2005; "DPM Calls Meeting of Authorities Concerned in Aftermath of Three Bomb Blasts in Hat Yai," *Thai News Agency*, 4 April 2005.

50 "2006-South Roundup: No End in Sight to Deadly Violence," *The Nation*, 27 December 2006; author's discussion with Thai police at the SB-PAC lunch pavilion in Yala and four Yala businessmen in Yala, April 2008.

51 "Two Soldiers Brutally Murdered after Held Hostages by Villagers," *The Nation*, 21 September 2005; "Another Suspect Held for Murder of Marines," People's Daily Online, 2 October 2005; "Muslim Schoolteacher Shot Dead," *The Nation*, 13 November 2005.

52 "Three BRN Men Wanted for Killings," *Bangkok Post*, 30 September 2005; "Three Held over Killing of Marines," *Bangkok Post*, 24 September 2005.

53 "Two Teenagers, Monk Killed in Southern Thailand," *Agence France-Presse*, 16 October 2005; "Three Killed in Southern Temple Attack," *Thai News Agency*, 16 October 2005; "Raid Splits Peaceful Village Community," *Bangkok Post*, 17 October 2005.

54 "2 Dead, 17 Wounded as Explosions Rock Far South," *Thai News Agency*, 15 June 2006; "PM Government Must Boost Counter-Insurgency Measures," *Thai News Agency*, 15 June 2006; "Caretaker PM Blames Police for Bomb Attacks in the South," *The Nation*, 15 June 2006; "Bombs Kill Two, Thaksin Raps Police," *Bangkok Post*, 15 June 2006; "Six Arrested after New Wave of Blasts," *Bangkok Post*, 17 June 2006.

55 "Six Dead in Series of Bombings, Shootings in Yala, Narathiwat," *The Nation*, 28 June 2006.

56 "Policy Shifts in the South," *Bangkok Post*, 4 July 2006; "Emergency Decree Extended Once More," *Bangkok Post*, 7 July 2006.

57 "Sonthi Out To Block Thaksin's Man," *Bangkok Post*, 18 July 2006; "Sonthi To Take Over in South," *The Nation*, 2 August 2006.

58 "Teacher Shot Dead in His Class," *Bangkok Post*, 25 July 2006; Michael Sheridan, "Thai Coup Sparked by Failed War on Islamists," *The Sunday Times*, 24 September 2006.

59 "Bombs Kill 4 in Thai Department Stores," *Associated Press*, 16 September 2006; "Series of Bombs Rock Hat Yai," *Bangkok Post*, 17 September 2006; "Canadian Teacher Dead in Hat Yai Bombings, Top Brass Fly South," *Thai News Agency*, 17 September 2006; "Hat Yai Bombs Detonated by Mobile Phones: Southern Army Chief," *The Nation*, 17 September 2006; "Rally of Reformed Separatists a Factor in Had Yai Bombings," translated and summarized from *Komchadluek*, 17 September 2006, posted on 2Bangkok.com, http://www.2bangkok.com/; "Six Blasts Rock Hat Yai," *The Nation*, 17 September 2006.

60 Michael Sheridan, "Thai Coup Sparked by Failed War on Islamists," *Sunday Times*, 24 September 2006; "Bombs Kill 4 in Thai Department Stores," *Associated Press*, 16 September 2006.

61 "2006-South Roundup: No End in Sight To Deadly Violence," *The Nation*.

62 Ibid.

63 Sutthi Sookying, United Nations Asia and Far East Institute for the Prevention of Crime website paper, "The Department of Special Investigations (DSI): Countermeasures in Regard to the Investigation of Economic Crimes and Special Crimes in Thailand," http://www.unafei.or.jp/english/pdf/RS_No66/No66_20PA_Sookying.pdf.

64 "Investigators Split over New Year's Bombings," *Bangkok Post*, 5 February 2007; "Thai Police Abandon Probe of Bangkok Blasts," *Agence France-Presse*, 20 March 2008.

65 "Four Dead, 49 Injured as Bombs Rip Through Thai Muslim South," *Agence France-Presse*, 18 February 2007; "Thai Army Paranoia Gives Muslim Militants Room," *Reuters*, 20 February 2007; "Death Toll Hits Nine in Thai Separatist Attacks," *The Nation*, 20 February 2007; "Sunday Bombers Bolstered by Drugs," *Bangkok Post*, 21 February 2007; "Aree Says South Strategy Flawed," *Bangkok Post*, 20 February 2007; "Bomb Attack inside 7-Eleven Shop in Yala Averted," *The Nation*, 20 February 2007; "Thailand Warns of More Terrorist Attacks," Agence France-Presse, 19 February 2007.

66 "Third Day of Bombings Rattles Hat Yai," *Thai News Agency*, 29 May 2007.

67 "53 Arrests in Raids in Far South; Dawn Swoops in Narathiwat and Yala," *Bangkok Post*, 30 July 2007.

68 "Busted: Hat Yai Bomb Plot," *Bangkok Post*, 6 October 2007.

69 Ibid.

70 "Suicide Killers," *Bangkok Post*, 6 December 2007.

71 "Three Held for Disco Bombs," *The Nation*, 1 January 2008; "31 People Injured in Explosions at Two Discotheques in Narathiwat," *The Nation*, 1 January 2007.

72 "Academic Raps Lack of Govt Action in South," *Bangkok Post*, 11 January 2008.

73 "Number of Attacks Drop, But Not the Threat," *Bangkok Post*, 25 December 2008.

74 "RKK Linked to Songkhla Bomb Blasts," *Bangkok Post*, 3 August 2008.

75 "Attack on a Narathiwat Mosque Kills 10," *The Nation*, 8 June 2009.

76 Norwegian Refugee Council, "Thailand: Buddhist Minority Declines in the 'Deep South' Due to Protracted Armed Conflict," 15 November 2011, http://www.internal-displacement.org/8025708F004BE3B1/(httpInfoFiles)/4A0999B1997970BFC12579490050FCCA/$file/thailand-overview-nov2011.pdf.

77 "Two Muslims Shot Dead at Prayers in Thai Mosque," *This Day Live*, 16 September 2011; "Three Bomb Blasts Rock Sungai Kolok," *Bangkok Post*, 17 September 2011.

78 "17 Ministries to be Grouped in 'Pentagon II' Plan for South," *The Nation*, 8 August 2012.

79 "Ties with Thaksin Not Behind Rise to Top of NSC: Paradorn," *The Nation*, 8 October 2012.

80 "A New Operations Center to Be Set Up to Tackle Problems in the Deep South," RTG Public Relations Department, 10 August 2012, http://thailand.prd.go.th/view_news.php?id=6403&a=2#.

81 UNCHR's version of the Thai Internal Security Act, 2007, http://www.unhcr.org/refworld/category,LEGAL,THA,482b01e82,0.html; see also the ISA at: http://rspas.anu.edu.au/rmap/newmandala/2007/10/19/thailands-revised-internal-security-act/.

82 "Government Bristles at OIC Resolution," *Pattaya Today*, 30 November 2012.

83 "South on Alert After Deadly Marine Ambush," *The Nation*, 14 February 2013; "Thai Military Base Attack Leaves 16 Gunmen Dead," *AFP*, 13 February 2013.

84 "Muslim Insurgents Launch 50 Attacks in Thailand's Deep South," *The Telegraph*, 18 February 2013.

85 "Toddler among Six Massacred in Pattani," *Khabar*, 3 May 2013.

86 "Thai Militants Adopting Al-Qaeda Tactics: General," *Agence France-Presse*, 21 March 2007.

87 "April 28 Raids: Militants' Guide Book from M'sia," *The Nation*, 3 June 2004; Gunaratna, Acharya, and Chua, 118–145.

88 Indonesia took over East Timor in 1975 after Portugal relinquished it from colonial status. In 1999, after years of insurgency and under the UN's act of self-determination, Jakarta released East Timor from its control.

89 Algerian insurgents in the 1950s revolted against their French colonial masters and used a triangular cell structure. There were but five commanders in charge of the entire movement; each had two personnel under him, each of these had a cell under him, and so forth. The structure kept cells from knowing much, if anything, about cells vertically and horizontally separated from each other.

90 "A Tale of Two Insurgents," *Bangkok Post*, 19 July 2009.

91 "Queen Vows To Protect Southerners," *Bangkok Post*, 18 March 2007; "Separatists Well Organised, Police Believe," *Bangkok Post*, 25 December 2008.

92 *Al Jazeera* interview (via Fringer) with Wan Kadir Che Man on 21 November 2006, posted by "Bangkok Pundit" on 21 February 2007.

93 "RKK Insurgents Admit They Trained in Indonesia, Says Army," *Bangkok Post*, 28 November 2005; "Government Rejects Insurgent Amnesty Proposal," *Thai News Agency*, 29 November 2005.

94 "A Tale of Two Insurgents," *Bangkok Post*, 19 July 2009.

95 "More Autonomy, Local Solutions Would Help End Crisis in Far South," *The Nation*, 14 August 2011.

96 "Spoilers on the Ground May Derail Peace Process," *The Nation*, 1 January 2011.

97 "Separatists Well Organised, Police Believe," *Bangkok Post*, 25 December 2008.

98 "Cyber War Army Website Paves Paths to Peace in Far South," *Thai News Agency*, 2 November 2005.

99 "Southern Thai Split on Emergency Decree Extension," *Bernama*, 1 July 2009; "Thai Separatists To Continue Fight," *Al Jazeera*, 9 June 2009.

100 "Police Intercept Weapons Heading for Deep South," *The Nation*, 19 October 2005; "Police Arrest 3, Find Arms, Ammunition in Southbound Truck," *Thai News Agency*, 19 October 2005.

101 "PM, Hunt Them Down," *Bangkok Post*, 28 October 2005.

102 "Security Forces Hunt for Armed Robbers in Deep South," *Thai News Agency*, 27 October 2005; "PM, Hunt Them Down," *Bangkok Post*, 28 October 2005; "Village Volunteer Attacks and Gun Robberies Linked to Takbai," *Thai News Agency*, 28 October 2005.

103 "Arms at the Ready; What Were Five Thai Militants Arrested in Malaysia Looking For?" *Time*, 1 May 2005; "Protest Against Senseless Violence," *Bangkok Post*, 5 December 2005.

104 "Calculating and Skilled: Bali Terror Recreated," *Sydney Morning Herald*, 2 November 2002; *Thai News Agency*, Customs Officers Seize 600kg Of Bomb-Making Chemical, 2005.

105 "Yala Attacks: 60 People Believed To Have Taken Part," *The Nation*, 16 July 2005.

106 "Police Arrest Two Men on Bomb Charges," *Bangkok Post*, 22 August 2005.

107 "Statement from a Member of the National Liberation Front of Patani," translated and summarized from *Issara News Centre*, 24 April 2009, posted on 2Bangkok.com, http://2Bangkok.com/09/National-Liberation-Front-of-Patani.shtml.

108 "Militants Getting Info from Websites," *The Nation*, 21 January 2008.

109 "Raids Lead to Valuable Haul," *The Nation*, 20 May 2005; "Students Say Weapons Training Held at School," *Bangkok Post*, 20 May 2005; "Al Qaeda Training Booklets Found," *Thai News Agency*, 20 May 2005; "Students Say Ustazes Gave Firearms Training," *Bangkok Post*, 24 May 2005.

110 "PM Cancels Rebel Boss Bounties," *Bangkok Post*, 7 April 2007.

111 "RKK Insurgents Admit They Trained in Indonesia, Says Army," *Bangkok Post*, 28 November 2005; "Government Rejects Insurgent Amnesty Proposal," *Thai News Agency*, 29 November 2005.

112 Lee Jay Walker, "Islamic Terrorists Kill More Buddhists in Southern Thailand," *Modern Tokyo Times*, reposted in *Worldwide Religious News*, 26 January 2011, http://wwrn.org/articles/34848/?&place=thai-myanmar.

113 "Interior Minister: Drug Dealers Supporting Insurgents Will Be Brought to Justice," *Thai News Agency*, 14 November 2005.

114 "Police Raise Vigilance Against Drug Dealers Supporting Insurgency in South," *Thai News Agency*, 17 November 2005.

115 "Dozens of Fighters to Surrender," *The Nation*, 28 August 2005.

116 "Amlo Plans To Seize Assets of Insurgent Sympathizers," *Bangkok Post*, 27 December 2005.

117 "RKK Insurgents Admit They Trained in Indonesia, Says Army," *Bangkok Post*, 28 November 2005.

118 "AMLO Eyes Cash Smuggling Backing Up Southern Insurgency," *Thai News Agency*, 10 November 2005.

119 John Funston, "Thailand's Southern Fires: The Malaysian Factor," Research School of Pacific and Asian Studies (RSPAS), Australian National University, Canberra (November 2006), 60.

120 "Statement from a Member of the National Liberation Front of Patani," *Issara News Centre*.

121 Simon Elegant, "Southern Front," *Time Asia*, 11 October 2004.

122 Ibid.

123 Ibid.

124 "Statement from a Member of the National Liberation Front of Patani," *Issara News Centre*.

125 Ibid.

126 PULO website, www.pulo.org (since shut down by the Thai government). Translated for the author by a native Thai speaker, 21 January 2005.

127 Gunaratna, Acharya, and Chua, 118–145.

128 "Book Found on Dead Militants a Call to Arms," *The Nation*, 5 June 2004.

129 "Militants' Guide Book from M'sia," *The Nation*, 3 June 2004.

130 "Book Found on Dead Militants a Call to Arms," *The Nation*.

131 "Leaflets Tell Muslims To Quit Gov't Jobs or Die," *Bangkok Post*, 7 July 2005.

132 "Three Shot Dead in The South," *Thai News Agency*, 4 August 2005.

133 "Militants Chop Off Plantation Worker's Head," *The Nation*, 7 June 2005.

134 Ibid.

135 "Three Killed by Insurgents in Narathiwat," *Bangkok Post*, 5 August 2005; "Rebel Threat Shutters Yala, Pattani Businesses," *Bangkok Post*, 6 August 2005; "Businesses in South Seek Return of Order," *The Nation*, 7 August 2005; "Bt 10,000 Reward for Tipoff on Leaflet Distributors in Pattani," *Thai News Agency*, 5 August 2005; "Almost Like Being There: Yala Closed," a pictorial description of the forced closing of businesses, 12 August 2005, http://www.2bangkok.com/south05August2.shtml.

136 "Thailand: Insurgents Target Leading Muslim Woman Activist," Human Rights Watch report, 18 March 2009, http://www.hrw.org/en/news/2009/03/18/thailand-insurgents-target-leading-muslim-woman-activist.

137 "Call for Return of Modern SBPAC," *Bangkok Post*, 13 October 2006.

138 "Situation Improves in Deep South," *Bangkok Post*, 22 January 2009.

139 The statistics regarding the number of assassinations, bombings, raids, ambushes, and arson attacks from the 2004–2006 time frame come from meticulous pattern analyses from news stories on violence in the south. For each line of operation, the author consulted hundreds of articles.

140 "Raids Lead to Valuable Haul," *The Nation*, 20 May 2005; "Thai Police Seize Al Qaeda Training Video," ABC.net, 20 May 2005, http://www.abc.net.au/news/newsitems/200505/s1373717.htm.

141 "19 Rebels Give Up Tak Bai Defendant Killed," *Bangkok Post*, 29 November 2005.

142 "Authorities Parade 46 Insurgent Spies," *The Nation*, 2 December 2005.

143 "Security Loopholes Endanger South; Decisive Measures Must Be Taken To Weed Out Spies, But Officials Should Ensure That Locals Are Not Prejudged," *The Nation*, 8 January 2008; "Army Chief Visits Violence-Plagued South," *Bangkok Post*, 11 January 2008.

144 "Yala Attacks: 60 People Believed To Have Taken Part," *The Nation*, 16 July 2005.

145 "Understanding Is the Key to Solutions in the South," *The Nation*, 20 January 2009.

146 "Three Bomb Blasts in Hat Yai Kill Two," *Thai News Agency*, 3 April 2005; "Two Dead, 40 Wounded as Bombs Rock Airport, Cities in Thai South: Police," *Agence France-Presse*, 3 April 2005; "Emergency Security Meeting Following Latest Bomb Attacks in South," *The Nation*, 4 April 2005; "Full Alert at Airports in the South after Bomb Attacks," *The Nation*, 4 April 2005; "Public Announcement, U.S. Department of State, Office of the Spokesman," 4 April 2005; "Blast Investigation: Police Announce Name of Suspect in Hotel Bombing," *The Nation*, 6 April 2005; "Bombs Kill Two, Wound Dozens in Thailand," *Associated Press*, 3 April 2005; "Lone Bomber Suspected," *The Nation*, 4 April 2005; "Two Die in Triple Hat Yai Blasts," *Bangkok Post*, 4 April 2005; "Terror in Hat Yai: Blasts Hit Airport, Hotel and Carrefour," *The Nation*, 4 April 2005; "DPM Calls Meeting of Authorities Concerned in Aftermath of Three Bomb Blasts in Hat Yai," *Thai News Agency*, 4 April 2005.

147 Author's personal observations from two trips to Hat Yai in March and April 2008 and casual conversations with hotel and nightclub staffs.

148 "Two Soldiers Brutally Murdered after Held Hostages by Villagers," *The Nation*, 21 September 2005; "Another Suspect Held for Murder of Marines," *People's Daily Online*, 2 October 2005; "Muslim Schoolteacher Shot Dead," *The Nation*, 13 November 2005.

149 "Teachers Freed from Pattani Hostage Beaten by Female Villagers," *The Nation*, 19 May 2006; "Security Forces Rescue Two Teachers Held Hostage in Narathiwat," *Bernama*, 19 May 2006; "Wife of Terrorist Suspect Arrested for Allegedly Inciting Villagers To Lynch Teachers," *The Nation*, 22 May 2006.

150 "Talks Between Thai Gov't, Separatists Have Been Going On Since June, 2005," *Bernama*, 22 April 2008; "Murdered Headman's Wife Killed in Drive-By Attack," *The Nation*, 7 November 2008.

151 "Sapae-ing Basor and the Peace Process," *The Nation*, 23 August 2011.

152 "Thailand Takes Battle to Deep-South's Islamic Schools," *Bangkok Post*, 24 August 2007.

153 "More Concerned about the South Than About Protecting His Job," *Bangkok Post*, 10 December 2007.

154 Abuza, *Conspiracy of Silence*, 104–106.

155 "Pulo Willing To Talk to Thai Government," *Bernama*, 24 January 2009.

156 "New Generation Insurgents Killing Teachers in Southern Thai," *Bernama*, 19 June 2009.

157 "Insurgents Kill Woman Teacher, Torch Schools," *Bangkok Post*, 28 August 2007.

158 Abuza, *Conspiracy of Silence*, 108.

159 "Murdered Headman's Wife Killed in Drive-By Attack," *The Nation*, 7 November 2008.

160 "Military Chiefs Join Forces," *Bangkok Post*, 8 April 2009.

161 Abuza, *Conspiracy of Silence*, 125.

162 "Pattani Killers 'Had Krue Se Connection,'" *Bangkok Post*, 24 January 2008.

163 "PM Cancels Rebel Boss Bounties," *Bangkok Post*, 7 April 2007.

164 Ibid.

165 Marc Askew, "Fighting with Ghosts: Confronting Thailand's Enigmatic 'Southern Fire,'" paper presented at the Institute for Southeast Asian Studies (ISEAS), "Conference on Southern Thailand: Anatomy of an Insurgency, 2004–2009," Singapore, 10–11 March 2009, 24.

166 Ibid.

167 Ibid., 26–27.

168 "Thailand May Extend Sharia Law in Violence-Ridden Muslim South," *Bloomberg*, 23 June 2009.

169 "Muslim Rebel Leader Calls for Referendum on Autonomy for Restive Southern Thailand," *Associated Press*, 22 February 2008.

170 "Thailand: How To Curb High Maternal Mortality in South?" *IRIN*, 31 December 2008, http://www.irinnews.org/Report.aspx?ReportId=82153.

171 Ibid.

172 "Public Health in the Crossfire," *Bangkok Post*, 3 August 2008.

173 "Cheap Thrills Down South," *Bangkok Post*, 27 January 2008.

174 "MPs Fly Down To Seek Out Solutions," *The Nation*, 1 March 2005.

175 "End Abuses for Peace: Thai Muslims," *IslamOnline*, 18 June 2009, http://www.islamonline.net/servlet/Satellite?c=Article_C&cid=1245159055507&pagename=Zone-English-News/NWELayout.

176 Ibid.

177 Ibid.

178 Ibid.

179 Mydans, "Tales of Black Ninjas."

180 Srisompob Jitsomprisi, ed., "Southern Border Provinces Poll," *Deep South Watch*, 18 May 2009.

181 Ibid.

182 Abuza, *Conspiracy of Silence*, 29.

183 Srisompob, "Southern Border Provinces Poll."

184 "Teaching 'Pure' Islam in South," *The Nation*, 6 March 2004.

185 "Yala Attacks: 60 People Believed To Have Taken Part," *The Nation*, 16 July 2005.

186 "Senior Police Testify Against Najmuddin," *Bangkok Post*, 6 April 2005.

187 "Gov't Denies One of 131 Thais Returned by M'sia," *The Nation*, 2 December 2005; "Students Say Ustazes Gave Firearms Training," *Bangkok Post*, 24 May 2005; "Seven Nabbed over Officer's Decapitation," *Bangkok Post*, 19 August 2005; "Army To Buy Phone Jammers," *Bangkok Post*, 18 August 2005; "Dismissed Religious Leader Killed," *Bangkok Post*, 30 August 2005.

188 "Separatists Well Organised," *Bangkok Post*.

189 Arun, author interview.

190 National News Bureau of Thailand, Public Relations Department, "Prime Minister Thaksin and the Southern Development," (Bangkok, 25 May 2004), http://thainews.prd.go.th/en/news.php?id=254705250001; see also "Prime Minister Thaksin and the Southern Development," http://202.47.224.92/en/news.php?id=254705250001.

191 Askew, "Fighting with Ghosts"; Chartchai Chaigasam (Colonel, RTA, SF), National Defense University master's thesis (he quoted a Thai military source, "Guideline for RTA's Troopers Working in the Deep South, 2005"); Chandra nuj Mahakanjana, "Decentralization, Local Government, and Socio-political Conflict in Southern Thailand" (Washington, DC: East West Center Working Paper No. 5, August 2006), 13 and footnote 84; National News Bureau of Thailand, Public Relations Department, "Prime Minister Thaksin and The Southern Development."

192 SBPPC website, http://www.southpeace.go.th/eng/vision.html.

193 Ibid.

194 "Thai PM Rules Out Militant Talks," BBC, 6 November 2004.

195 "Thai Queen Urges Nation To Unite To End Southern Violence," *Agence France-Presse*, 17 November 2004.

196 "Thai Premier Visits Deaths Town," BBC, 7 November 2004.

197 "Thailand Boosts Security in South," BBC, 3 May 2004.

198 "Thailand Boosts Security in South," BBC; Dillon, "Insurgency in Thailand," "Thai Violence ahead of Key Talks," BBC, 13 October 2004.

199 "Thai Troop Reduction in South," World News, 1 April 2005, http://www9.sbs.com.au/theworldnews/region.php?id=108529&region=2.

200 "PM Rules Out Violence To Solve Insurgency," *Thai News Agency*, 4 April 2005; "Thai Panel Says It May Take a Year To Find Solution for Unrest," *Bloomberg*, 9 April 2005; "Emergency Security Meeting Following Latest Bomb Attacks in South," *The Nation*, 4 April 2005.

201 "Putting Peace in the Hands of the People," *Bangkok Post*, 11 April 2005; "Critics Doubt Thai PM's Openness on Muslim South," *Reuters*, 1 March 2005; "Report of the National Reconciliation Commission (NRC): Overcoming Violence Through the Power of Reconciliation, Unofficial Translation," 16 May 2006.

202 "New Security Law for Deep South," *Thai News Agency*, 6 May 2005; "Anand Expects End to Martial Law in Deep South," *The Nation*, 10 May 2005; "Executive Decree Sails Through in Senate Vote," *Bangkok Post*, 30 August 2005.

203 "Gov't To End Martial Law," *The Nation*, 12 May 2005; "Thais Lambast New Emergency Sweeping Powers," *Islamonline*, 16 July 2005; "Diplomats Press Government over Absolute-Power Grab," *The Nation*, 19 July 2005; "Zachary Abuza: Thai Democrats Can't See Insurgency for What It Is," *New Straits Times*, 15 March 2009, http://www.nst.com.my/Current_News/NST/Sunday/Columns/2504958/Article/pppull_index_html.

204 "New Security Law for Deep South," *Thai News Agency*; "Anand Expects End to Martial Law," *The Nation*.

205 "Gov't Needs Force To Fight Southern Unrest," *Thai News Agency*, 24 June 2005; "Thailand To Offer Cheap Guns to Teachers in Restive South," *Agence France-Presse*, 25 June 2005.

206 "New Army Chief To Merge Southern Commands," *Thai News Agency*, 1 October 2005.

207 "PM Stakes Political Future on Ending Unrest in Deep South" *Thai News Agency*, 24 September 2005; "PM Tells Top Brass To Map New Plan To Curb Violence," *The Nation*, 2 October 2005; "Sonthi: Authorities Still in Dark," *Bangkok Post*, 19 October 2005.

208 Western Resistance.com blog hosting a combination of articles from Thai English dailies titled, "November 4, 2006, Thailand: Schools Burn in the Muslim South," http://www.westernresistance.com/blog/archives/003310.html, (website defunct as of 11 October 2009); "Rebels Signal They May Talk To End Unrest," *Bangkok Post*, 5 October 2006; "Southern Border Administration Centre May Be Revived: Deputy Interior Minister," *The Nation*, 10 October 2006; "Renewed Southern Security Agency Coming, Thai Army Chief Says," *Thai News Agency*, 12 October 2006.

209 Prakij Prajonpujjanug, "Security Problems in the Most Southern Provinces" (Speech Document, National Security Council, Bangkok, December 23, 2007), provided by COL Chartchai Chaigasam; "Policy for Peace-building the Southern Border Provinces," Royal Thai Ministry of Foreign Affairs information, link found via http://www.thai2arab.com/eng/content.php?page=content&id=421&kword=ec.

210 Ibid.

211 Ibid.

212 "Suspected Insurgent Shoots Villagers in Narathiwat," *Thai News Agency*, 18 January 2007.

213 "New Ranger Units for Deep South," *Bangkok Post*, 26 August 2006.

214 "Time Is Needed To Quell Southern Insurgency, Says Army Chief," *Thai News Agency*, 7 March 2006.

215 "PM: Al Qaeda Not Funding Muslim Insurgents in Deep South," *Thai News Agency*, 18 January 2008.

216 "Time is Needed to Quell Southern Insurgency," *Thai News Agency*.

217 "To Win People's Hearts Is Key To Resolve Southern Unrest: Army Chief," *Thai News Agency*, 22 August 2006.

218 "Time Is Needed To Quell Southern Insurgency," *Thai News Agency*.

219 "Suicide Bombers May Hit South, Says Sonthi Warns of 'Infiltration' Rousing Locals' Hatred, *Bangkok Post*, 26 April 2006.

220 "Army Chief Backs Unarmed Peace Units in South," *Thai News Agency*, 7 June 2006.

221 "Political Solutions Become Core Strategy in Solving Southern Unrest," *Thai News Agency*, 3 July 2006.

222 "New Ranger Units for Deep South," *Bangkok Post*, "Time Is Needed To Quell Southern Insurgency," *Thai News Agency*.

223 "Suicide Bombers May Hit South, Says Sonthi; Warns of 'Infiltration' Rousing Locals' Hatred," *Bangkok Post*, 26 April 2006; Chartchai Chaigasam, National Defense University master's thesis, 2009; "Political Solutions Become Core Strategy in Solving Southern Unrest," *Thai News Agency*, 3 July 2006.

224 "Army Offers Amnesty to Insurgents," *Bangkok Post*, 12 August 2006; "Deep South: Army Wants Peace Talks but Unsure Who With," *Bangkok Post*, 19 September 2006.

225 "More Concerned about the South than about Protecting His Job," *Bangkok Post*, 10 December 2007.

226 Abuza, *Conspiracy of Silence*, 96.

227 "Army Chief Gen. Anupong Phaochinda and His New Role in Tackling Mistrust and Unrest in the Far South," *Issara News Centre*, 29 December 2007.

228 Comment by an anonymous RTA officer, National Defense University, 3 September 2009, Washington, DC.

229 Professor Bhumarat, author interview, 3 March 2008.

230 "Thai Separatists To Continue Fight," *Al Jazeera*, 9 June 2009.

231 "Southern Border Provinces Development Policy, 2012–2014," *Thai News Update*, 13 February 2012.

232 Southern Border Provinces Peace-building Command (SBPPC) website, http://www.southpeace.go.th/eng/vision.html.

233 "Management Policy for Peace-Building in the Southernmost Provinces," 6 March 2005, http://thailand.prd.go.th/the_inside_view.php?id=755; "Peace-building in the Three Southern

Border Provinces," *Inside Thailand Review*, 27 June 2005, http://thailand.prd.go.th/ebook/review/content.php?chapterID=20.

234 "Peace Is The Objective of New Southern Provinces Administrative Committee," *Thai News Agency*, 6 October 2005.

235 "New Thai Army Chief Promises Soft Line on Insurgency," *Reuters*, 9 September 2005; Gerald Walker, "Thailand: Mollifying the Muslim, Pacification by PR," *Sobaka*, 9 September 2005.

236 "Thai Tactics Win Fear, Not Favor," *Asia Times*, 26 February 2005.

237 "Distrust 'Needs Urgent Solution,'" *Bangkok Post*, 13 March 2005.

238 General Waipot Srinual, Director-General, Office of Policy and Planning, RTA, author interview, Bangkok, Thailand, 4 March 2008.

239 Ibid.

240 *Royal Gazette*, "Office of the Prime Minister's Regulation in Peace-building in the Southern Border Provinces of Thailand 2008," Issue 125, Special Section, 21 *Ngor*, 31 January 2008.

241 "ISOC Expands to All 76 Provinces To Block Turmoil in the Southern Border Region and Halt Political Undercurrents," *Thai Daily*, 12 December 2006.

242 Professor Bhumarat, author interview, 3 March 2008.

243 "ISOC Expands to All 76 Provinces," *Thai Daily*.

244 Ibid.

245 Surayud Chulanon, "The Office of the Prime Minister's Order 207/2549, Subject: The Public Administration in the Southern Border Provinces, 30 October 2006," unofficial translation; anonymous.

246 Ibid.

247 "PM Says Interior and Defense Ministries Cooperate in Announcing the SBPAC Structure," *Thais News.com*, 23 October 2006.

248 "ISOC Expands to All 76 Provinces," *Thai Daily*.

249 "Southern Border Province Administration To Be Revived: Sonthi," *The Nation*, 16 October 2006.

250 "PM Says Interior and Defense Ministries Cooperate in Announcing the SBPAC Structure," *Thais News.com*, 23 October 2006.

251 Surayud, "Office of the Prime Minister's Order 207/2549"; anonymous.

252 Pranai, author interview.

253 "Border Provinces Peace Centre To Resume Operations Soon," *Thai News Agency*, 27 October 2006.

254 "ISOC Expands to All 76 Provinces," *Thai Daily*.

255 Surayud, "Office of the Prime Minister's Order 207/2549."

256 Pranai, author interview.

257 Anonymous.

258 Pranai, author interview.

259 Anonymous.

260 Anonymous; Surayud, "Office of the Prime Minister's Order 207/2549."

261 Pranai, author interview.

262 Anonymous.

263 Anonymous.

264 *Royal Thai Government Gazette*, "Office of the Prime Minister's Regulation on Peace-Building in the Southern Border Provinces of Thailand 2008," Issue 125, Special Section, 21 *Ngor*, 31 January 2008.

265 "PM Defends South Policy But Admits More Needs To Be Done," *The Nation*, 18 March 2011.

266 "Bombers Strike SB-PAC Office Complex in Yala; Six Explosions Rock the Provincial Capital," *Bangkok Post*, 28 November 2007.

267 "Army Chief Gen. Anupong Phaochinda and His New Role in Tackling Mistrust and Unrest in the Far South," *Issara News Center*, 29 December 2007, "More Concerned about the South"; "Newly Appointed Pattani Military Task Force Will Not Use Martial Law—Narathiwat Governor Moves on Solving Economic and Educational Problems," posted on 2Bangkok.com, translated and summarized from *Issara News Center*, 2 October 2008.

268 "Separatists Well Organised," *Bangkok Post*.

269 "Police Unit To Be Upgraded," South Thailand.org, *Bangkok Post*, 20 August 2008.

270 "Police Close In on South Car Bomb Suspect," *The Nation*, 11 March 2011.

271 Thai Government Public Relations Department website, Southern Border Provinces Administrative Center Restructured to Improve Peace-building Operations, http://thailand.prd.go.th/ebook/review/content.php?chapterID=179; author's direct observations in March 2011.

272 International Crisis Group, "Thailand: The Evolving Conflict in the South," *Report No. 241*, 11 December 2012, 17.

273 "Three Separatists Killed in Southern Battle," *Bangkok Post*, 21 December 2007; "4,000 More Troops for the Far South," *Bangkok Post*.

274 Abhisit Vejjajiva, Head of Democratic Party, author interview, 30 April 2008, Bangkok, Thailand, 30 April 2012; anonymous.

275 Abhisit Vejjajiva, Head of Democratic Party, author interview, 30 April 2008, Bangkok, Thailand, 30 April 2012; anonymous.

276 Anonymous.

277 "4,000 More Troops for the far South," *Bangkok Post*, 13 March 2009.

278 "Army Chief Visits the South," *Bangkok Post*, 22 April 2008.

279 Anonymous.

280 Anonymous.

281 Anonymous.

282 Anonymous.

283 "PM Cancels Rebel Boss Bounties," *Bangkok Post,* 7 April 2007.

284 February 2011 conversation with an anonymous Thai RTA captain, Bangkok, Thailand.

285 Abuza, *Conspiracy of Silence,* 174.

286 Nick Nostiz, Thailand-based professional photographer and author, author interview, Bangkok, Thailand, 29 January 2008.

287 Anonymous.

288 Conversation with Thai emergency medical workers, 4 April 2008, Bangkok, Thailand.

289 "OIC Members To Be Lobbied; Man Loses Legs in Blast," *Bangkok Post,* 30 January 2009.

290 Anonymous.

291 Anonymous.

292 "A Tale of Two Insurgents," *Bangkok Post.*

293 Ibid.

294 Ibid.

295 See 2Bangkok.com's pictorial of wanted posters at http://www.2bangkok.com/07/south07mar.shtml. The author observed wanted posters in the employees' section of the JB Hotel's downstairs nightclub in Hat Yai in March 2008.

296 Anonymous.

297 Anonymous.

298 "Army Finds Shot Sergeant's Head," *Bangkok Post,* 5 January 2006.

299 Anonymous.

300 Nostiz, author interview.

301 Anonymous.

302 Group interview with four businessmen in Yala: Tharom, a wood factory owner in Yala; Arwut, owner of the Park View hotel; an anonymous local government official; and Pong Anusat, purveyor of a travel company, 10 April 2008, Yala town, Yala province.

303 Srisompob, author interview, 7 April 2008.

304 Nostiz, author interview; Srisompob, author interview, 7 April 2008.

305 "Thailand's War Without an Audience: How a Deadly Insurgency Stays Beneath Our Radar," Boston Globe.com, http://www.bostonglobe.com/ideas/2012/07/21/thailand-conflict/5mKHjwxLL3Hqrw5eDfgskI/story.html, 22 July 2012; "Buddhist Minority Declines in the 'deep south' due to protracted armed conflict," a 15 November 2011 report by the Internal Displacement Monitoring Centre, Norwegian Refugee Council, asserts that by 2011, perhaps 30 percent of Buddhists and 10 percent of Thai Malay Muslims had been forced from the south.

306 Nostiz, author interview.

307 Srisompob, author interview, 7 April 2008.

308 Anonymous.

309 Srisompob, author interview, 7 April 2008.

310 "Army Offers Amnesty to Insurgents," *Bangkok Post*, 12 August 2006; "Army To Readjust Policy in South," *Bangkok Post*, 3 August 2006; "Sonthi Sends Another 5,000 Troops," *Bangkok Post*, 19 August 2006.

311 "Army Explains Amnesty for Insurgents," DPA, 14 August 2006.

312 "4,000 Troops To Join ISOC's Forward Command in Deep South," *The Nation*, 12 March 2009.

313 "4,000 More Troops for the Far South," *Bangkok Post*, 13 March 2009.

314 Srisompob, author interview, 7 April 2008.

315 Nostiz, author interview.

316 "Southern Projects Approved," *Bangkok Post*, 29 January 2009.

317 Srisompob, author interview, 7 April 2008.

318 Nostiz, author interview.

319 Anonymous.

320 Anonymous.

321 Anonymous.

322 "Chavalit To Test Peace Project To Stem Ills in South," *Bangkok Post*, 28 September 2008.

323 Ibid.

324 "Govt Beefs Up Forces in South; Focus Put on Winning Hearts and Minds," *Bangkok Post*, 13 March 2009.

325 Ibid.

326 Ibid.

327 Ghazali, author interview.

328 Ibid.

329 Anonymous.

330 "Military Chiefs Join Forces," *Bangkok Post*, 8 April 2009.

331 "Thai, Malaysian PMs Confer on Violence in Thailand's Southern Border Provinces," *Thai News Agency*, 11 April 2009.

332 Tritot, author interview.

333 Charnchao Chaiyanukij, Deputy Permanent Secretary of Justice, author interview, 31 March 2008, Bangkok, Thailand.

334 Anonymous.

335 Anonymous.

336 Anonymous.

337 Anonymous.

338 Anonymous.

339 Nostiz, author interview.

340 Ibid.

341 Professor Bhumarat, author interview, 3 March 2008.

342 Somchai, author interview, 24 February 2008.

343 Anonymous.

344 "The EM General Who Is Making a Difference," *The Nation*, 29 June 2009; "Pineapple Eye Network Is Turning Volunteers into Fighters," *The Nation*, 3 July 2009.

345 Ibid.

346 Ibid.

347 "Border Town Enjoys Peace Amid Insurgency," *Inter Press Service*, 24 August 2009.

348 Srisompob, author interview, 7 April 2008.

349 "Advisers Suggest National Islamic Affairs Office," *Bangkok Post*, 10 January 2007.

350 Srisompob, author interview, 7 April 2008.

351 Ibid.

352 "Yala Task Force Holds Meeting With Members from Human Rights Group Aimed To Create Trust, Confidence," *Issara News Centre*, 22 January 2008.

353 "A Wake-up Call for Bangkok," *The Malay Insider*, 22 June 2009.

354 "Sonthi To Provide Evidence to Wada," *Bangkok Post*, 3 April 2007.

355 "A New Face for Islamic Teaching," *Bangkok Post*, 12 July 2007.

356 "Surin Calls for Reform in Muslim Schools," *The Nation*, 24 August 2008.

357 "Tadika Teachers Want Better Training; Distortion of Islamic Teachings Regretted," *Bangkok Post*, 27 April 2008.

358 Ibid.

359 "Islamic Groups Raise Funds for Teachers Jailed in Cambodia," *Bangkok Post*, 17 June 2008; "SCB Donates to the 'San jai thai su jai tai' Project," press release by Siam Commercial Bank, 16 October 2008, http://www.scb.co.th/en/csr/csr_nws_081016-ns.shtml; "Mouth-watering Bouts in Store," news from thebestmuaythai.com website, 23 February 2007, http://www.bestmuaythai.com/muaythai_news_07_02_23b.html.

360 Professor Bhumarat, author interview, 3 March 2008.

361 Ibid.

362 "Surin Calls for Reform in Muslim Schools," *The Nation*, 24 August 2008.

363 Perapong, author interview.

364 Anonymous.

365 "Talks Betweben Thai Govt, Separatists Been Going On Since June," *Bernama*, 22 April 2008.

366 "Thai Foreign Ministry Not Aware of Talks in Jakarta," *Antara*, 23 September 2008.

367 "Indonesia Hosts Talk between Thai Govt and South Group," *The Nation*, 22 September 2008; "President SBY Welcomes Thai Muslim Delegates," *The Jakarta Post*, 22 September 2008.

368 "South Thailand Conflict: Ceasefire Terms in 10 days," *Malaysian Digest*, 15 June 2013, http://malaysiandigest.com/news/36-local2/371502-south-thailand-conflict-ceasefire-terms-in-10-days.html, and "BRN Demands 'Drawing Scant Support,'" *Bangkok Post*, 13 June 2013, and "Patience 'Wearing Thin' in BRN Talks," *Bangkok Post*, 13 June 2013, and "Sukumpol Blasts BRN Chiefs, Calls them Liars," *Bangkok Post*, 30 May 2013.

369 "Thai Peace Talks Brokered by M'sia Hit a Dead End," *The Nation*, 1 July 2013, and "Thailand's Turn for Peace in Troubled South Offers Little Hope, So Far," *The Irrawaddy*, 1 July 2013.

370 "Soldiers to Lie Low During Ramadan," *The Nation*, 11 July 2013.

371 "Government Misreads the Religion Factor in South," *The Nation*, 19 July 2013.

372 "Ball now in Govt's Court as BRN Peace Talks Look to be Over," *The Nation*, 10 August 2013.

373 Arun, author interview.

374 General Waipot Srinual, Director-General, Office of Policy and Planning, RTA, author interview, 4 March 2008, Bangkok, Thailand.

375 "Pessimism over Samak's Visit," *Bangkok Post*, 24 April 2008.

376 "Thai, Malaysian PMs Confer on Violence," *Thai News Agency*.

377 Arun, author interview.

378 "Unrest Tops Agenda for Nitya's Arab Visit; Bid To Offset Criticism at Next OIC Meeting," *Bangkok Post*, 20 April 2007.

379 Ibid.

380 "Sonthi: OIC Understands South Situation," *Bangkok Post*, 2 May 2007.

381 "OIC Rewrite Brings Sigh of Relief," *Bangkok Post*, 21 May 2007.

382 Ibid.

383 Ibid.

384 "Sonthi: OIC Understands South Situation," *Bangkok Post*.

385 "World Muslim Body Praises Thai Approach To Solve Violence," *Thai News Agency*, 18 May 2007; "OIC Rewrite Brings Sigh of Relief," *Bangkok Post*.

386 "World Muslim Body Praises Thai Approach," *Thai News Agency*; "OIC Rewrite Brings Sigh of Relief," *Bangkok Post*.

387 Ibid.

388 "Government Bristles at OIC Resolution," *Pattaya Today*, 30 November 2012.

389 Ibid.

390 Anonymous.

391 "Minister Backs Amnesty Plan," *The Nation*, 23 April 2007.

392 "Muslim Leaders Welcome Amnesty Offer," *Bangkok Post*, 2 May 2007.

393 "Militants Surrender Because of POC: Yala's Deputy Governor," *The Nation*, 9 March 2008.

394 "ISOC Welcomes Separatists Turning Themselves In," *Bangkok Post*, 11 March 2008; "80 Insurgents Surrender in Yala," *Bangkok Post*, 7 March 2008.

395 "Militants Surrender Because of POC: Yala's Deputy Governor," *The Nation*, 9 March 2008.

396 "ISOC Welcomes Separatists Turning Themselves In," *Bangkok Post*, "80 Insurgents Surrender in Yala," *Bangkok Post*.

397 "Separatist Group Surrenders," *The Nation*, 25 March 2011.

398 Charnchao, author interview.

399 Ibid.

400 Pranai, author interview.

401 Ibid.

402 Professor Bhumarat, author interview, 3 March 2008.

403 Pranai, author interview.

404 Anonymous.

405 Anonymous.

406 Anonymous.

407 Anonymous.

408 Anonymous.

409 Anonymous.

410 Anonymous.

411 Anonymous.

412 Anonymous.

413 Nostiz, author interview.

414 Anonymous.

415 Anonymous.

416 Anonymous.

417 "Raids Net 9 Locals in Deep South," *The Nation*, 11 June 2008.

418 Charnchao, author interview.

419 "3 Separatists Sentenced to Life Imprisonment by Thai Court," *Xinhuanet*, 16 October 2002.

420 "Thailand Uses 'Re-education' To Fight Muslim Separatists," *Agence France-Presse*, 16 July 2008.

421 Ibid.

422 Anonymous.

423 Anonymous.

424 Chuan, author interview.

425 Anonymous.

426 Anonymous.

427 Anonymous.

428 "Kasit Leads EU Envoys Visit Islamic College in Yala," *The Nation*, 4 May 2009; "Diplomats Take Note of Angkhana's Work," *Bangkok Post*, 5 May 2009.

429 Colonel Suwan Chirdshai, RTA, ISOC, Chief of Office of Coordination for Mass Strategies to Solve the Problem of Narcotics in the Three Southern Border Provinces, author interview, Pattani, Thailand, 9 April 2008.

430 Ibid.

431 Ibid.

432 "Special Privileges for Investment in South," *Thai News Agency*, 21 January 2006.

433 "Development Plans for Deep South Likely To Be Implemented Next Year," *Thai News Agency*, 5 October 2005.

434 "Violent Areas Want More Tax Breaks," *Bangkok Post*, 8 January 2007.

435 "PM: Soldiers To Work in Southern Businesses," *Bangkok Post*, 22 March 2008.

436 "Thai Cabinet Adopts Growth Plan for Southern Region," *Asia Pulse Data Source* via COMTEX, 10 April 2008.

437 Abhisit, author interview.

438 "Govt Beefs Up Forces in South; Focus Put on Winning Hearts and Minds," *Bangkok Post*, 13 March 2009.

439 Ibid.

440 "Egyptian Spiritual Leader to Visit," *The Nation*, 19 April 2007.

441 Ibid.

442 Pranai, author interview.

443 "Winning the Southern Thai Conflict Through Hearts and Minds," *Bernama*, 3 March 2009.

444 Ibid.

445 Pranai, author interview.

446 "Islamic Study Hours To Rise in Schools," *Bangkok Post*, 25 July 2008.

447 "Bilingual Teaching Deemed Necessary," *Bangkok Post*, 16 October 2007.

448 Ibid.

449 "New Incentives To Stimulate the South; Measures Include Eight-Year Tax Holiday," *Bangkok Post*, 16 June 2007.

450 Pranai, author interview.

451 "Thai PM Hopes Restive South Will Improve Soon," *Thai News Agency*, 14 January 2007.

452 "Babel To Host IMT-GT Meeting on Halal Food," *Antara*, 7 May 2008.

453 Pranai, author interview.

454 Ibid.

455 Ibid.

456 Ibid.

457 "New Centre To Teach Kids about Peace," *Bangkok Post*, 8 May 2008.

458 "Rubber Loses Bounce, Farmers Growing More Rice in Narathiwat," *Thai News Agency*, 19 May 2008.

459 Ibid.

460 Anonymous.

461 Anonymous.

462 "Army to Tell Thaksin its Plan for South," *Bangkok Post*, 14 March 2005.

463 Anonymous.

464 Anonymous.

465 Anonymous.

466 "The EM General," *The Nation*.

467 Anonymous.

468 Anonymous.

469 Anonymous.

470 Anonymous.

471 Anonymous.

472 "Statement from a Member of the National Liberation Front of Patani," *Issara News Centre*.

473 "Counter-Insurgency Success Backfires," *Bangkok Post*, 1 January 2009.

474 "Shelter for Single Mums in Kampung Bujang," *Bernama*, 3 June 2009; "Village of Hope for Widows of War," *New Straits Times*, 25 May 2009.

475 "Shelter for Single Mums," *Bernama*.

476 "Village of Hope for Widows of War," *New Straits Times*.

Conclusion

1 David Galula, *Counterinsurgency Warfare: Theory and Practice* (New York: Praeger, 2006); Robert Thompson, *Defeating Communist Insurgency: Experiences from Malaya and Vietnam* (Houndmills Basingstoke Hampshire: Palgrave Macmillan, 1978). All the following Galula and Thompson quotes, ideas, and theories come from these respective books.

References and Resources

Interviews

January 2008
Gothom Arya, Director, Mahidol University Research Centre on Peace Building and Chairman of the Second National Economic and Social Advisory Council, Bangkok, Thailand, 24 January 2008.

Denny Lane, Assistant US Army Attaché to Thailand (retired), Bangkok, Thailand, 26 January 2008.

Somchai Rakwijit (formerly Somsak Rakwijit), communist war-era intelligence official and COIN advisor to General Prem (retired), Bangkok, Thailand, 27 January 2008.

Nick Nostiz, freelance photographer who has covered the far south on combat patrols, Bangkok, Thailand, 29 January 2008.

February 2008
Professor Bhumarat Taksadipong, Chief, National Intelligence Agency (retired), Bangkok, Thailand, 1 February 2008.

Somchai Rakwijit, former high-ranking intelligence official during the CPT COIN, Bangkok, Thailand, 24 February 2008.

Ahmed Ghazali, Colonel, Malaysian Army (retired), Faculty of Defence Studies and Management, National Defence University of Malaysia, Bangkok, Thailand, 26 February 2008.

Amara Pongsapich, Chair, Thai Rotary Club, Chulalongkorn University, Rotary Peace and Conflict Studies Program, Bangkok, Thailand, 29 February 2008.

Jeffrey Race, author of *War Comes to Long An: Revolutionary Conflict in a Vietnamese Province*, Thai cultural and politico-military expert, and former Thai COIN consultant, Bangkok, Thailand, 29 February 2008.

March 2008
Professor Bhumarat Taksadipong, Chief, National Intelligence Agency (retired), Bangkok, Thailand, 3 March 2008.

Waipot Srinual, Lieutenant General, Director General, Office of Policy and Planning, RTA, Bangkok, Thailand, 4 March 2008.

Tritot Ronnaritivichai, Police Major General, Deputy Commissioner, Special Branch, Bangkok, Thailand, 13 March 2008.

John Cole, Colonel, US Army (retired), former US Army Attaché to Thailand, Bangkok, Thailand, 14 March 2008.

Srisompob Jitpiromsri, Professor, Prince of Songkhla University, Hat Yai, Songkhla, Thailand, 22 March 2008.

Perapong Manakit, Major General, Thai National Security Council, Bangkok, Thailand, 24 March 2008.

Henrik Fredborg Larsen, United Nations Policy Advisor for Democratic Governance, Decentralization and Local Governance, Bangkok, Thailand, 27 March 2008.

Arun Bhunupong, Thai Ambassador to Moscow, Washington, DC, and Paris; former Undersecretary of Ministry of Foreign Affairs; former Assistant Minister of Foreign Affairs (retired), present professor in International Law, Thammasat University, Bangkok, Thailand, 28 March 2008.

Kitti Rattanachaya, Lieutenant General (retired), Fourth Army Area Commander, RTA, Bangkok, Thailand, 28 March 2008.

Pranai Suwannarat, Deputy Permanent Secretary for Interior Director General, Southern Border Provinces Administrative Centre (SB-PAC), Bangkok, Thailand, 28 March 2008.

Charnchao Chaiyanukij, Deputy Permanent Secretary of Justice, Bangkok, Thailand, 31 March 2008.

April 2008
Harn Pathai, Brigadier General (retired), Special Army Advisor, RTA, Bangkok, Thailand, 1 April 2008.

Chuan Leekpai, twice former Thai Prime Minister, Democratic Party, Bangkok, Thailand, 3 April 2008.

Samacha Potavorn," Deputy Director of 1980s–1990s SB-PAC, Ministry of Interior, Bangkok, Thailand, 4 April 2008.

Sascha Helbardt, PhD student, Fakultät für Soziologie, Universität Bielefeld, Narathiwat, Thailand, 6 April 2008.

Srisompob Jitpiromsri, Professor, Prince of Songkhla University, Pattani, Thailand, 7 April 2008.

Suwan Chirdshai, Colonel, RTA, ISOC officer, Chief of Office of Coordination for Mass Strategies to Solve the Problem of Narcotics in the Three Southern Border Provinces, Pattani, Thailand, 9 April 2008.

Group interview with Tharom, a wood factory owner in Yala; Arwut, owner of the Park View Hotel; an anonymous local government official; and Pong Anusat, purveyor of a travel company, Yala, Thailand, 10 April 2008.

Akanit Munsewat, General, RTA Intelligence Chief, Malaysia Coordination Office, Bangkok, Thailand, 21 April 2008.

Khunying Pornthip Rojanasunand, Justice Ministry's Forensic Science Institute, Bangkok, Thailand, 24 April 2008.

Abhisit Vejjajiva, Head, Democratic Party, Bangkok, Thailand, 30 April 2008.

Select Bibliography

Abuza, Zachary. "A Breakdown of Southern Thailand's Insurgent Groups." *Terrorism Monitor* (Jamestown Foundation), 4/17 (8 September 2006). http://www.jamestown.org/single/?no_cache=1&tx_ttnews%5Btt_news%5D=893.

Abuza, Zachary. "The Islamist Insurgency in Thailand." *Current Trends in Islamist Ideology* 4 (1 November 2006).

Abuza, Zachary. *Conspiracy of Silence: The Insurgency in Southern Thailand.* Washington, DC: United States Institute of Peace Press, 2009.

Anand, Chaiwat Satha. "Islam and Violence: A Case Study of Violent Events in the Four Southern Provinces," *USF Monographs in Religion and Public Policy, No. 2.* Tampa, FL: University of South Florida, 1987.

Antiterrorism. Joint Publication 3-07.2. http://www.fas.org/irp/doddir/dod/jp3_07_2.pdf.

Anurugsa, Panomporn. "Political Integration Policy in Thailand: The Case of the Malay Muslim Minority." PhD dissertation, University of Texas at Austin, 1984.

Aphornsuvan, Thanet. *History and Politics of the Muslims in Thailand.* Bangkok: Thammasat University, 2003. Document 3. http://www.einaudi.cornell.edu/SoutheastAsia/outreach/resources/MuslimThailand.pdf.

Aphornsuvan, Thanet. *Origins of Malay Muslim "Separatism" in Southern Thailand.* Working Paper Series, No. 32. Singapore: Asia Research Institute, National University of Singapore, October 2004.

ASEAN website. Biography of Minister Surin. http://www.aseansec.org/drsurin-biodata.pdf.

Askew, Marc. "Fighting with Ghosts: Confronting Thailand's Enigmatic 'Southern Fire.'" Paper presented at the Institute for Southeast Asian Studies (ISEAS), "Conference on Southern Thailand: Anatomy of an Insurgency, 2004–2009," Singapore, 10–11 March 2009.

Bajunid, Omar Farouk. "Islam, Nationalism, and the Thai State." In *Dynamic Diversity in Southern Thailand,* edited by Wattana Sungunnasil. Pattani, Thailand: Prince of Songkhla University, 2005.

Ball, Desmond, and David Scott Mathieson. *Militia Redux: Or Sor and the Revival of Paramilitarism in Thailand.* Bangkok: White Lotus Press, 2007.

Ball, Desmond. *The Boys in Black: The Thahan Phran (Rangers), Thailand's Para-military Border Guards.* Bangkok: White Lotus Press, 2004.

Bowie, Katherine A. *Rituals of National Loyalty: An Anthropology of the State and the Village Scout Movement in Thailand.* New York: Columbia University Press, 1997.

Bunbongkarn, Suchit. *The Military in Thai Politics, 1981–86.* Singapore: ISEAS, 1986.

Central Intelligence Agency. "A Look Back…'Free Thai' Movement Is Born." 3 July 2008. https://www.cia.gov/news-information/featured-story-archive/free-thai-movement.html.

Central Intelligence Agency. "Intelligence Report: Peking's Support of Insurgencies in Southeast Asia." Reference Title: POLO LIII. Washington, DC: CIA, April 1973.

Chalk, Peter. "The Malay-Muslim Insurgency in Southern Thailand: Understanding the Conflict's Evolving Dynamic." Washington, DC: RAND Corporation, prepared for the Office of the Secretary of Defense, 2008. http://www.rand.org/pubs/occasional_papers/2008/RAND_OP198.pdf.

Chalk, Peter, Angel Rabasa, William Rosenau, and Leanne Piggott. "The Evolving Terrorist Threat to Southeast Asia: A Net Assessment." Washington, DC: RAND Corporation, prepared for the Office of the Secretary of Defense, 2009.

Che Man, Wan Kadir. *Muslim Separatism: The Moros of Southern Philippines and the Malays of Southern Thailand.* Manila: Ateneo de Manila University Press, 1990.

Cheah Boon Kheng, ed. "From PKI to the Comintern, 1924–1941: The Apprenticeship of the Malayan Communist Party." *Southeast Asia Program Series,* No. 8. Ithaca, NY: Cornell University Press, 1992.

Chutima, Gawin. "The Rise and Fall of the Communist Party of Thailand, 1973–1987." Occasional Paper No. 12. Canterbury, UK: University of Kent, Centre of Southeast Asian Studies, 1990.

Clutterbuck, Richard. *The Long, Long War: The Emergency in Malaya, 1948–1960.* Singapore: Cultured Lotus, 2005.

Cornish, Andrew. *Whose Place Is This? Malay Rubber Producers and Thai Government Officials in Yala.* Bangkok: White Lotus, 1997.

Dillon, Dana R. "Insurgency in Thailand: The U.S. Should Support the Government." Heritage Foundation, Executive Memorandum 936, 10 June 2004. http://www.heritage.org/research/asiaandthepacific/upload/64842_1.pdf.

Dulyakasem, Utai, and Lertchai Sirichai, eds. *Knowledge and Conflict Resolution: The Crisis of the Border Region of Southern Thailand.* Bangkok: School of Liberal Arts, Walailak University, December 2005.

Economic and Social Commission for Asia and the Pacific (ESCAP). "Participatory Approach to Transport Infrastructure Development." *Economic and Social Commission for Asia and the Pacific, Transport and Communications Bulletin for Asia and the Pacific.* New York: United Nations, 1999. http://www.unescap.org/TTDW/Publications/TPTS_pubs/bulletin69_fulltext.pdf.

Elegant, Simon. "Southern Front." *Time Asia* 164/1618 (October 2004).

Ettinger, Glenn. "Thailand's Defeat of Its Communist Party." *International Journal of Intelligence and Counterintelligence* 20/4 (2007).

Fairclough, Gordon. "Hidden Hands: Politicians and Army Blamed for Bombings in the South." *Far Eastern Economic Review* 20 (9 June 1994).

Ferry, Alexandra. "The Laotian Crisis of 1960–62: Birth of the Rusk-Thanat Joint Communique." In *International Affairs Journal* (University of California at Davis), 1/1 (Winter 2005). http://davisiaj.com/content/view/378/86/.

Funston, John. "Thailand's Southern Fires: The Malaysian Factor." Research School of Pacific and Asian Studies, Australian National University, Canberra (November 2006): 60.

Gilquin, Michel. *The Muslims of Thailand,* translated by Michael Smithies. Bangkok: Silkworm Books, 2002.

Gunaratna, Rohan, Arabinda Acharya, and Sabrina Chua. *Conflict and Terrorism in Southern Thailand.* Singapore: Times Academic Press, 2005.

Haberkorn, Tyrell Caroline. "States of Transgression: Politics, Violence, and Agrarian Transformation in Northern Thailand." PhD dissertation, Cornell University, August 2007.

Handley, Paul M. *The King Never Smiles: A Biography of Thailand's Bhumibol Adulyadej.* New Haven, CT: Yale University Press, 2006.

Haseman, John B. "Thailand and the Realities of Southeast Asia." *Military Review* (May 1977). http://calldp.leavenworth.army.mil/eng_mr/txts/VOL57/00000005/art10.pdf.

Heaton, William R., and Richard MacLeod. "People's War in Thailand." In *Insurgency in the Modern World,* edited by Bard E. O'Neil, William Heaton, and Donald J. Roberts. Boulder, CO: Westview Press, 1980.

Hillcourt, William. *The Official Boy Scout Handbook*. Boy Scouts of America, 1979.

Human Rights Watch. "No One Is Safe." 27 August 2007.
http://www.hrw.org/en/reports/2007/08/27/no-one-safe.

Human Rights Watch. "Thailand: Insurgents Target Leading Muslim Woman Activist." 18 March
2009. http://www.hrw.org/en/news/2009/03/18/thailand-insurgents-target-leading-muslim-
woman-activist.

Institute for Defense Analyses. *Counterinsurgency in Thailand* (Report R-146), volume 1, *Summary
and Evaluation*. Washington, DC: US Government Printing Office, 1968.

Institute for Defense Analyses. *Counterinsurgency in Thailand* (WSEG Report 133), volume 4:
*Appendixes: The Insurgent Threat and the RTG Counterinsurgency Effort, Including IDA Report
R-146*. Washington, DC: US Government Printing Office, 1968.

Internal Displacement Monitoring Centre. "Buddhist Minority Declines in the 'deep south' due to
protracted armed conflict." Report by the Internal Displacement Monitoring Centre, Norwegian
Refugee Council, 15 November 2011.

International Crisis Group. "Southern Thailand: Insurgency, Not Jihad," *Asia Report No. 98*.
Jakarta/Brussels: ICG, 18 May 2005.

International Crisis Group. "Southern Thailand: The Problem with Paramilitaries," *Asia Report No.
140*. Jakarta/Brussels: ICG, 23 October 2007.

Jitsomprisi, Srisompob, ed. "Southern Border Provinces Poll." In *Deep South Watch* (18 May 2009).

Jory, Patrick. "Multiculturism in Thailand? Cultural and Regional Resurgence in a Diverse Kingdom."
Harvard Asia Pacific Review, 2002.
http://www.hcs.harvard.edu/~hapr/winter00_millenium/Thailand.html.

Karnchanapee, Char. "Thai Politics and Foreign Aid in Rural Isan: Development and Modernization
in 1990s." Rutgers University paper. http://www.rci.rutgers.edu/~karnchan/thai_isa.txt.

Kelly, Mark. "Special Press Summary: Unrest in Southern Thailand." Prepared by defense contractor
Virtual Information Center for US Commander in Chief, Pacific, 9 January 2004.

Kerdphol, Saiyud. *The Struggle for Thailand: Counterinsurgency 1965–1985*. Bangkok: S. Research
Center, 1986.

Kittaworn, Piya. "Voices from the Grassroots." In *Dynamic Diversity in Southern Thailand*, edited
by Wattana Sungunnasil. Pattani, Thailand: Prince of Songkhla University, 2005.

LePoer, Barbara Leitch, ed. *Thailand, a Country Study*. Washington, DC: Federal Research Division,
Library of Congress, 1987.

Mahakanjana, Chandra nuj. "Decentralization, Local Government, and Socio-political Conflict in
Southern Thailand." Washington, DC: East West Center, Working Paper No. 5 (August 2006).

Mansurnoor, Iik A. "Muslims in Modern Southeast Asia: Radicalism in Historical Perspectives."
Taiwan Journal of Southeast Asian Studies 2/2 (2005).
http://www.cseas.ncnu.edu.tw/journal/v02_no2/pp3-54.pdf.

Marks, Thomas A., Sebastian L. V. Gorka, and Bob Sharp. "Getting the Next War Right: Beyond
Population Centric Warfare." *PRISM* 1/3 (June 2010): 79–98.

Marks, Tom. *Making Revolution: The Insurgency of the Communist Party of Thailand in Structural
Perspective*. Bangkok: White Lotus, 1994.

McCargo, Duncan. "Southern Thai Politics." In *Dynamic Diversity in Southern Thailand*, edited by
Wattana Sungunnasil. Pattani, Thailand: Prince of Songkhla University, 2005.

McCargo, Duncan. *Tearing Apart the Land: Islam and Legitimacy in Southern Thailand.* Ithaca, NY: Cornell University Press, 2008.

McCoy, Alfred W. *The Politics of Heroin in Southeast Asia.* New York: Harper and Row, 1972.

Nagai, Fumio, Nakharin Mektrairat, and Tsuruyo Funatsu. "Local Government in Thailand: Analysis of the Local Administrative Organization Survey." JRP Series 147. Wakaba Mihama-ku Chiba-s. Japan, Institute of Developing Economies, 2008. http://www.ide-jetro.jp/English/Publish/Download/Jrp/147.html.

National News Bureau of Thailand, Public Relations Department. "Prime Minister Thaksin and the Southern Development." 25 May 2004. http://thainews.prd.go.th/en/news.php?id=254705250001.

Noiwong, Ornanong. "Political Integration Policies and Strategies of the Thai Government Toward the Malay-Muslims of Southernmost Thailand (1973–2000)." PhD dissertation, Northern Illinois University, 2001.

Nuechterlein, Donald E. *Thailand and the Struggle for Southeast Asia.* Ithaca, New York: Cornell University Press, 1966.

"Peace-building in the Three Southern Border Provinces." *Inside Thailand Review,* 27 June 2005. http://thailand.prd.go.th/ebook/review/content.php?chapterID=20.

Pike, Douglas. *PAVN: People's Army of Vietnam.* Novato, CA: Presidio Press, 1986.

Pitsuwan, Surin. "Islam and Malay Nationalism: A Case Study of the Malay-Muslims of Southern Thailand." PhD dissertation, Harvard University, 1982.

Prajonpujjanug, Prakij. "Security Problems in the Most Southern Provinces" (Speech Document, National Security Council, Bangkok, 23 December 2007).

"Principles of Royally Initiated Projects." *Inside Thailand Review,* n.d. http://thailand.prd.go.th/ebook/review/content.php?chapterID=35&PHPSESSID=1c5e22987e66 5e511bf6059fb9be3680.

Rabasa, Angel, and Peter Chalk. "Muslim Separatist Movements in the Philippines and Thailand." In *Indonesia's Transformation and the Stability of Southeast Asia.* RAND Corporation, 2001. http://www.rand.org/pubs/monograph_reports/MR1344/MR1344.ch9.pdf.

Race, Jeffrey. "The War in Northern Thailand." *Modern Asian Studies, 8.* University of Cambridge. January 1974.

Rakwijit, Somchai. "Problems of Thai Internal Security." Singapore: ISEAS, Heinmann Educational Books (Asia), 1977.

Rattanachaya, General Kitti. *The Last Role of Chin Peng; The Communist Party of Malaya, Malaysia, and Thailand.* Sahadhammika, Thailand: n.p., 2007.

Rattanachaya, General Kitti. *Thailand's Southern Insurgency: Creation of Pattani State.* Bangkok: Sor. Pichit Publication Company, 2004.

Royal Thai Government. Secretariat of the Cabinet web page. http://www.cabinet.thaigov.go.th/eng/pm_20.htm.

Royal Thai Government. "Minister of Agriculture and Co-operatives, Wan Muhammad Noor Matha." http://www.cabinet.thaigov.go.th/eng/WanMuhamadNoor47_1.htm.

Royal Thai Government, Ministry of Foreign Affairs. "Policy for Peace-building the Southern Border Provinces." http://www.thai2arab.com/eng/content.php?page=content&id=421&kword=ec.

Royal Thai Government. "Management Policy for Peace-Building in the Southernmost Provinces." 6 March 2005. http://thailand.prd.go.th/the_inside_view.php?id=755.

Royal Thai Government. "Office of the Prime Minister's Regulation on Peace-Building in the Southern Border Provinces of Thailand 2008." *Royal Gazette.* Issue 125, Special Section, 21 Ngor. 31 January 2008.

Royal Thai Government. "Royal Project Foundation." Royal Thai website. http://www.royalprojectthailand.com/general/english/index.html.

Royal Thai Government. "Southern Border Provinces Administrative Centre (SB-PAC)," 1991.

Royal Thai Government. "Unofficial Translation, The Office of the Prime Minister's Order 207/2549, Subject: The Public Administration in the Southern Border Provinces." 30 October 2006.

Royal Thai Government. *Krue Se* report. Translated by *The Nation.* http://www.nationmultimedia.com/specials/takbai/p2.htm.

Royal Thai Government. *Tak Bai* report. Translated by *The Nation.* http://www.nationmultimedia.com/specials/takbai/p1.htm.

Royal Thai Military press conference web page. "The Royal Thai Army (RTA) Organic Units Meeting 4/2003." http://armysecretary.rta.mi.th/pressconferencee.htm.

Royal Thai military website, SBPPC. "Origin of the Southern Border Provinces Peace-Building Command." http://www.southpeace.go.th/eng/Origin_of_SBPPC.htm.

Royal Thai military website, SBPPC. "Vision, Mission." http://www.southpeace.go.th/eng/vision.html.

Samudavanija, Chai-Anan, and Sukhumbhand Paribatra. "In Search of Balance: Prospects for Stability in Thailand During the Post-CPT Era." In *Durable Stability in Southeast Asia,* edited by Kusuma Snitwongse and Sukhumbhand Paribatra. Singapore: ISEAS, 1987.

Samudavanija, Chai-Anan, Kusuma Snitwongse, and Suchit Bunbongkarn. *From Armed Suppression to Political Offensive.* Bangkok: Aksornsiam Press, 1990.

Saniwa, Suria. "Democracy and Elections: A Case Study of the Malay-Muslims in Southern Thailand." http://gotoknow.org/blog/niksof/101398.

Schlight, John. *The United States Air Force in Southeast Asia: The War in South Vietnam, The Years of the Offensive: 1965–1968.* Washington, DC: Office of Air Force History, 1988.

Service, Robert. *Comrades! A History of World Communism.* Boston: Harvard University Press, 2007.

Sookying, Sutthi. "The Department of Special Investigation (DSI): Countermeasures in Regard to the Investigation of Economic Crimes and Special Crimes in Thailand." http://www.unafei.or.jp/english/pdf/RS_No66/No66_20PA_Sookying.pdf.

Storey, Ian. "Ethnic Separatism in Southern Thailand: Kingdom Fraying at the Edge?" Asia-Pacific Center for Security Studies, March 2007. http://www.jamestown.org/terrorism/news/article.php?articleid=2370121.

Syukri, Ibrahim. *History of the Malay Kingdom of Pattani,* translated by Conner Bailey and John N. Miksic. Bangkok: Silkworm Books, 1985.

Tan, Andrew Tian Huat. *Handbook of Terrorism and Insurgency in Southeast Asia: The Emergence of Postmodern Terrorism.* University of New South Wales: Edward Elgar Publishing, 2007.

Tanham, George K. *Trial in Thailand.* New York: Crane, Russak & Company, 1974.

Thai Muslims. Bangkok: Royal Thai Ministry of Foreign Affairs, 1979.

Thomas, M. Ladd. "Political Violence in the Muslim Provinces of Southern Thailand." Occasional Paper No. 28. Singapore: ISEAS, 1975.

Thomas, M. Ladd. "Thai Muslim Separatism in South Thailand." In *The Muslims of Thailand*, volume 2: *Politics of the Malay-Speaking South*, edited by Andrew D. W. Forbes. Bihar, India: Centre for Southeast Asian Studies, 1989.

Tinsulanonda, General Prem, official website. "Thai Experience in Combating Insurgency." http://www.generalprem.com/Speech4.html.

Turnbull, Wayne. "A Tangled Web of Southeast Asian Islamic Terrorism: The Jemaah Islamiyah Terrorist Network." Monterey, CA: Monterey Institute of International Studies, 31 July 2003.

US Department of Justice website, Al Qaeda. "Declaration of Jihad (Holy War) Against the Country's Tyrants, Military Series." UK/BM-8. http://www.justice.gov/ag/manualpart1_1.pdf.

US Department of State. "Public Announcement, U.S. Department of State, Office of the Spokesman," 4 April 2005 (State Department travel advisory on the violence in Thailand).

Union of Democratic Thais. *Thailand: Songs for Life Sung by Caravan: Songs of the Peasant, Student and Worker Struggle for Democratic Rights*. Brooklyn, NY: Paredon Records, 1978.

United Nations. "UNCHR's Version of the Thai Internal Security Act, 2007." http://www.unhcr.org/refworld/category, LEGAL, THA,482b01e82,0.html.

Urban, Mark. *Big Boy's Rules: The SAS and the Secret Struggle Against the IRA*. London: Faber and Faber, 1992.

Valsesia, Angelo Carlo. "Thailand: Insurgency in the South." Equilibri.net, 19 May 2007. http://uk.equilibri.net/article/6794/Thailand__insurgency_in_the_South.

Vatikiotis, Michael. "Resolving Internal Conflicts in Southeast Asia: Domestic Challenges and Regional Perspectives." In *Contemporary Southeast Asia*, 28/1 (2006). Singapore: ISEAS.

Virtual Information Center. "Primer: Muslim Separatism in Southern Thailand." Prepared by defense contractor Virtual Information Center for US Commander in Chief, Pacific, 3 July 2002.

Wedel, Yuangrat. "The Thai Radicals and the Communist Party: Interaction of Ideology and Nationalism in the Forest, 1975–1980." Occasional Paper No. 72. Singapore: ISEAS, 1983.

Wongtrangan, Kanok. "Change and Persistence in Thai Counter-Insurgency Policy." Occasional Paper No. 1. Bangkok: Institute of Security and International Studies, Chulalongkorn University, 1983.

Yegar, Moshe. *Between Integration and Secession: The Muslim Communities of the Southern Philippines, Southern Thailand, and Western Burma/Myanmar*. Lanham, MD: Lexington Books, 2002.

Index

(Thai and other Asian names listed as first and last names, not last and first)

"Buy Thai!," 34–35

Internal Security Act (ISA), 247, 292, 367

Internal Security Operations Command (ISOC), 16, 21, 62, 73, 81–82, 102, 110, 112, 175, 181, 183, 190, 203, 218, 236, 242, 247, 286, 290–94, 297–99, 318, 330–31, 339–40, 346, 354

Islamist, 26, 140, 151–57, 160, 164, 168, 198, 227–28, 230–36, 250–52, 257, 260–61, 264, 266, 268, 272, 274, 279, 300, 325, 329, 331–32, 357, 359–61, 371

Issan, 3–4, 6–8, 26, 29, 40, 47, 70, 76, 87, 108, 122, 125, 128, 130, 217, 221, 246, 349, 358

J

Jemaah Islamiyah (JI, the Islamic Congregation), 228–30, 232–33, 237, 341, 254, 266

Jemaah Salafiya (JS, the Salafist Congregation), 230

Jihad, 152, 157, 162, 198, 228–31, 250, 257–58, 266, 268, 274, 332, 358, 361

Joint Security Center (JSC), 102

Joint Security Teams (JSTs), 94

K

Kafir, 157

Kamnan, 186

Kampung Bujang, (Unmarried Widow), 350

Kampung Janda (Widow Village), 350

Karunthep ("Cooperators in National Development"), 113

Kedah, 209, 256, 313

Kelantan, 145, 156, 209, 211, 229, 255, 312–13

Khaiseng Suksai, 20

Khao Chong Chang, 45

Khao Kho, 18, 20, 45, 89–90, 185, 368

Khek, 167

Khmer Rouge (KR), 29, 32, 118

Khru, 77

Kilcullen, David, xv, xvii, xix

Kilo 11 Incident, 6

Kitti Rattanachaya, 99, 141–42, 150, 153–54, 172–76, 183, 185, 190, 203, 207–8, 212–13, 216, 218, 222, 235, 281, 354

Komchai (musical group), 42

Komg Asa Raksa Dindaen (*Or Sor*, Volunteer Defense Corps, VDC), 78, 88, 94, 110, 189, 303, 308, 310

Kriangsak Chomanand, 18, 62–63, 70, 114, 116–17, 120, 137–38, 175, 364, 367–68

Krong Kahn, 212–13

Krue Se mosque, 235–36, 239, 279, 281

Kukrit Pramoj, 56, 116–17

Kumpulan Militan Malaysia (KMM), 228–29

Kuomintang (KMT), 89–90

Kuruthayat, 220

Kwam-pen Thai, 3. *See also* "Thainess"

L

Laos, 7–8, 11, 13–14, 17, 24, 26, 29, 31–32, 41–42, 45, 47, 59, 72, 76, 79, 90, 99, 117, 122, 230, 361

Lenin, Vladimir, 5, 27

Long Mu, 32

Luce, Don, 36

M

Makkh-thayok, 77

Malaysian Special Branch, 145, 189, 207–8

Maoism, Maoist, 22, 24–26, 34–35, 38–41, 51, 54–55, 151

440

Propaganda, 9–13, 20, 24–27, 33–43, 50, 61, 73, 86, 88, 103, 144, 146, 153, 161, 171, 183, 186, 191, 206, 216, 218, 233, 250, 255, 257, 260–61, 267–68, 278–79, 287, 313, 321, 323, 326–34, 344, 357, 359

PAO Act, 198

Provincial Administrative Organizations (PAOs), 198, 201, 249, 319

Provincial Police (PP), 54, 88, 90–92, 306–7

Psychological Operations (psyops), 8, 11, 16, 61, 64, 72–75, 79, 94, 99, 106–8, 112, 136, 160, 173, 183–88, 194, 217–18, 222, 265, 269, 312, 316, 332, 335–39, 353, 356–57, 368

Public Relations (PR), 106, 108, 140, 173, 180, 216–17, 238, 250, 276, 279, 312, 316, 323, 332, 338–39, 350, 353, 357, 359, 365, 368

Public Welfare Department, 45

Q

Quick Reaction Force (QRF), 46, 79, 85–88, 94, 185, 300, 307

Queen Sirikit, 122, 309

R

Race, Jeffrey, 31, 45, 48, 54, 113, 358

Radio 909, 108–9

Radio Hanoi, 9

Radio Peking, 9

Rama III, 334

Rama IV, 3

Rama V, 3

Red Gaurs, 15

Riduan Isamuddin "Hambali," 228

Rotary Club in Thailand, 122, 126, 224

Royal Initiatives Project (RIP), 178, 225–26

Royal Keg Basin Development Project, 89

Royal Thai Air Force (RTAF), 58, 84, 88, 184, 300

Royal Thai Army (RTA), 10–20, 29, 39, 57–114, 121–26, 136–43, 172–93, 203, 206, 218, 220–69, 277–372

Royal Thai Government (RTG), 9–12, 16, 39–41, 45, 48, 54, 56, 65, 69, 74–75, 90, 92–93, 101–3, 106, 109, 115, 124, 132–33, 146, 153, 162, 173, 187, 194, 198, 204–5, 217, 220, 245–48, 251, 253, 260, 262, 265, 267, 276, 288–89, 291, 308, 313, 316, 322–24, 328–32, 337, 342, 344, 354, 359, 361–62, 365, 368

Royal Thai Marines (RTM), 84–85, 131, 184, 233, 247, 300–1, 364

Royal Thai Navy (RTN), 84, 243, 246–47, 300

Royal Thai Police (RTP), 6, 10–11, 59, 69, 79, 84, 88, 90–92, 102, 107, 176, 182–88, 191, 229, 235, 244, 246, 249, 252, 255, 262, 280, 289, 291, 296–98, 306–7, 312–13, 324, 355–56, 359, 365, 369

Runda Kumpulan Kecil (RKK, Small Unit Tactics), 238, 242, 252, 256, 262, 266–67, 275, 331–32, 338

S

Sadao (district in Songkhla), 249–50

Saiyud Kerdphol, 10–14, 17, 28, 39, 47, 50–54, 57, 61–62, 66, 69, 75, 77, 80–82, 109–10, 126–28, 291, 352

Sakdi na, 1–2, 35, 37, 50, 215

Salafist, 230, 236, 251, 268

San Chitpatima, 12, 17

Sangha, 2

San Jai Thai Su Jai Tai (Uniting Thai Hearts for the South), 320

Santi Suk (Peace and Happiness), 108

Sarit Thanarat, 10, 59

Y

Yala (province), 99, 130, 133, 141, 151, 159–62, 166, 172, 177, 187, 190, 195, 210, 215, 218, 220–22, 230, 233, 235–36, 239–40, 250, 252, 254–56, 260–61, 267, 271, 273–74, 295–96, 304, 309–11, 316, 318–19, 330–31, 339, 342, 345, 349

Yala Santisuk, 318

Yasothon, 20

Yingluck Shinawatra, 246–47, 276, 287–88, 298, 355, 366

Yunnan Province, 8

Made in the USA
Charleston, SC
06 August 2014